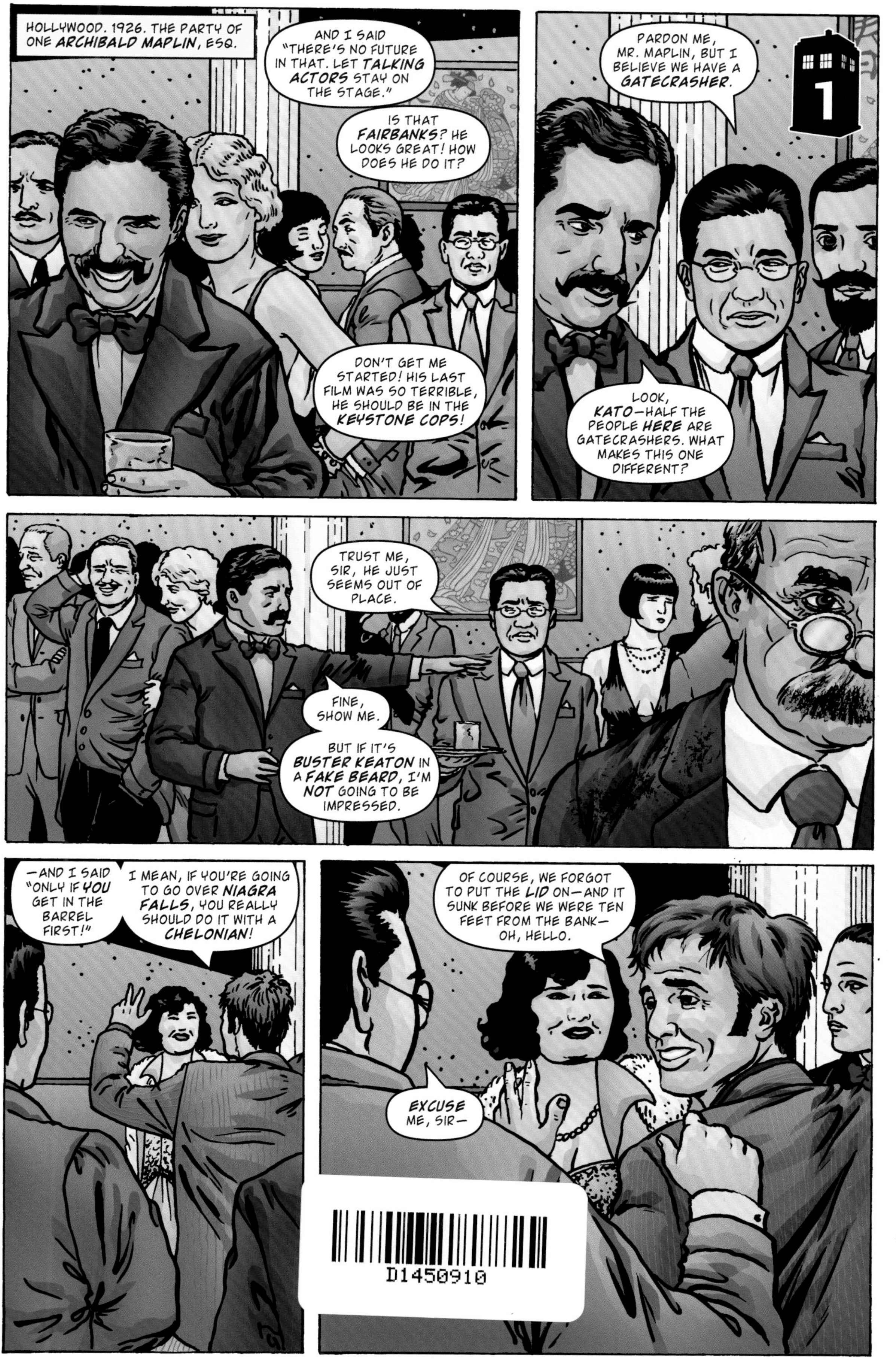
HOLLYWOOD. 1926. THE PARTY OF ONE ARCHIBALD MAPLIN, ESQ.
AND I SAID "THERE'S NO FUTURE IN THAT. LET TALKING ACTORS STAY ON THE STAGE."
IS THAT FAIRBANKS? HE LOOKS GREAT! HOW DOES HE DO IT?
DON'T GET ME STARTED! HIS LAST FILM WAS SO TERRIBLE, HE SHOULD BE IN THE KEYSTONE COPS!
PARDON ME, MR. MAPLIN, BUT I BELIEVE WE HAVE A GATECRASHER.
1
LOOK, KATO—HALF THE PEOPLE HERE ARE GATECRASHERS. WHAT MAKES THIS ONE DIFFERENT?
TRUST ME, SIR, HE JUST SEEMS OUT OF PLACE.
FINE, SHOW ME.
BUT IF IT'S BUSTER KEATON IN A FAKE BEARD, I'M NOT GOING TO BE IMPRESSED.
—AND I SAID "ONLY IF YOU GET IN THE BARREL FIRST!"
I MEAN, IF YOU'RE GOING TO GO OVER NIAGRA FALLS, YOU REALLY SHOULD DO IT WITH A CHELONIAN!
OF COURSE, WE FORGOT TO PUT THE LID ON—AND IT SUNK BEFORE WE WERE TEN FEET FROM THE BANK—OH, HELLO.
EXCUSE ME, SIR—

D1450910

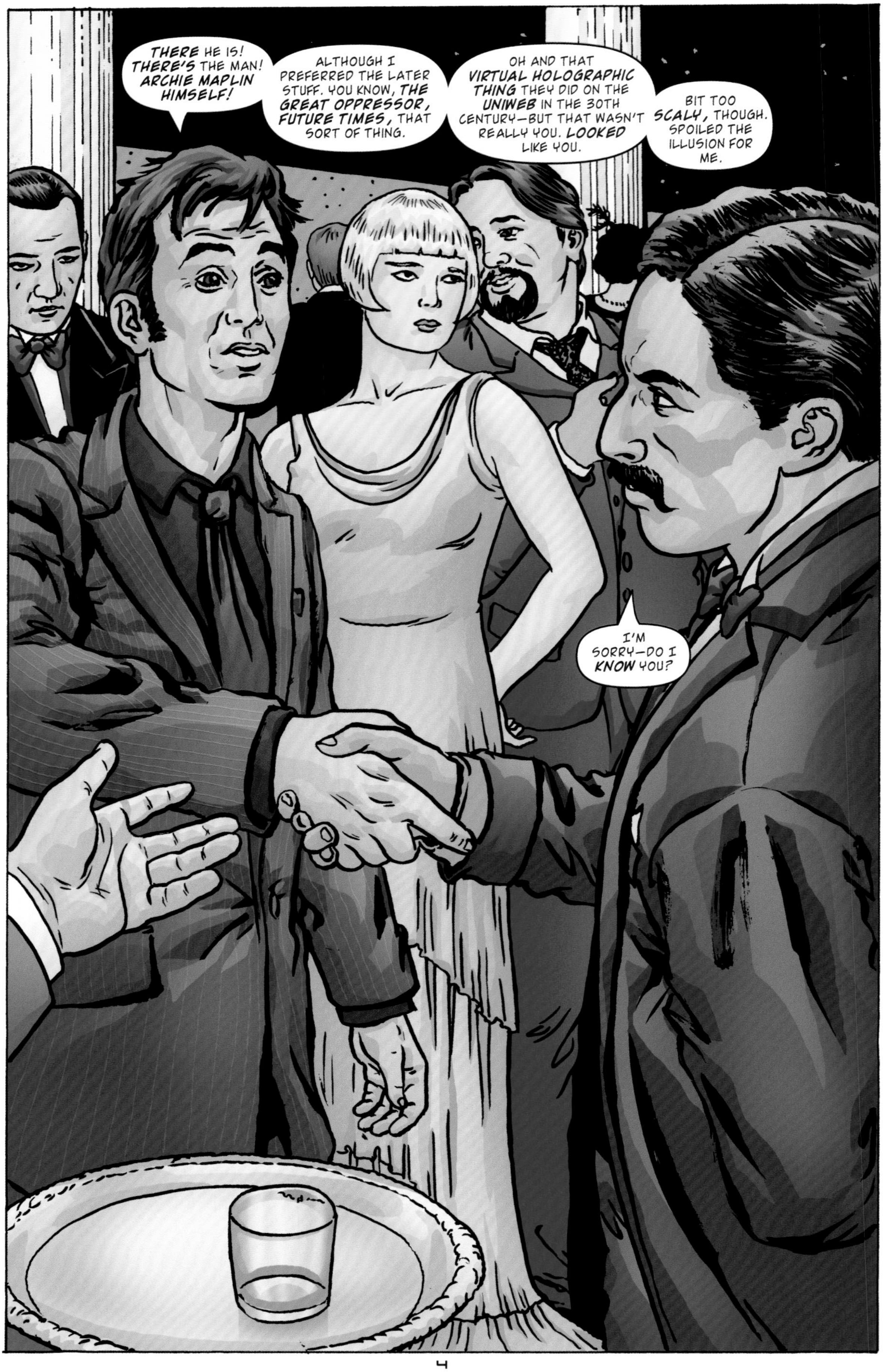
THERE HE IS! THERE'S THE MAN! ARCHIE MAPLIN HIMSELF!
ALTHOUGH I PREFERRED THE LATER STUFF. YOU KNOW, THE GREAT OPPRESSOR, FUTURE TIMES, THAT SORT OF THING.
OH AND THAT VIRTUAL HOLOGRAPHIC THING THEY DID ON THE UNIWEB IN THE 30TH CENTURY—BUT THAT WASN'T REALLY YOU. LOOKED LIKE YOU.
BIT TOO SCALY, THOUGH. SPOILED THE ILLUSION FOR ME.
I'M SORRY—DO I KNOW YOU?

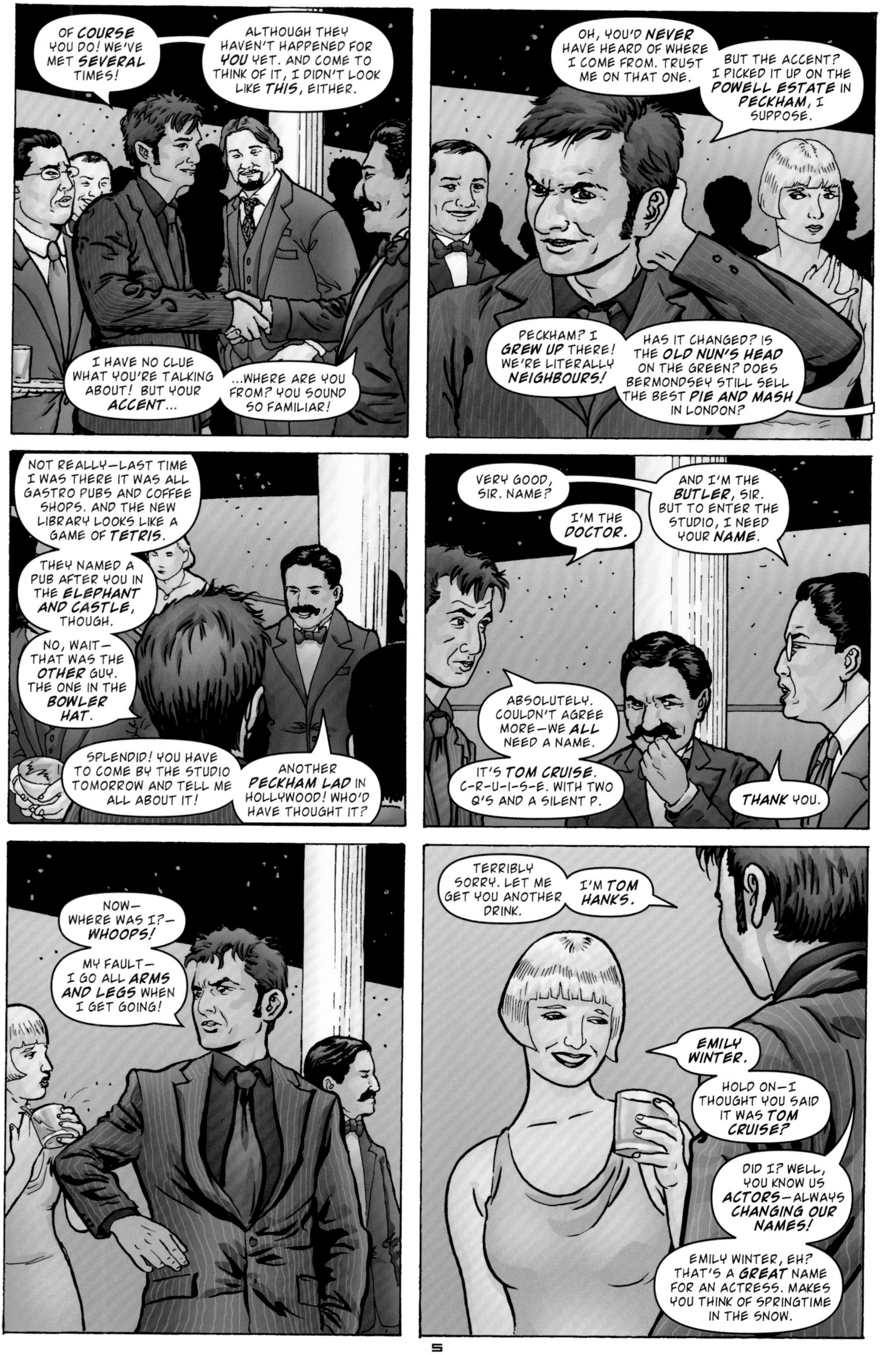
OF COURSE YOU DO! WE'VE MET SEVERAL TIMES!
ALTHOUGH THEY HAVEN'T HAPPENED FOR YOU YET. AND COME TO THINK OF IT, I DIDN'T LOOK LIKE THIS, EITHER.
I HAVE NO CLUE WHAT YOU'RE TALKING ABOUT! BUT YOUR ACCENT...
...WHERE ARE YOU FROM? YOU SOUND SO FAMILIAR!
OH, YOU'D NEVER HAVE HEARD OF WHERE I COME FROM. TRUST ME ON THAT ONE.
BUT THE ACCENT? I PICKED IT UP ON THE POWELL ESTATE IN PECKHAM, I SUPPOSE.
PECKHAM? I GREW UP THERE! WE'RE LITERALLY NEIGHBOURS!
HAS IT CHANGED? IS THE OLD NUN'S HEAD ON THE GREEN? DOES BERMONDSEY STILL SELL THE BEST PIE AND MASH IN LONDON?
NOT REALLY—LAST TIME I WAS THERE IT WAS ALL GASTRO PUBS AND COFFEE SHOPS. AND THE NEW LIBRARY LOOKS LIKE A GAME OF TETRIS.
THEY NAMED A PUB AFTER YOU IN THE ELEPHANT AND CASTLE, THOUGH.
NO, WAIT— THAT WAS THE OTHER GUY. THE ONE IN THE BOWLER HAT.
SPLENDID! YOU HAVE TO COME BY THE STUDIO TOMORROW AND TELL ME ALL ABOUT IT!
ANOTHER PECKHAM LAD IN HOLLYWOOD! WHO'D HAVE THOUGHT IT?
VERY GOOD, SIR. NAME?
I'M THE DOCTOR.
AND I'M THE BUTLER, SIR. BUT TO ENTER THE STUDIO, I NEED YOUR NAME.
ABSOLUTELY. COULDN'T AGREE MORE—WE ALL NEED A NAME.
IT'S TOM CRUISE. C-R-U-I-S-E. WITH TWO Q'S AND A SILENT P.
THANK YOU.
NOW— WHERE WAS I?— WHOOPS!
MY FAULT— I GO ALL ARMS AND LEGS WHEN I GET GOING!
TERRIBLY SORRY. LET ME GET YOU ANOTHER DRINK.
I'M TOM HANKS.
EMILY WINTER.
HOLD ON—I THOUGHT YOU SAID IT WAS TOM CRUISE?
DID I? WELL, YOU KNOW US ACTORS—ALWAYS CHANGING OUR NAMES!
EMILY WINTER, EH? THAT'S A GREAT NAME FOR AN ACTRESS. MAKES YOU THINK OF SPRINGTIME IN THE SNOW.

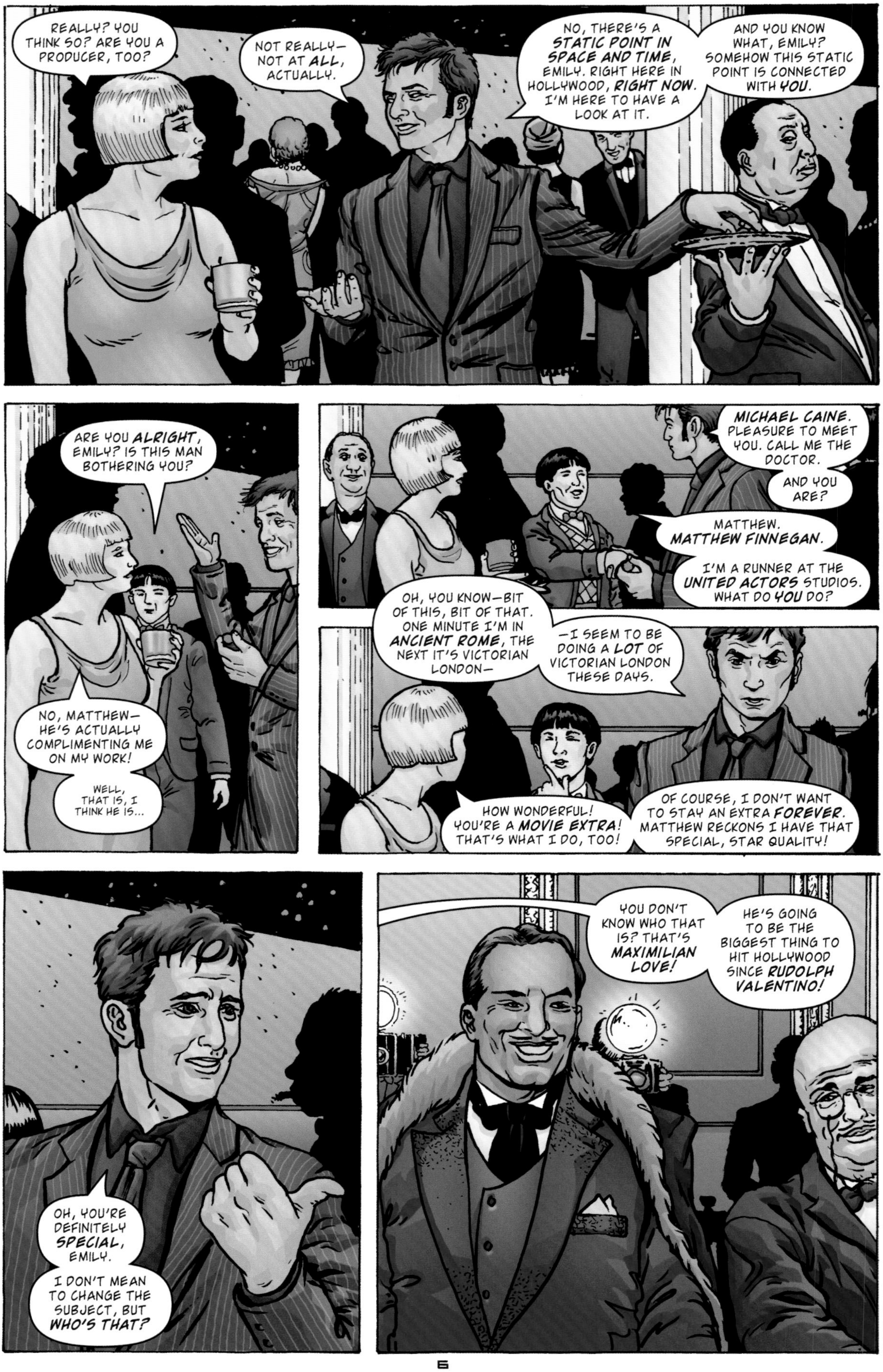
REALLY? YOU THINK SO? ARE YOU A PRODUCER, TOO?
NOT REALLY— NOT AT ALL, ACTUALLY.
NO, THERE'S A STATIC POINT IN SPACE AND TIME, EMILY. RIGHT HERE IN HOLLYWOOD, RIGHT NOW. I'M HERE TO HAVE A LOOK AT IT.
AND YOU KNOW WHAT, EMILY? SOMEHOW THIS STATIC POINT IS CONNECTED WITH YOU.
ARE YOU ALRIGHT, EMILY? IS THIS MAN BOTHERING YOU?
NO, MATTHEW— HE'S ACTUALLY COMPLIMENTING ME ON MY WORK!
WELL, THAT IS, I THINK HE IS...
MICHAEL CAINE. PLEASURE TO MEET YOU. CALL ME THE DOCTOR.
AND YOU ARE?
MATTHEW. MATTHEW FINNEGAN.
I'M A RUNNER AT THE UNITED ACTORS STUDIOS. WHAT DO YOU DO?
OH, YOU KNOW—BIT OF THIS, BIT OF THAT. ONE MINUTE I'M IN ANCIENT ROME, THE NEXT IT'S VICTORIAN LONDON—
—I SEEM TO BE DOING A LOT OF VICTORIAN LONDON THESE DAYS.
HOW WONDERFUL! YOU'RE A MOVIE EXTRA! THAT'S WHAT I DO, TOO!
OF COURSE, I DON'T WANT TO STAY AN EXTRA FOREVER. MATTHEW RECKONS I HAVE THAT SPECIAL, STAR QUALITY!
OH, YOU'RE DEFINITELY SPECIAL, EMILY.
I DON'T MEAN TO CHANGE THE SUBJECT, BUT WHO'S THAT?
YOU DON'T KNOW WHO THAT IS? THAT'S MAXIMILIAN LOVE!
HE'S GOING TO BE THE BIGGEST THING TO HIT HOLLYWOOD SINCE RUDOLPH VALENTINO!

REALLY? NEVER HEARD OF HIM. AND FOR *ME* TO NOT KNOW HIM...

...MEANS THAT HE'S *WRONG.* AND SO CLOSE TO A STATIC POINT IN SPACE IN TIME...

...MEANS THAT I JUST *HAVE* TO MEET HIM.

TOM! *DOCTOR!* WHATEVER YOUR NAME IS—

—WAIT FOR US!

MAX LOVE! *PEE-WEE HERMAN,* BRITISH PRESS CORPS! ANY CHANCE OF AN INTERVIEW?

I'M SORRY, MR. *HERMAN,* BUT MAXIMILIAN DOESN'T DO INTERVIEWS AT PARTIES.

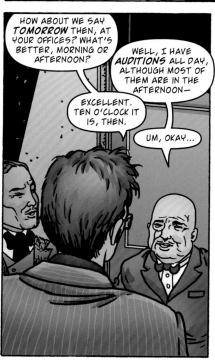

HOW ABOUT WE SAY *TOMORROW* THEN, AT YOUR OFFICES? WHAT'S BETTER, MORNING OR AFTERNOON?

WELL, I HAVE *AUDITIONS* ALL DAY, ALTHOUGH MOST OF THEM ARE IN THE AFTERNOON—

EXCELLENT. TEN O'CLOCK IT IS, THEN.

UM, OKAY...

EMILY WINTER, MR. MILLER. I JUST WANTED TO SAY HOW MUCH OF AN *HONOR* IT IS TO BE AUDITIONING FOR YOU TOMORROW MORNING!

WELL, AREN'T *YOU* JUST FULL OF LIFE, MISS WINTER?! YOU MIGHT BE *EXACTLY* WHAT WE'RE LOOKING FOR!

HEY! FIRST YOU'RE *TOM,* THEN *MICHAEL,* THEN YOU'RE AN *EXTRA,* THEN YOU'RE A *REPORTER*—

OH, I'M A *LOT OF THINGS,* MATTHEW.

AND SO IS *LEO MILLER.*

MORNING! IS THIS THE *UNITED ACTORS* STUDIO? I HAVE A MEETING WITH LEO MILLER ON YOUR BACKLOT.

HE'S *EXPECTING* ME.

MR. *HERMAN?* YES, MR. MILLER TOLD ME TO APOLOGISE TO YOU, BUT I CAN'T ALLOW YOU *ENTRANCE* TO THE OFFICES.

THEY'RE *VERY BUSY* TODAY.

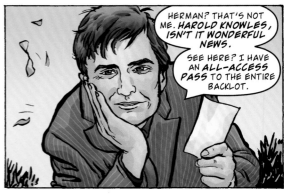

HERMAN? THAT'S NOT ME. *HAROLD KNOWLES,* ISN'T IT WONDERFUL NEWS.

SEE HERE? I HAVE AN *ALL-ACCESS PASS* TO THE ENTIRE BACKLOT.

OH, SORRY, MR. KNOWLES. I'LL SIGN YOU THROUGH.

CALL ME HARRY.

AH, THE *ROAR* OF THE GREASEPAINT, THE *SMELL* OF THE CROWDS.

AH, MR. *CRUISE!* YOU MADE IT!

HELLO, ARCHIE. JUST CALL ME THE *DOCTOR.* FAR EASIER FOR ME TO REMEMBER, YOU KNOW?

I'LL BE HONEST, ARCHIE, I'M ONLY HERE REALLY BECAUSE OF A FRIEND.

DONNA NOBLE. HER NAME ECHOED IN THE STARS EVERY NIGHT, SUNG BY THE PEOPLE WHOSE LIVES SHE CHANGED.

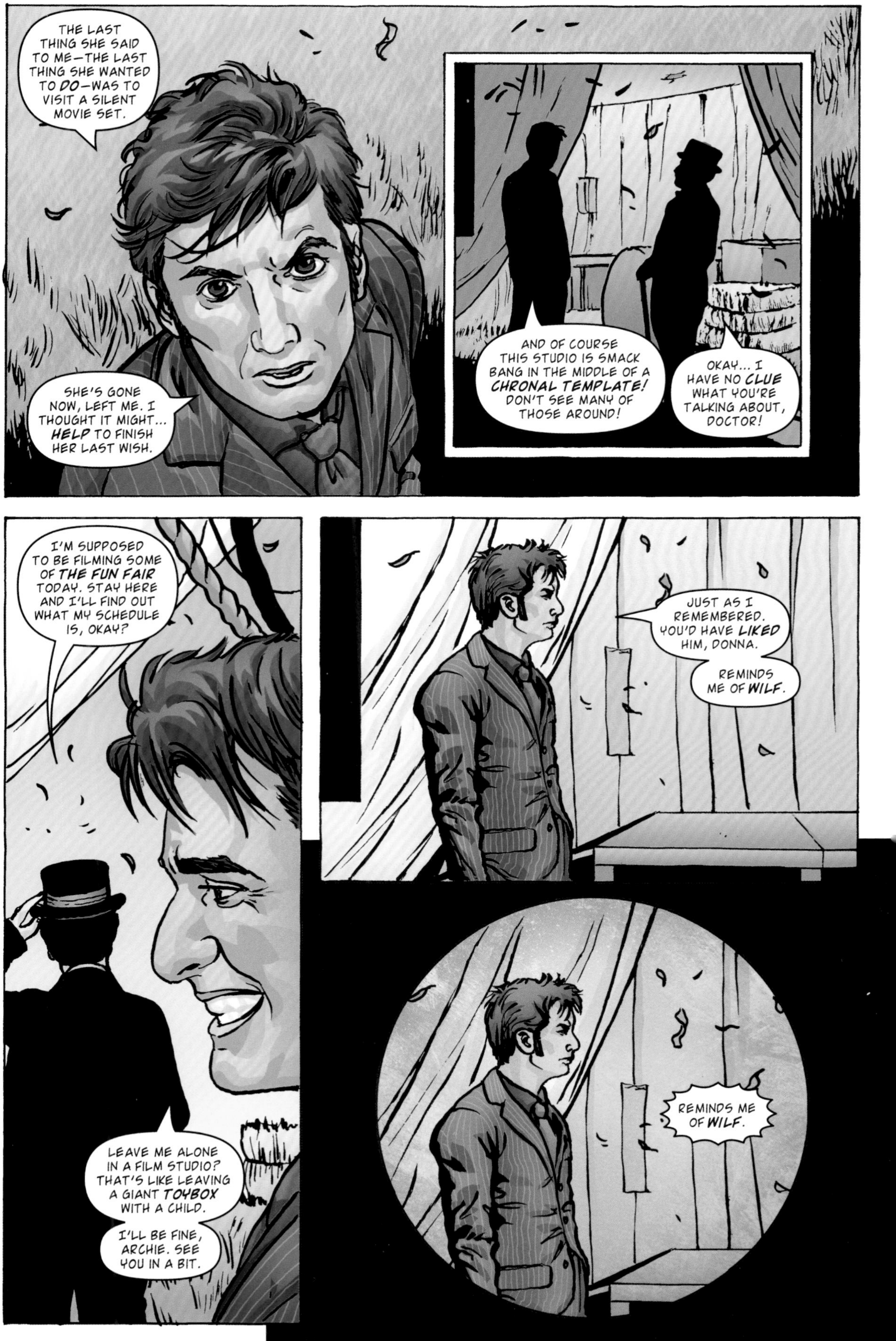
THE LAST THING SHE SAID TO ME—THE LAST THING SHE WANTED TO *DO*—WAS TO VISIT A SILENT MOVIE SET.
SHE'S GONE NOW, LEFT ME. I THOUGHT IT MIGHT... ***HELP*** TO FINISH HER LAST WISH.
AND OF COURSE THIS STUDIO IS SMACK BANG IN THE MIDDLE OF A ***CHRONAL TEMPLATE!*** DON'T SEE MANY OF THOSE AROUND!
OKAY... I HAVE NO ***CLUE*** WHAT YOU'RE TALKING ABOUT, DOCTOR!
I'M SUPPOSED TO BE FILMING SOME OF ***THE FUN FAIR*** TODAY. STAY HERE AND I'LL FIND OUT WHAT MY SCHEDULE IS, OKAY?
LEAVE ME ALONE IN A FILM STUDIO? THAT'S LIKE LEAVING A GIANT ***TOYBOX*** WITH A CHILD.
I'LL BE FINE, ARCHIE. SEE YOU IN A BIT.
JUST AS I REMEMBERED. YOU'D HAVE ***LIKED*** HIM, DONNA.
REMINDS ME OF ***WILF***.
REMINDS ME OF ***WILF***.

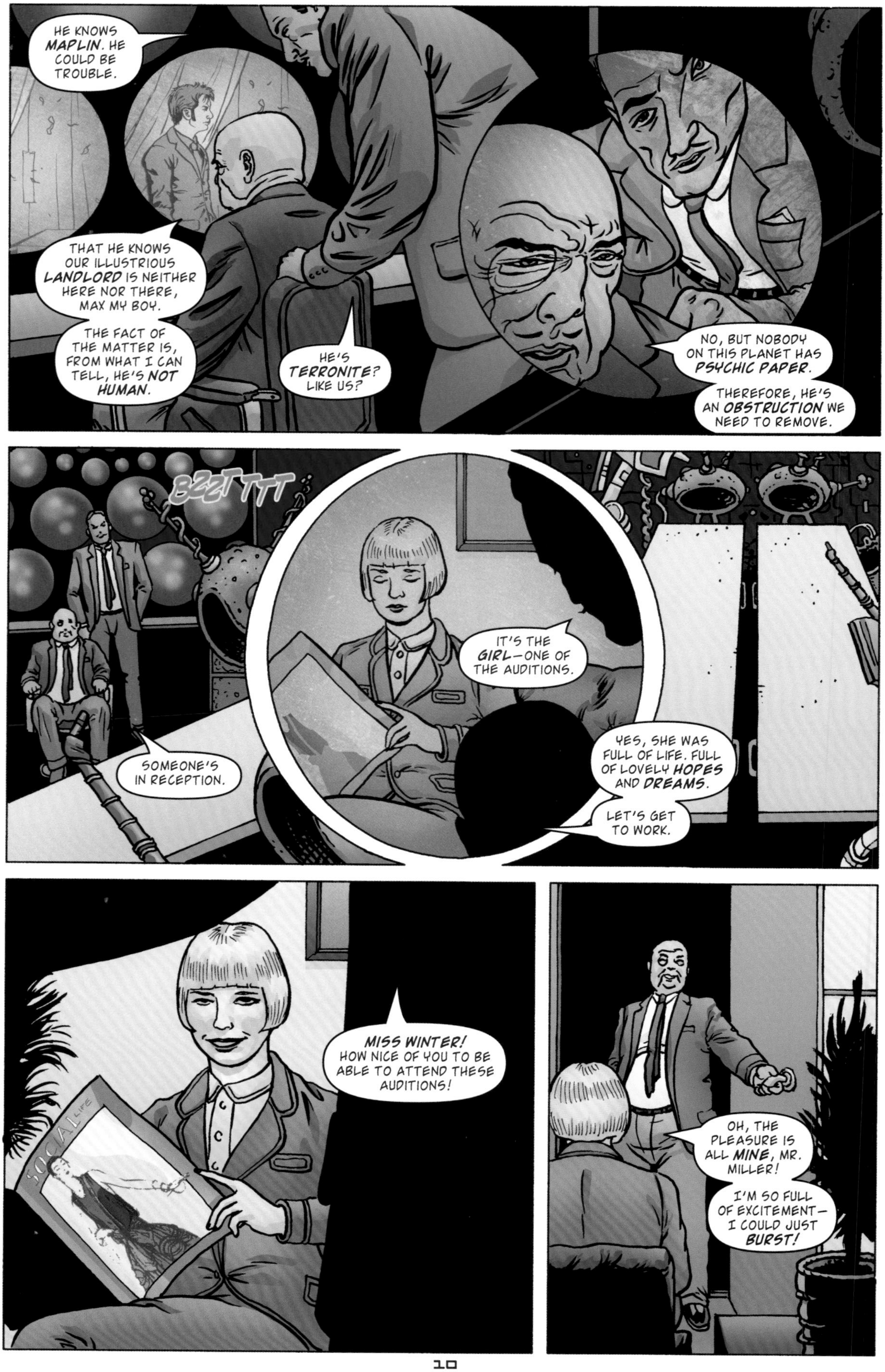

HE KNOWS MAPLIN. HE COULD BE TROUBLE.
THAT HE KNOWS OUR ILLUSTRIOUS LANDLORD IS NEITHER HERE NOR THERE, MAX MY BOY.
THE FACT OF THE MATTER IS, FROM WHAT I CAN TELL, HE'S NOT HUMAN.
HE'S TERRONITE? LIKE US?
NO, BUT NOBODY ON THIS PLANET HAS PSYCHIC PAPER.
THEREFORE, HE'S AN OBSTRUCTION WE NEED TO REMOVE.
BZZTTTT
SOMEONE'S IN RECEPTION.
IT'S THE GIRL—ONE OF THE AUDITIONS.
YES, SHE WAS FULL OF LIFE. FULL OF LOVELY HOPES AND DREAMS.
LET'S GET TO WORK.
MISS WINTER! HOW NICE OF YOU TO BE ABLE TO ATTEND THESE AUDITIONS!
OH, THE PLEASURE IS ALL MINE, MR. MILLER!
I'M SO FULL OF EXCITEMENT— I COULD JUST BURST!

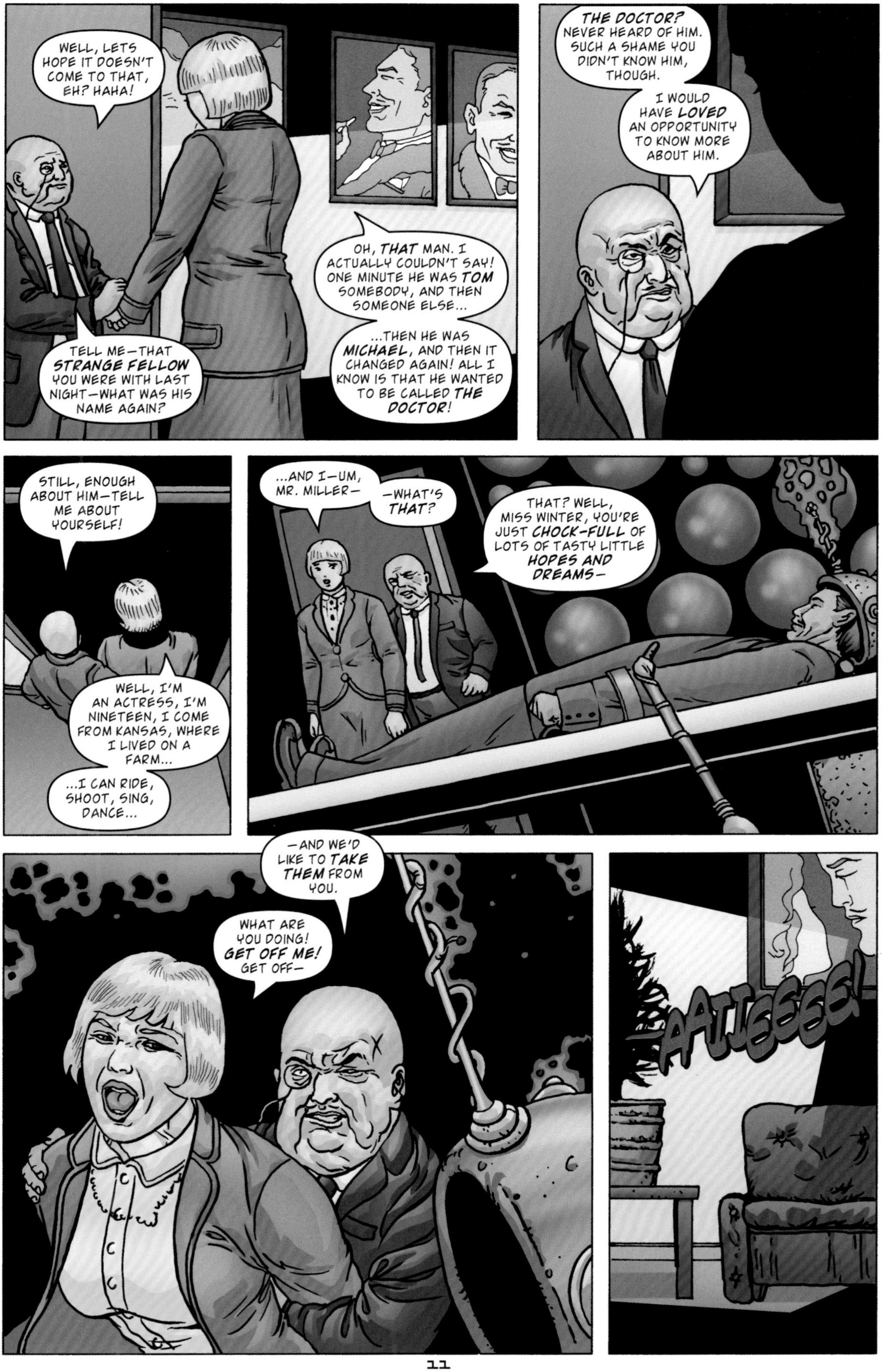

WELL, LETS HOPE IT DOESN'T COME TO THAT, EH? HAHA!
TELL ME—THAT STRANGE FELLOW YOU WERE WITH LAST NIGHT—WHAT WAS HIS NAME AGAIN?
OH, THAT MAN. I ACTUALLY COULDN'T SAY! ONE MINUTE HE WAS TOM SOMEBODY, AND THEN SOMEONE ELSE...
...THEN HE WAS MICHAEL, AND THEN IT CHANGED AGAIN! ALL I KNOW IS THAT HE WANTED TO BE CALLED THE DOCTOR!
THE DOCTOR? NEVER HEARD OF HIM. SUCH A SHAME YOU DIDN'T KNOW HIM, THOUGH.
I WOULD HAVE LOVED AN OPPORTUNITY TO KNOW MORE ABOUT HIM.
STILL, ENOUGH ABOUT HIM—TELL ME ABOUT YOURSELF!
WELL, I'M AN ACTRESS, I'M NINETEEN, I COME FROM KANSAS, WHERE I LIVED ON A FARM...
...I CAN RIDE, SHOOT, SING, DANCE...
...AND I—UM, MR. MILLER—
—WHAT'S THAT?
THAT? WELL, MISS WINTER, YOU'RE JUST CHOCK-FULL OF LOTS OF TASTY LITTLE HOPES AND DREAMS—
—AND WE'D LIKE TO TAKE THEM FROM YOU.
WHAT ARE YOU DOING! GET OFF ME! GET OFF—
AAIIEEEE!

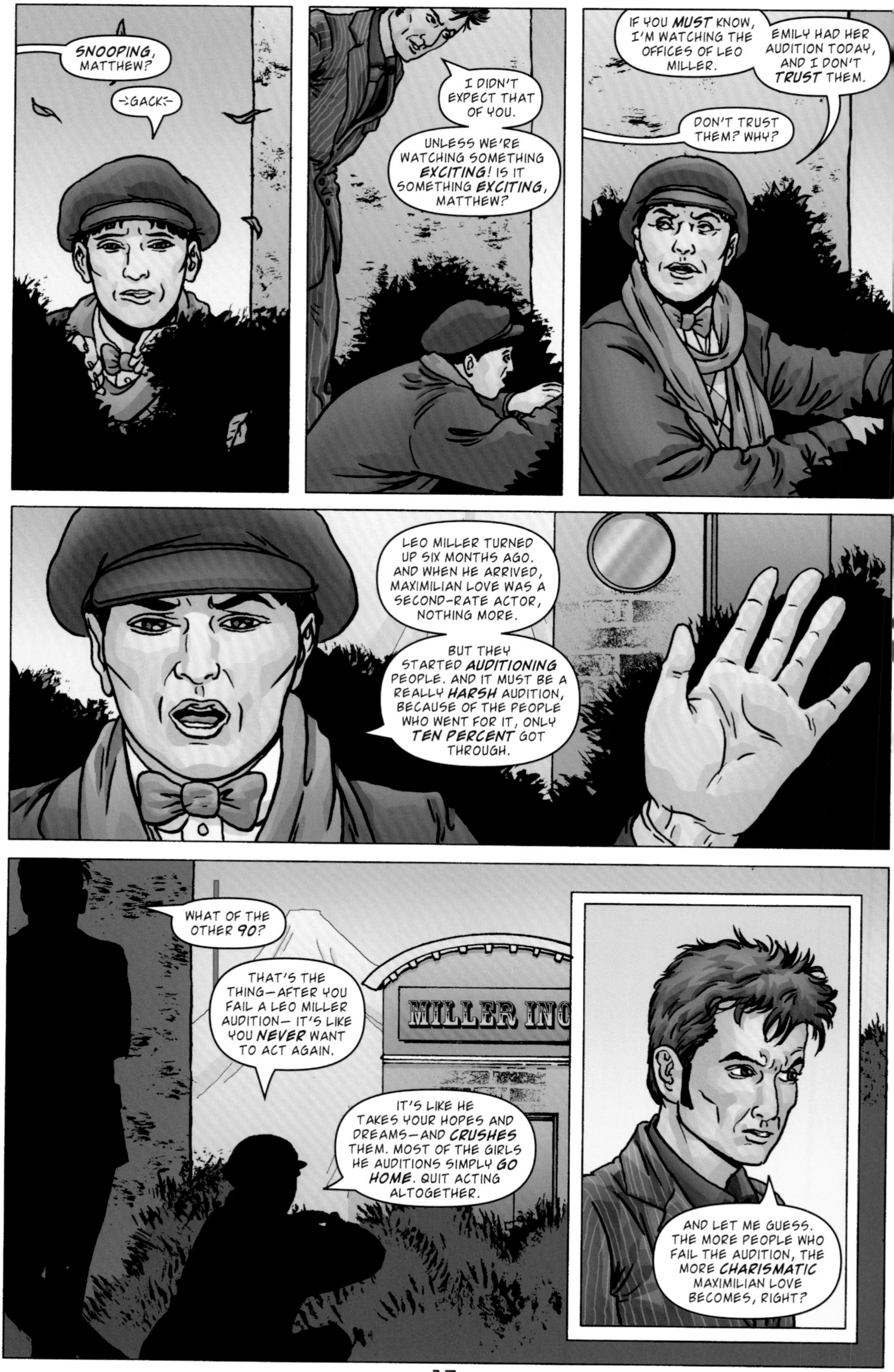
SNOOPING, MATTHEW?
-GACK-
I DIDN'T EXPECT THAT OF YOU.
UNLESS WE'RE WATCHING SOMETHING EXCITING! IS IT SOMETHING EXCITING, MATTHEW?
IF YOU MUST KNOW, I'M WATCHING THE OFFICES OF LEO MILLER.
EMILY HAD HER AUDITION TODAY, AND I DON'T TRUST THEM.
DON'T TRUST THEM? WHY?
LEO MILLER TURNED UP SIX MONTHS AGO. AND WHEN HE ARRIVED, MAXIMILIAN LOVE WAS A SECOND-RATE ACTOR, NOTHING MORE.
BUT THEY STARTED AUDITIONING PEOPLE. AND IT MUST BE A REALLY HARSH AUDITION, BECAUSE OF THE PEOPLE WHO WENT FOR IT, ONLY TEN PERCENT GOT THROUGH.
WHAT OF THE OTHER 90?
THAT'S THE THING—AFTER YOU FAIL A LEO MILLER AUDITION— IT'S LIKE YOU NEVER WANT TO ACT AGAIN.
MILLER INC
IT'S LIKE HE TAKES YOUR HOPES AND DREAMS—AND CRUSHES THEM. MOST OF THE GIRLS HE AUDITIONS SIMPLY GO HOME. QUIT ACTING ALTOGETHER.
AND LET ME GUESS. THE MORE PEOPLE WHO FAIL THE AUDITION, THE MORE CHARISMATIC MAXIMILIAN LOVE BECOMES, RIGHT?

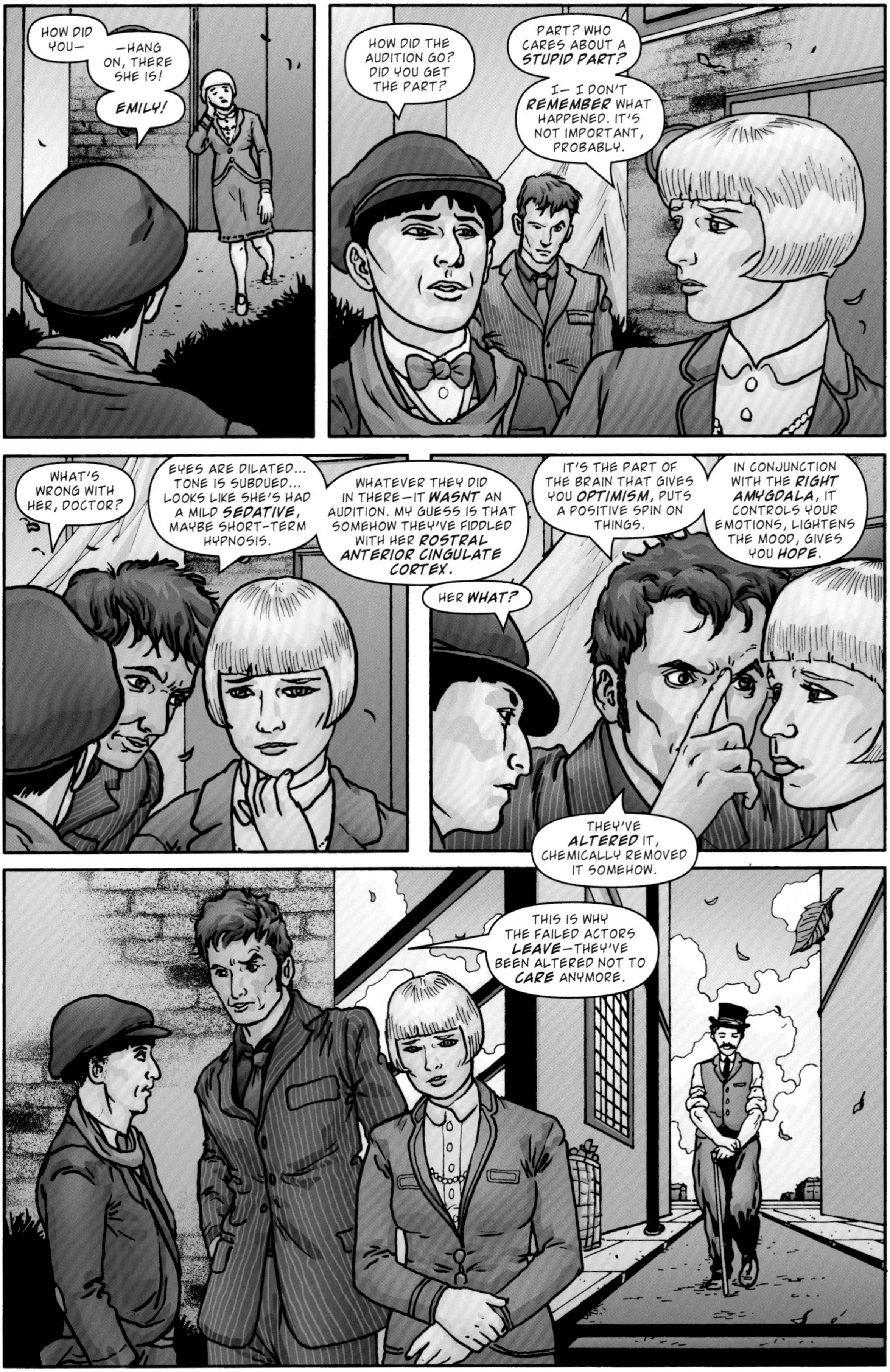

HOW DID YOU—
—HANG ON, THERE SHE IS!
EMILY!
HOW DID THE AUDITION GO? DID YOU GET THE PART?
PART? WHO CARES ABOUT A STUPID PART?
I— I DON'T REMEMBER WHAT HAPPENED. IT'S NOT IMPORTANT, PROBABLY.
WHAT'S WRONG WITH HER, DOCTOR?
EYES ARE DILATED... TONE IS SUBDUED... LOOKS LIKE SHE'S HAD A MILD SEDATIVE, MAYBE SHORT-TERM HYPNOSIS.
WHATEVER THEY DID IN THERE—IT WASNT AN AUDITION. MY GUESS IS THAT SOMEHOW THEY'VE FIDDLED WITH HER ROSTRAL ANTERIOR CINGULATE CORTEX.
HER WHAT?
IT'S THE PART OF THE BRAIN THAT GIVES YOU OPTIMISM, PUTS A POSITIVE SPIN ON THINGS.
IN CONJUNCTION WITH THE RIGHT AMYGDALA, IT CONTROLS YOUR EMOTIONS, LIGHTENS THE MOOD, GIVES YOU HOPE.
THEY'VE ALTERED IT, CHEMICALLY REMOVED IT SOMEHOW.
THIS IS WHY THE FAILED ACTORS LEAVE—THEY'VE BEEN ALTERED NOT TO CARE ANYMORE.

IS THAT THE LASS FROM YESTERDAY? SHE DOESN'T LOOK TOO GOOD.

AH, ARCHIE, WHAT MADE YOU LEASE OUT OFFICE SPACE TO MILLER?

AH. WELL, THAT'S A BIT OF A STORY, REALLY.

I'M GOING THROUGH A MESSY *DIVORCE* AT THE MOMENT—IT'S CAUSING MAJOR PROBLEMS WITH *THE FUN FAIR*, THE FILM I'M SHOOTING.

I'D HAD SOME MONEY ISSUES—WE HAD FILM THAT WAS *BURNED*, SETS WERE DESTROYED—THE WHOLE FILM WAS *CURSED*.

MATTHEW, TAKE EMILY TO THE INFIRMARY. SEE IF WE CAN'T DO SOMETHING ABOUT HER *SEROTONIN LEVELS*.

AND THEN LEO MILLER TURNED UP. OFFERED TO RENT A BLOCK JUST OFF THE SET, OFFERED TO PAY *CASH IN HAND*.

AND ANYTHING MAXIMILIAN LOVE FILMS IS DISTRIBUTED THROUGH *UNITED ACTORS*, SO I'LL MAKE EXTRA MONEY THERE.

OKAY, DOCTOR. WHAT WILL YOU DO?

OH, I DON'T KNOW—

MILLER INC

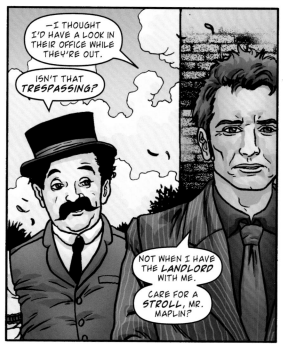

—I THOUGHT I'D HAVE A LOOK IN THEIR OFFICE WHILE THEY'RE OUT.

ISN'T THAT *TRESPASSING*?

NOT WHEN I HAVE THE *LANDLORD* WITH ME.

CARE FOR A *STROLL*, MR. MAPLIN?

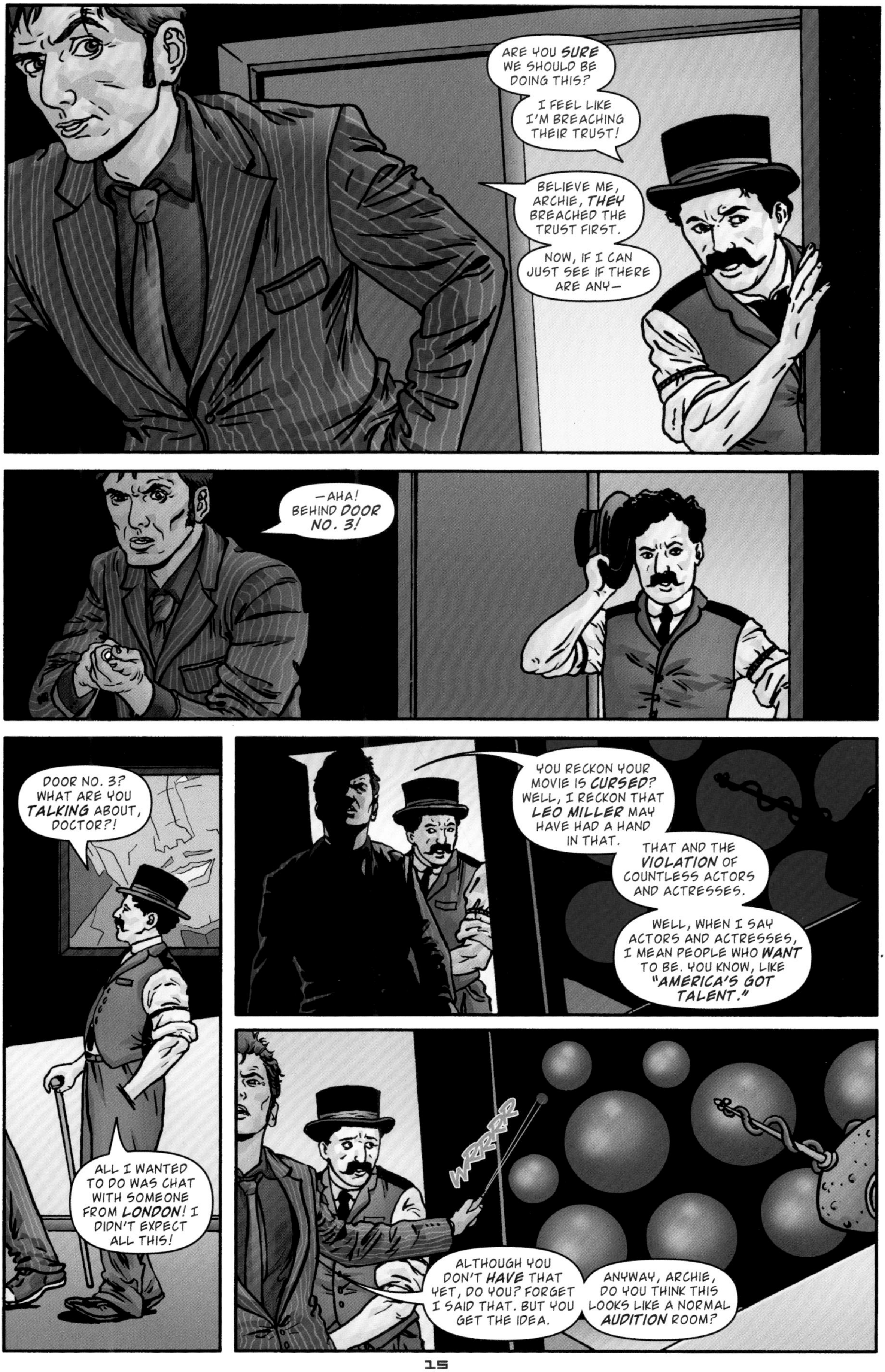
ARE YOU SURE WE SHOULD BE DOING THIS?
I FEEL LIKE I'M BREACHING THEIR TRUST!
BELIEVE ME, ARCHIE, THEY BREACHED THE TRUST FIRST.
NOW, IF I CAN JUST SEE IF THERE ARE ANY—
—AHA! BEHIND DOOR NO. 3!
DOOR NO. 3? WHAT ARE YOU TALKING ABOUT, DOCTOR?!
ALL I WANTED TO DO WAS CHAT WITH SOMEONE FROM LONDON! I DIDN'T EXPECT ALL THIS!
YOU RECKON YOUR MOVIE IS CURSED? WELL, I RECKON THAT LEO MILLER MAY HAVE HAD A HAND IN THAT.
THAT AND THE VIOLATION OF COUNTLESS ACTORS AND ACTRESSES.
WELL, WHEN I SAY ACTORS AND ACTRESSES, I MEAN PEOPLE WHO WANT TO BE. YOU KNOW, LIKE "AMERICA'S GOT TALENT."
WRRRR
ALTHOUGH YOU DON'T HAVE THAT YET, DO YOU? FORGET I SAID THAT. BUT YOU GET THE IDEA.
ANYWAY, ARCHIE, DO YOU THINK THIS LOOKS LIKE A NORMAL AUDITION ROOM?

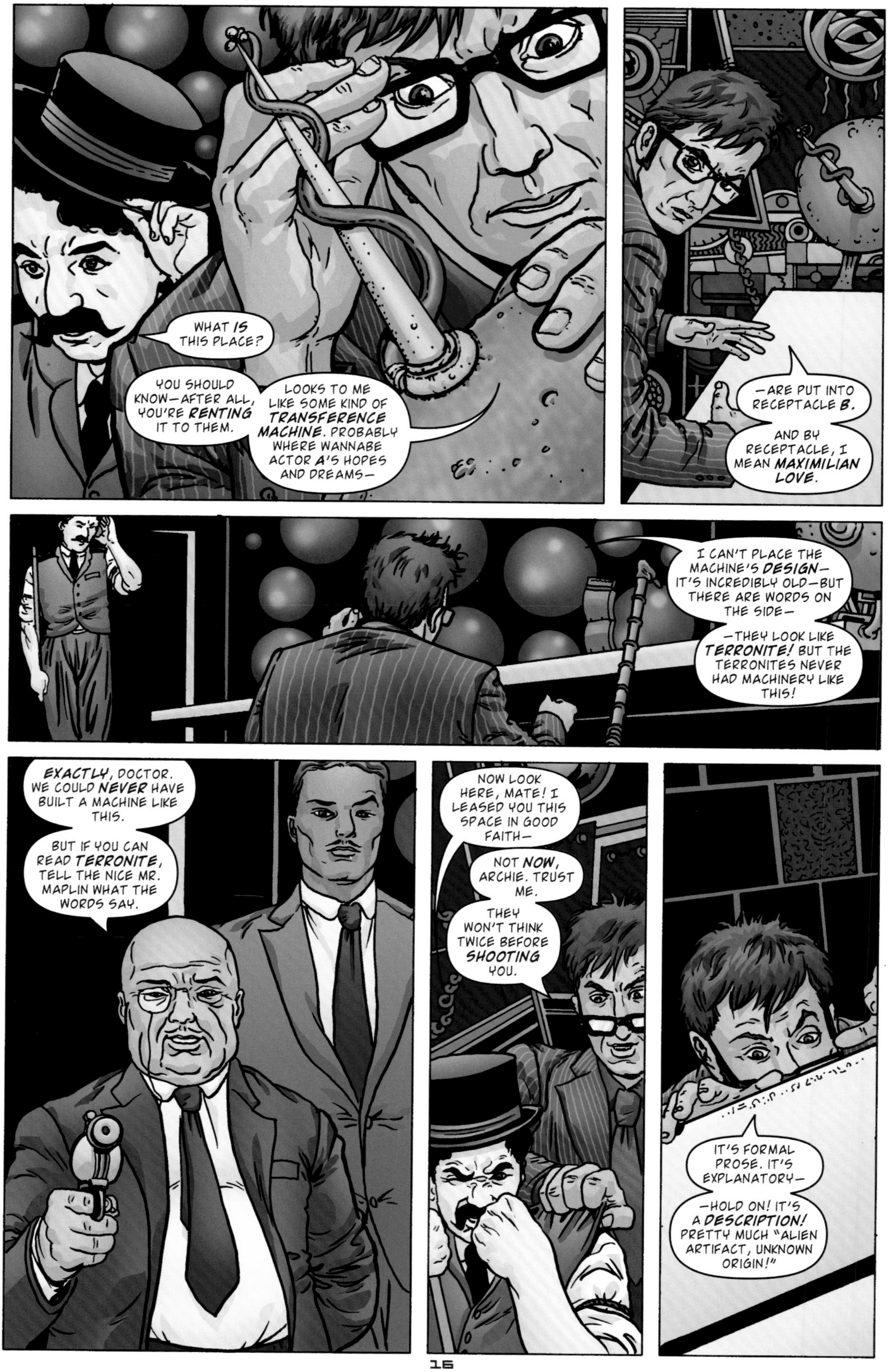
WHAT *IS* THIS PLACE?
YOU SHOULD KNOW—AFTER ALL, YOU'RE *RENTING* IT TO THEM.
LOOKS TO ME LIKE SOME KIND OF *TRANSFERENCE MACHINE*. PROBABLY WHERE WANNABE ACTOR *A*'S HOPES AND DREAMS—
—ARE PUT INTO RECEPTACLE *B.*
AND BY RECEPTACLE, I MEAN *MAXIMILIAN LOVE*.
I CAN'T PLACE THE MACHINE'S *DESIGN*—IT'S INCREDIBLY OLD—BUT THERE ARE WORDS ON THE SIDE—
—THEY LOOK LIKE *TERRONITE!* BUT THE TERRONITES NEVER HAD MACHINERY LIKE THIS!
EXACTLY, DOCTOR. WE COULD *NEVER* HAVE BUILT A MACHINE LIKE THIS.
BUT IF YOU CAN READ *TERRONITE*, TELL THE NICE MR. MAPLIN WHAT THE WORDS SAY.
NOW LOOK HERE, MATE! I LEASED YOU THIS SPACE IN GOOD FAITH—
NOT *NOW*, ARCHIE. TRUST ME.
THEY WON'T THINK TWICE BEFORE *SHOOTING* YOU.
IT'S FORMAL PROSE. IT'S EXPLANATORY—
—HOLD ON! IT'S A *DESCRIPTION!* PRETTY MUCH "ALIEN ARTIFACT, UNKNOWN ORIGIN!"

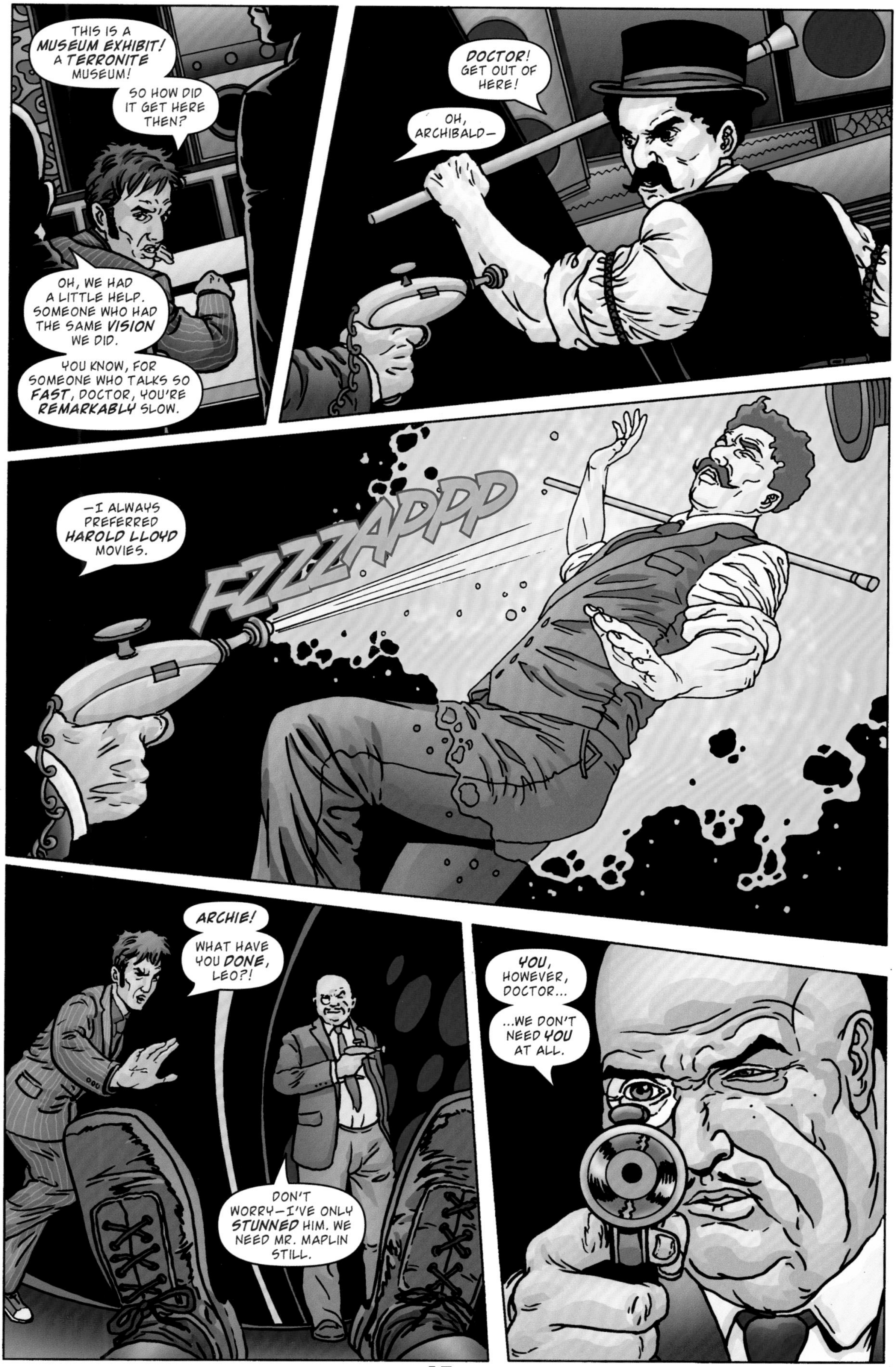
THIS IS A MUSEUM EXHIBIT! A TERRONITE MUSEUM!
SO HOW DID IT GET HERE THEN?
OH, WE HAD A LITTLE HELP. SOMEONE WHO HAD THE SAME VISION WE DID.
YOU KNOW, FOR SOMEONE WHO TALKS SO FAST, DOCTOR, YOU'RE REMARKABLY SLOW.
DOCTOR! GET OUT OF HERE!
OH, ARCHIBALD—
—I ALWAYS PREFERRED HAROLD LLOYD MOVIES.
FZZZAPPP
ARCHIE!
WHAT HAVE YOU DONE, LEO?!
DON'T WORRY—I'VE ONLY STUNNED HIM. WE NEED MR. MAPLIN STILL.
YOU, HOWEVER, DOCTOR...
...WE DON'T NEED YOU AT ALL.

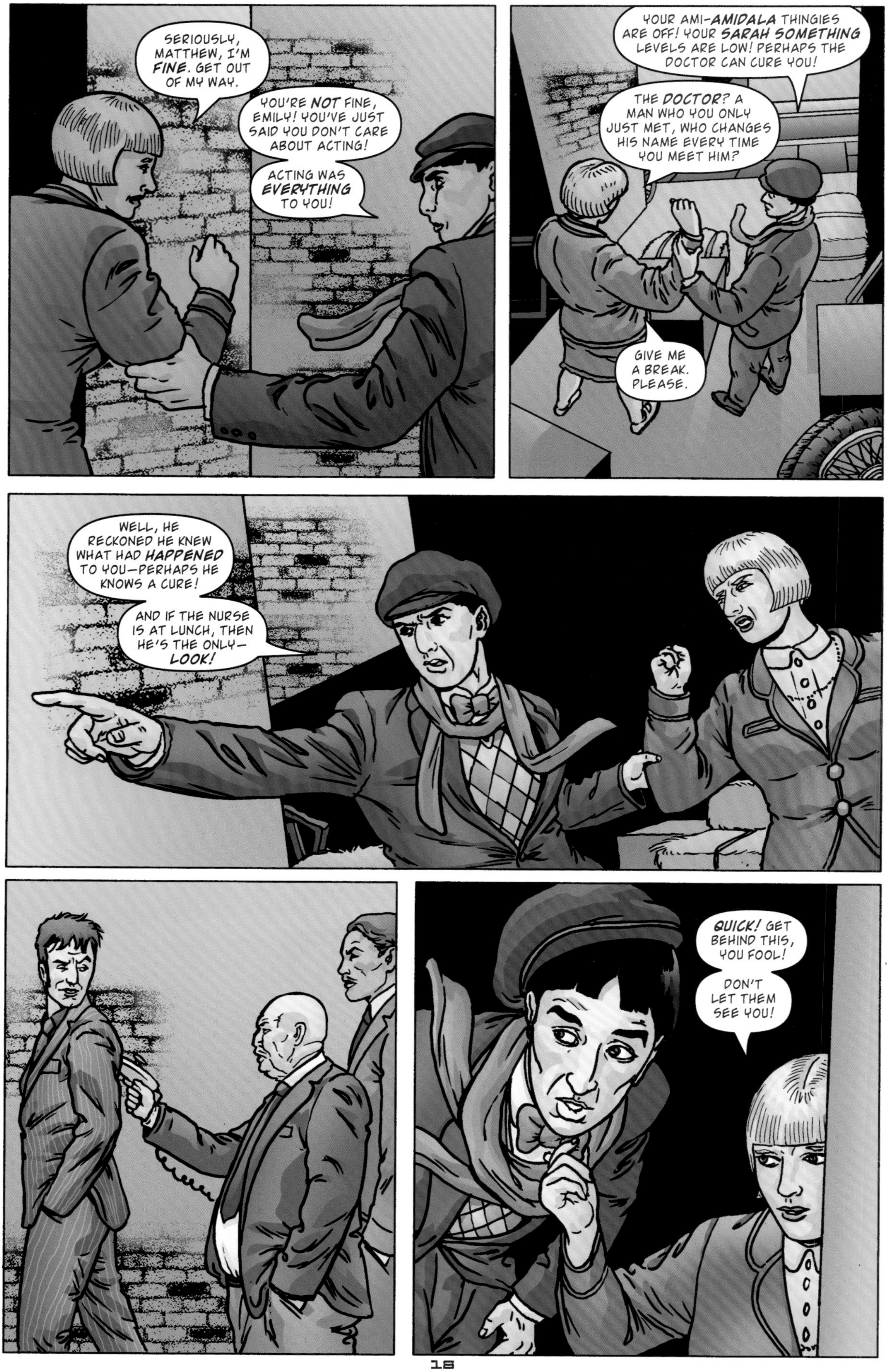
SERIOUSLY, MATTHEW, I'M FINE. GET OUT OF MY WAY.
YOU'RE NOT FINE, EMILY! YOU'VE JUST SAID YOU DON'T CARE ABOUT ACTING!
ACTING WAS EVERYTHING TO YOU!
YOUR AMI-AMIDALA THINGIES ARE OFF! YOUR SARAH SOMETHING LEVELS ARE LOW! PERHAPS THE DOCTOR CAN CURE YOU!
THE DOCTOR? A MAN WHO YOU ONLY JUST MET, WHO CHANGES HIS NAME EVERY TIME YOU MEET HIM?
GIVE ME A BREAK. PLEASE.
WELL, HE RECKONED HE KNEW WHAT HAD HAPPENED TO YOU—PERHAPS HE KNOWS A CURE!
AND IF THE NURSE IS AT LUNCH, THEN HE'S THE ONLY— LOOK!
QUICK! GET BEHIND THIS, YOU FOOL!
DON'T LET THEM SEE YOU!

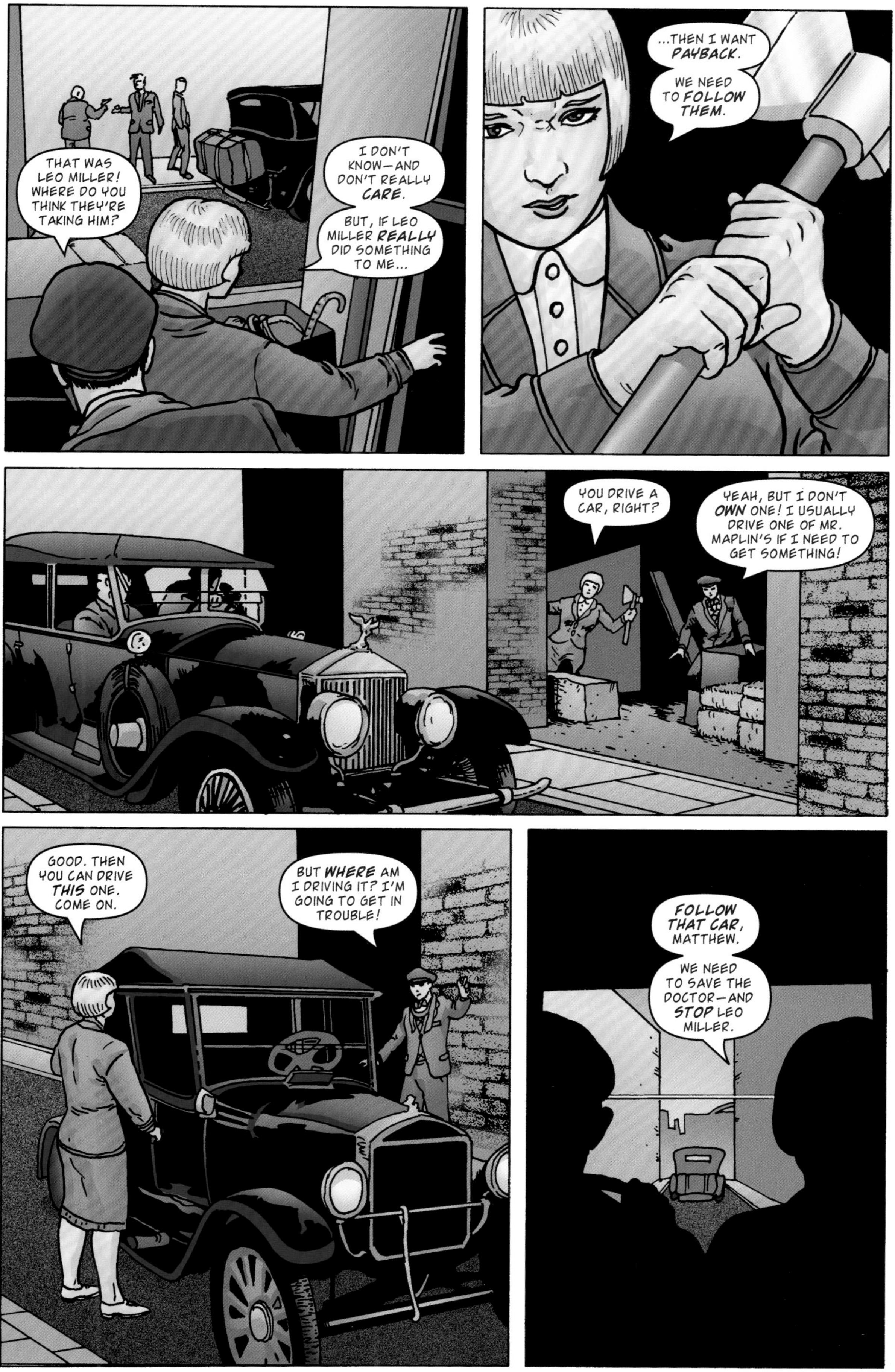
THAT WAS LEO MILLER! WHERE DO YOU THINK THEY'RE TAKING HIM?
I DON'T KNOW—AND DON'T REALLY **CARE**.
BUT, IF LEO MILLER **REALLY** DID SOMETHING TO ME...
...THEN I WANT **PAYBACK**.
WE NEED TO **FOLLOW THEM**.
YOU DRIVE A CAR, RIGHT?
YEAH, BUT I DON'T **OWN** ONE! I USUALLY DRIVE ONE OF MR. MAPLIN'S IF I NEED TO GET SOMETHING!
GOOD. THEN YOU CAN DRIVE **THIS** ONE. COME ON.
BUT **WHERE** AM I DRIVING IT? I'M GOING TO GET IN TROUBLE!
FOLLOW THAT CAR, MATTHEW.
WE NEED TO SAVE THE DOCTOR—AND **STOP** LEO MILLER.

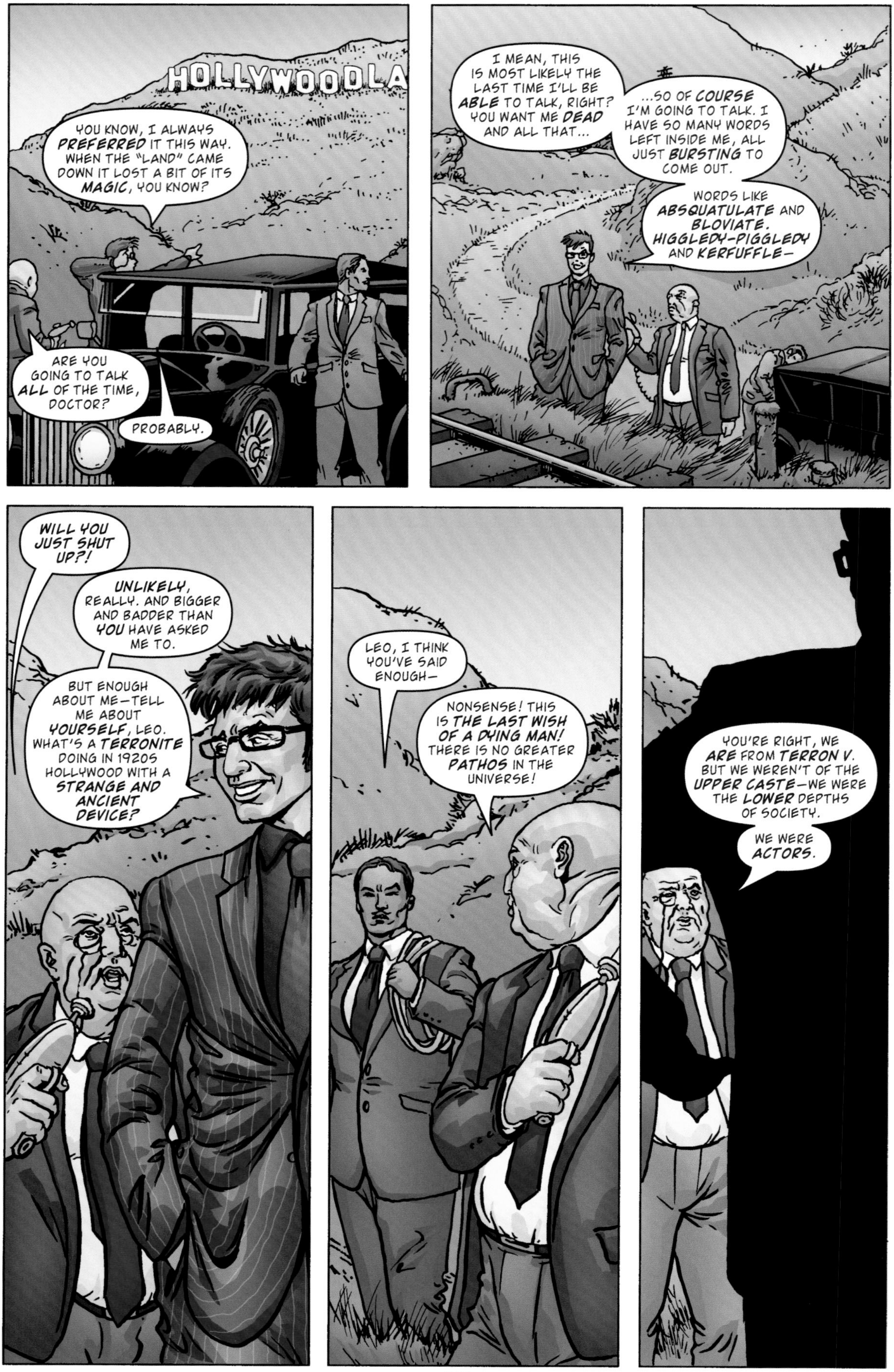
HOLLYWOODLA
YOU KNOW, I ALWAYS PREFERRED IT THIS WAY. WHEN THE "LAND" CAME DOWN IT LOST A BIT OF ITS MAGIC, YOU KNOW?
ARE YOU GOING TO TALK ALL OF THE TIME, DOCTOR?
PROBABLY.
I MEAN, THIS IS MOST LIKELY THE LAST TIME I'LL BE ABLE TO TALK, RIGHT? YOU WANT ME DEAD AND ALL THAT...
...SO OF COURSE I'M GOING TO TALK. I HAVE SO MANY WORDS LEFT INSIDE ME, ALL JUST BURSTING TO COME OUT.
WORDS LIKE ABSQUATULATE AND BLOVIATE. HIGGLEDY-PIGGLEDY AND KERFUFFLE—
WILL YOU JUST SHUT UP?!
UNLIKELY, REALLY. AND BIGGER AND BADDER THAN YOU HAVE ASKED ME TO.
BUT ENOUGH ABOUT ME—TELL ME ABOUT YOURSELF, LEO. WHAT'S A TERRONITE DOING IN 1920S HOLLYWOOD WITH A STRANGE AND ANCIENT DEVICE?
LEO, I THINK YOU'VE SAID ENOUGH—
NONSENSE! THIS IS THE LAST WISH OF A DYING MAN! THERE IS NO GREATER PATHOS IN THE UNIVERSE!
YOU'RE RIGHT, WE ARE FROM TERRON V. BUT WE WEREN'T OF THE UPPER CASTE—WE WERE THE LOWER DEPTHS OF SOCIETY.
WE WERE ACTORS.

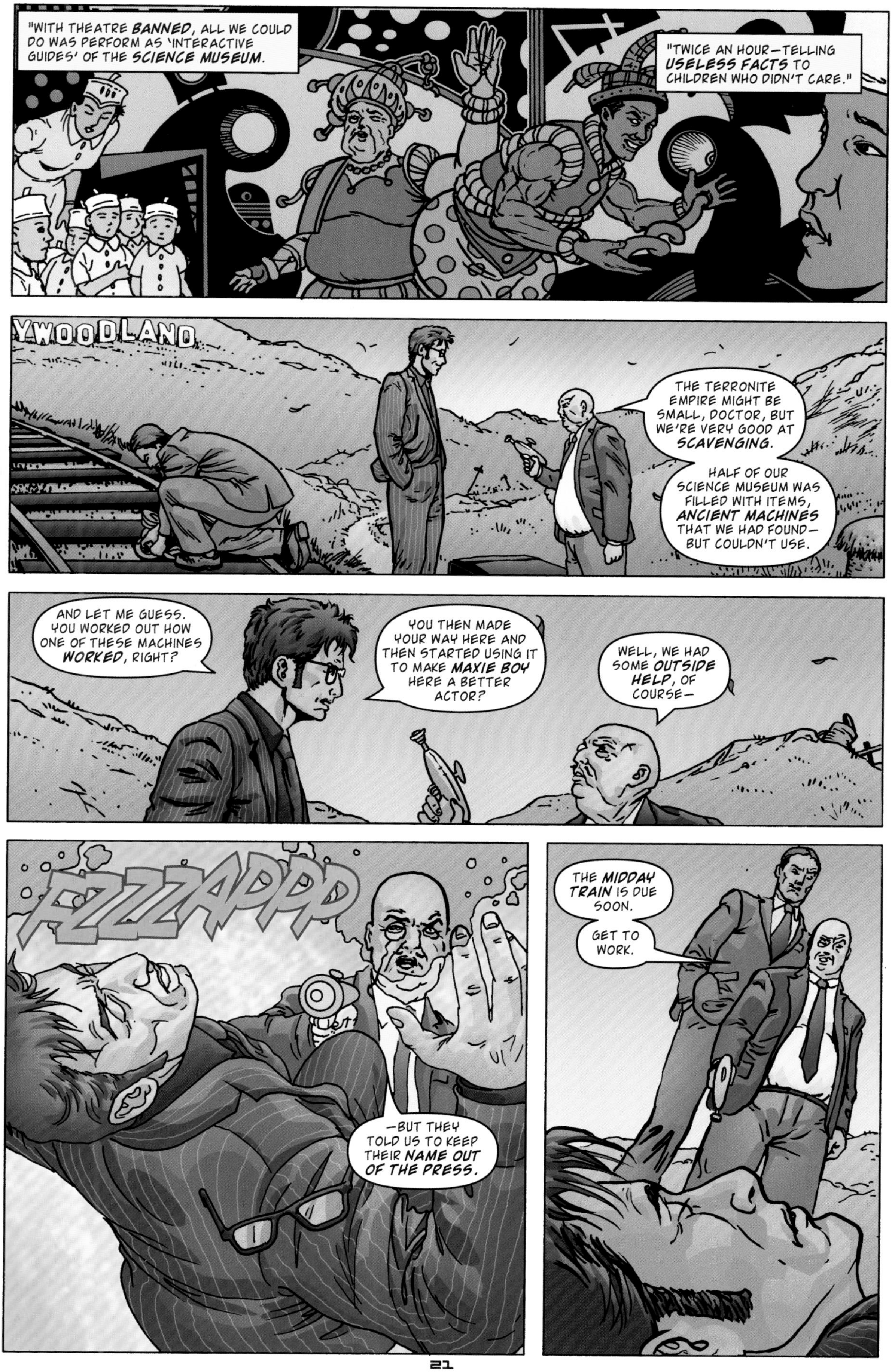
"WITH THEATRE BANNED, ALL WE COULD DO WAS PERFORM AS 'INTERACTIVE GUIDES' OF THE SCIENCE MUSEUM.
"TWICE AN HOUR—TELLING USELESS FACTS TO CHILDREN WHO DIDN'T CARE."
YWOODLAND
THE TERRONITE EMPIRE MIGHT BE SMALL, DOCTOR, BUT WE'RE VERY GOOD AT SCAVENGING.
HALF OF OUR SCIENCE MUSEUM WAS FILLED WITH ITEMS, ANCIENT MACHINES THAT WE HAD FOUND—BUT COULDN'T USE.
AND LET ME GUESS. YOU WORKED OUT HOW ONE OF THESE MACHINES WORKED, RIGHT?
YOU THEN MADE YOUR WAY HERE AND THEN STARTED USING IT TO MAKE MAXIE BOY HERE A BETTER ACTOR?
WELL, WE HAD SOME OUTSIDE HELP, OF COURSE—
FZZZAPPP
—BUT THEY TOLD US TO KEEP THEIR NAME OUT OF THE PRESS.
THE MIDDAY TRAIN IS DUE SOON.
GET TO WORK.

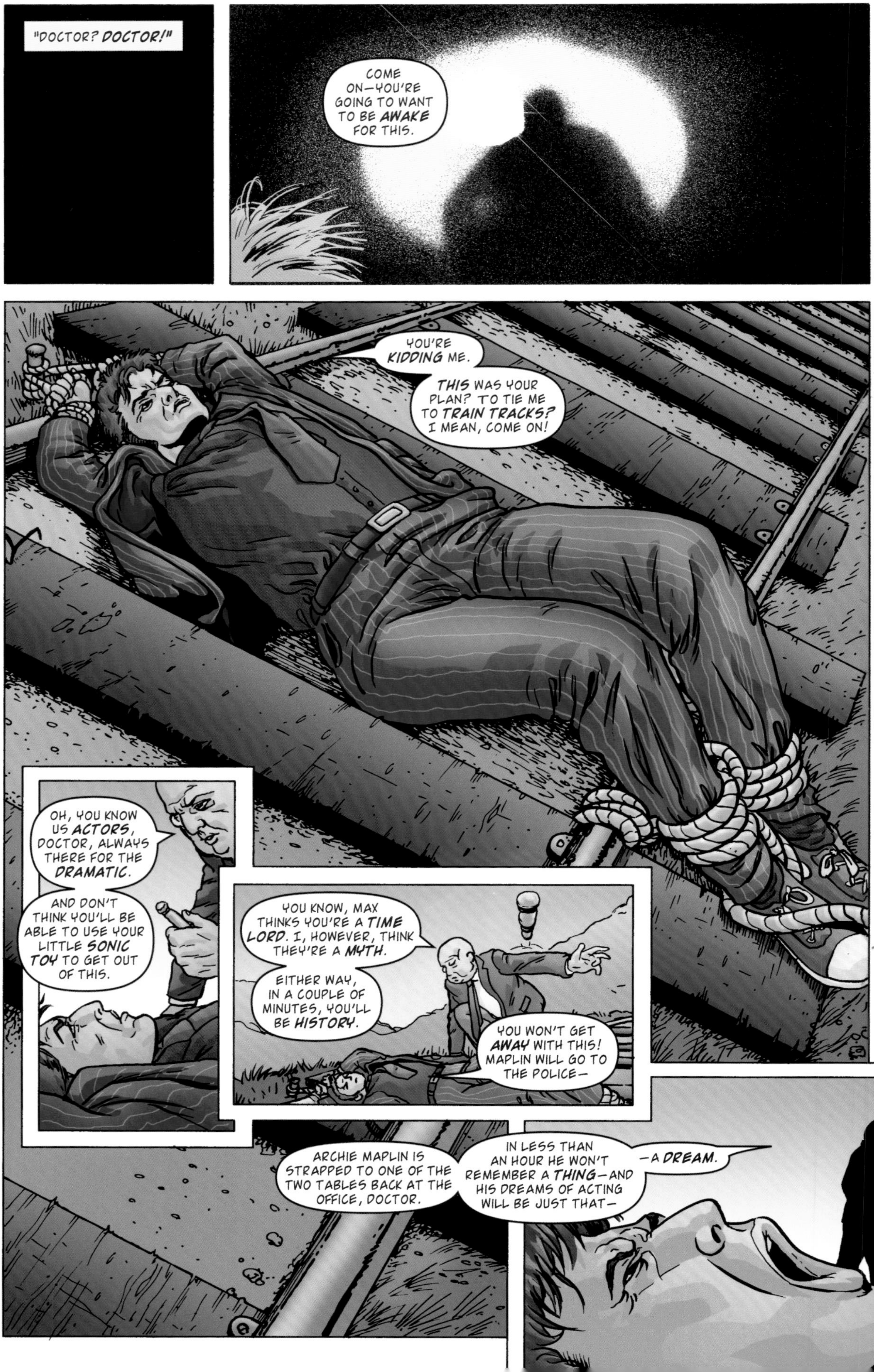
"DOCTOR? DOCTOR!"
COME ON—YOU'RE GOING TO WANT TO BE AWAKE FOR THIS.
YOU'RE KIDDING ME.
THIS WAS YOUR PLAN? TO TIE ME TO TRAIN TRACKS? I MEAN, COME ON!
OH, YOU KNOW US ACTORS, DOCTOR, ALWAYS THERE FOR THE DRAMATIC.
AND DON'T THINK YOU'LL BE ABLE TO USE YOUR LITTLE SONIC TOY TO GET OUT OF THIS.
YOU KNOW, MAX THINKS YOU'RE A TIME LORD. I, HOWEVER, THINK THEY'RE A MYTH.
EITHER WAY, IN A COUPLE OF MINUTES, YOU'LL BE HISTORY.
YOU WON'T GET AWAY WITH THIS! MAPLIN WILL GO TO THE POLICE—
ARCHIE MAPLIN IS STRAPPED TO ONE OF THE TWO TABLES BACK AT THE OFFICE, DOCTOR.
IN LESS THAN AN HOUR HE WON'T REMEMBER A THING—AND HIS DREAMS OF ACTING WILL BE JUST THAT—
—A DREAM.

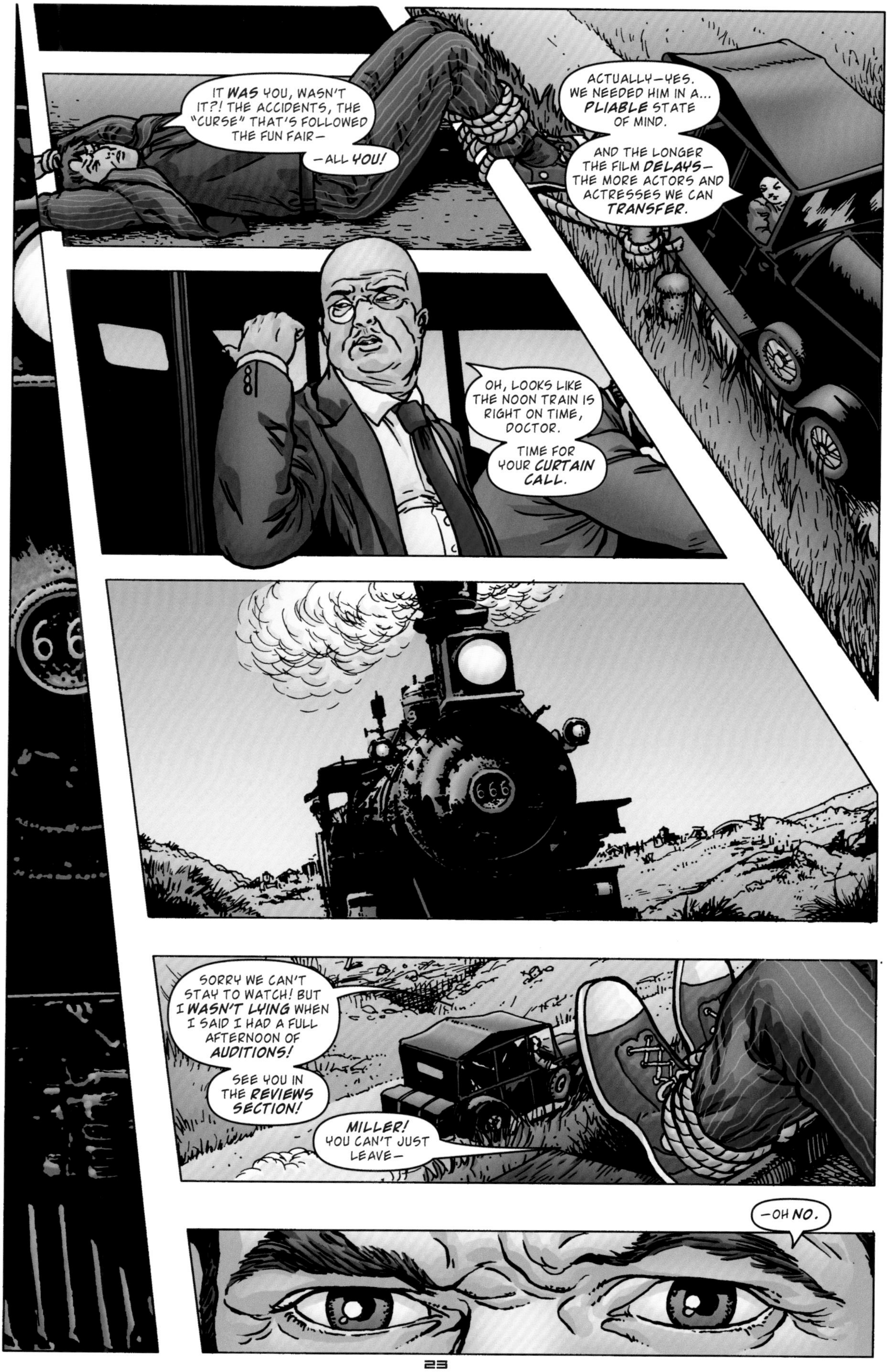
IT WAS YOU, WASN'T IT?! THE ACCIDENTS, THE "CURSE" THAT'S FOLLOWED THE FUN FAIR—
—ALL YOU!
ACTUALLY—YES. WE NEEDED HIM IN A... PLIABLE STATE OF MIND.
AND THE LONGER THE FILM DELAYS—THE MORE ACTORS AND ACTRESSES WE CAN TRANSFER.
OH, LOOKS LIKE THE NOON TRAIN IS RIGHT ON TIME, DOCTOR.
TIME FOR YOUR CURTAIN CALL.
666
SORRY WE CAN'T STAY TO WATCH! BUT I WASN'T LYING WHEN I SAID I HAD A FULL AFTERNOON OF AUDITIONS!
SEE YOU IN THE REVIEWS SECTION!
MILLER! YOU CAN'T JUST LEAVE—
—OH NO.

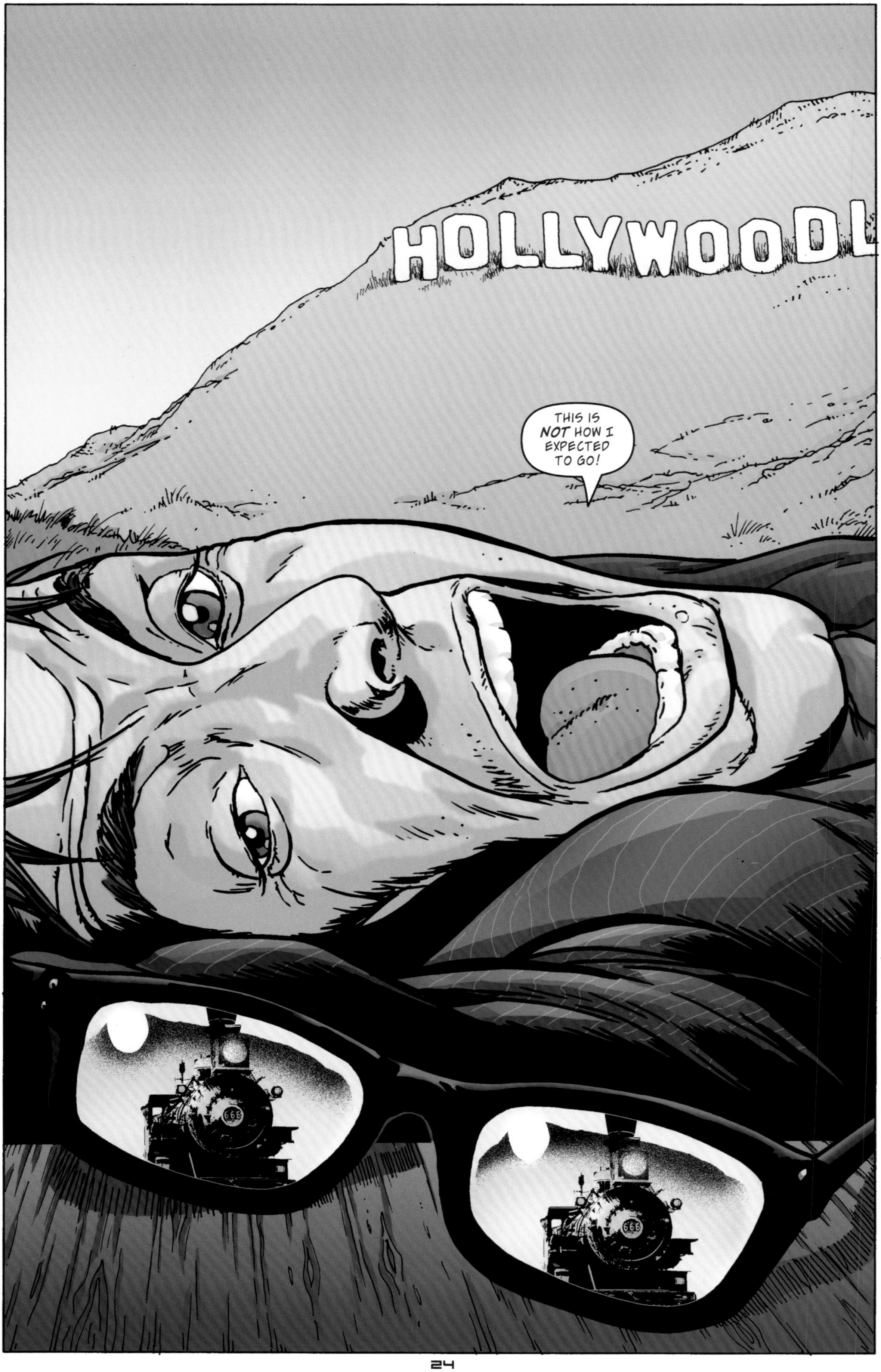
HOLLYWOOD
THIS IS NOT HOW I EXPECTED TO GO!

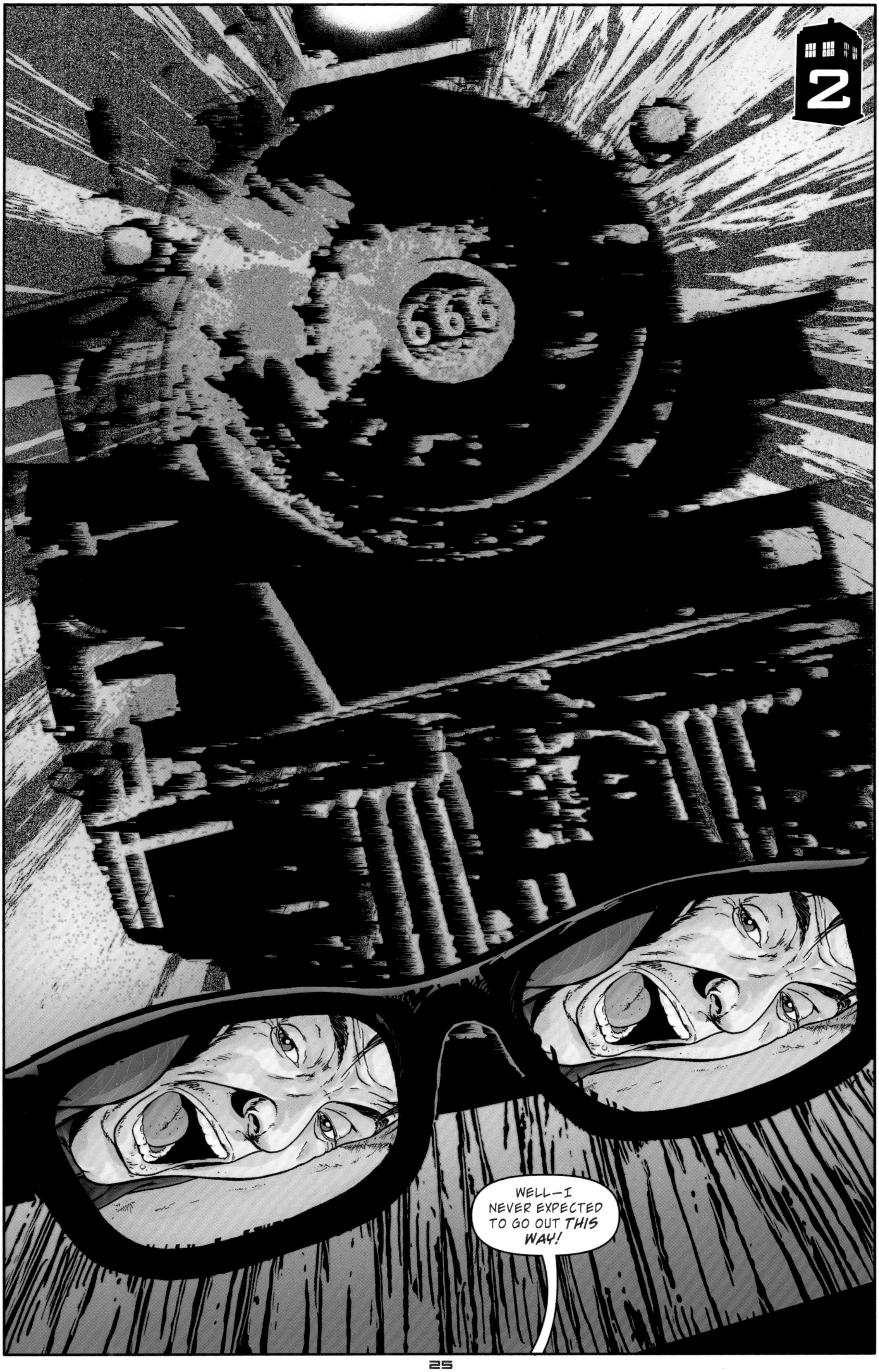
2
666
WELL—I NEVER EXPECTED TO GO OUT *THIS WAY!*

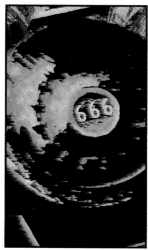

QUICK,
DOCTOR! YOUR
LEGS!

QUICKLY!
GRAB AN ARM,
MATTHEW!

FWOOSH

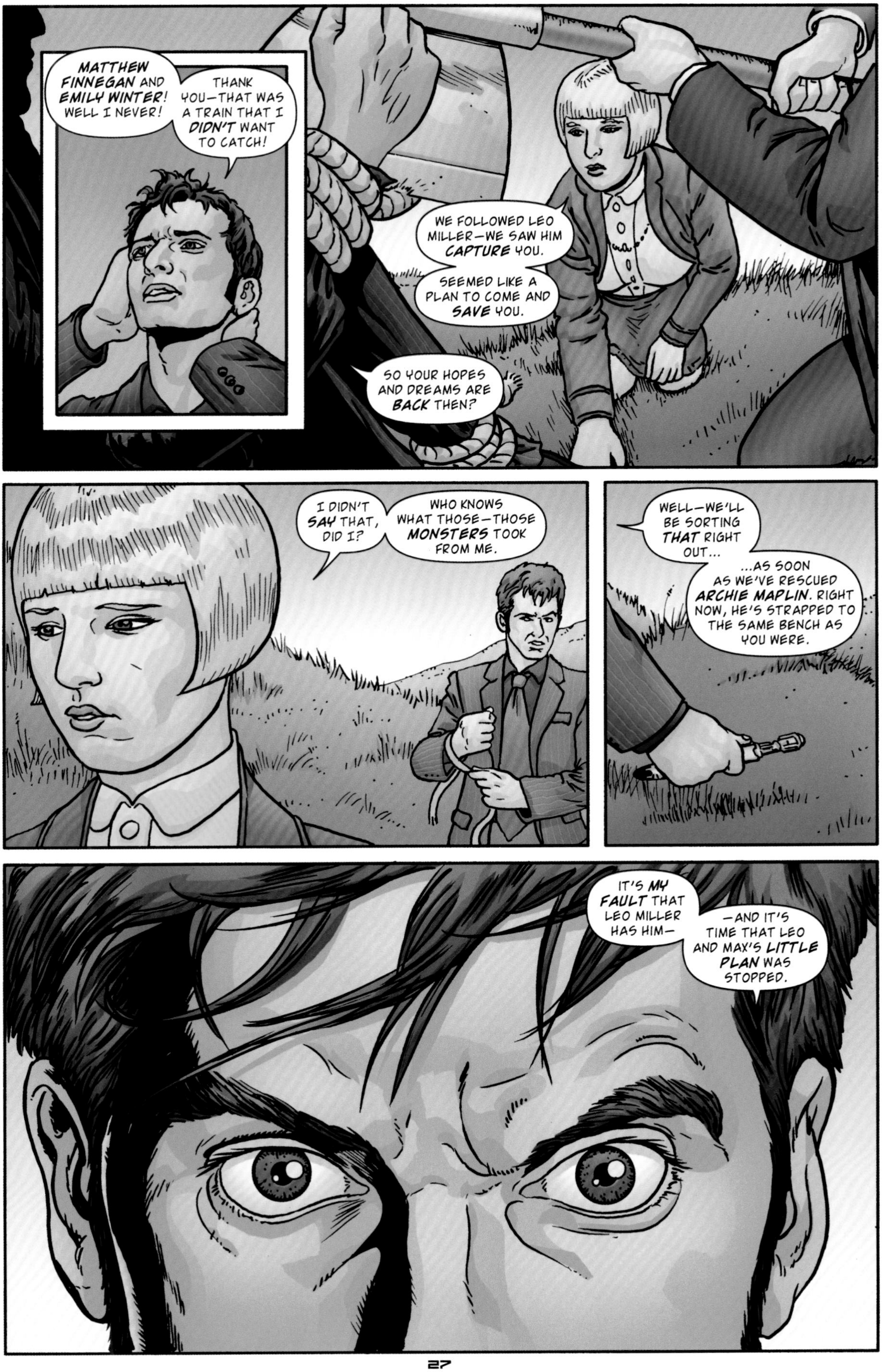
MATTHEW FINNEGAN AND EMILY WINTER! WELL I NEVER!
THANK YOU—THAT WAS A TRAIN THAT I DIDN'T WANT TO CATCH!
WE FOLLOWED LEO MILLER—WE SAW HIM CAPTURE YOU.
SEEMED LIKE A PLAN TO COME AND SAVE YOU.
SO YOUR HOPES AND DREAMS ARE BACK THEN?
I DIDN'T SAY THAT, DID I?
WHO KNOWS WHAT THOSE—THOSE MONSTERS TOOK FROM ME.
WELL—WE'LL BE SORTING THAT RIGHT OUT...
...AS SOON AS WE'VE RESCUED ARCHIE MAPLIN. RIGHT NOW, HE'S STRAPPED TO THE SAME BENCH AS YOU WERE.
IT'S MY FAULT THAT LEO MILLER HAS HIM—
—AND IT'S TIME THAT LEO AND MAX'S LITTLE PLAN WAS STOPPED.

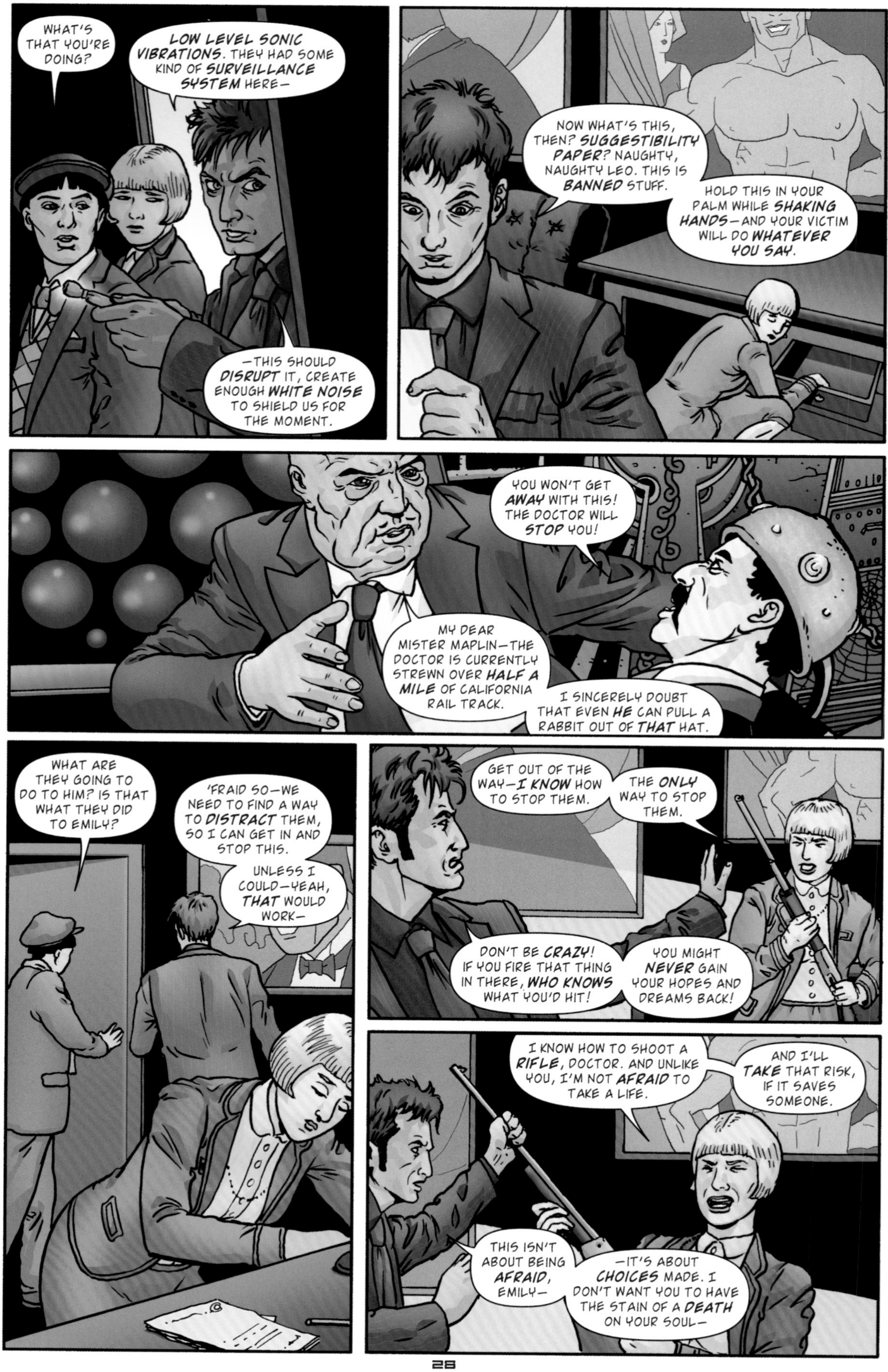
WHAT'S THAT YOU'RE DOING?
LOW LEVEL SONIC VIBRATIONS. THEY HAD SOME KIND OF SURVEILLANCE SYSTEM HERE—
—THIS SHOULD DISRUPT IT, CREATE ENOUGH WHITE NOISE TO SHIELD US FOR THE MOMENT.
NOW WHAT'S THIS, THEN? SUGGESTIBILITY PAPER? NAUGHTY, NAUGHTY LEO. THIS IS BANNED STUFF.
HOLD THIS IN YOUR PALM WHILE SHAKING HANDS—AND YOUR VICTIM WILL DO WHATEVER YOU SAY.
YOU WON'T GET AWAY WITH THIS! THE DOCTOR WILL STOP YOU!
MY DEAR MISTER MAPLIN—THE DOCTOR IS CURRENTLY STREWN OVER HALF A MILE OF CALIFORNIA RAIL TRACK.
I SINCERELY DOUBT THAT EVEN HE CAN PULL A RABBIT OUT OF THAT HAT.
WHAT ARE THEY GOING TO DO TO HIM? IS THAT WHAT THEY DID TO EMILY?
'FRAID SO—WE NEED TO FIND A WAY TO DISTRACT THEM, SO I CAN GET IN AND STOP THIS.
UNLESS I COULD—YEAH, THAT WOULD WORK—
GET OUT OF THE WAY—I KNOW HOW TO STOP THEM.
THE ONLY WAY TO STOP THEM.
DON'T BE CRAZY! IF YOU FIRE THAT THING IN THERE, WHO KNOWS WHAT YOU'D HIT!
YOU MIGHT NEVER GAIN YOUR HOPES AND DREAMS BACK!
I KNOW HOW TO SHOOT A RIFLE, DOCTOR. AND UNLIKE YOU, I'M NOT AFRAID TO TAKE A LIFE.
AND I'LL TAKE THAT RISK, IF IT SAVES SOMEONE.
THIS ISN'T ABOUT BEING AFRAID, EMILY—
—IT'S ABOUT CHOICES MADE. I DON'T WANT YOU TO HAVE THE STAIN OF A DEATH ON YOUR SOUL—

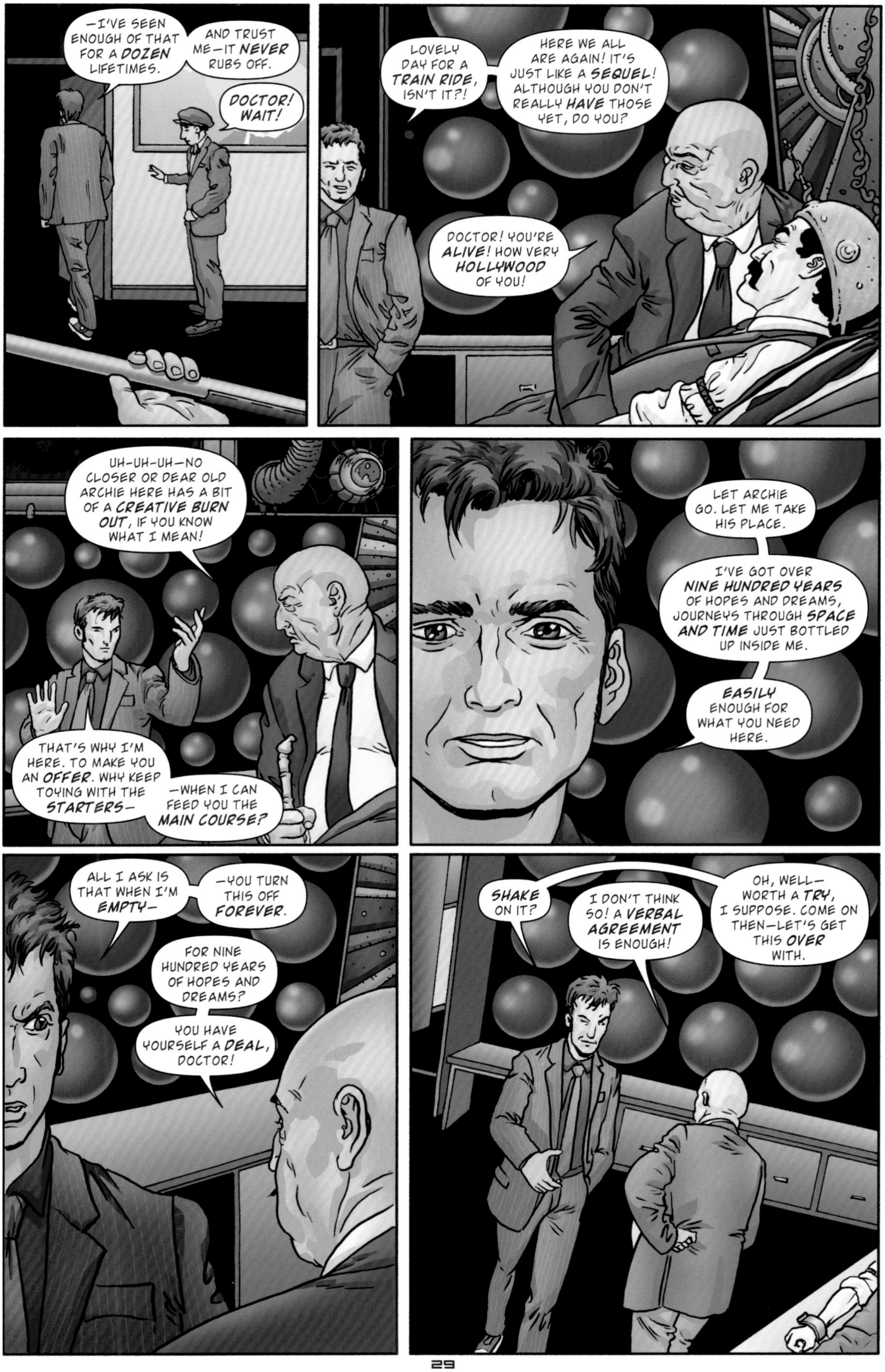
—I'VE SEEN ENOUGH OF THAT FOR A DOZEN LIFETIMES.
AND TRUST ME—IT NEVER RUBS OFF.
DOCTOR! WAIT!
LOVELY DAY FOR A TRAIN RIDE, ISN'T IT?!
HERE WE ALL ARE AGAIN! IT'S JUST LIKE A SEQUEL! ALTHOUGH YOU DON'T REALLY HAVE THOSE YET, DO YOU?
DOCTOR! YOU'RE ALIVE! HOW VERY HOLLYWOOD OF YOU!
UH-UH-UH—NO CLOSER OR DEAR OLD ARCHIE HERE HAS A BIT OF A CREATIVE BURN OUT, IF YOU KNOW WHAT I MEAN!
THAT'S WHY I'M HERE. TO MAKE YOU AN OFFER. WHY KEEP TOYING WITH THE STARTERS—
—WHEN I CAN FEED YOU THE MAIN COURSE?
LET ARCHIE GO. LET ME TAKE HIS PLACE.
I'VE GOT OVER NINE HUNDRED YEARS OF HOPES AND DREAMS, JOURNEYS THROUGH SPACE AND TIME JUST BOTTLED UP INSIDE ME.
EASILY ENOUGH FOR WHAT YOU NEED HERE.
ALL I ASK IS THAT WHEN I'M EMPTY—
—YOU TURN THIS OFF FOREVER.
FOR NINE HUNDRED YEARS OF HOPES AND DREAMS?
YOU HAVE YOURSELF A DEAL, DOCTOR!
SHAKE ON IT?
I DON'T THINK SO! A VERBAL AGREEMENT IS ENOUGH!
OH, WELL—WORTH A TRY, I SUPPOSE. COME ON THEN—LET'S GET THIS OVER WITH.

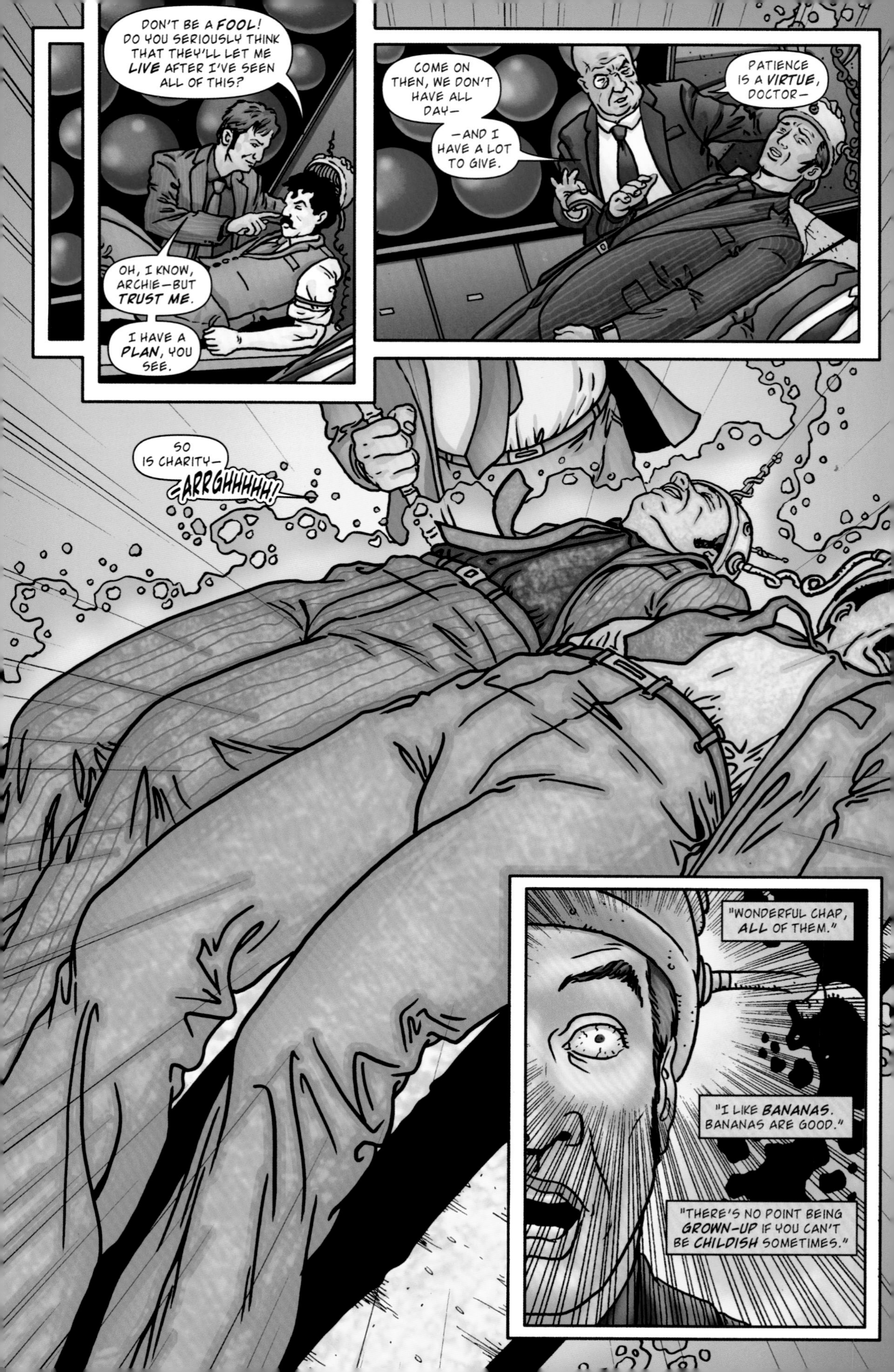
DON'T BE A FOOL! DO YOU SERIOUSLY THINK THAT THEY'LL LET ME LIVE AFTER I'VE SEEN ALL OF THIS?
OH, I KNOW, ARCHIE—BUT TRUST ME.
I HAVE A PLAN, YOU SEE.
COME ON THEN, WE DON'T HAVE ALL DAY—
—AND I HAVE A LOT TO GIVE.
PATIENCE IS A VIRTUE, DOCTOR—
SO IS CHARITY—
ARRGHHHHH!
"WONDERFUL CHAP, ALL OF THEM."
"I LIKE BANANAS. BANANAS ARE GOOD."
"THERE'S NO POINT BEING GROWN-UP IF YOU CAN'T BE CHILDISH SOMETIMES."

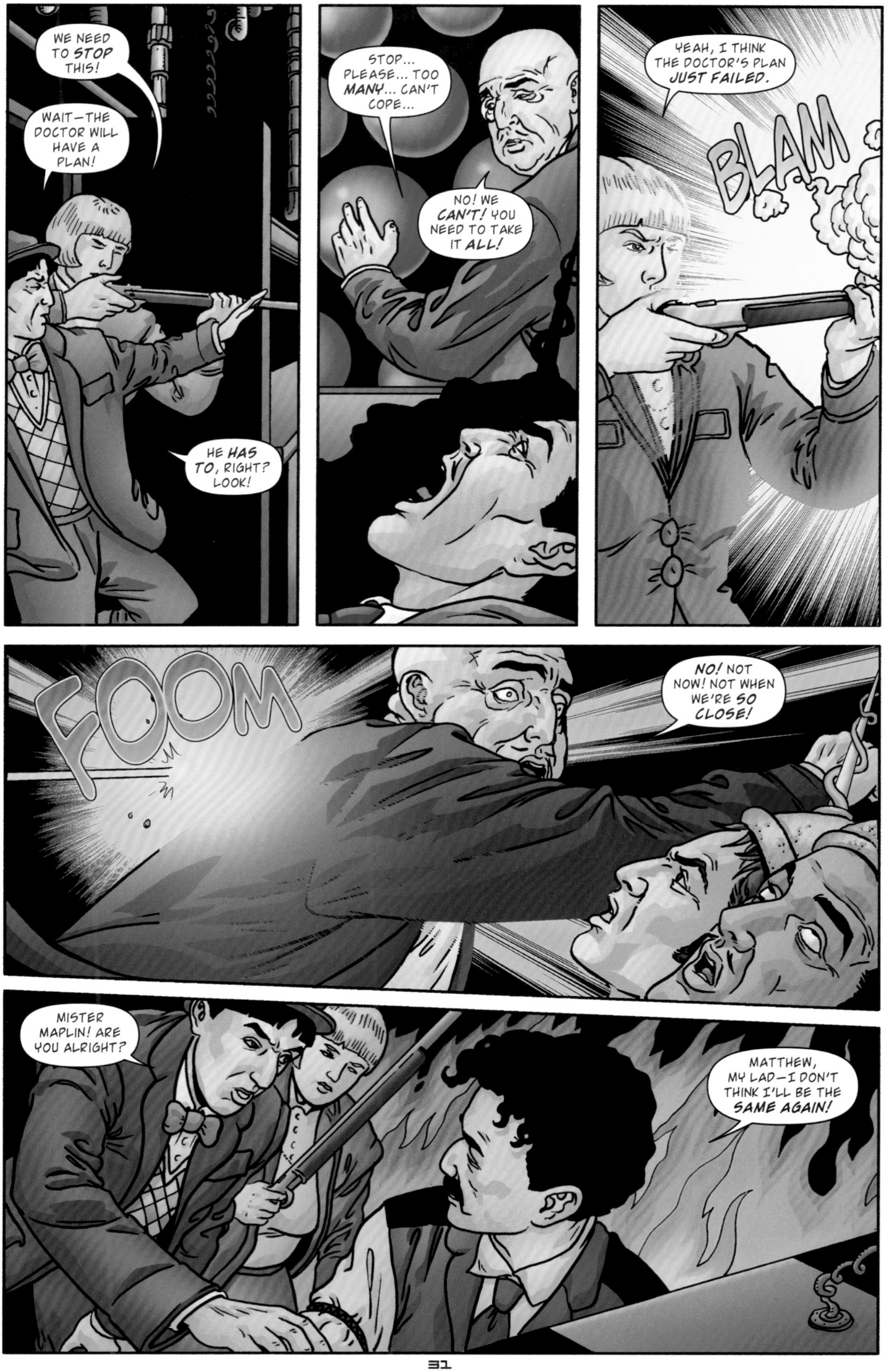
WE NEED TO STOP THIS!
WAIT—THE DOCTOR WILL HAVE A PLAN!
HE HAS TO, RIGHT? LOOK!
STOP... PLEASE... TOO MANY... CAN'T COPE...
NO! WE CAN'T! YOU NEED TO TAKE IT ALL!
YEAH, I THINK THE DOCTOR'S PLAN JUST FAILED.
BLAM
FOOM
NO! NOT NOW! NOT WHEN WE'RE SO CLOSE!
MISTER MAPLIN! ARE YOU ALRIGHT?
MATTHEW, MY LAD—I DON'T THINK I'LL BE THE SAME AGAIN!

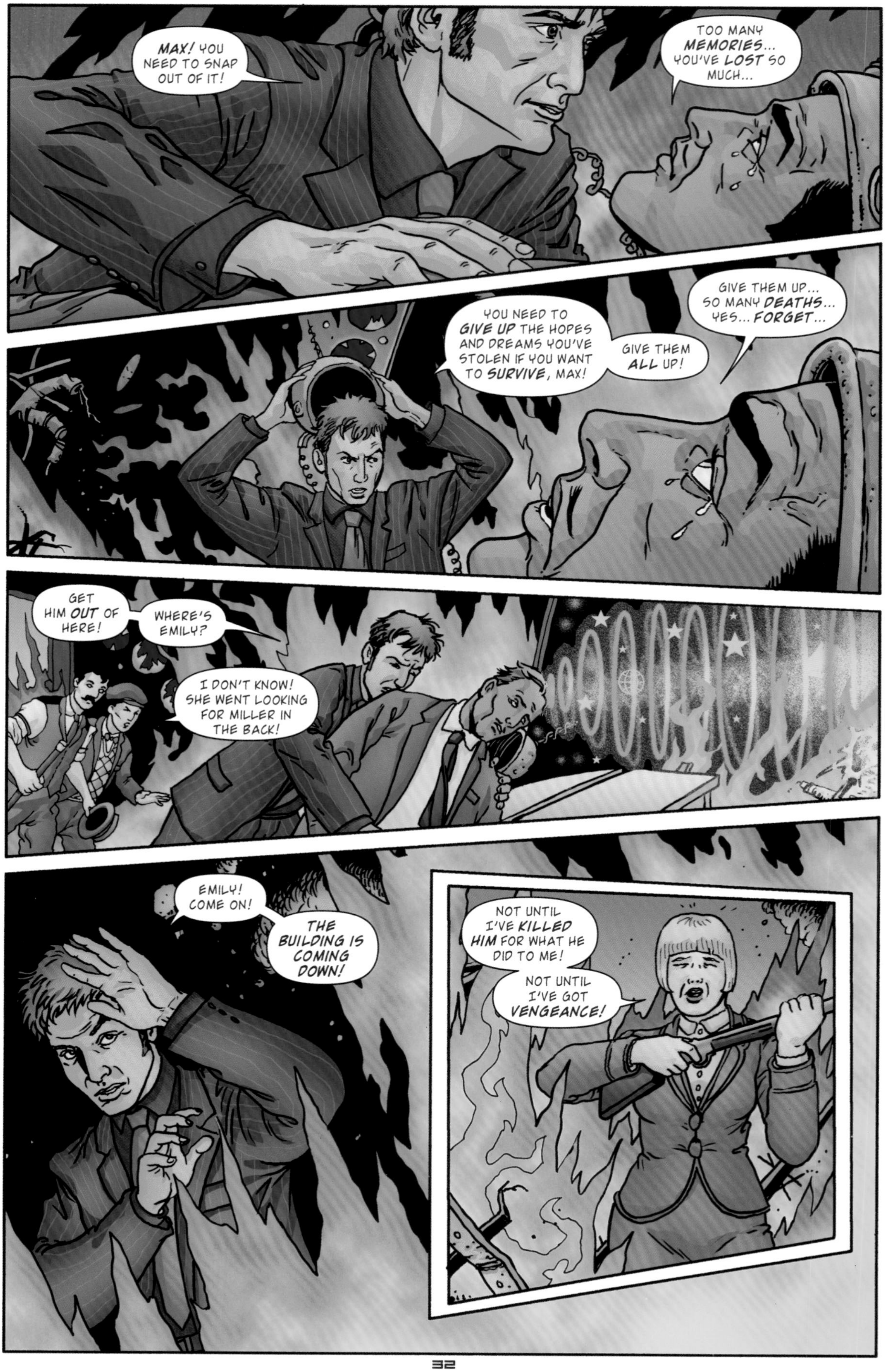
MAX! YOU NEED TO SNAP OUT OF IT!
TOO MANY MEMORIES... YOU'VE LOST SO MUCH...
YOU NEED TO GIVE UP THE HOPES AND DREAMS YOU'VE STOLEN IF YOU WANT TO SURVIVE, MAX!
GIVE THEM ALL UP!
GIVE THEM UP... SO MANY DEATHS... YES... FORGET...
GET HIM OUT OF HERE!
WHERE'S EMILY?
I DON'T KNOW! SHE WENT LOOKING FOR MILLER IN THE BACK!
EMILY! COME ON!
THE BUILDING IS COMING DOWN!
NOT UNTIL I'VE KILLED HIM FOR WHAT HE DID TO ME!
NOT UNTIL I'VE GOT VENGEANCE!

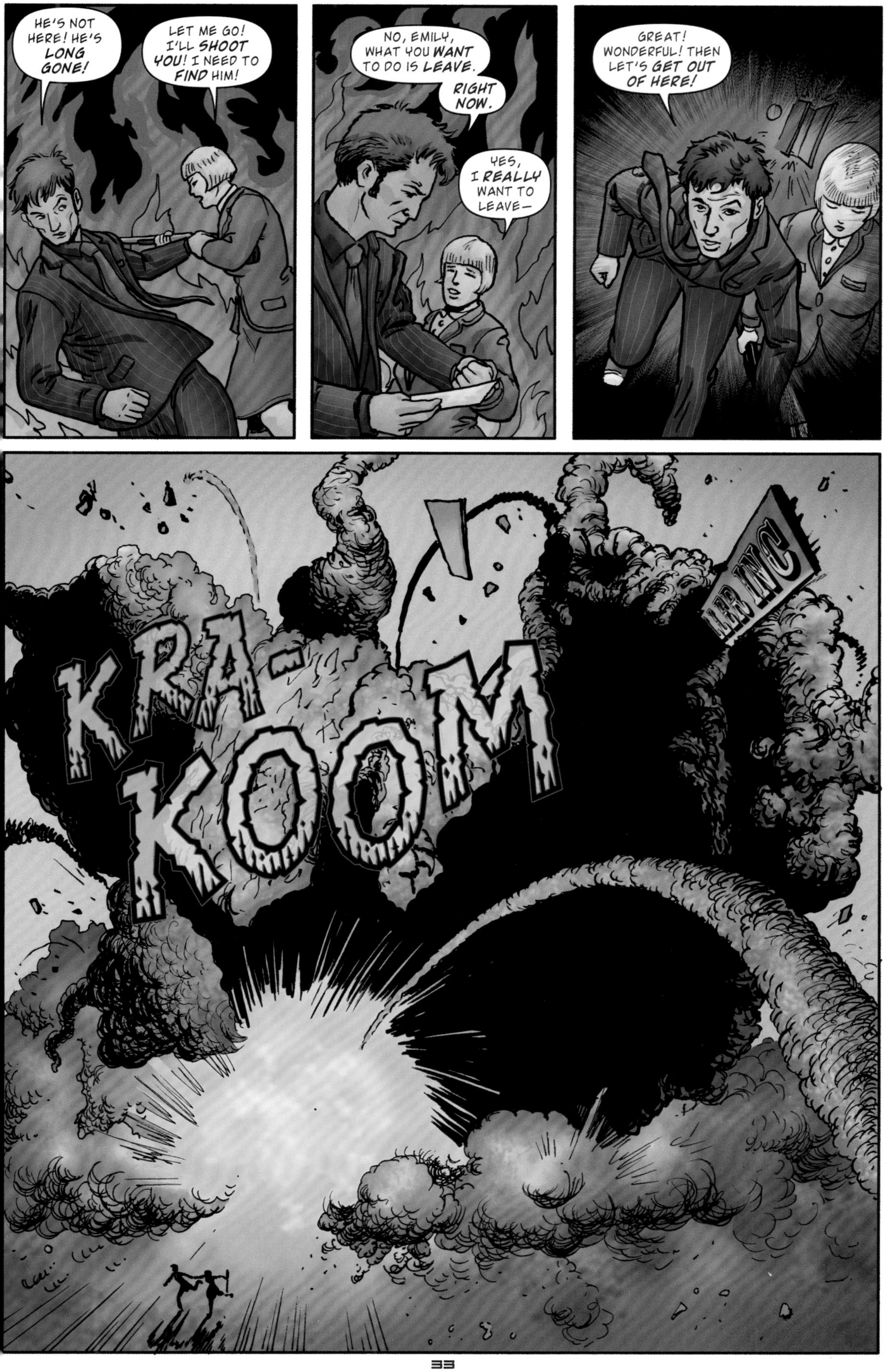
HE'S NOT HERE! HE'S LONG GONE!
LET ME GO! I'LL SHOOT YOU! I NEED TO FIND HIM!
NO, EMILY, WHAT YOU WANT TO DO IS LEAVE.
RIGHT NOW.
YES, I REALLY WANT TO LEAVE—
GREAT! WONDERFUL! THEN LET'S GET OUT OF HERE!
KRA-KOOM

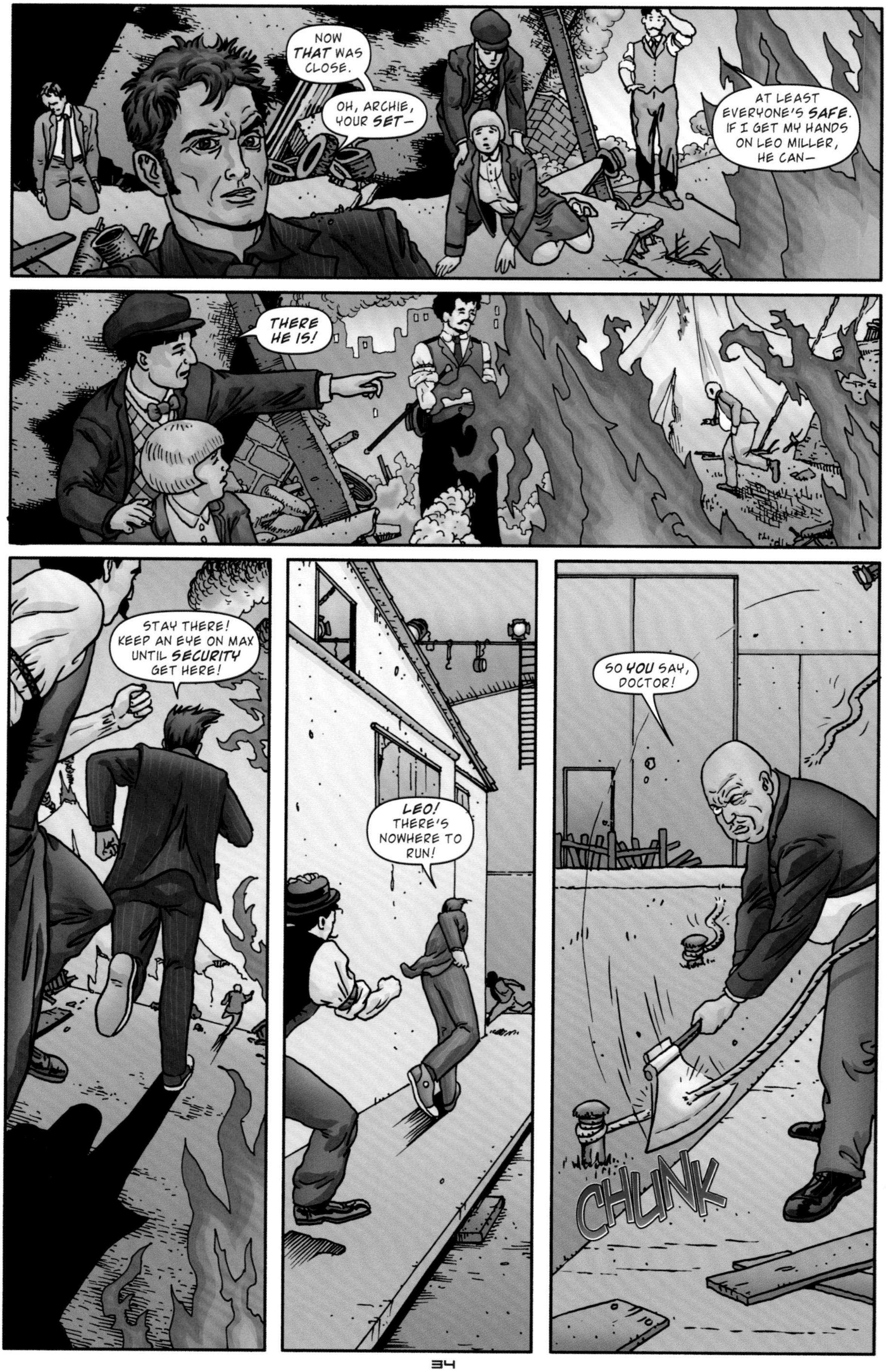
NOW THAT WAS CLOSE.
OH, ARCHIE, YOUR SET—
AT LEAST EVERYONE'S SAFE. IF I GET MY HANDS ON LEO MILLER, HE CAN—
THERE HE IS!
STAY THERE! KEEP AN EYE ON MAX UNTIL SECURITY GET HERE!
LEO! THERE'S NOWHERE TO RUN!
SO YOU SAY, DOCTOR!
CHUNK

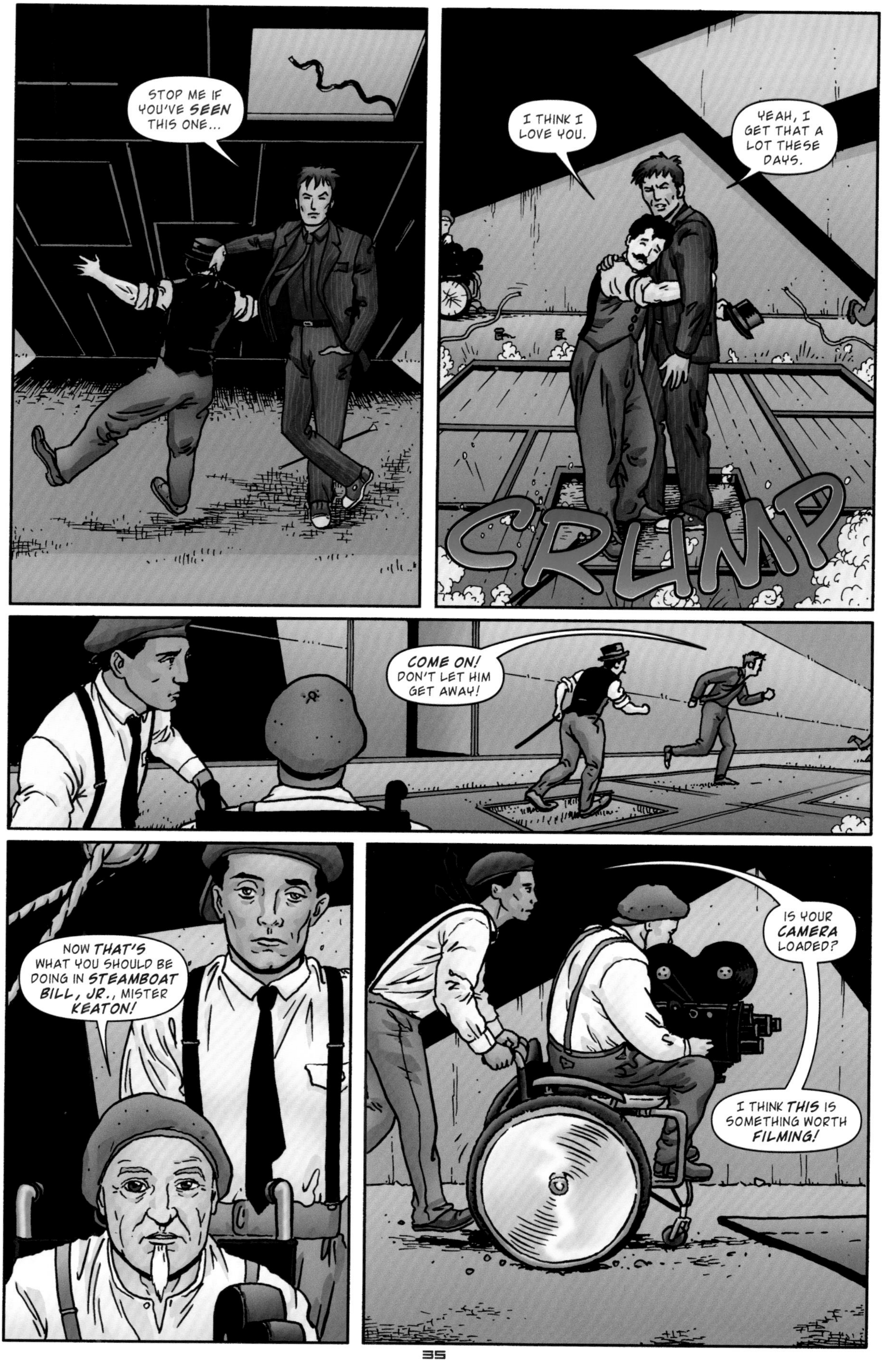
STOP ME IF YOU'VE SEEN THIS ONE...
I THINK I LOVE YOU.
YEAH, I GET THAT A LOT THESE DAYS.
CRUMP
COME ON! DON'T LET HIM GET AWAY!
NOW THAT'S WHAT YOU SHOULD BE DOING IN STEAMBOAT BILL, JR., MISTER KEATON!
IS YOUR CAMERA LOADED?
I THINK THIS IS SOMETHING WORTH FILMING!

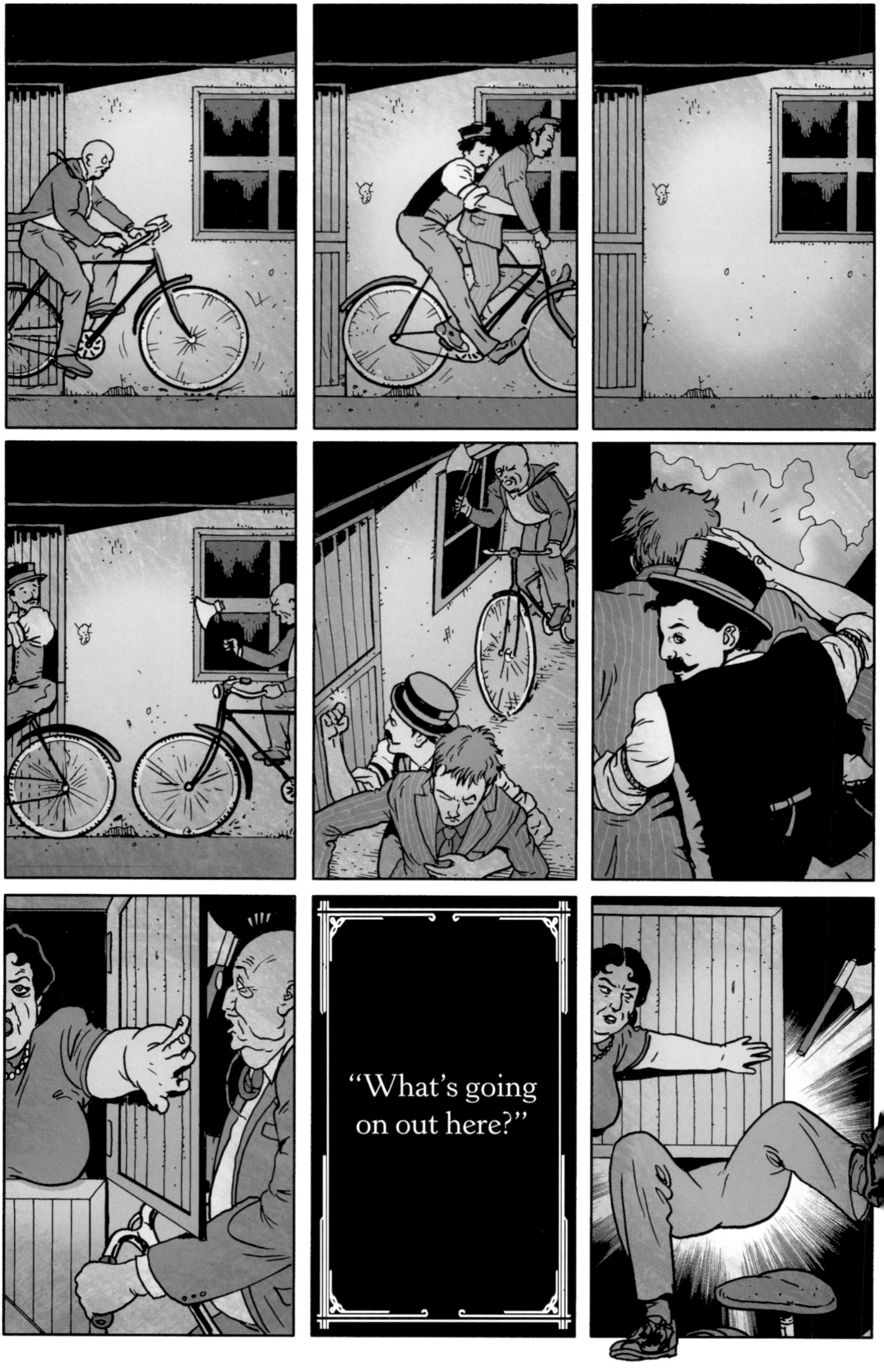

"What's going on out here?"

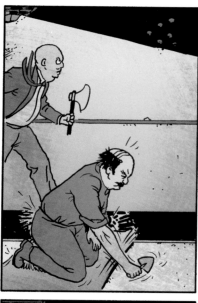

"You're really
stopping
to do *this*?
I mean, *really*?"

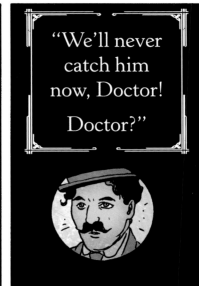

"We'll never
catch him
now, Doctor!

Doctor?"

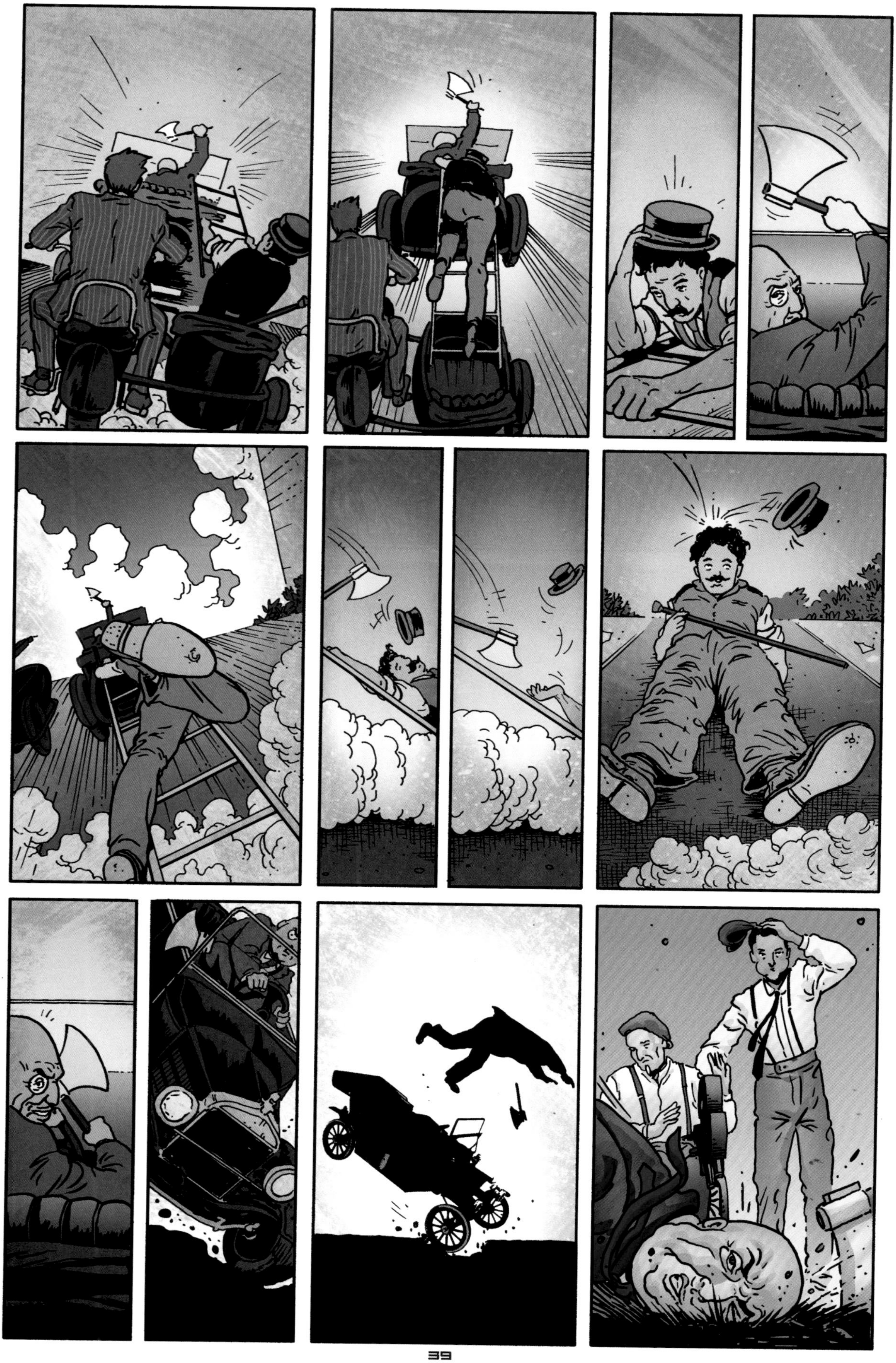

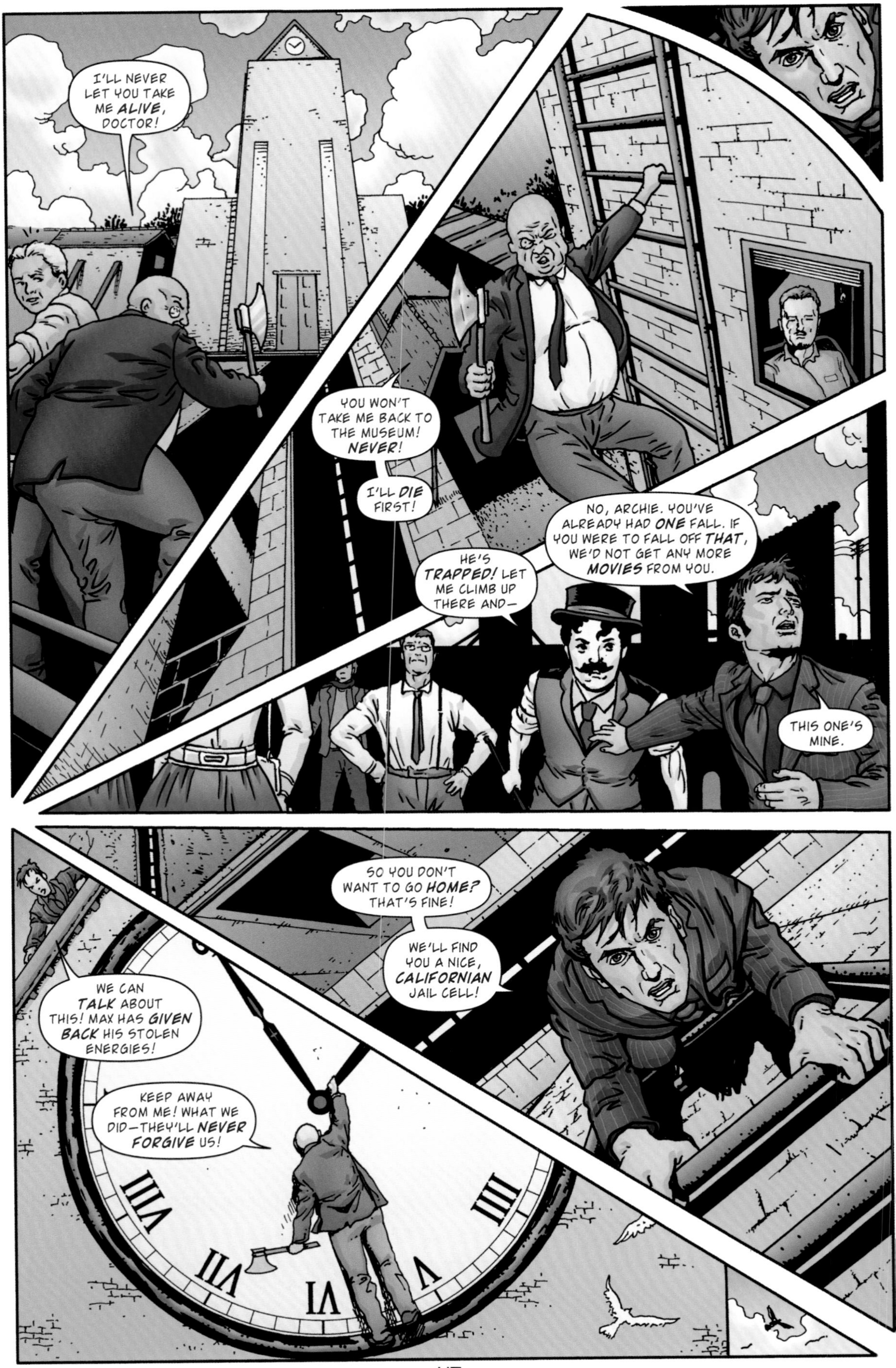
I'LL NEVER LET YOU TAKE ME ALIVE, DOCTOR!
YOU WON'T TAKE ME BACK TO THE MUSEUM! NEVER!
I'LL DIE FIRST!
HE'S TRAPPED! LET ME CLIMB UP THERE AND—
NO, ARCHIE. YOU'VE ALREADY HAD ONE FALL. IF YOU WERE TO FALL OFF THAT, WE'D NOT GET ANY MORE MOVIES FROM YOU.
THIS ONE'S MINE.
SO YOU DON'T WANT TO GO HOME? THAT'S FINE!
WE'LL FIND YOU A NICE, CALIFORNIAN JAIL CELL!
WE CAN TALK ABOUT THIS! MAX HAS GIVEN BACK HIS STOLEN ENERGIES!
KEEP AWAY FROM ME! WHAT WE DID—THEY'LL NEVER FORGIVE US!

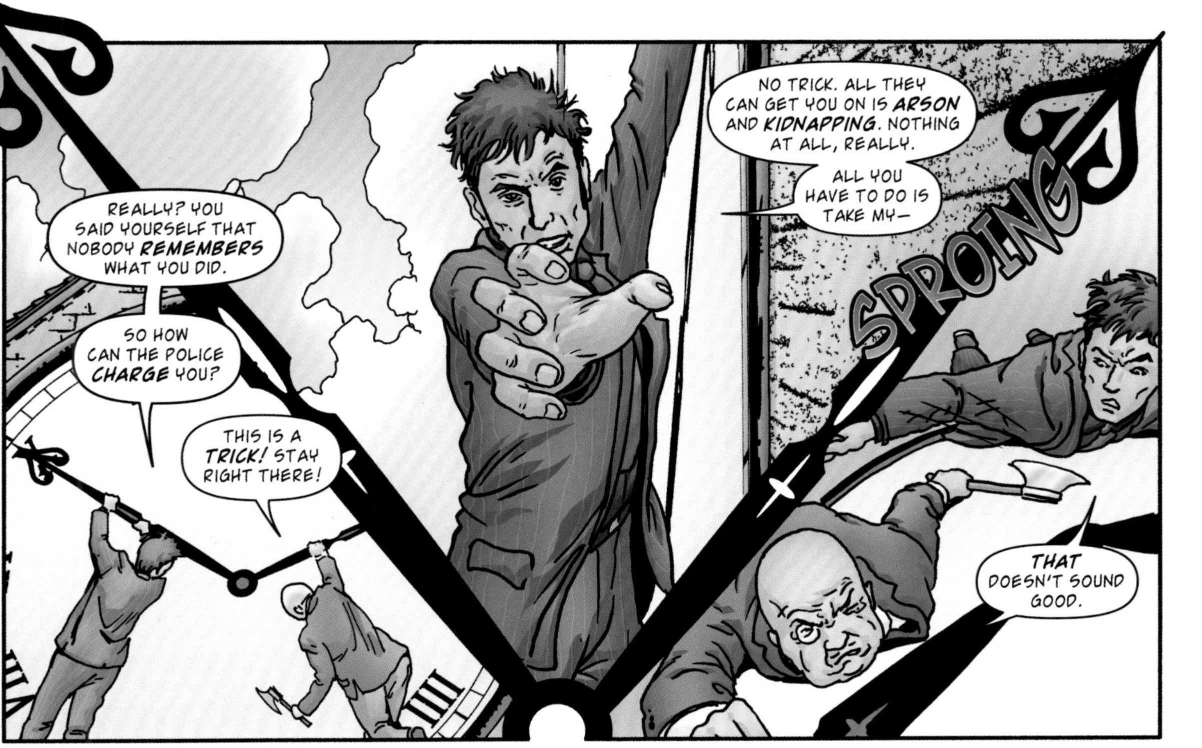
REALLY? YOU SAID YOURSELF THAT NOBODY REMEMBERS WHAT YOU DID.
SO HOW CAN THE POLICE CHARGE YOU?
THIS IS A TRICK! STAY RIGHT THERE!
NO TRICK. ALL THEY CAN GET YOU ON IS ARSON AND KIDNAPPING. NOTHING AT ALL, REALLY.
ALL YOU HAVE TO DO IS TAKE MY—
SPROING
THAT DOESN'T SOUND GOOD.

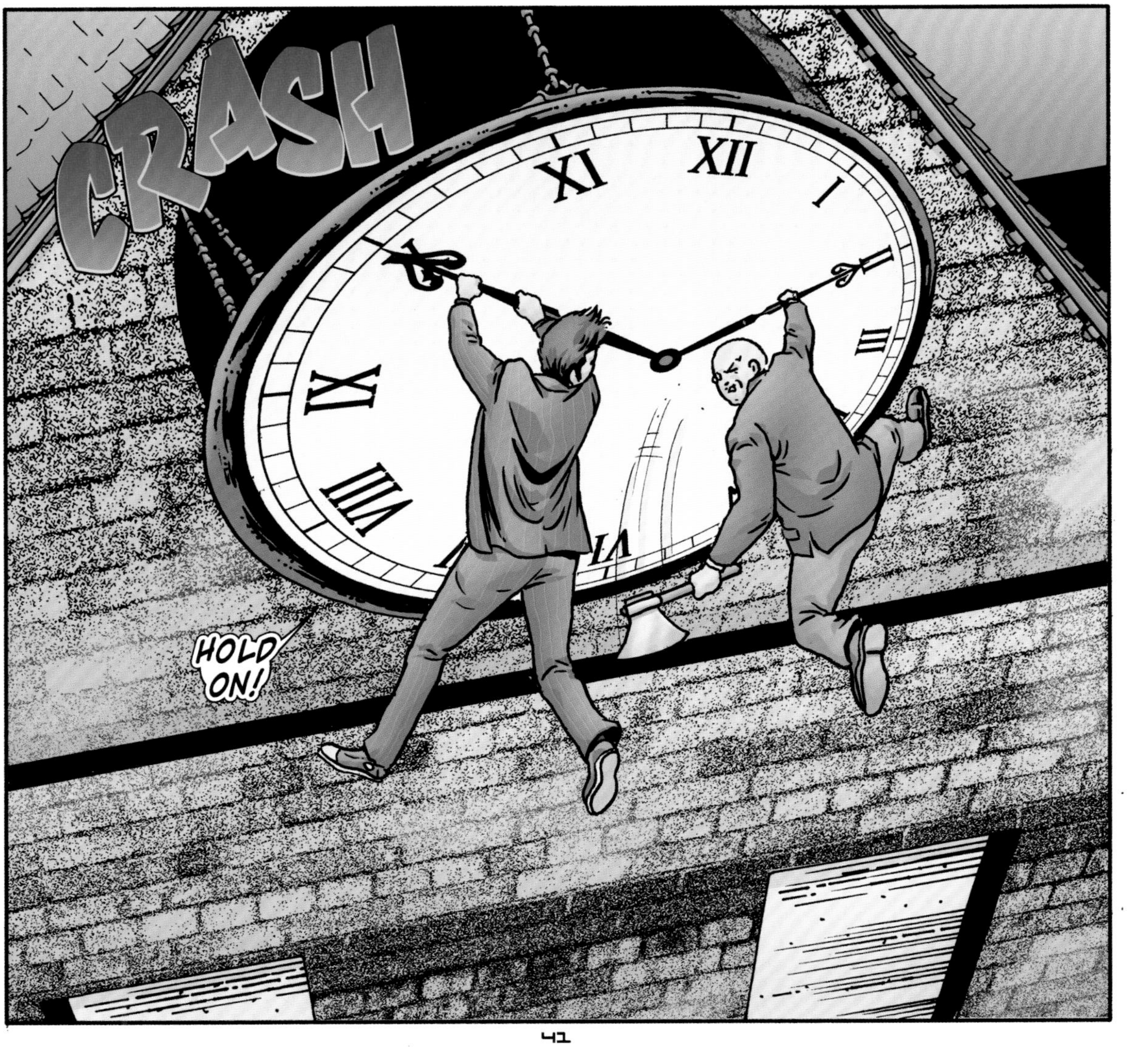
CRASH
HOLD ON!

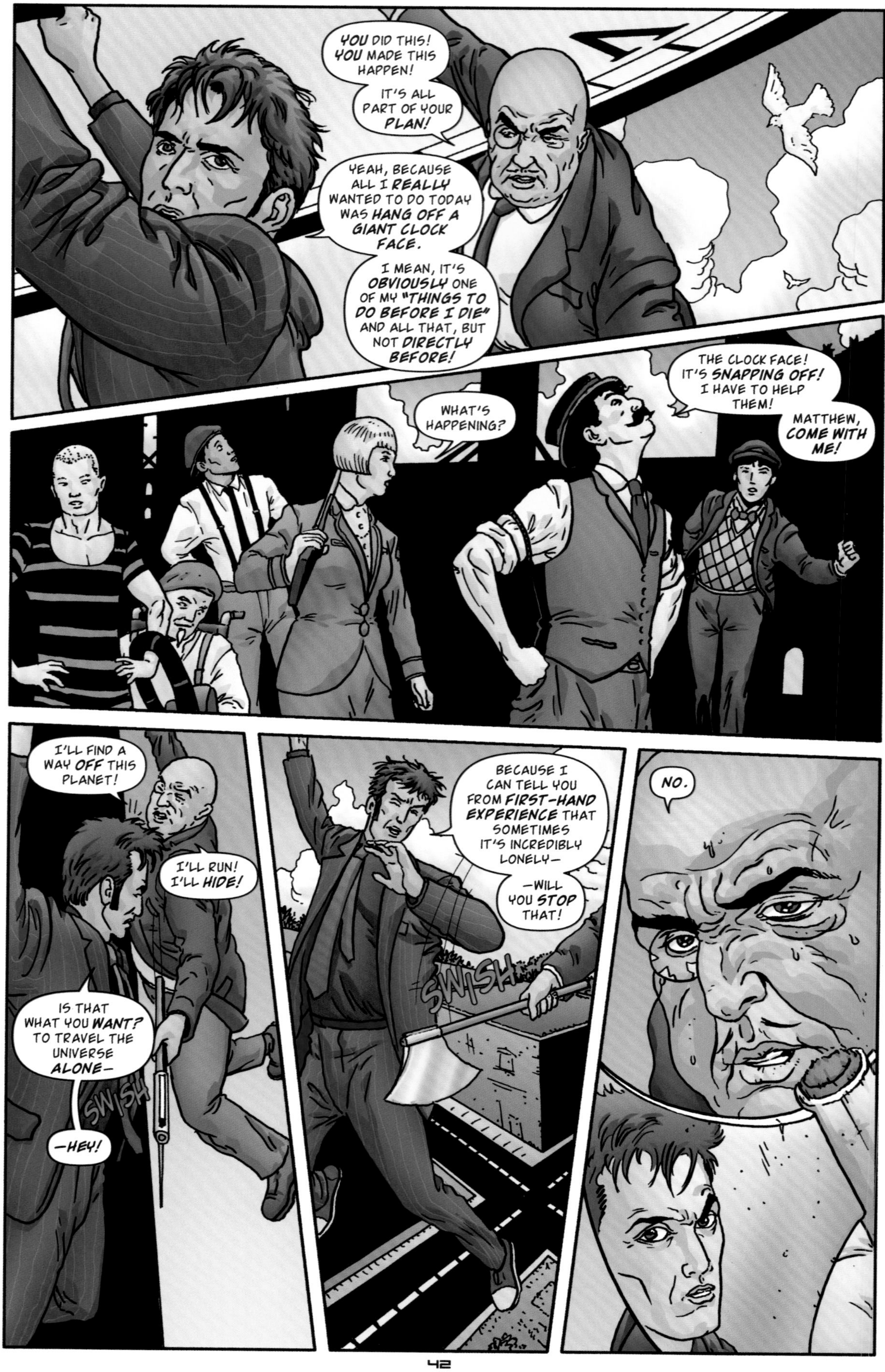
YOU DID THIS! YOU MADE THIS HAPPEN!
IT'S ALL PART OF YOUR PLAN!
YEAH, BECAUSE ALL I REALLY WANTED TO DO TODAY WAS HANG OFF A GIANT CLOCK FACE.
I MEAN, IT'S OBVIOUSLY ONE OF MY "THINGS TO DO BEFORE I DIE" AND ALL THAT, BUT NOT DIRECTLY BEFORE!
WHAT'S HAPPENING?
THE CLOCK FACE! IT'S SNAPPING OFF! I HAVE TO HELP THEM!
MATTHEW, COME WITH ME!
I'LL FIND A WAY OFF THIS PLANET!
I'LL RUN! I'LL HIDE!
IS THAT WHAT YOU WANT? TO TRAVEL THE UNIVERSE ALONE—
SWISH
—HEY!
BECAUSE I CAN TELL YOU FROM FIRST-HAND EXPERIENCE THAT SOMETIMES IT'S INCREDIBLY LONELY—
—WILL YOU STOP THAT!
SWISH
NO.

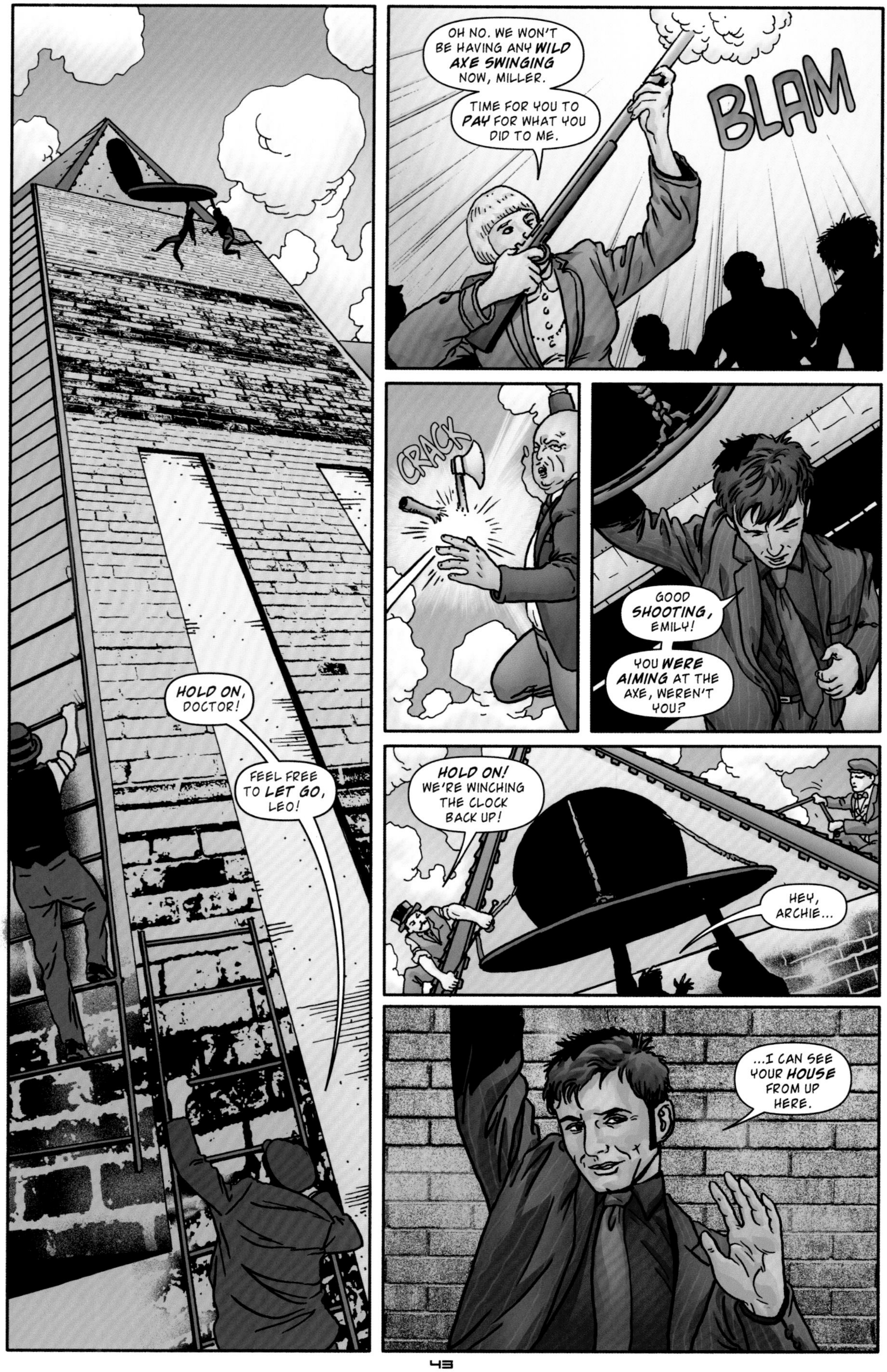
HOLD ON, DOCTOR!
FEEL FREE TO LET GO, LEO!
OH NO. WE WON'T BE HAVING ANY WILD AXE SWINGING NOW, MILLER.
TIME FOR YOU TO PAY FOR WHAT YOU DID TO ME.
BLAM
CRACK
GOOD SHOOTING, EMILY!
YOU WERE AIMING AT THE AXE, WEREN'T YOU?
HOLD ON! WE'RE WINCHING THE CLOCK BACK UP!
HEY, ARCHIE...
...I CAN SEE YOUR HOUSE FROM UP HERE.

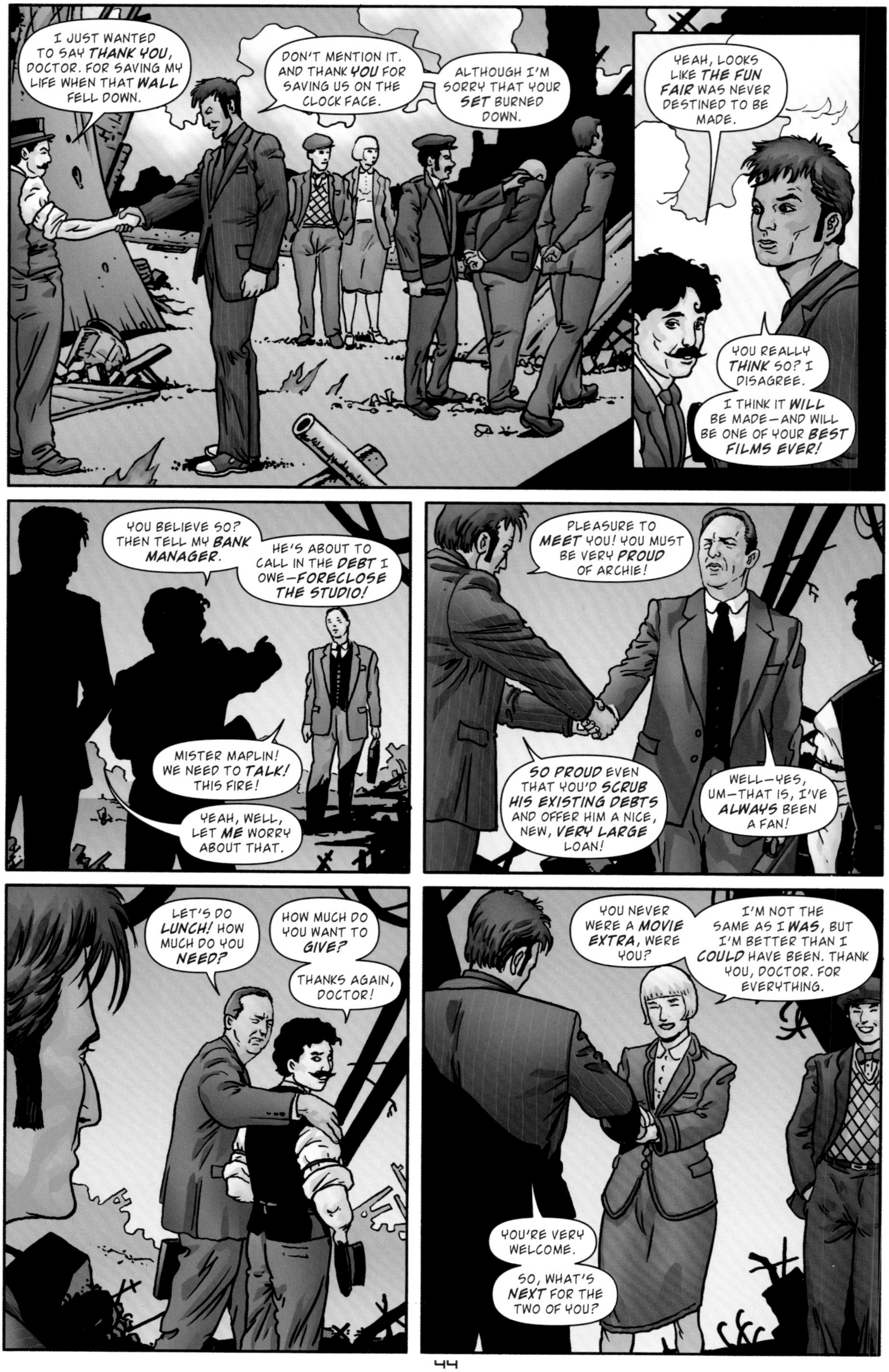
I JUST WANTED TO SAY THANK YOU, DOCTOR. FOR SAVING MY LIFE WHEN THAT WALL FELL DOWN.
DON'T MENTION IT. AND THANK YOU FOR SAVING US ON THE CLOCK FACE.
ALTHOUGH I'M SORRY THAT YOUR SET BURNED DOWN.
YEAH, LOOKS LIKE THE FUN FAIR WAS NEVER DESTINED TO BE MADE.
YOU REALLY THINK SO? I DISAGREE.
I THINK IT WILL BE MADE—AND WILL BE ONE OF YOUR BEST FILMS EVER!
YOU BELIEVE SO? THEN TELL MY BANK MANAGER.
HE'S ABOUT TO CALL IN THE DEBT I OWE—FORECLOSE THE STUDIO!
MISTER MAPLIN! WE NEED TO TALK! THIS FIRE!
YEAH, WELL, LET ME WORRY ABOUT THAT.
PLEASURE TO MEET YOU! YOU MUST BE VERY PROUD OF ARCHIE!
SO PROUD EVEN THAT YOU'D SCRUB HIS EXISTING DEBTS AND OFFER HIM A NICE, NEW, VERY LARGE LOAN!
WELL—YES, UM—THAT IS, I'VE ALWAYS BEEN A FAN!
LET'S DO LUNCH! HOW MUCH DO YOU NEED?
HOW MUCH DO YOU WANT TO GIVE?
THANKS AGAIN, DOCTOR!
YOU NEVER WERE A MOVIE EXTRA, WERE YOU?
I'M NOT THE SAME AS I WAS, BUT I'M BETTER THAN I COULD HAVE BEEN. THANK YOU, DOCTOR. FOR EVERYTHING.
YOU'RE VERY WELCOME.
SO, WHAT'S NEXT FOR THE TWO OF YOU?

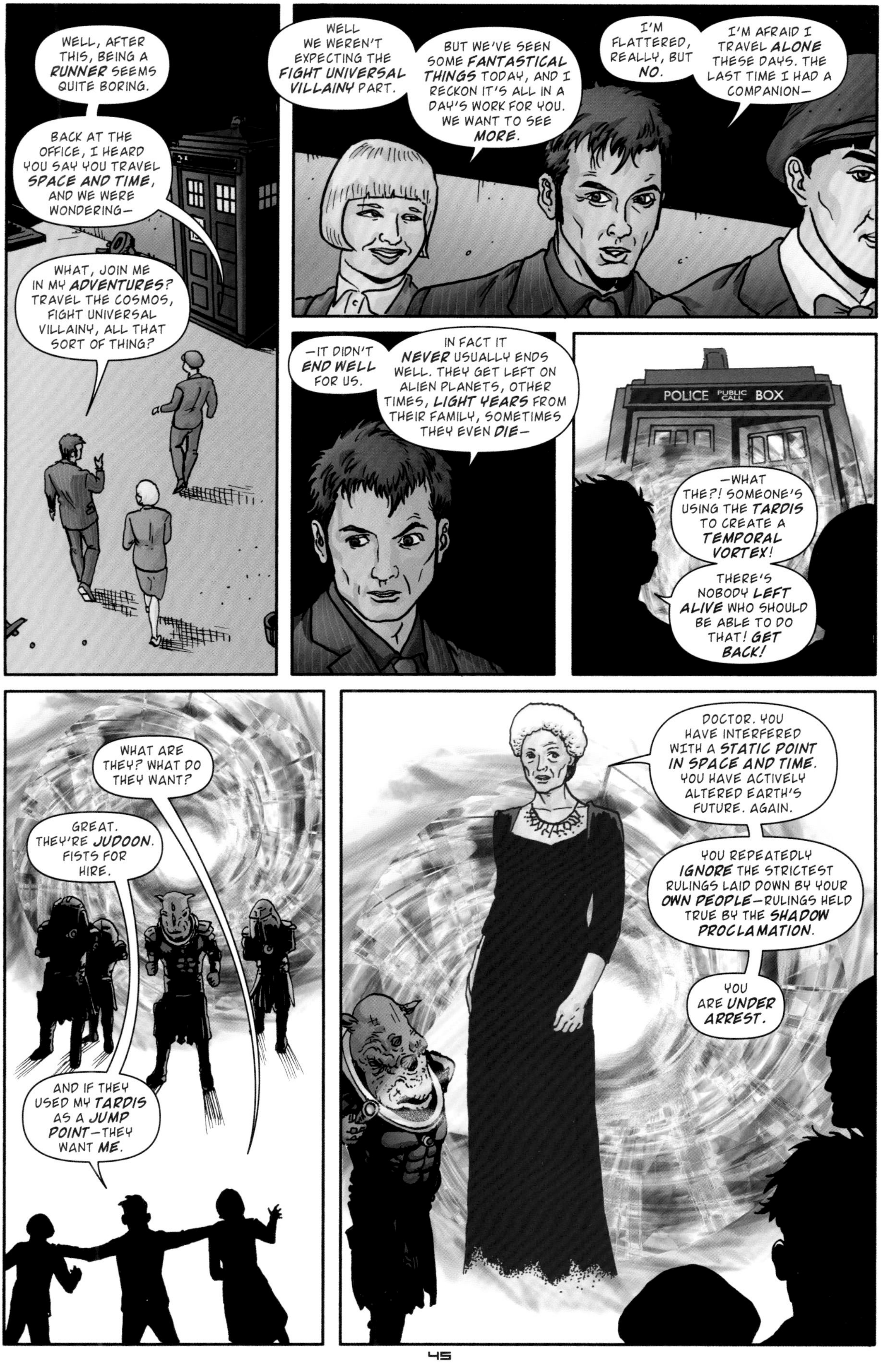

WELL, AFTER THIS, BEING A RUNNER SEEMS QUITE BORING.
BACK AT THE OFFICE, I HEARD YOU SAY YOU TRAVEL SPACE AND TIME, AND WE WERE WONDERING—
WHAT, JOIN ME IN MY ADVENTURES? TRAVEL THE COSMOS, FIGHT UNIVERSAL VILLAINY, ALL THAT SORT OF THING?
WELL WE WEREN'T EXPECTING THE FIGHT UNIVERSAL VILLAINY PART.
BUT WE'VE SEEN SOME FANTASTICAL THINGS TODAY, AND I RECKON IT'S ALL IN A DAY'S WORK FOR YOU. WE WANT TO SEE MORE.
I'M FLATTERED, REALLY, BUT NO.
I'M AFRAID I TRAVEL ALONE THESE DAYS. THE LAST TIME I HAD A COMPANION—
—IT DIDN'T END WELL FOR US.
IN FACT IT NEVER USUALLY ENDS WELL. THEY GET LEFT ON ALIEN PLANETS, OTHER TIMES, LIGHT YEARS FROM THEIR FAMILY, SOMETIMES THEY EVEN DIE—
POLICE PUBLIC CALL BOX
—WHAT THE?! SOMEONE'S USING THE TARDIS TO CREATE A TEMPORAL VORTEX!
THERE'S NOBODY LEFT ALIVE WHO SHOULD BE ABLE TO DO THAT! GET BACK!
WHAT ARE THEY? WHAT DO THEY WANT?
GREAT. THEY'RE JUDOON. FISTS FOR HIRE.
AND IF THEY USED MY TARDIS AS A JUMP POINT—THEY WANT ME.
DOCTOR. YOU HAVE INTERFERED WITH A STATIC POINT IN SPACE AND TIME. YOU HAVE ACTIVELY ALTERED EARTH'S FUTURE. AGAIN.
YOU REPEATEDLY IGNORE THE STRICTEST RULINGS LAID DOWN BY YOUR OWN PEOPLE—RULINGS HELD TRUE BY THE SHADOW PROCLAMATION.
YOU ARE UNDER ARREST.

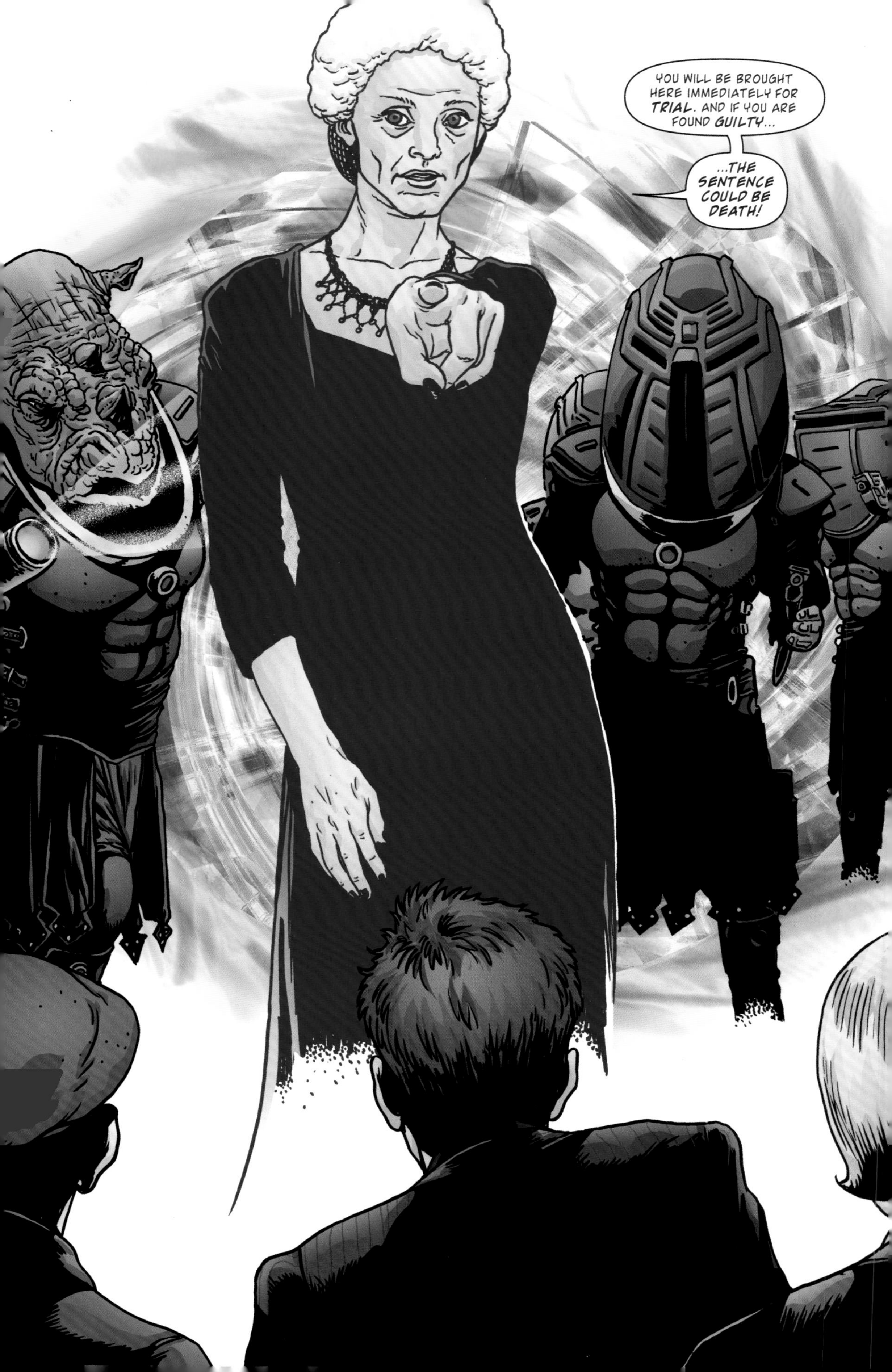
YOU WILL BE BROUGHT HERE IMMEDIATELY FOR TRIAL. AND IF YOU ARE FOUND GUILTY...
...THE SENTENCE COULD BE DEATH!

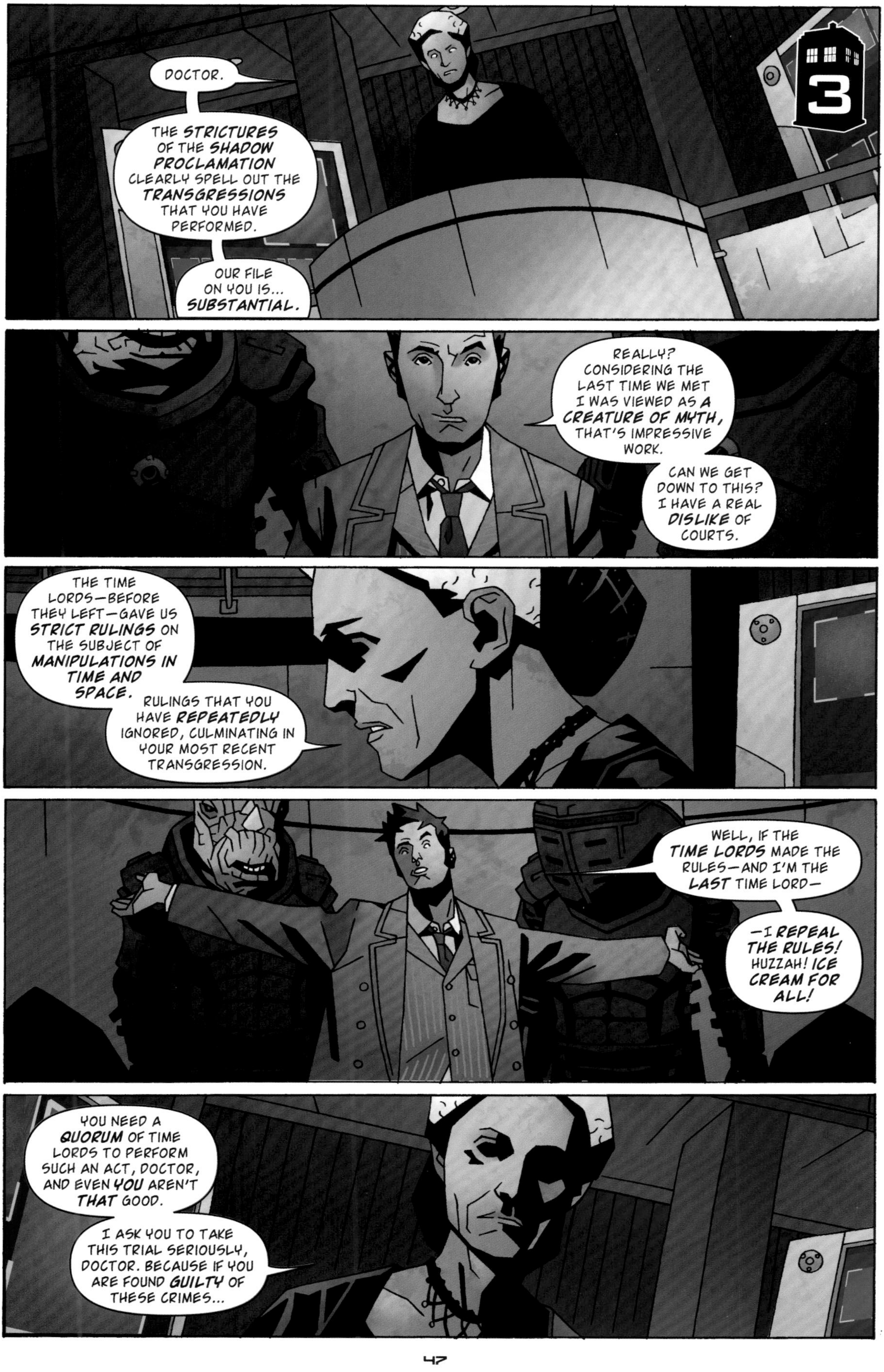
3
DOCTOR.
THE STRICTURES OF THE SHADOW PROCLAMATION CLEARLY SPELL OUT THE TRANSGRESSIONS THAT YOU HAVE PERFORMED.
OUR FILE ON YOU IS... SUBSTANTIAL.
REALLY? CONSIDERING THE LAST TIME WE MET I WAS VIEWED AS A CREATURE OF MYTH, THAT'S IMPRESSIVE WORK.
CAN WE GET DOWN TO THIS? I HAVE A REAL DISLIKE OF COURTS.
THE TIME LORDS—BEFORE THEY LEFT—GAVE US STRICT RULINGS ON THE SUBJECT OF MANIPULATIONS IN TIME AND SPACE.
RULINGS THAT YOU HAVE REPEATEDLY IGNORED, CULMINATING IN YOUR MOST RECENT TRANSGRESSION.
WELL, IF THE TIME LORDS MADE THE RULES—AND I'M THE LAST TIME LORD—
—I REPEAL THE RULES! HUZZAH! ICE CREAM FOR ALL!
YOU NEED A QUORUM OF TIME LORDS TO PERFORM SUCH AN ACT, DOCTOR, AND EVEN YOU AREN'T THAT GOOD.
I ASK YOU TO TAKE THIS TRIAL SERIOUSLY, DOCTOR. BECAUSE IF YOU ARE FOUND GUILTY OF THESE CRIMES...

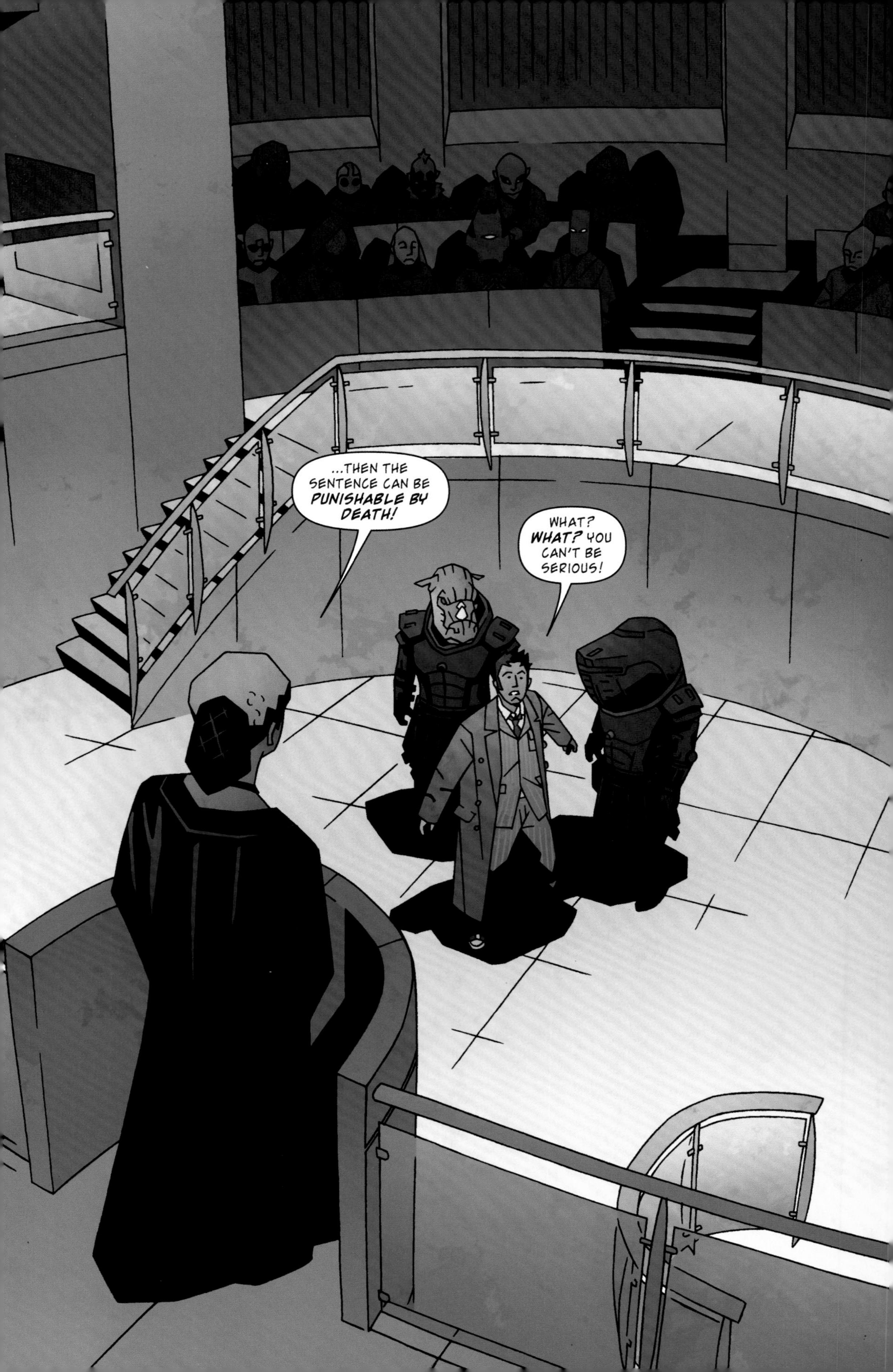
...THEN THE SENTENCE CAN BE PUNISHABLE BY DEATH!
WHAT? WHAT? YOU CAN'T BE SERIOUS!

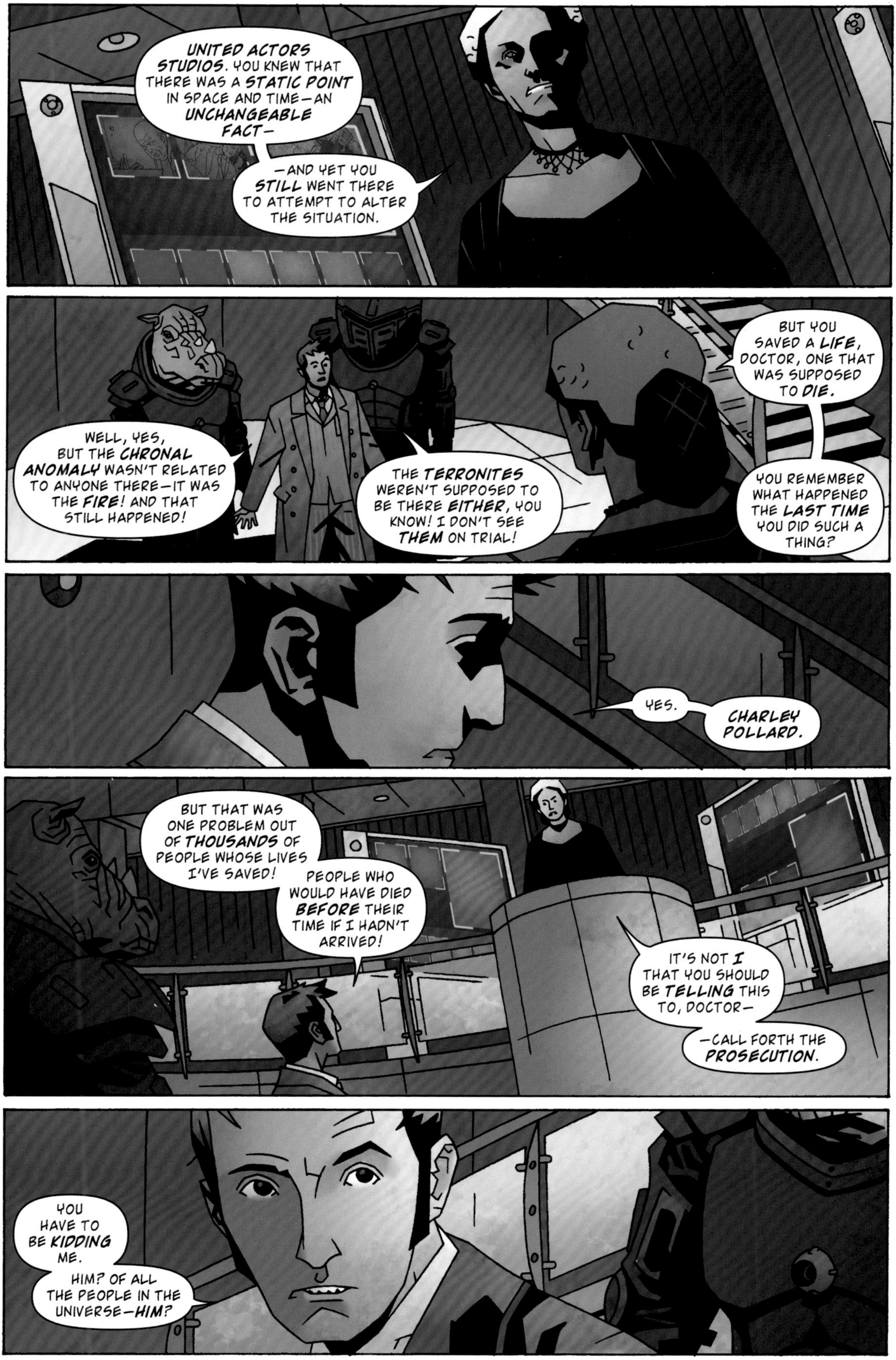
UNITED ACTORS STUDIOS. YOU KNEW THAT THERE WAS A STATIC POINT IN SPACE AND TIME—AN UNCHANGEABLE FACT—
—AND YET YOU STILL WENT THERE TO ATTEMPT TO ALTER THE SITUATION.
BUT YOU SAVED A LIFE, DOCTOR, ONE THAT WAS SUPPOSED TO DIE.
WELL, YES, BUT THE CHRONAL ANOMALY WASN'T RELATED TO ANYONE THERE—IT WAS THE FIRE! AND THAT STILL HAPPENED!
THE TERRONITES WEREN'T SUPPOSED TO BE THERE EITHER, YOU KNOW! I DON'T SEE THEM ON TRIAL!
YOU REMEMBER WHAT HAPPENED THE LAST TIME YOU DID SUCH A THING?
YES.
CHARLEY POLLARD.
BUT THAT WAS ONE PROBLEM OUT OF THOUSANDS OF PEOPLE WHOSE LIVES I'VE SAVED!
PEOPLE WHO WOULD HAVE DIED BEFORE THEIR TIME IF I HADN'T ARRIVED!
IT'S NOT I THAT YOU SHOULD BE TELLING THIS TO, DOCTOR—
—CALL FORTH THE PROSECUTION.
YOU HAVE TO BE KIDDING ME.
HIM? OF ALL THE PEOPLE IN THE UNIVERSE—HIM?

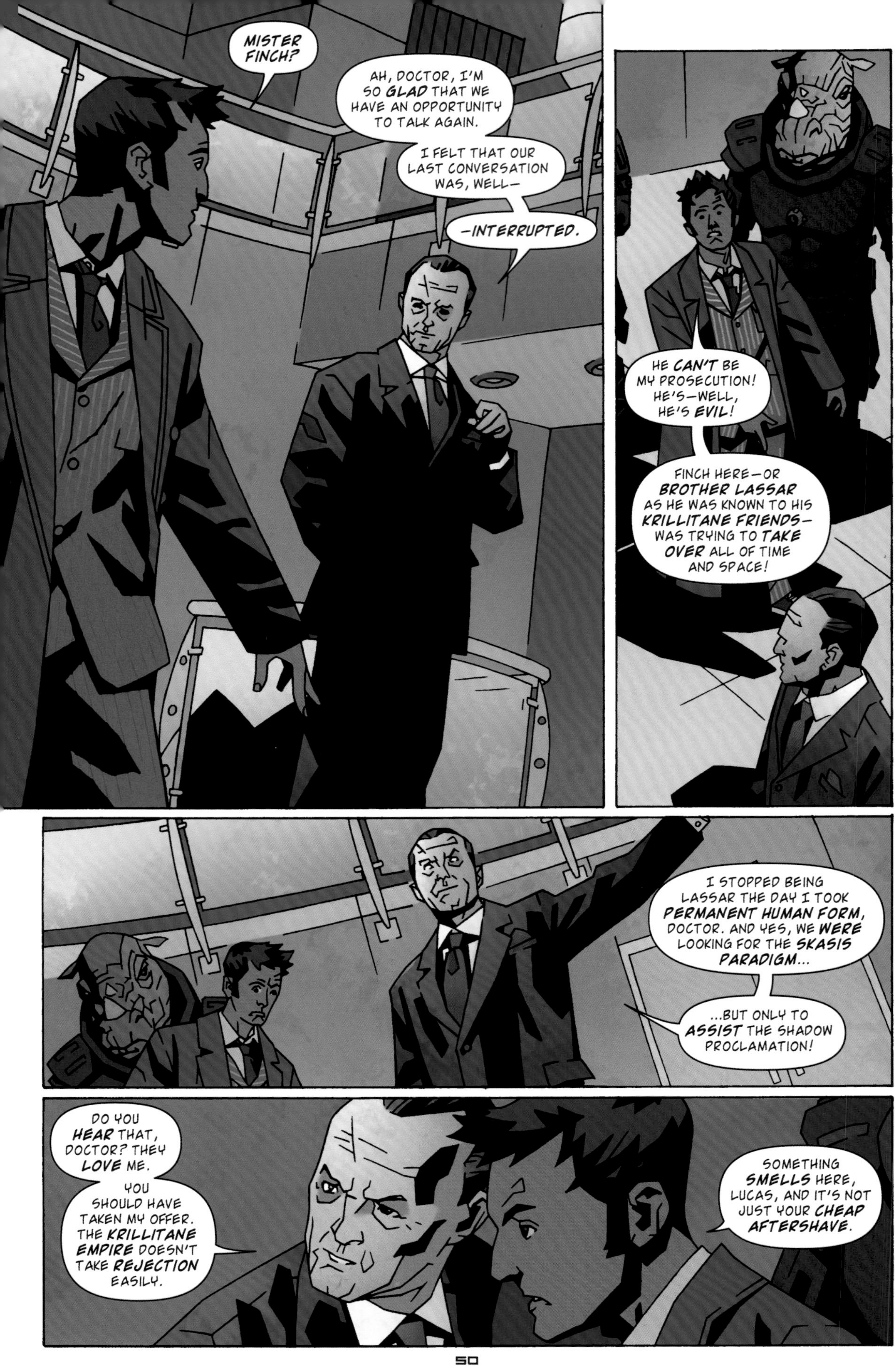
MISTER FINCH?
AH, DOCTOR, I'M SO GLAD THAT WE HAVE AN OPPORTUNITY TO TALK AGAIN.
I FELT THAT OUR LAST CONVERSATION WAS, WELL—
—INTERRUPTED.
HE CAN'T BE MY PROSECUTION! HE'S—WELL, HE'S EVIL!
FINCH HERE—OR BROTHER LASSAR AS HE WAS KNOWN TO HIS KRILLITANE FRIENDS—WAS TRYING TO TAKE OVER ALL OF TIME AND SPACE!
I STOPPED BEING LASSAR THE DAY I TOOK PERMANENT HUMAN FORM, DOCTOR. AND YES, WE WERE LOOKING FOR THE SKASIS PARADIGM...
...BUT ONLY TO ASSIST THE SHADOW PROCLAMATION!
DO YOU HEAR THAT, DOCTOR? THEY LOVE ME.
YOU SHOULD HAVE TAKEN MY OFFER. THE KRILLITANE EMPIRE DOESN'T TAKE REJECTION EASILY.
SOMETHING SMELLS HERE, LUCAS, AND IT'S NOT JUST YOUR CHEAP AFTERSHAVE.

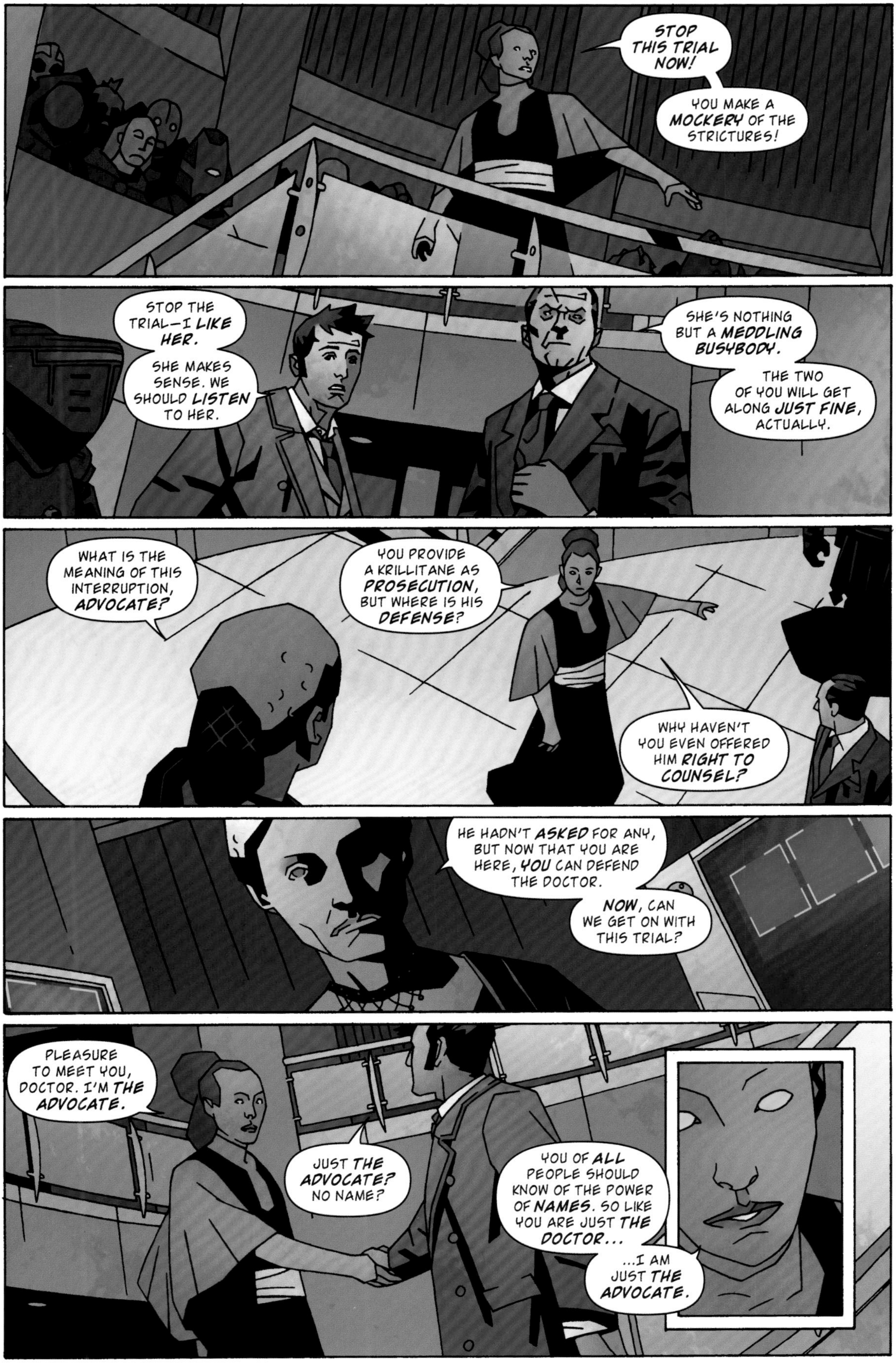

STOP THIS TRIAL NOW!
YOU MAKE A MOCKERY OF THE STRICTURES!
STOP THE TRIAL—I LIKE HER.
SHE MAKES SENSE. WE SHOULD LISTEN TO HER.
SHE'S NOTHING BUT A MEDDLING BUSYBODY.
THE TWO OF YOU WILL GET ALONG JUST FINE, ACTUALLY.
WHAT IS THE MEANING OF THIS INTERRUPTION, ADVOCATE?
YOU PROVIDE A KRILLITANE AS PROSECUTION, BUT WHERE IS HIS DEFENSE?
WHY HAVEN'T YOU EVEN OFFERED HIM RIGHT TO COUNSEL?
HE HADN'T ASKED FOR ANY, BUT NOW THAT YOU ARE HERE, YOU CAN DEFEND THE DOCTOR.
NOW, CAN WE GET ON WITH THIS TRIAL?
PLEASURE TO MEET YOU, DOCTOR. I'M THE ADVOCATE.
JUST THE ADVOCATE? NO NAME?
YOU OF ALL PEOPLE SHOULD KNOW OF THE POWER OF NAMES. SO LIKE YOU ARE JUST THE DOCTOR...
...I AM JUST THE ADVOCATE.

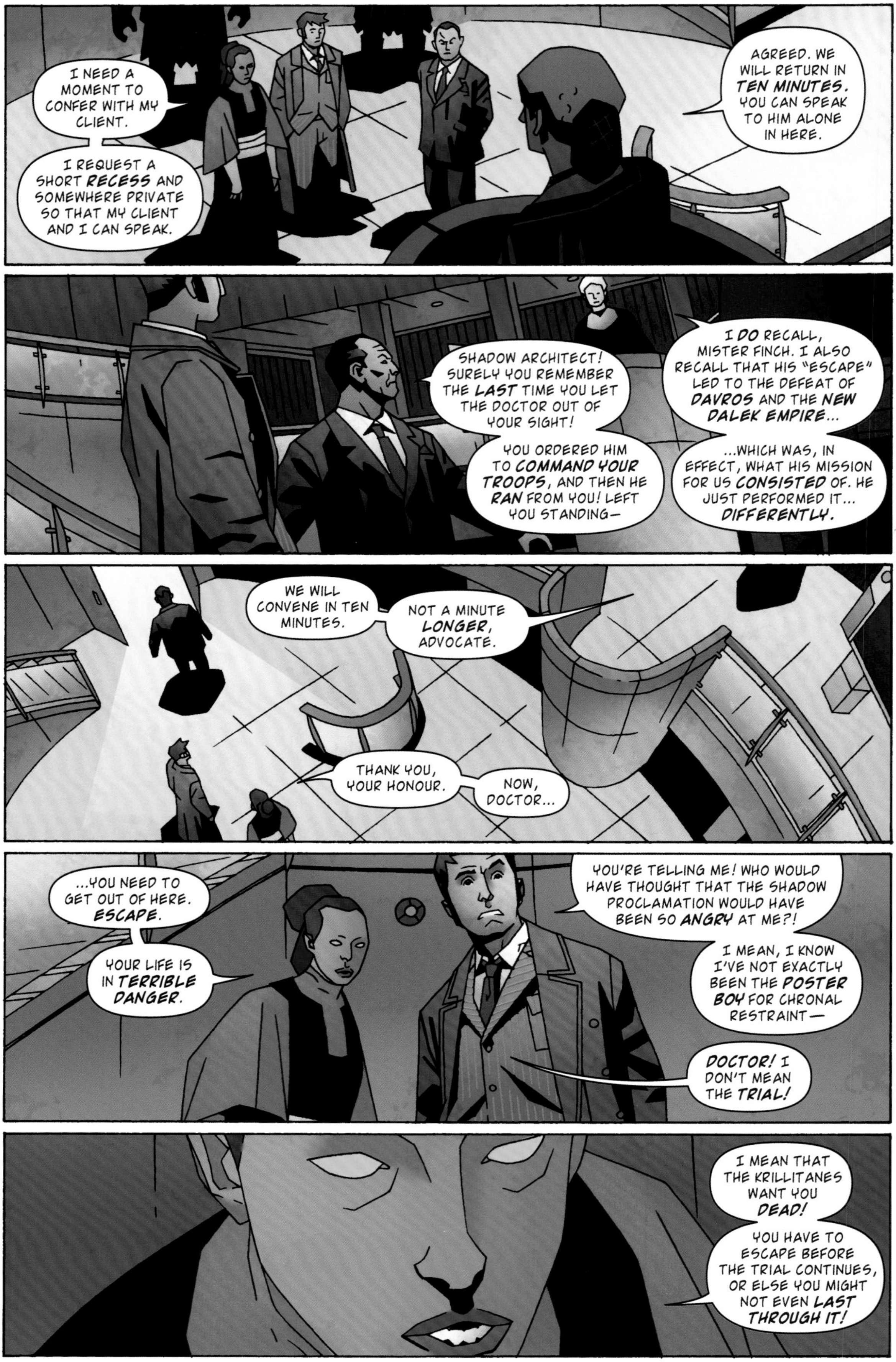
I NEED A MOMENT TO CONFER WITH MY CLIENT.
I REQUEST A SHORT RECESS AND SOMEWHERE PRIVATE SO THAT MY CLIENT AND I CAN SPEAK.
AGREED. WE WILL RETURN IN TEN MINUTES. YOU CAN SPEAK TO HIM ALONE IN HERE.
SHADOW ARCHITECT! SURELY YOU REMEMBER THE LAST TIME YOU LET THE DOCTOR OUT OF YOUR SIGHT!
YOU ORDERED HIM TO COMMAND YOUR TROOPS, AND THEN HE RAN FROM YOU! LEFT YOU STANDING—
I DO RECALL, MISTER FINCH. I ALSO RECALL THAT HIS "ESCAPE" LED TO THE DEFEAT OF DAVROS AND THE NEW DALEK EMPIRE...
...WHICH WAS, IN EFFECT, WHAT HIS MISSION FOR US CONSISTED OF. HE JUST PERFORMED IT... DIFFERENTLY.
WE WILL CONVENE IN TEN MINUTES.
NOT A MINUTE LONGER, ADVOCATE.
THANK YOU, YOUR HONOUR.
NOW, DOCTOR...
...YOU NEED TO GET OUT OF HERE. ESCAPE.
YOUR LIFE IS IN TERRIBLE DANGER.
YOU'RE TELLING ME! WHO WOULD HAVE THOUGHT THAT THE SHADOW PROCLAMATION WOULD HAVE BEEN SO ANGRY AT ME?!
I MEAN, I KNOW I'VE NOT EXACTLY BEEN THE POSTER BOY FOR CHRONAL RESTRAINT—
DOCTOR! I DON'T MEAN THE TRIAL!
I MEAN THAT THE KRILLITANES WANT YOU DEAD!
YOU HAVE TO ESCAPE BEFORE THE TRIAL CONTINUES, OR ELSE YOU MIGHT NOT EVEN LAST THROUGH IT!

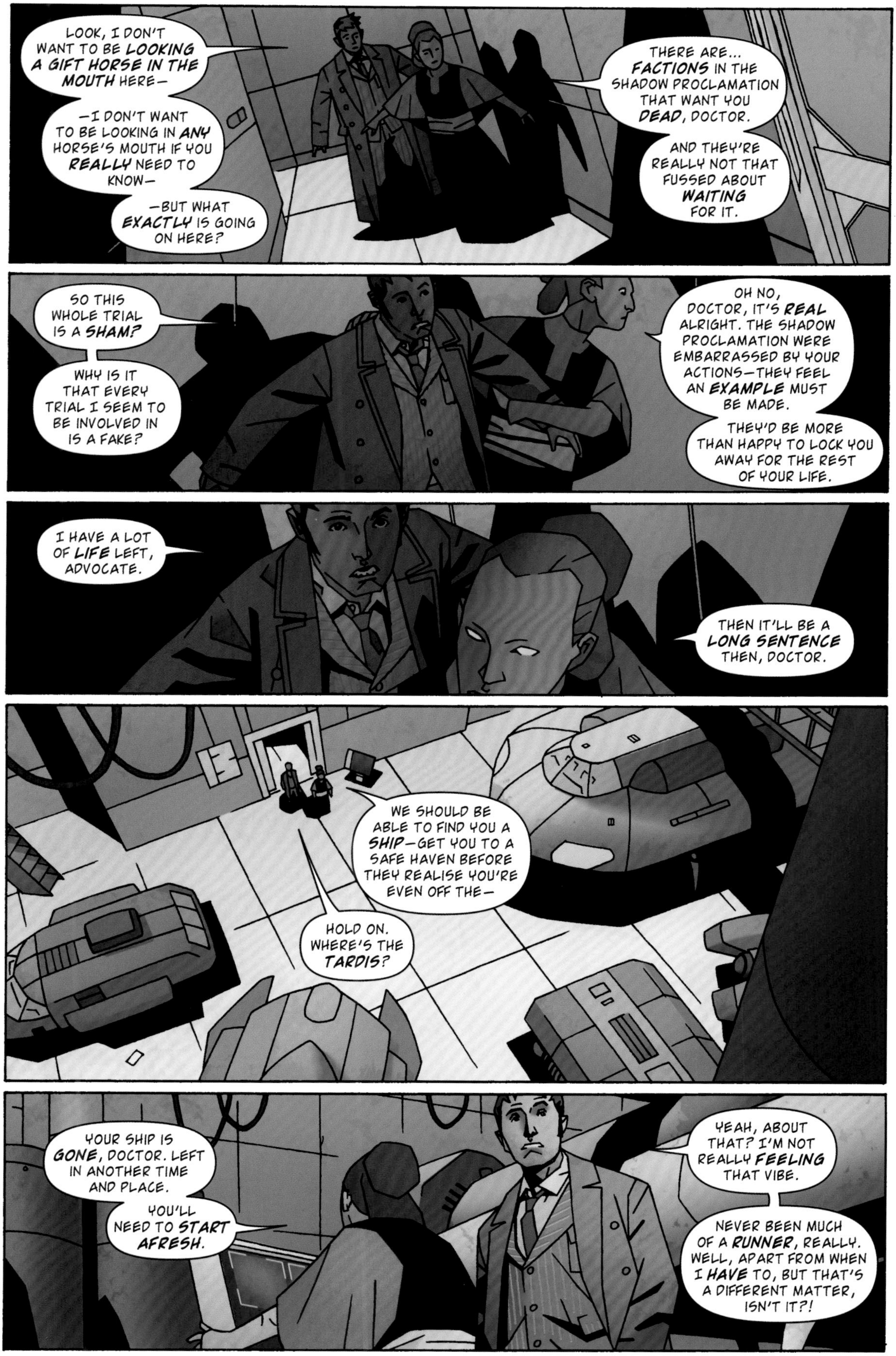
LOOK, I DON'T WANT TO BE LOOKING A GIFT HORSE IN THE MOUTH HERE—
—I DON'T WANT TO BE LOOKING IN ANY HORSE'S MOUTH IF YOU REALLY NEED TO KNOW—
—BUT WHAT EXACTLY IS GOING ON HERE?
THERE ARE... FACTIONS IN THE SHADOW PROCLAMATION THAT WANT YOU DEAD, DOCTOR.
AND THEY'RE REALLY NOT THAT FUSSED ABOUT WAITING FOR IT.
SO THIS WHOLE TRIAL IS A SHAM?
WHY IS IT THAT EVERY TRIAL I SEEM TO BE INVOLVED IN IS A FAKE?
OH NO, DOCTOR, IT'S REAL ALRIGHT. THE SHADOW PROCLAMATION WERE EMBARRASSED BY YOUR ACTIONS—THEY FEEL AN EXAMPLE MUST BE MADE.
THEY'D BE MORE THAN HAPPY TO LOCK YOU AWAY FOR THE REST OF YOUR LIFE.
I HAVE A LOT OF LIFE LEFT, ADVOCATE.
THEN IT'LL BE A LONG SENTENCE THEN, DOCTOR.
WE SHOULD BE ABLE TO FIND YOU A SHIP—GET YOU TO A SAFE HAVEN BEFORE THEY REALISE YOU'RE EVEN OFF THE—
HOLD ON. WHERE'S THE TARDIS?
YOUR SHIP IS GONE, DOCTOR. LEFT IN ANOTHER TIME AND PLACE.
YOU'LL NEED TO START AFRESH.
YEAH, ABOUT THAT? I'M NOT REALLY FEELING THAT VIBE.
NEVER BEEN MUCH OF A RUNNER, REALLY. WELL, APART FROM WHEN I HAVE TO, BUT THAT'S A DIFFERENT MATTER, ISN'T IT?!

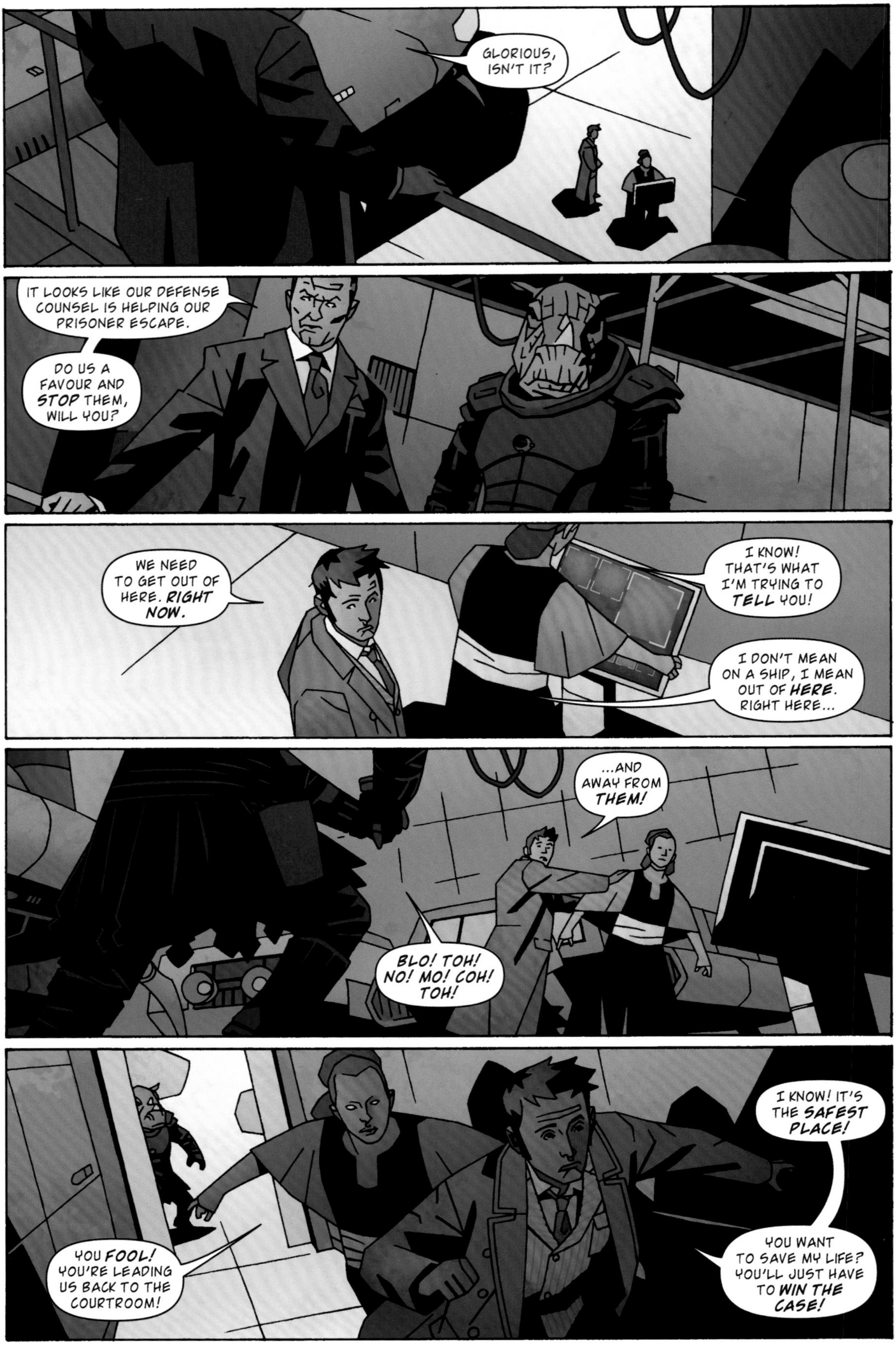
GLORIOUS, ISN'T IT?
IT LOOKS LIKE OUR DEFENSE COUNSEL IS HELPING OUR PRISONER ESCAPE.
DO US A FAVOUR AND **STOP** THEM, WILL YOU?
WE NEED TO GET OUT OF HERE. **RIGHT NOW.**
I KNOW! THAT'S WHAT I'M TRYING TO **TELL** YOU!
I DON'T MEAN ON A SHIP, I MEAN OUT OF **HERE**. RIGHT HERE...
...AND AWAY FROM **THEM!**
BLO! TOH! NO! MO! COH! TOH!
YOU **FOOL!** YOU'RE LEADING US BACK TO THE COURTROOM!
I KNOW! IT'S THE **SAFEST PLACE!**
YOU WANT TO SAVE MY LIFE? YOU'LL JUST HAVE TO **WIN THE CASE!**

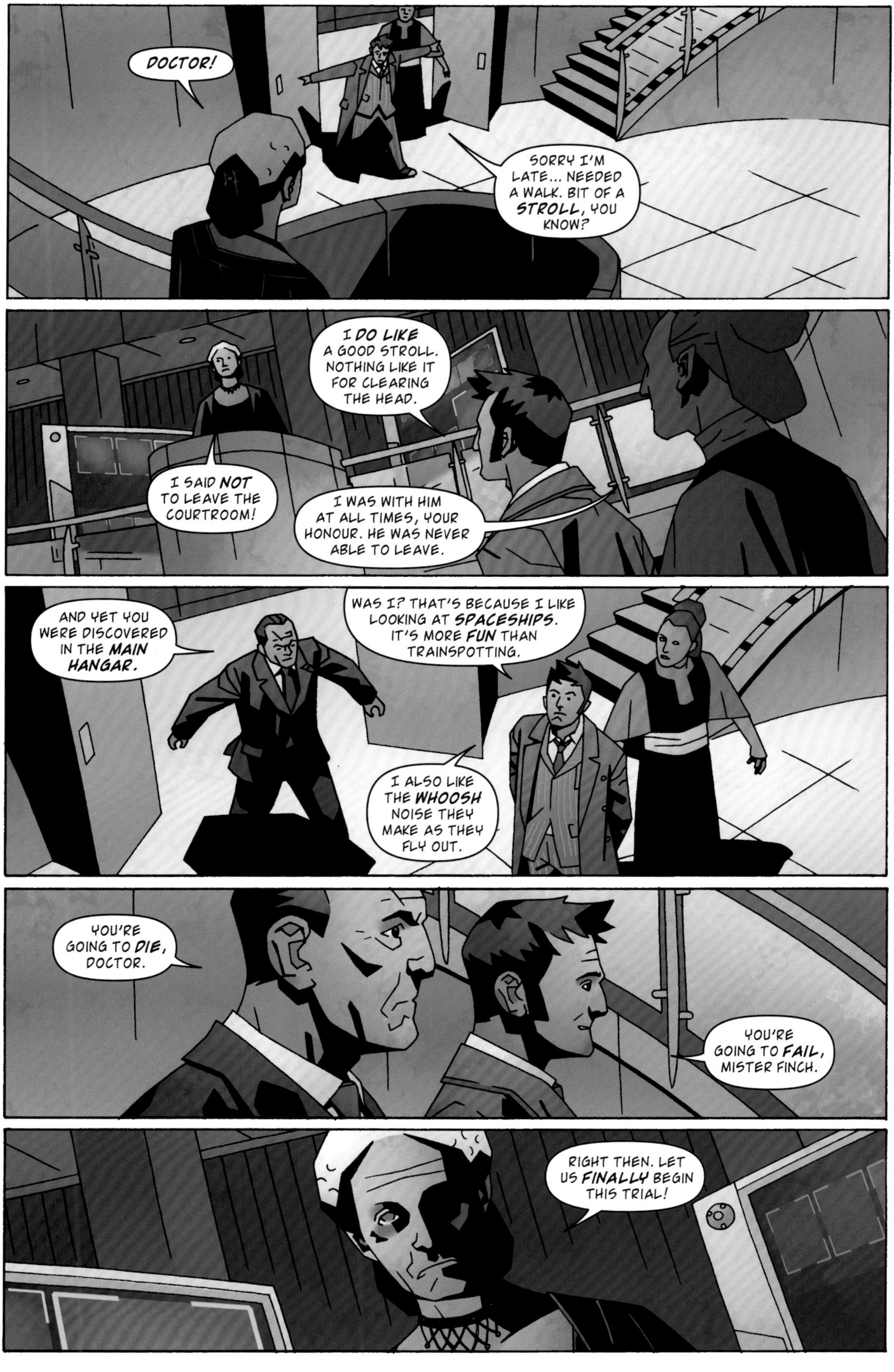
DOCTOR!
SORRY I'M LATE... NEEDED A WALK. BIT OF A STROLL, YOU KNOW?
I DO LIKE A GOOD STROLL. NOTHING LIKE IT FOR CLEARING THE HEAD.
I SAID NOT TO LEAVE THE COURTROOM!
I WAS WITH HIM AT ALL TIMES, YOUR HONOUR. HE WAS NEVER ABLE TO LEAVE.
AND YET YOU WERE DISCOVERED IN THE MAIN HANGAR.
WAS I? THAT'S BECAUSE I LIKE LOOKING AT SPACESHIPS. IT'S MORE FUN THAN TRAINSPOTTING.
I ALSO LIKE THE WHOOSH NOISE THEY MAKE AS THEY FLY OUT.
YOU'RE GOING TO DIE, DOCTOR.
YOU'RE GOING TO FAIL, MISTER FINCH.
RIGHT THEN. LET US FINALLY BEGIN THIS TRIAL!

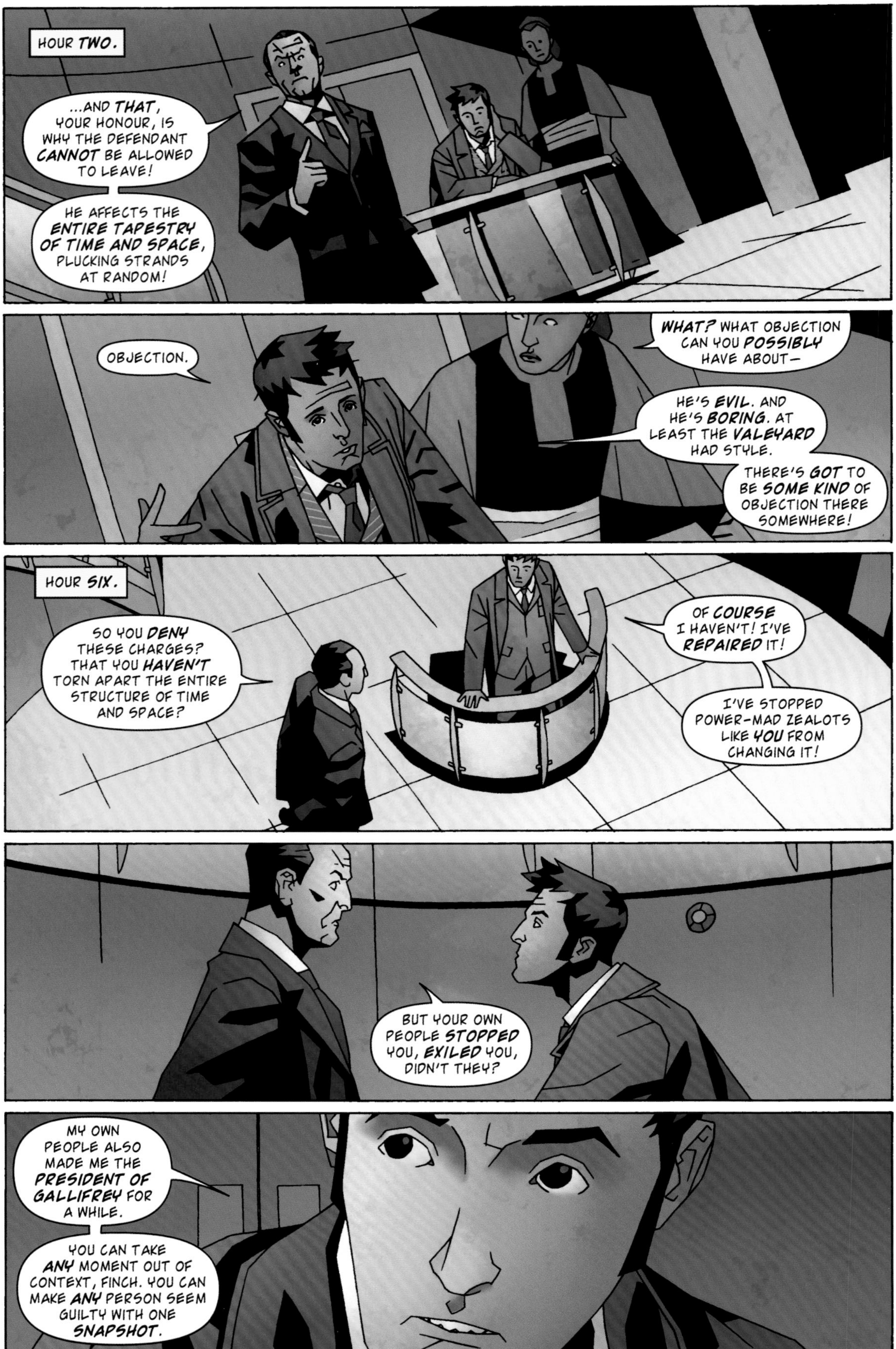
HOUR TWO.
...AND THAT, YOUR HONOUR, IS WHY THE DEFENDANT CANNOT BE ALLOWED TO LEAVE!
HE AFFECTS THE ENTIRE TAPESTRY OF TIME AND SPACE, PLUCKING STRANDS AT RANDOM!
OBJECTION.
WHAT? WHAT OBJECTION CAN YOU POSSIBLY HAVE ABOUT—
HE'S EVIL. AND HE'S BORING. AT LEAST THE VALEYARD HAD STYLE.
THERE'S GOT TO BE SOME KIND OF OBJECTION THERE SOMEWHERE!
HOUR SIX.
SO YOU DENY THESE CHARGES? THAT YOU HAVEN'T TORN APART THE ENTIRE STRUCTURE OF TIME AND SPACE?
OF COURSE I HAVEN'T! I'VE REPAIRED IT!
I'VE STOPPED POWER-MAD ZEALOTS LIKE YOU FROM CHANGING IT!
BUT YOUR OWN PEOPLE STOPPED YOU, EXILED YOU, DIDN'T THEY?
MY OWN PEOPLE ALSO MADE ME THE PRESIDENT OF GALLIFREY FOR A WHILE.
YOU CAN TAKE ANY MOMENT OUT OF CONTEXT, FINCH. YOU CAN MAKE ANY PERSON SEEM GUILTY WITH ONE SNAPSHOT.

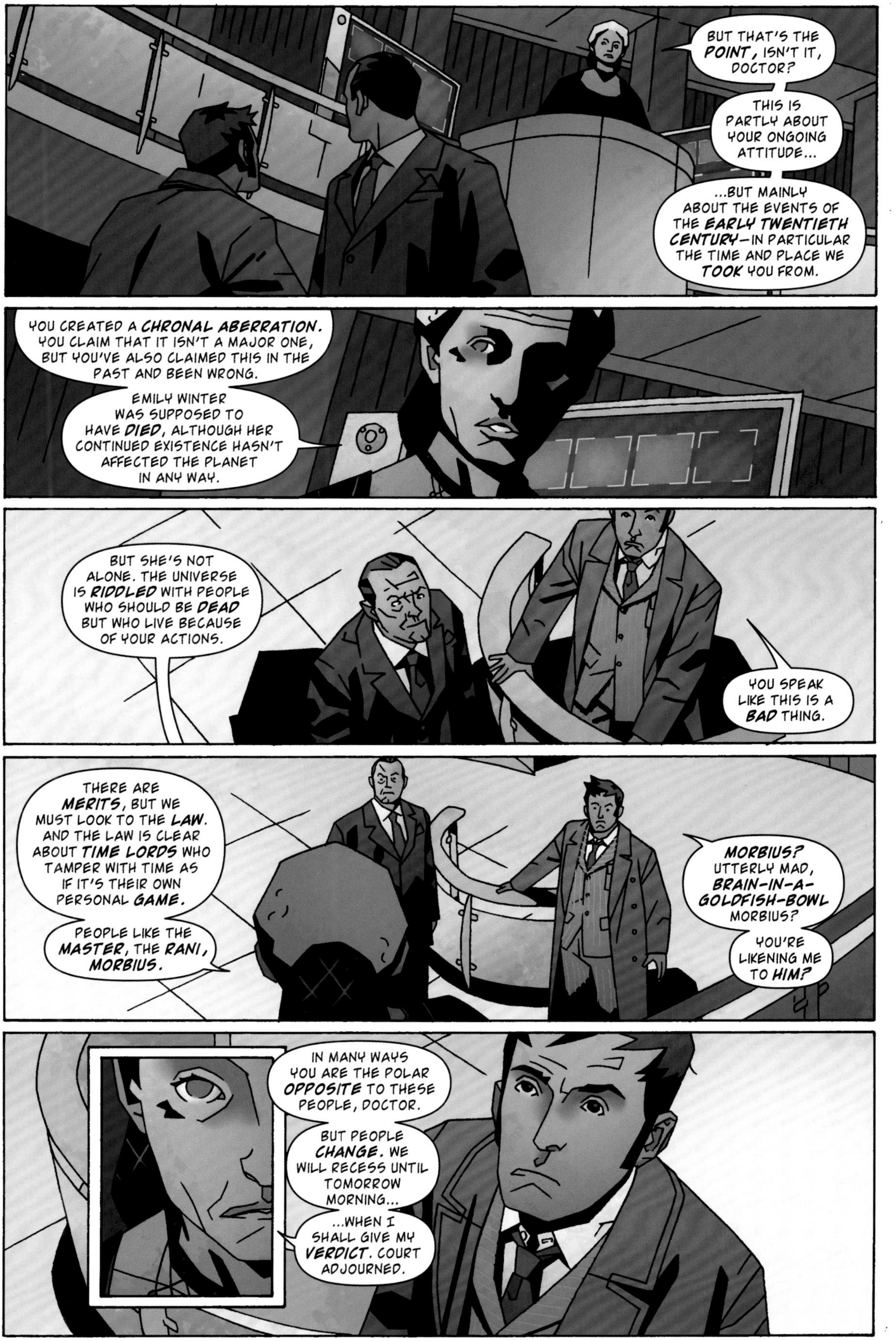
BUT THAT'S THE POINT, ISN'T IT, DOCTOR?
THIS IS PARTLY ABOUT YOUR ONGOING ATTITUDE...
...BUT MAINLY ABOUT THE EVENTS OF THE EARLY TWENTIETH CENTURY—IN PARTICULAR THE TIME AND PLACE WE TOOK YOU FROM.
YOU CREATED A CHRONAL ABERRATION. YOU CLAIM THAT IT ISN'T A MAJOR ONE, BUT YOU'VE ALSO CLAIMED THIS IN THE PAST AND BEEN WRONG.
EMILY WINTER WAS SUPPOSED TO HAVE DIED, ALTHOUGH HER CONTINUED EXISTENCE HASN'T AFFECTED THE PLANET IN ANY WAY.
BUT SHE'S NOT ALONE. THE UNIVERSE IS RIDDLED WITH PEOPLE WHO SHOULD BE DEAD BUT WHO LIVE BECAUSE OF YOUR ACTIONS.
YOU SPEAK LIKE THIS IS A BAD THING.
THERE ARE MERITS, BUT WE MUST LOOK TO THE LAW. AND THE LAW IS CLEAR ABOUT TIME LORDS WHO TAMPER WITH TIME AS IF IT'S THEIR OWN PERSONAL GAME.
PEOPLE LIKE THE MASTER, THE RANI, MORBIUS.
MORBIUS? UTTERLY MAD, BRAIN-IN-A-GOLDFISH-BOWL MORBIUS?
YOU'RE LIKENING ME TO HIM?
IN MANY WAYS YOU ARE THE POLAR OPPOSITE TO THESE PEOPLE, DOCTOR.
BUT PEOPLE CHANGE. WE WILL RECESS UNTIL TOMORROW MORNING...
...WHEN I SHALL GIVE MY VERDICT. COURT ADJOURNED.

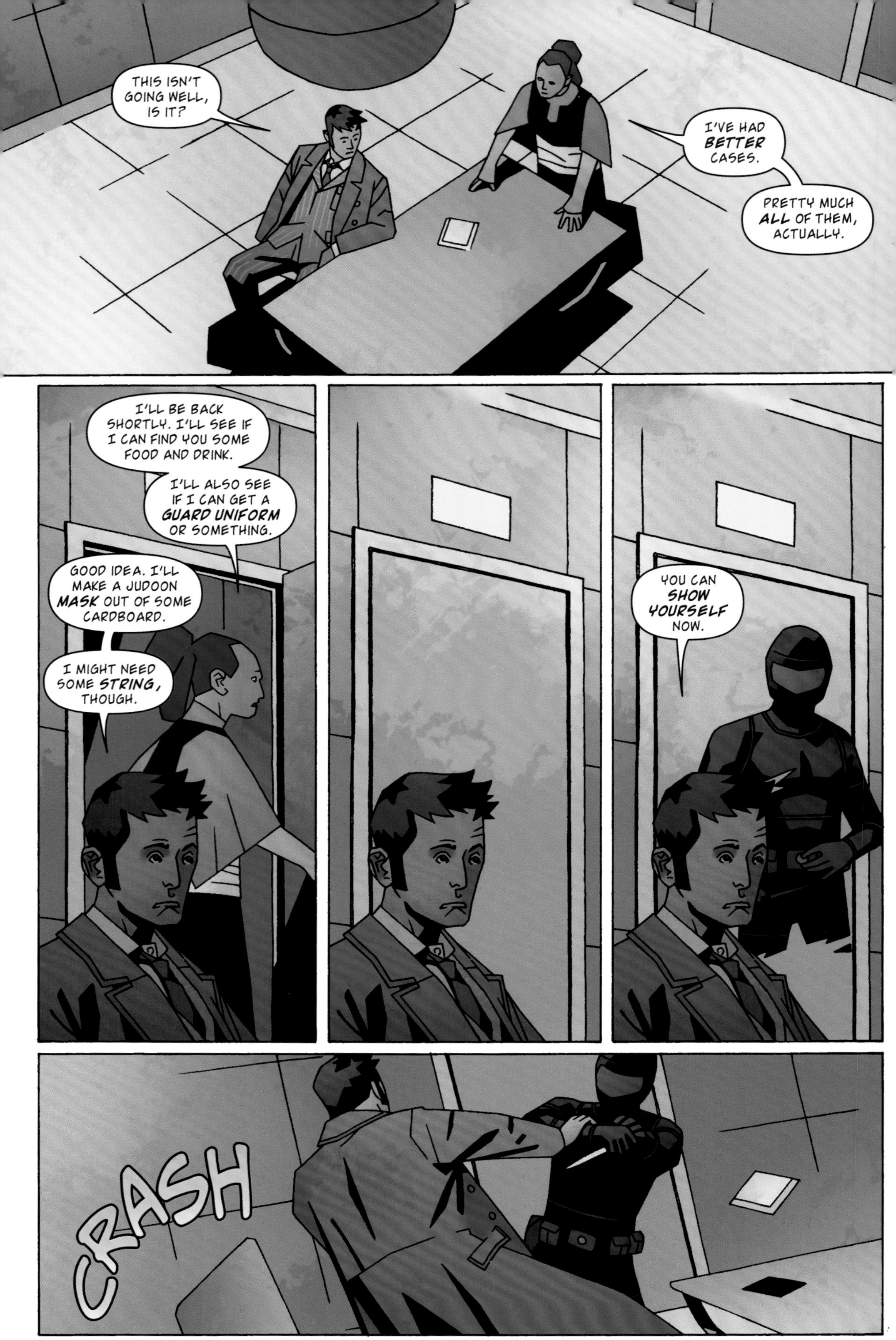
THIS ISN'T GOING WELL, IS IT?
I'VE HAD BETTER CASES.
PRETTY MUCH ALL OF THEM, ACTUALLY.
I'LL BE BACK SHORTLY. I'LL SEE IF I CAN FIND YOU SOME FOOD AND DRINK.
I'LL ALSO SEE IF I CAN GET A GUARD UNIFORM OR SOMETHING.
GOOD IDEA. I'LL MAKE A JUDOON MASK OUT OF SOME CARDBOARD.
I MIGHT NEED SOME STRING, THOUGH.
YOU CAN SHOW YOURSELF NOW.
CRASH

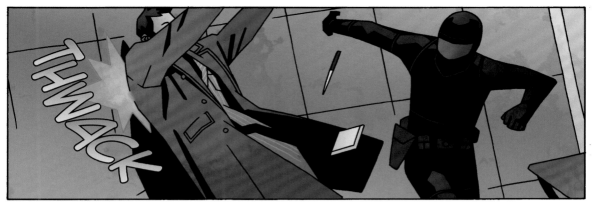

THWACK

ARGH!

CRACK

GRAARGHH!

HELP! I NEED SOME HELP IN *HERE!*

THERE'S *NEVER* A JUDOON AROUND WHEN YOU *NEED—*

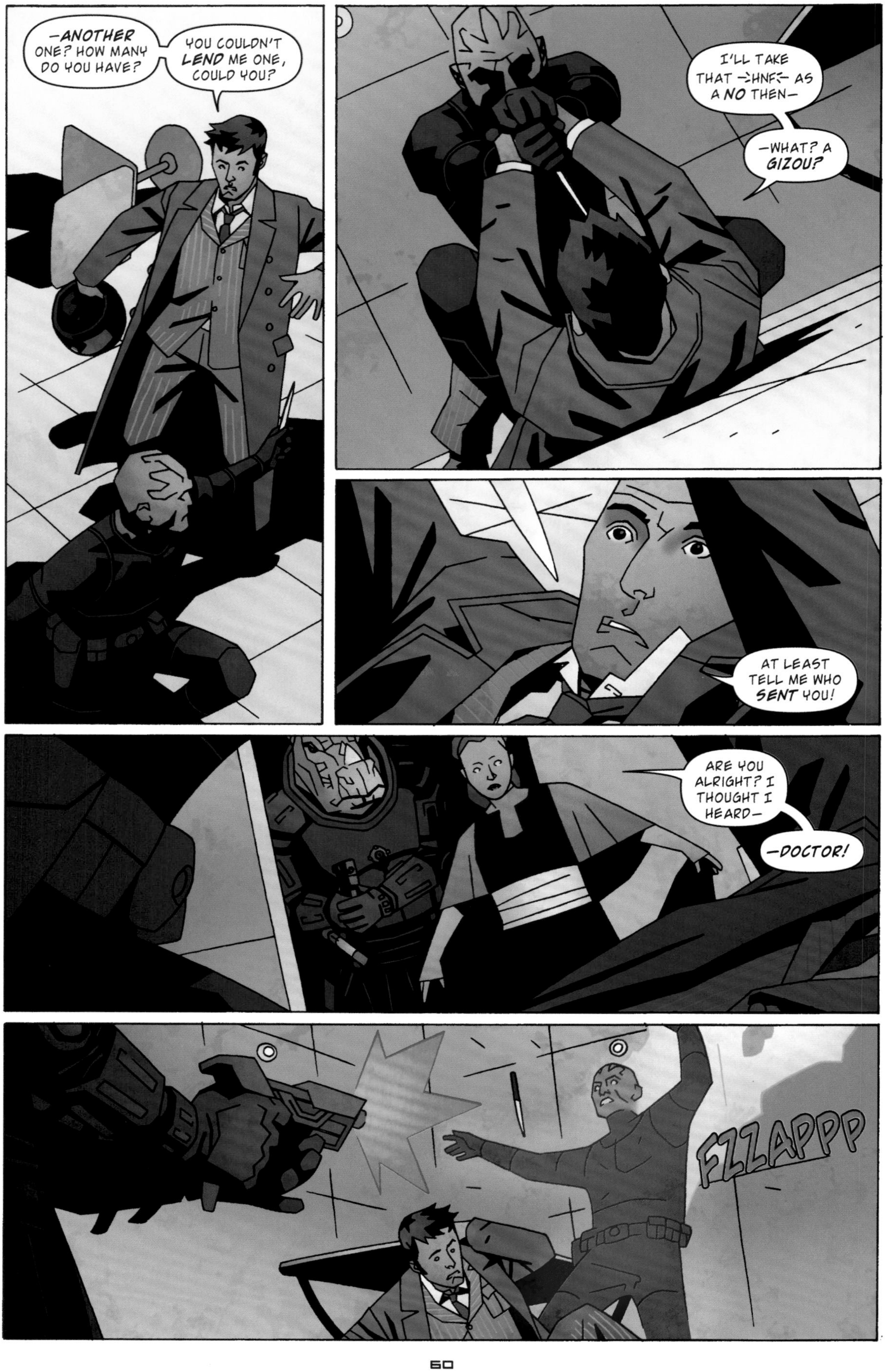
—ANOTHER ONE? HOW MANY DO YOU HAVE?
YOU COULDN'T LEND ME ONE, COULD YOU?
I'LL TAKE THAT —HNF— AS A NO THEN—
—WHAT? A GIZOU?
AT LEAST TELL ME WHO SENT YOU!
ARE YOU ALRIGHT? I THOUGHT I HEARD—
—DOCTOR!
FZZAPPP

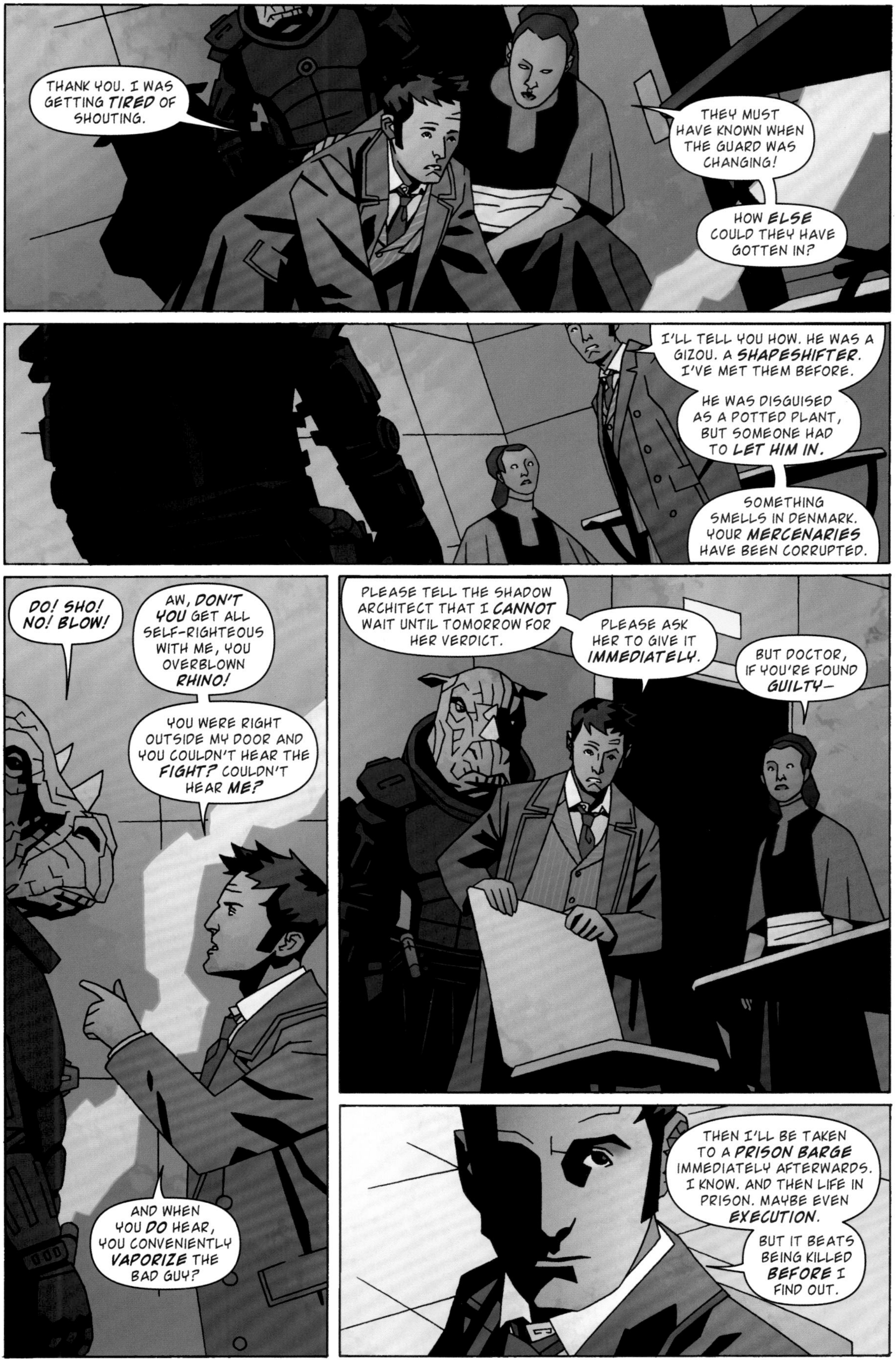
THANK YOU. I WAS GETTING TIRED OF SHOUTING.
THEY MUST HAVE KNOWN WHEN THE GUARD WAS CHANGING!
HOW ELSE COULD THEY HAVE GOTTEN IN?
I'LL TELL YOU HOW. HE WAS A GIZOU. A SHAPESHIFTER. I'VE MET THEM BEFORE.
HE WAS DISGUISED AS A POTTED PLANT, BUT SOMEONE HAD TO LET HIM IN.
SOMETHING SMELLS IN DENMARK. YOUR MERCENARIES HAVE BEEN CORRUPTED.
DO! SHO! NO! BLOW!
AW, DON'T YOU GET ALL SELF-RIGHTEOUS WITH ME, YOU OVERBLOWN RHINO!
YOU WERE RIGHT OUTSIDE MY DOOR AND YOU COULDN'T HEAR THE FIGHT? COULDN'T HEAR ME?
AND WHEN YOU DO HEAR, YOU CONVENIENTLY VAPORIZE THE BAD GUY?
PLEASE TELL THE SHADOW ARCHITECT THAT I CANNOT WAIT UNTIL TOMORROW FOR HER VERDICT.
PLEASE ASK HER TO GIVE IT IMMEDIATELY.
BUT DOCTOR, IF YOU'RE FOUND GUILTY—
THEN I'LL BE TAKEN TO A PRISON BARGE IMMEDIATELY AFTERWARDS. I KNOW. AND THEN LIFE IN PRISON. MAYBE EVEN EXECUTION.
BUT IT BEATS BEING KILLED BEFORE I FIND OUT.

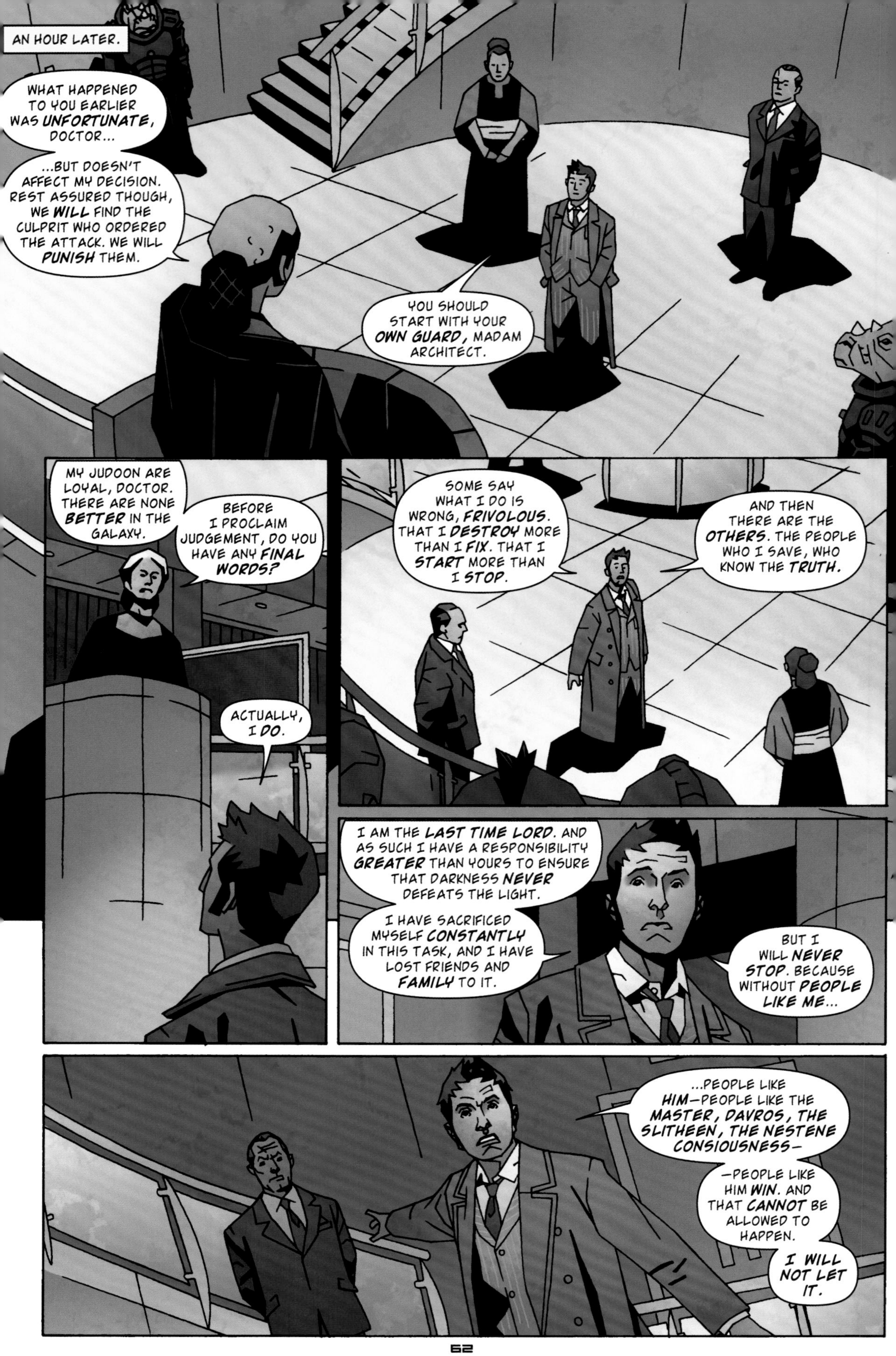
AN HOUR LATER.
WHAT HAPPENED TO YOU EARLIER WAS UNFORTUNATE, DOCTOR...
...BUT DOESN'T AFFECT MY DECISION. REST ASSURED THOUGH, WE WILL FIND THE CULPRIT WHO ORDERED THE ATTACK. WE WILL PUNISH THEM.
YOU SHOULD START WITH YOUR OWN GUARD, MADAM ARCHITECT.
MY JUDOON ARE LOYAL, DOCTOR. THERE ARE NONE BETTER IN THE GALAXY.
BEFORE I PROCLAIM JUDGEMENT, DO YOU HAVE ANY FINAL WORDS?
ACTUALLY, I DO.
SOME SAY WHAT I DO IS WRONG, FRIVOLOUS. THAT I DESTROY MORE THAN I FIX. THAT I START MORE THAN I STOP.
AND THEN THERE ARE THE OTHERS. THE PEOPLE WHO I SAVE, WHO KNOW THE TRUTH.
I AM THE LAST TIME LORD. AND AS SUCH I HAVE A RESPONSIBILITY GREATER THAN YOURS TO ENSURE THAT DARKNESS NEVER DEFEATS THE LIGHT.
I HAVE SACRIFICED MYSELF CONSTANTLY IN THIS TASK, AND I HAVE LOST FRIENDS AND FAMILY TO IT.
BUT I WILL NEVER STOP. BECAUSE WITHOUT PEOPLE LIKE ME...
...PEOPLE LIKE HIM—PEOPLE LIKE THE MASTER, DAVROS, THE SLITHEEN, THE NESTENE CONSIOUSNESS—
—PEOPLE LIKE HIM WIN. AND THAT CANNOT BE ALLOWED TO HAPPEN.
I WILL NOT LET IT.

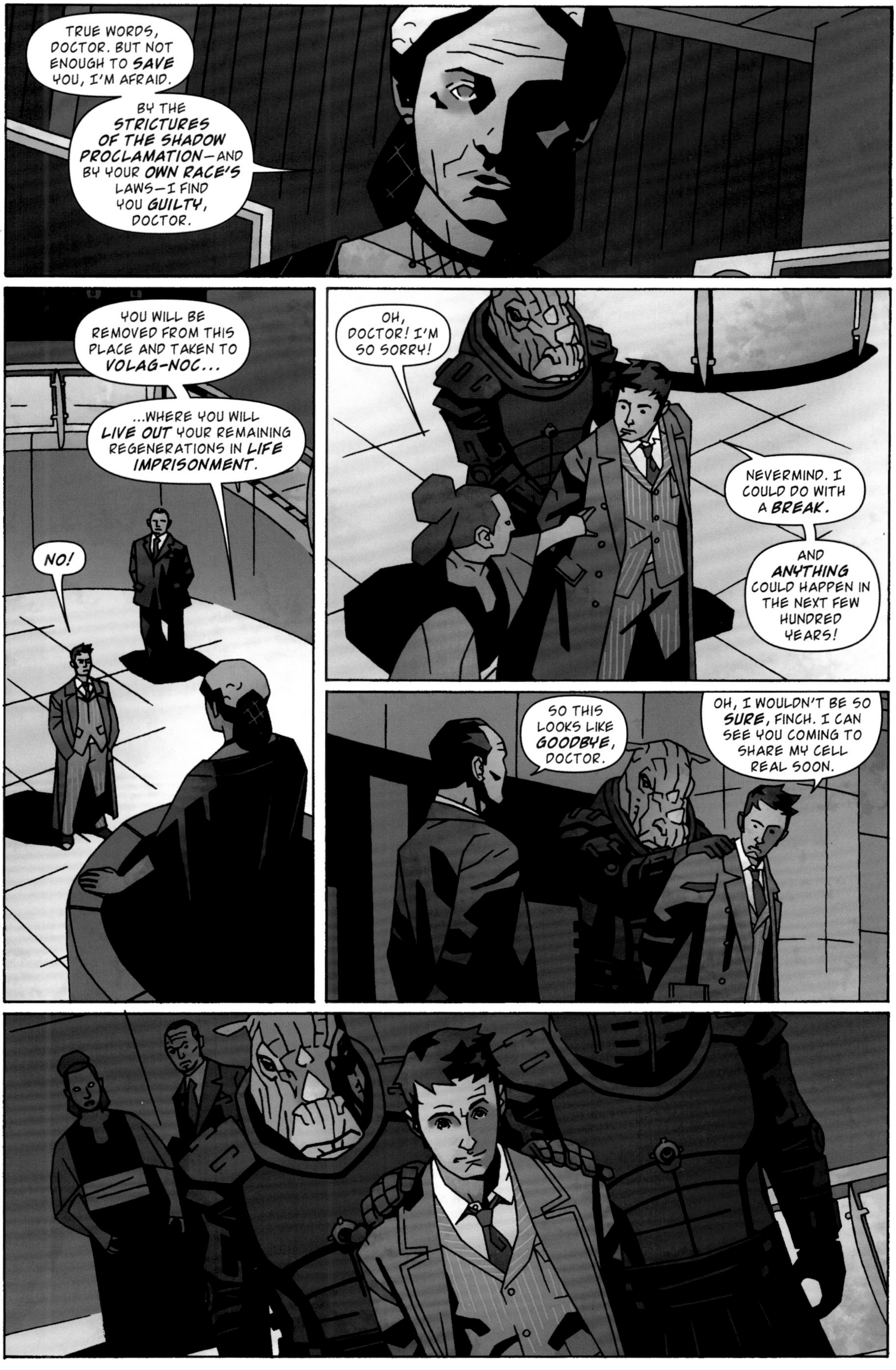
TRUE WORDS, DOCTOR. BUT NOT ENOUGH TO SAVE YOU, I'M AFRAID.
BY THE STRICTURES OF THE SHADOW PROCLAMATION—AND BY YOUR OWN RACE'S LAWS—I FIND YOU GUILTY, DOCTOR.
YOU WILL BE REMOVED FROM THIS PLACE AND TAKEN TO VOLAG-NOC...
...WHERE YOU WILL LIVE OUT YOUR REMAINING REGENERATIONS IN LIFE IMPRISONMENT.
NO!
OH, DOCTOR! I'M SO SORRY!
NEVERMIND. I COULD DO WITH A BREAK.
AND ANYTHING COULD HAPPEN IN THE NEXT FEW HUNDRED YEARS!
SO THIS LOOKS LIKE GOODBYE, DOCTOR.
OH, I WOULDN'T BE SO SURE, FINCH. I CAN SEE YOU COMING TO SHARE MY CELL REAL SOON.

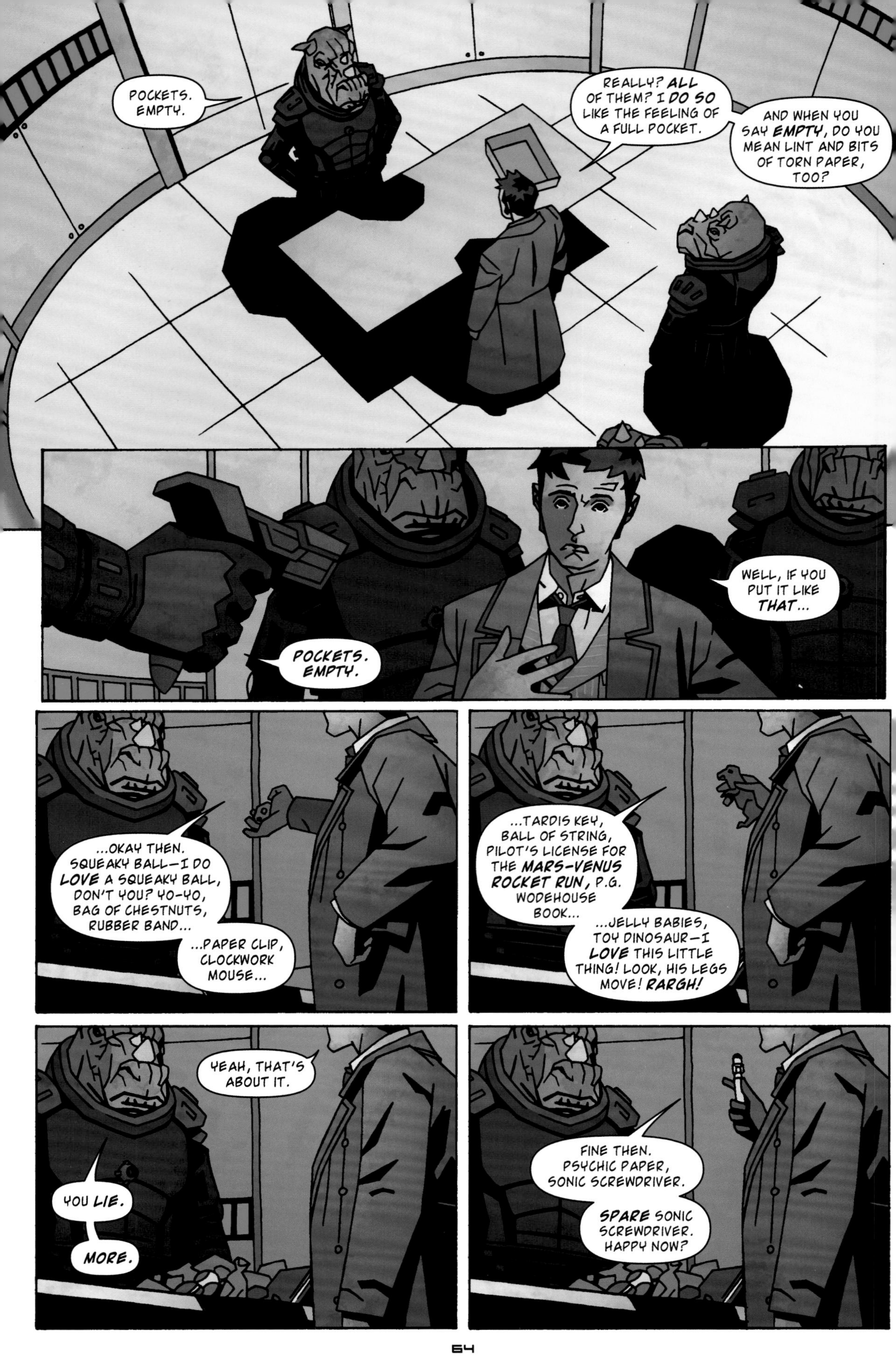
POCKETS. EMPTY.
REALLY? ALL OF THEM? I DO SO LIKE THE FEELING OF A FULL POCKET.
AND WHEN YOU SAY EMPTY, DO YOU MEAN LINT AND BITS OF TORN PAPER, TOO?
POCKETS. EMPTY.
WELL, IF YOU PUT IT LIKE THAT...
...OKAY THEN. SQUEAKY BALL—I DO LOVE A SQUEAKY BALL, DON'T YOU? YO-YO, BAG OF CHESTNUTS, RUBBER BAND...
...PAPER CLIP, CLOCKWORK MOUSE...
...TARDIS KEY, BALL OF STRING, PILOT'S LICENSE FOR THE MARS-VENUS ROCKET RUN, P.G. WODEHOUSE BOOK...
...JELLY BABIES, TOY DINOSAUR—I LOVE THIS LITTLE THING! LOOK, HIS LEGS MOVE! RARGH!
YEAH, THAT'S ABOUT IT.
YOU LIE.
MORE.
FINE THEN. PSYCHIC PAPER, SONIC SCREWDRIVER.
SPARE SONIC SCREWDRIVER. HAPPY NOW?

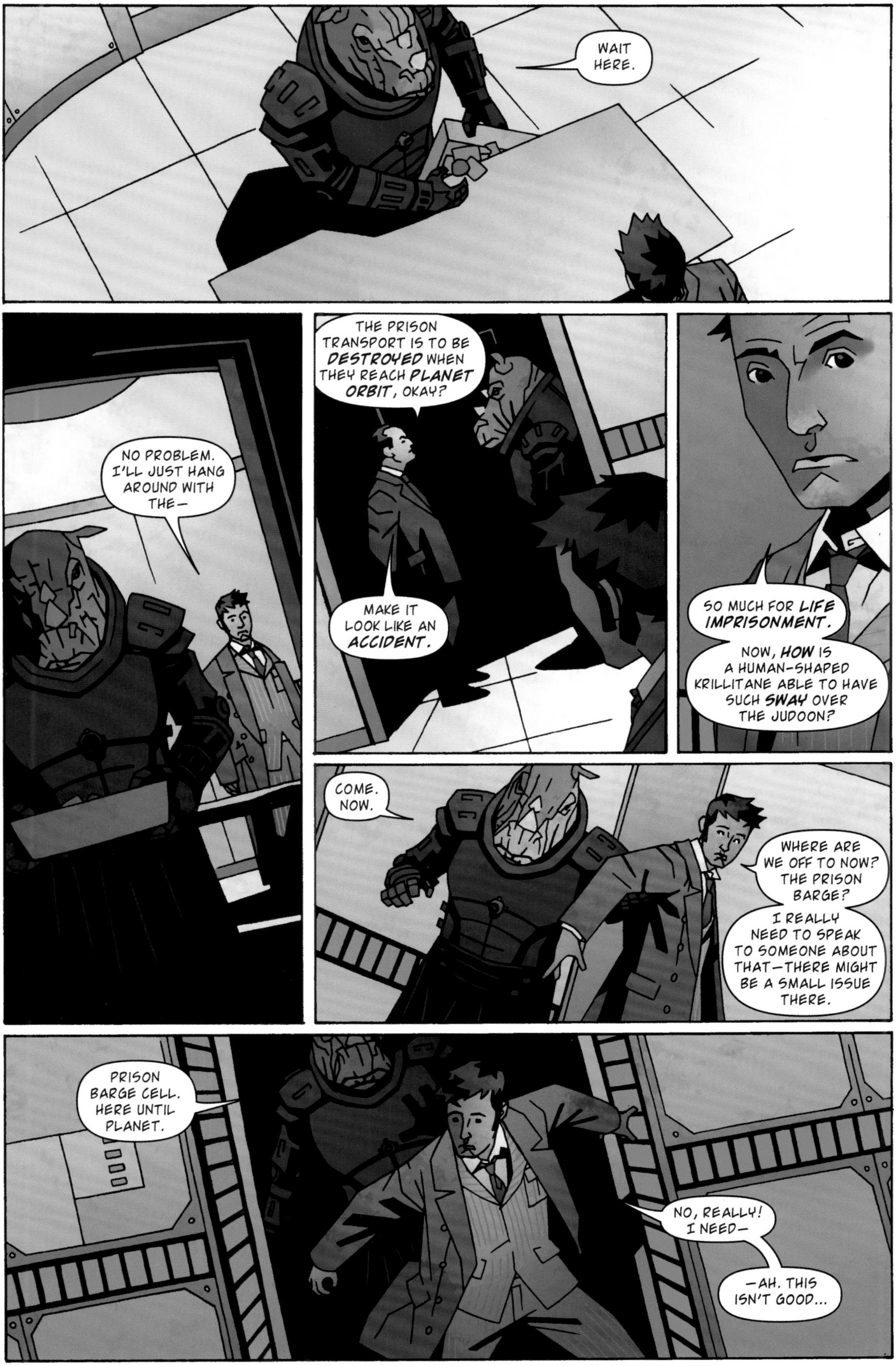
WAIT HERE.
NO PROBLEM. I'LL JUST HANG AROUND WITH THE—
THE PRISON TRANSPORT IS TO BE DESTROYED WHEN THEY REACH PLANET ORBIT, OKAY?
MAKE IT LOOK LIKE AN ACCIDENT.
SO MUCH FOR LIFE IMPRISONMENT.
NOW, HOW IS A HUMAN-SHAPED KRILLITANE ABLE TO HAVE SUCH SWAY OVER THE JUDOON?
COME. NOW.
WHERE ARE WE OFF TO NOW? THE PRISON BARGE?
I REALLY NEED TO SPEAK TO SOMEONE ABOUT THAT—THERE MIGHT BE A SMALL ISSUE THERE.
PRISON BARGE CELL. HERE UNTIL PLANET.
NO, REALLY! I NEED—
—AH. THIS ISN'T GOOD...

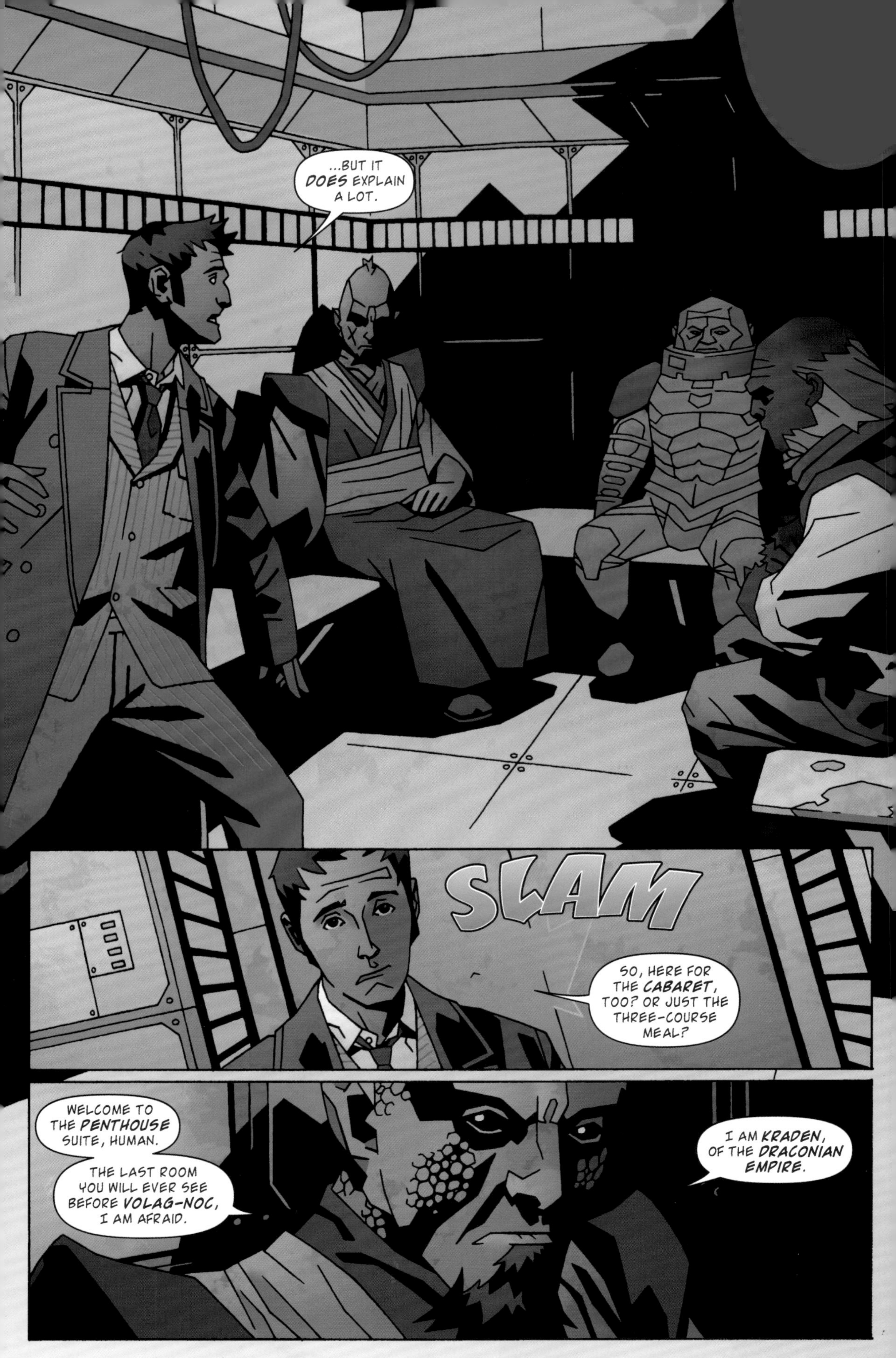
...BUT IT DOES EXPLAIN A LOT.
SLAM
SO, HERE FOR THE CABARET, TOO? OR JUST THE THREE-COURSE MEAL?
WELCOME TO THE PENTHOUSE SUITE, HUMAN.
THE LAST ROOM YOU WILL EVER SEE BEFORE VOLAG-NOC, I AM AFRAID.
I AM KRADEN, OF THE DRACONIAN EMPIRE.

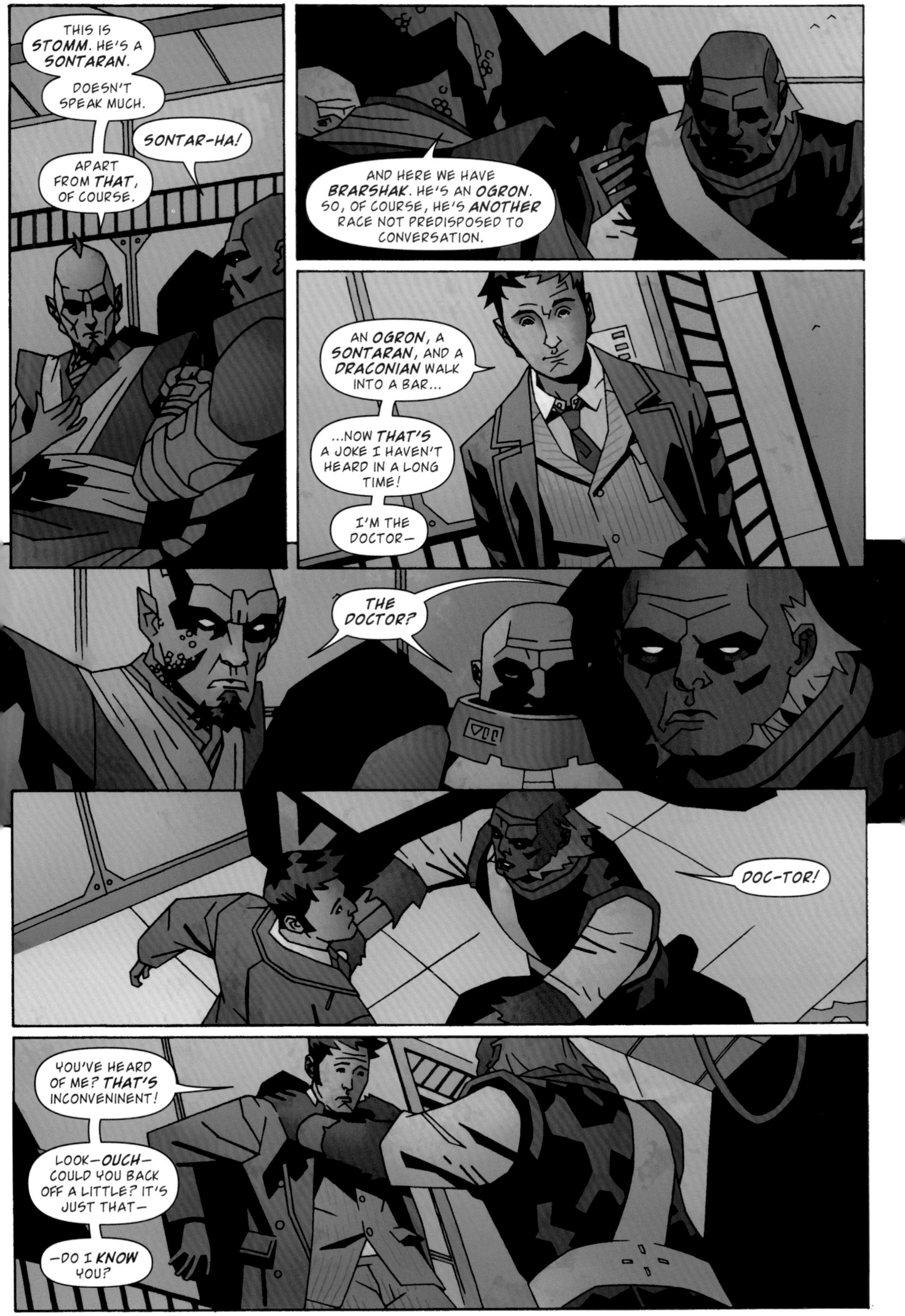

THIS IS STOMM. HE'S A SONTARAN.
DOESN'T SPEAK MUCH.
SONTAR-HA!
APART FROM THAT, OF COURSE.
AND HERE WE HAVE BRARSHAK. HE'S AN OGRON. SO, OF COURSE, HE'S ANOTHER RACE NOT PREDISPOSED TO CONVERSATION.
AN OGRON, A SONTARAN, AND A DRACONIAN WALK INTO A BAR...
...NOW THAT'S A JOKE I HAVEN'T HEARD IN A LONG TIME!
I'M THE DOCTOR—
THE DOCTOR?
DOC-TOR!
YOU'VE HEARD OF ME? THAT'S INCONVENINENT!
LOOK—OUCH—COULD YOU BACK OFF A LITTLE? IT'S JUST THAT—
—DO I KNOW YOU?

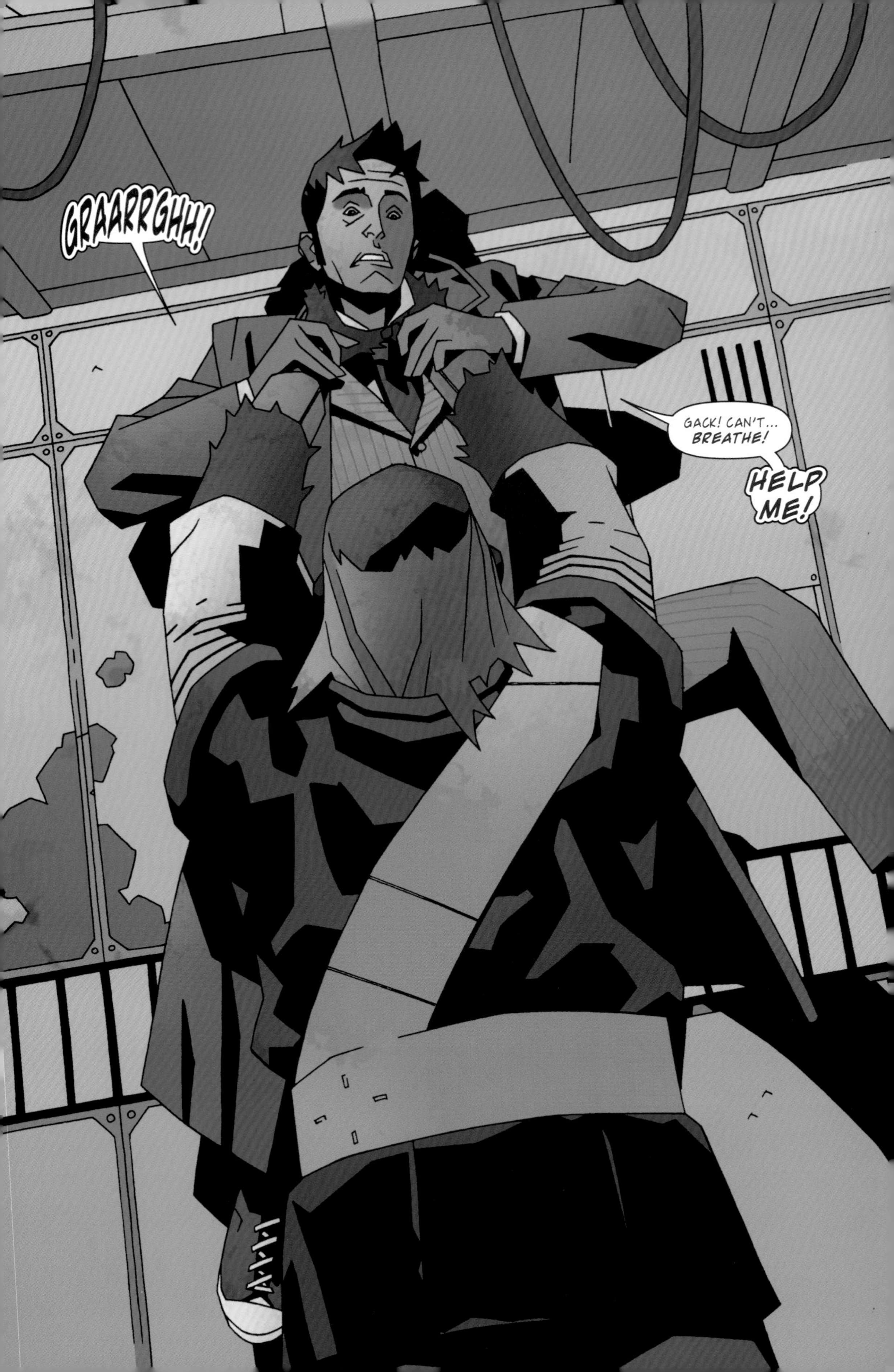
GRAARRGHH!
GACK! CAN'T... BREATHE!
HELP ME!

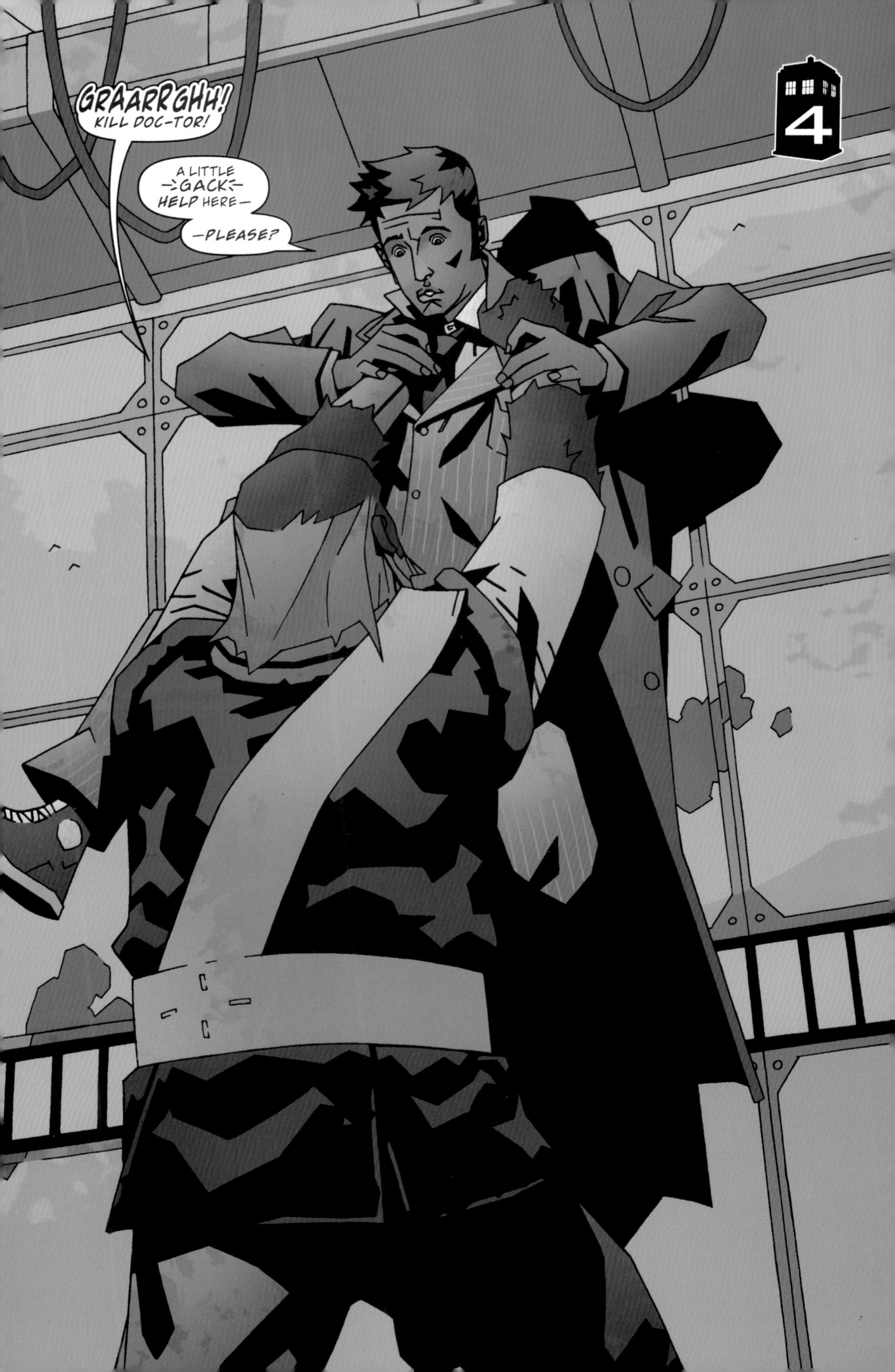
GRAARRGHH! KILL DOC-TOR!
A LITTLE -GACK- HELP HERE—
—PLEASE?
4

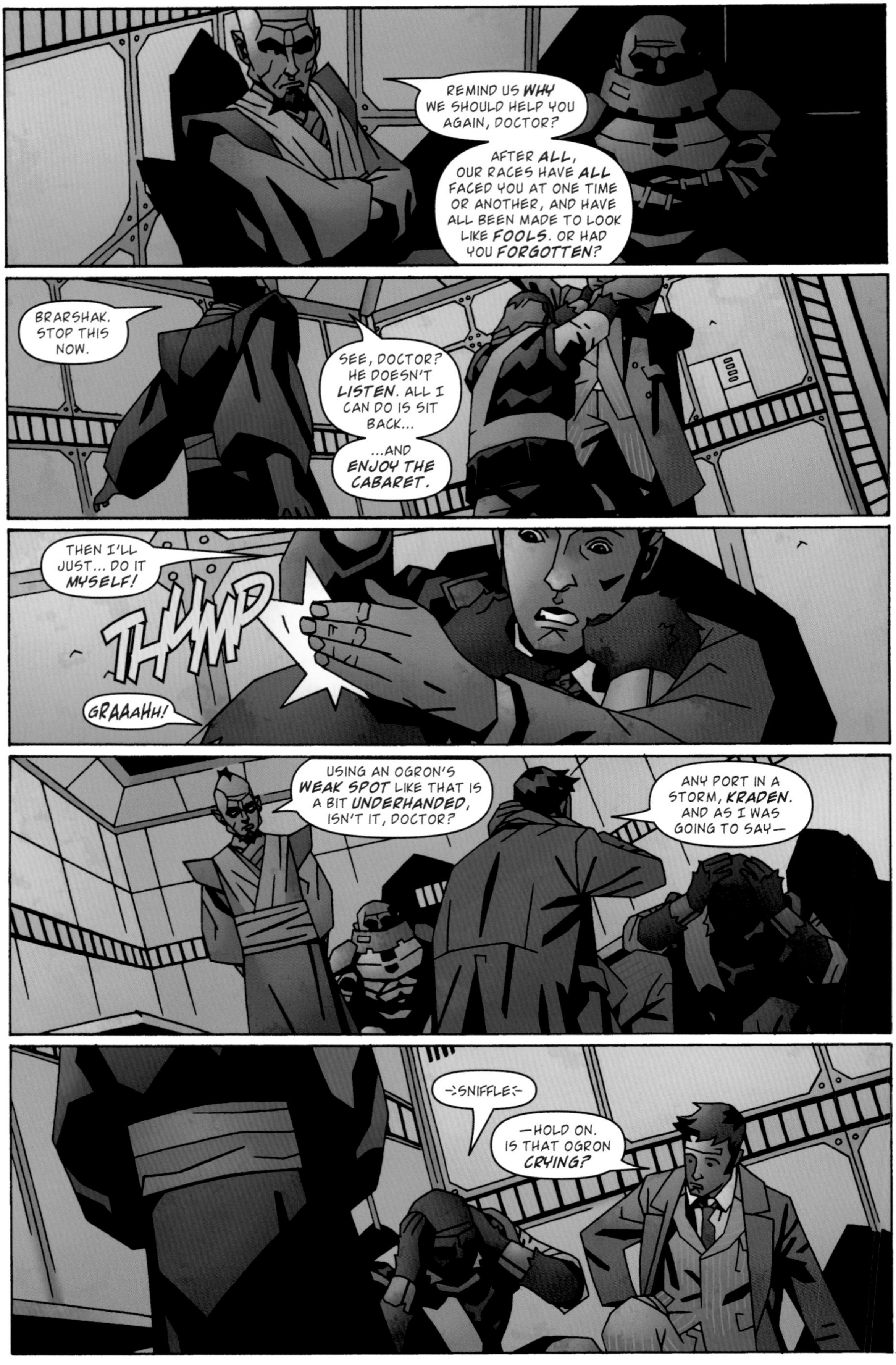
REMIND US WHY WE SHOULD HELP YOU AGAIN, DOCTOR?
AFTER ALL, OUR RACES HAVE ALL FACED YOU AT ONE TIME OR ANOTHER, AND HAVE ALL BEEN MADE TO LOOK LIKE FOOLS. OR HAD YOU FORGOTTEN?
BRARSHAK. STOP THIS NOW.
SEE, DOCTOR? HE DOESN'T LISTEN. ALL I CAN DO IS SIT BACK...
...AND ENJOY THE CABARET.
THEN I'LL JUST... DO IT MYSELF!
THUMP
GRAAAHH!
USING AN OGRON'S WEAK SPOT LIKE THAT IS A BIT UNDERHANDED, ISN'T IT, DOCTOR?
ANY PORT IN A STORM, KRADEN. AND AS I WAS GOING TO SAY—
-SNIFFLE-
—HOLD ON. IS THAT OGRON CRYING?

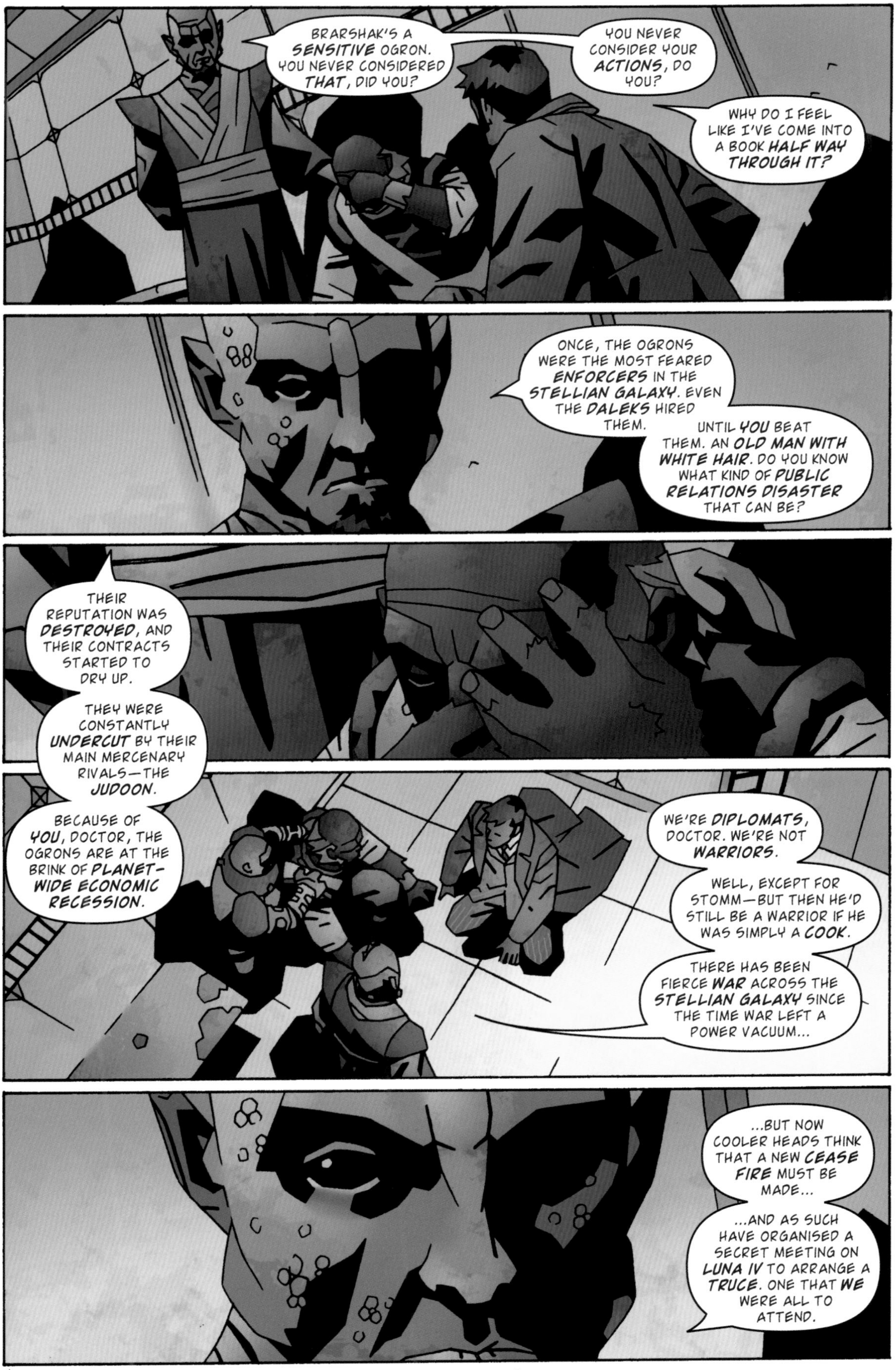
BRARSHAK'S A SENSITIVE OGRON. YOU NEVER CONSIDERED THAT, DID YOU?
YOU NEVER CONSIDER YOUR ACTIONS, DO YOU?
WHY DO I FEEL LIKE I'VE COME INTO A BOOK HALF WAY THROUGH IT?
ONCE, THE OGRONS WERE THE MOST FEARED ENFORCERS IN THE STELLIAN GALAXY. EVEN THE DALEKS HIRED THEM.
UNTIL YOU BEAT THEM. AN OLD MAN WITH WHITE HAIR. DO YOU KNOW WHAT KIND OF PUBLIC RELATIONS DISASTER THAT CAN BE?
THEIR REPUTATION WAS DESTROYED, AND THEIR CONTRACTS STARTED TO DRY UP.
THEY WERE CONSTANTLY UNDERCUT BY THEIR MAIN MERCENARY RIVALS—THE JUDOON.
BECAUSE OF YOU, DOCTOR, THE OGRONS ARE AT THE BRINK OF PLANET-WIDE ECONOMIC RECESSION.
WE'RE DIPLOMATS, DOCTOR. WE'RE NOT WARRIORS.
WELL, EXCEPT FOR STOMM—BUT THEN HE'D STILL BE A WARRIOR IF HE WAS SIMPLY A COOK.
THERE HAS BEEN FIERCE WAR ACROSS THE STELLIAN GALAXY SINCE THE TIME WAR LEFT A POWER VACUUM...
...BUT NOW COOLER HEADS THINK THAT A NEW CEASE FIRE MUST BE MADE...
...AND AS SUCH HAVE ORGANISED A SECRET MEETING ON LUNA IV TO ARRANGE A TRUCE. ONE THAT WE WERE ALL TO ATTEND.

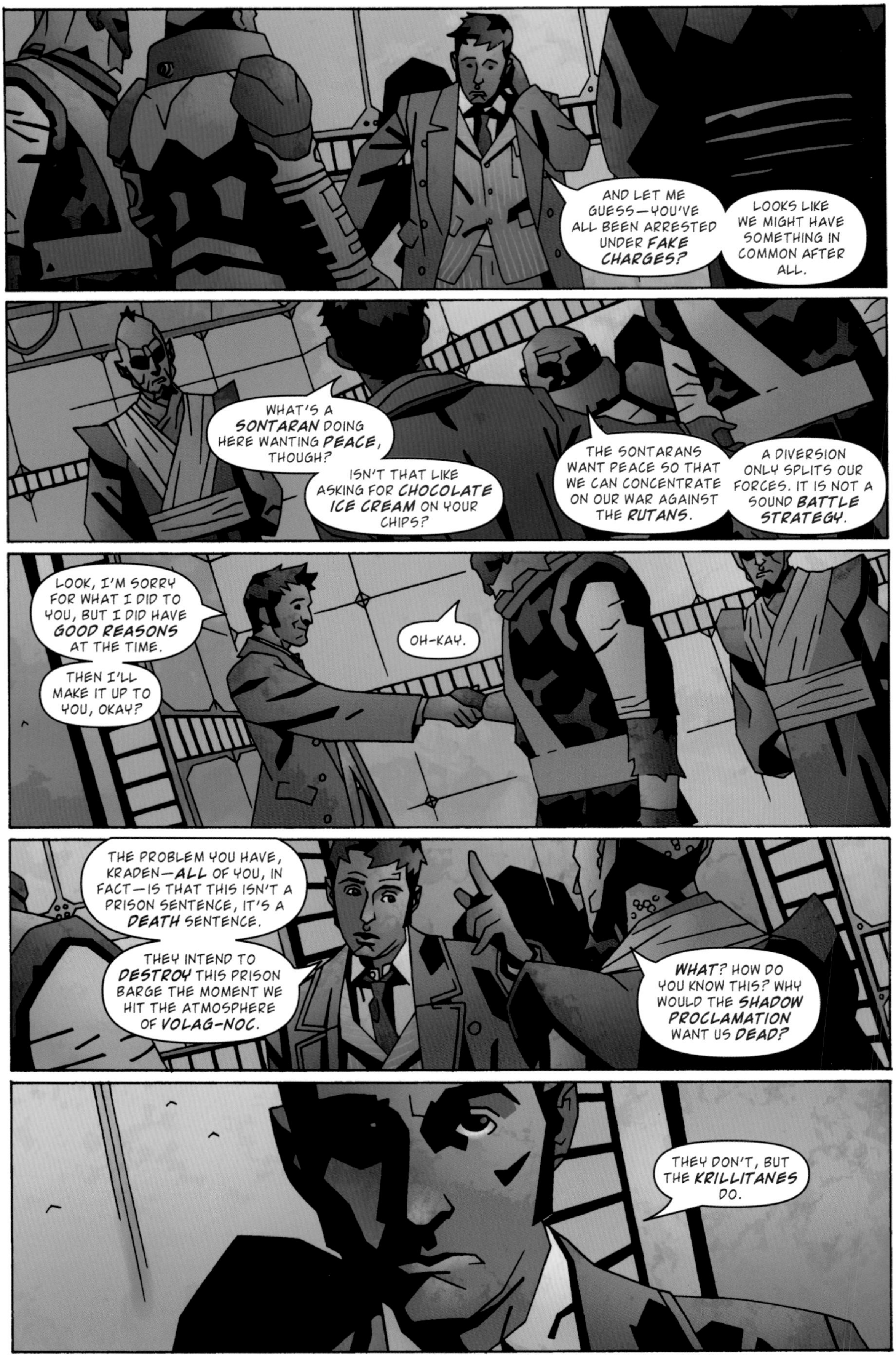
AND LET ME GUESS—YOU'VE ALL BEEN ARRESTED UNDER FAKE CHARGES?
LOOKS LIKE WE MIGHT HAVE SOMETHING IN COMMON AFTER ALL.
WHAT'S A SONTARAN DOING HERE WANTING PEACE, THOUGH?
ISN'T THAT LIKE ASKING FOR CHOCOLATE ICE CREAM ON YOUR CHIPS?
THE SONTARANS WANT PEACE SO THAT WE CAN CONCENTRATE ON OUR WAR AGAINST THE RUTANS.
A DIVERSION ONLY SPLITS OUR FORCES. IT IS NOT A SOUND BATTLE STRATEGY.
LOOK, I'M SORRY FOR WHAT I DID TO YOU, BUT I DID HAVE GOOD REASONS AT THE TIME.
THEN I'LL MAKE IT UP TO YOU, OKAY?
OH-KAY.
THE PROBLEM YOU HAVE, KRADEN—ALL OF YOU, IN FACT—IS THAT THIS ISN'T A PRISON SENTENCE, IT'S A DEATH SENTENCE.
THEY INTEND TO DESTROY THIS PRISON BARGE THE MOMENT WE HIT THE ATMOSPHERE OF VOLAG-NOC.
WHAT? HOW DO YOU KNOW THIS? WHY WOULD THE SHADOW PROCLAMATION WANT US DEAD?
THEY DON'T, BUT THE KRILLITANES DO.

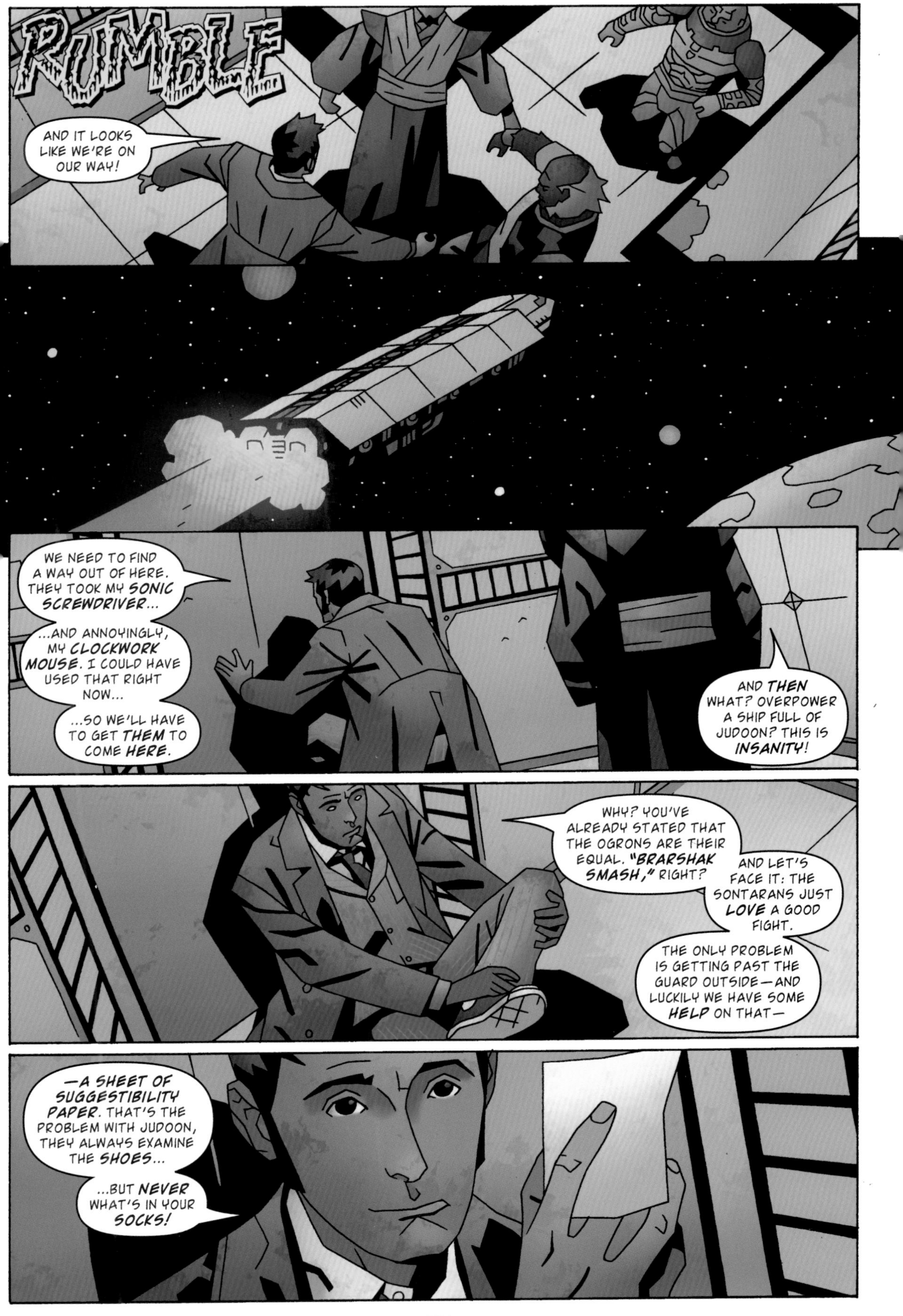
RUMBLE
AND IT LOOKS LIKE WE'RE ON OUR WAY!
WE NEED TO FIND A WAY OUT OF HERE. THEY TOOK MY SONIC SCREWDRIVER...
...AND ANNOYINGLY, MY CLOCKWORK MOUSE. I COULD HAVE USED THAT RIGHT NOW...
...SO WE'LL HAVE TO GET THEM TO COME HERE.
AND THEN WHAT? OVERPOWER A SHIP FULL OF JUDOON? THIS IS INSANITY!
WHY? YOU'VE ALREADY STATED THAT THE OGRONS ARE THEIR EQUAL. "BRARSHAK SMASH," RIGHT?
AND LET'S FACE IT: THE SONTARANS JUST LOVE A GOOD FIGHT.
THE ONLY PROBLEM IS GETTING PAST THE GUARD OUTSIDE—AND LUCKILY WE HAVE SOME HELP ON THAT—
—A SHEET OF SUGGESTIBILITY PAPER. THAT'S THE PROBLEM WITH JUDOON, THEY ALWAYS EXAMINE THE SHOES...
...BUT NEVER WHAT'S IN YOUR SOCKS!

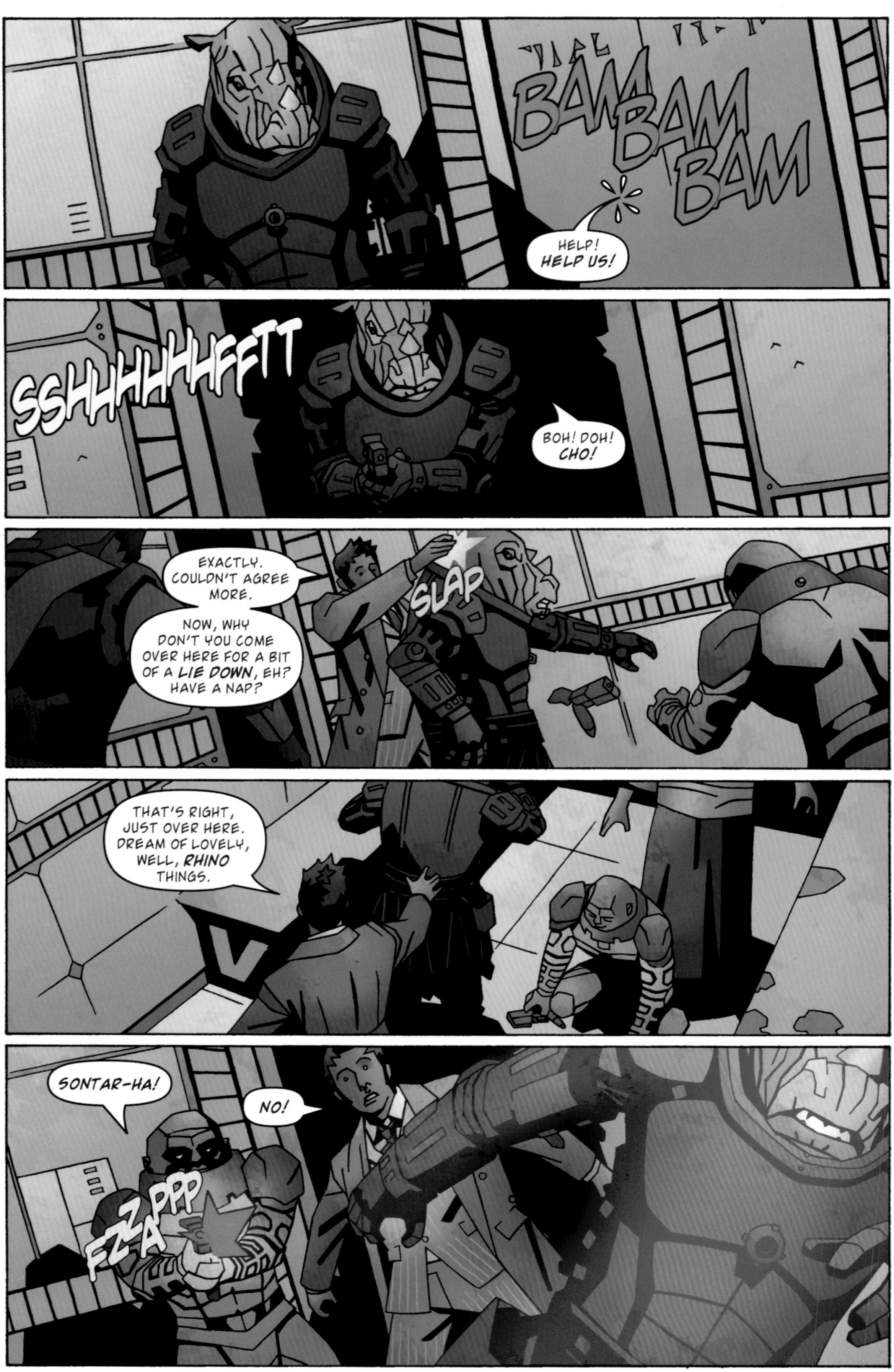
BAM BAM BAM
HELP! HELP US!
SSHHHHHHFFTT
BOH! DOH! CHO!
EXACTLY. COULDN'T AGREE MORE.
NOW, WHY DON'T YOU COME OVER HERE FOR A BIT OF A LIE DOWN, EH? HAVE A NAP?
SLAP
THAT'S RIGHT, JUST OVER HERE. DREAM OF LOVELY, WELL, RHINO THINGS.
SONTAR-HA!
NO!
FZZAPPP

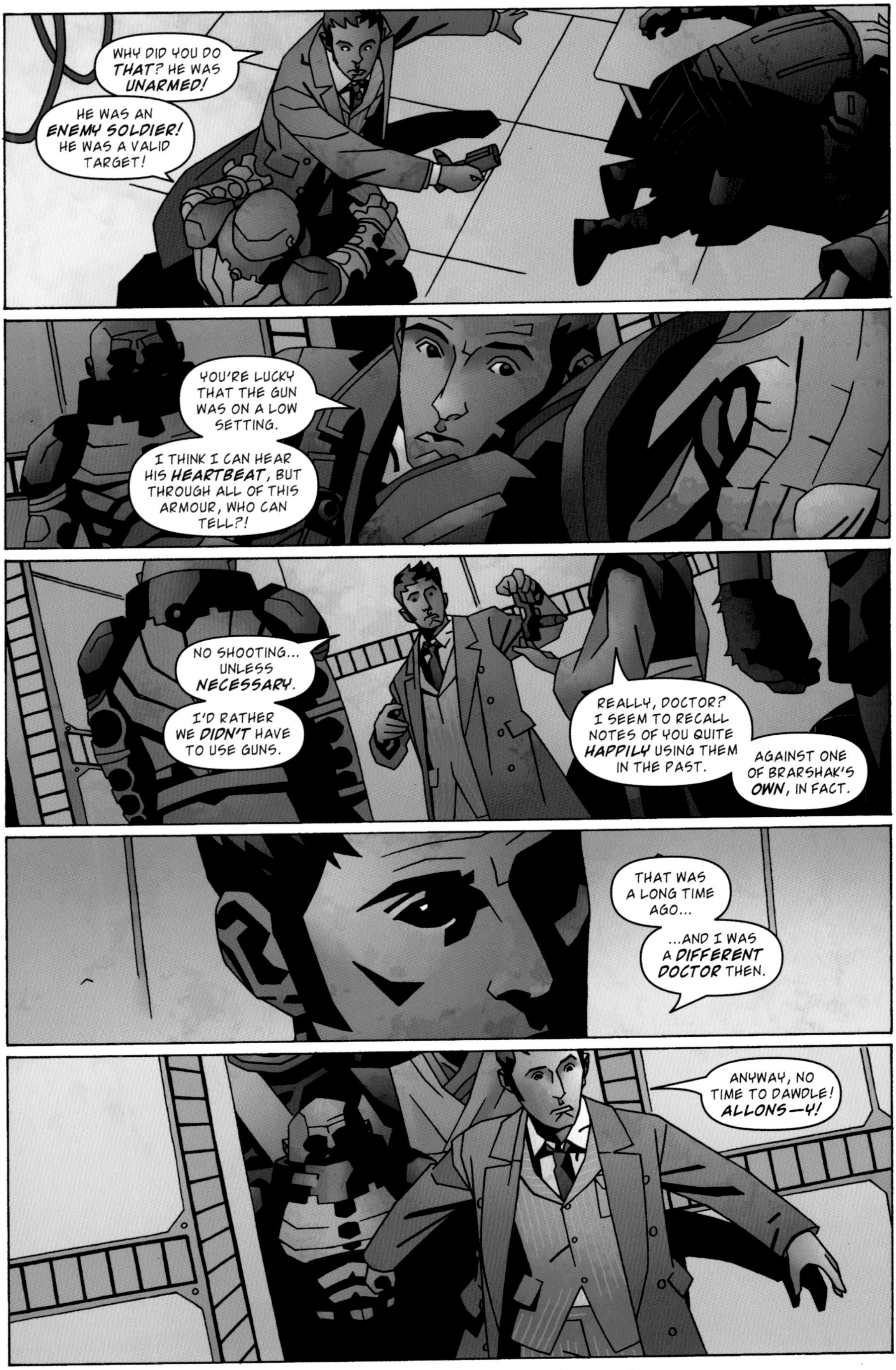
WHY DID YOU DO THAT? HE WAS UNARMED!
HE WAS AN ENEMY SOLDIER! HE WAS A VALID TARGET!
YOU'RE LUCKY THAT THE GUN WAS ON A LOW SETTING.
I THINK I CAN HEAR HIS HEARTBEAT, BUT THROUGH ALL OF THIS ARMOUR, WHO CAN TELL?!
NO SHOOTING... UNLESS NECESSARY.
I'D RATHER WE DIDN'T HAVE TO USE GUNS.
REALLY, DOCTOR? I SEEM TO RECALL NOTES OF YOU QUITE HAPPILY USING THEM IN THE PAST.
AGAINST ONE OF BRARSHAK'S OWN, IN FACT.
THAT WAS A LONG TIME AGO...
...AND I WAS A DIFFERENT DOCTOR THEN.
ANYWAY, NO TIME TO DAWDLE! ALLONS—Y!

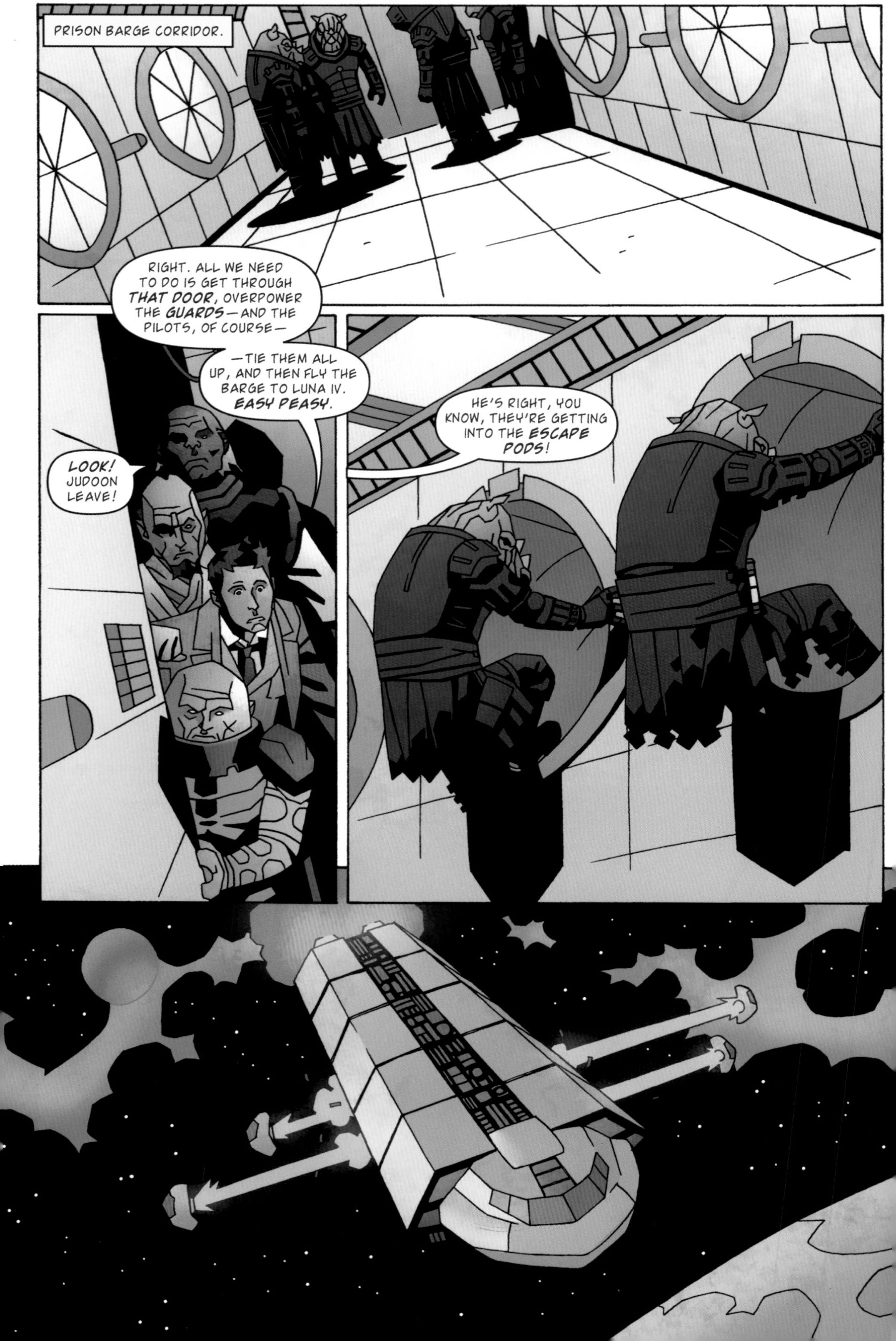
PRISON BARGE CORRIDOR.
RIGHT. ALL WE NEED TO DO IS GET THROUGH THAT DOOR, OVERPOWER THE GUARDS—AND THE PILOTS, OF COURSE—
—TIE THEM ALL UP, AND THEN FLY THE BARGE TO LUNA IV. EASY PEASY.
LOOK! JUDOON LEAVE!
HE'S RIGHT, YOU KNOW, THEY'RE GETTING INTO THE ESCAPE PODS!

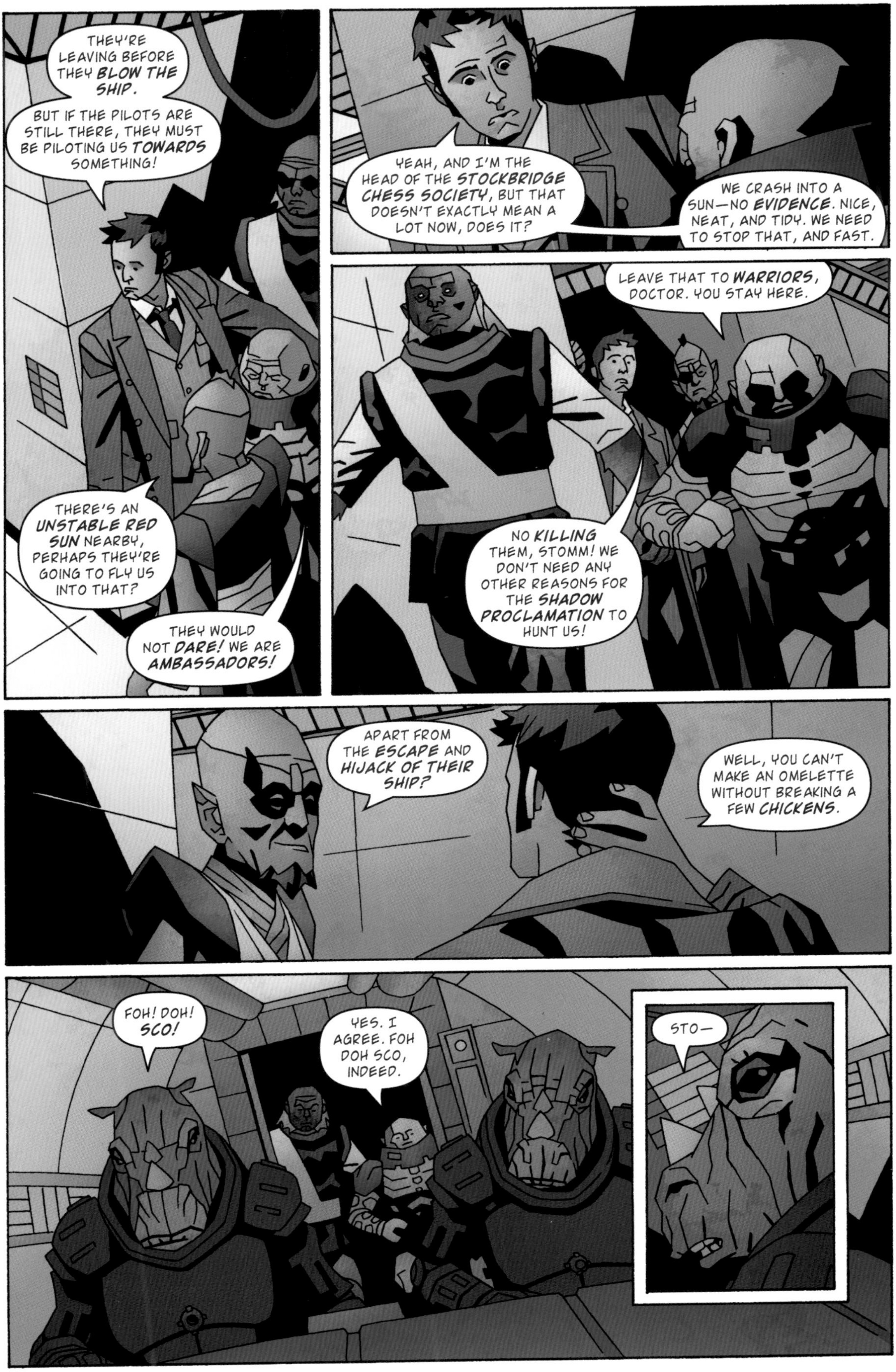
THEY'RE LEAVING BEFORE THEY BLOW THE SHIP.
BUT IF THE PILOTS ARE STILL THERE, THEY MUST BE PILOTING US TOWARDS SOMETHING!
YEAH, AND I'M THE HEAD OF THE STOCKBRIDGE CHESS SOCIETY, BUT THAT DOESN'T EXACTLY MEAN A LOT NOW, DOES IT?
WE CRASH INTO A SUN—NO EVIDENCE. NICE, NEAT, AND TIDY. WE NEED TO STOP THAT, AND FAST.
THERE'S AN UNSTABLE RED SUN NEARBY, PERHAPS THEY'RE GOING TO FLY US INTO THAT?
THEY WOULD NOT DARE! WE ARE AMBASSADORS!
LEAVE THAT TO WARRIORS, DOCTOR. YOU STAY HERE.
NO KILLING THEM, STOMM! WE DON'T NEED ANY OTHER REASONS FOR THE SHADOW PROCLAMATION TO HUNT US!
APART FROM THE ESCAPE AND HIJACK OF THEIR SHIP?
WELL, YOU CAN'T MAKE AN OMELETTE WITHOUT BREAKING A FEW CHICKENS.
FOH! DOH! SCO!
YES. I AGREE. FOH DOH SCO, INDEED.
STO—

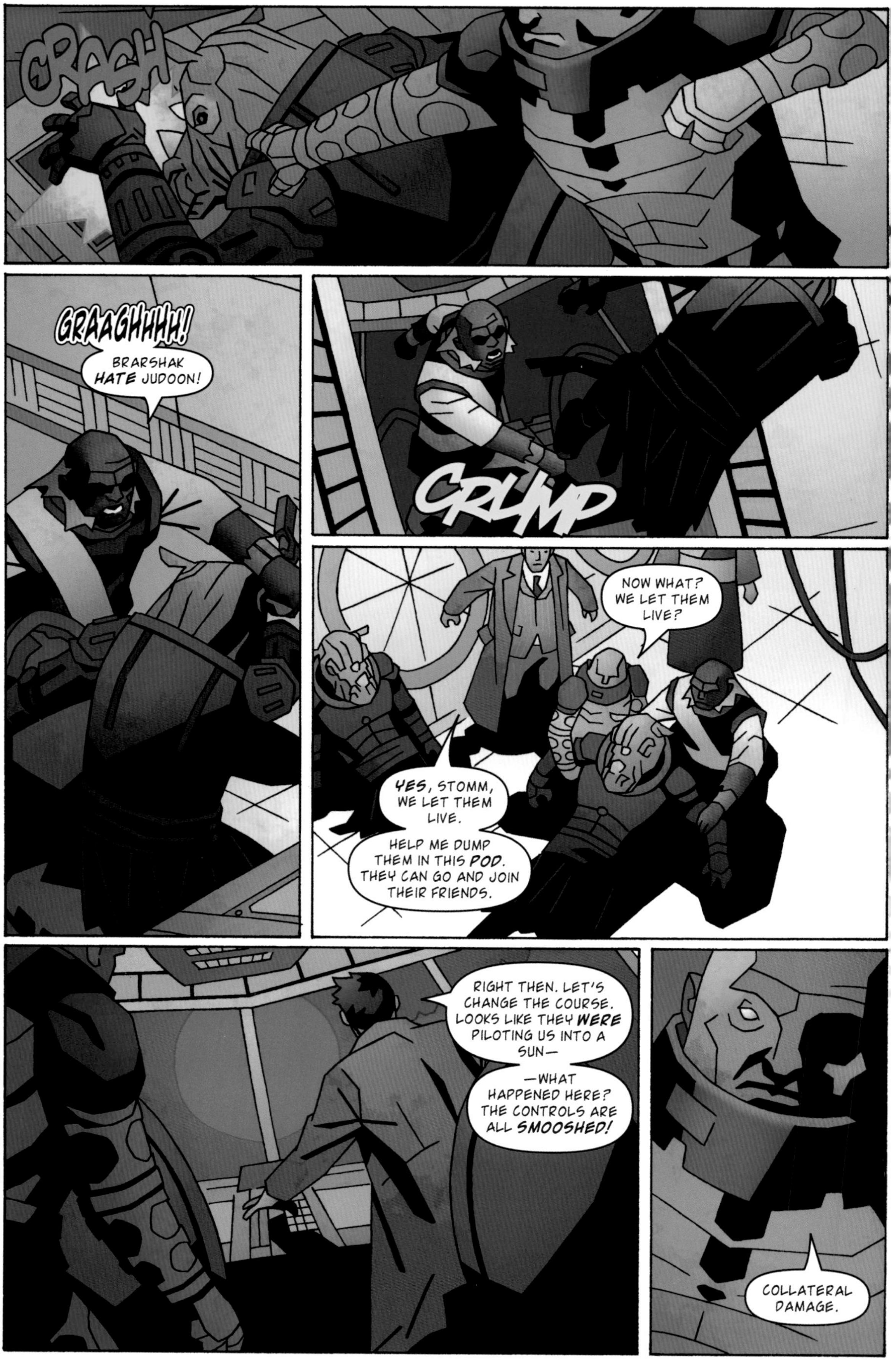
CRASH
GRAAGHHHH!
BRARSHAK HATE JUDOON!
CRUMP
NOW WHAT? WE LET THEM LIVE?
YES, STOMM, WE LET THEM LIVE.
HELP ME DUMP THEM IN THIS POD. THEY CAN GO AND JOIN THEIR FRIENDS.
RIGHT THEN. LET'S CHANGE THE COURSE. LOOKS LIKE THEY WERE PILOTING US INTO A SUN—
—WHAT HAPPENED HERE? THE CONTROLS ARE ALL SMOOSHED!
COLLATERAL DAMAGE.

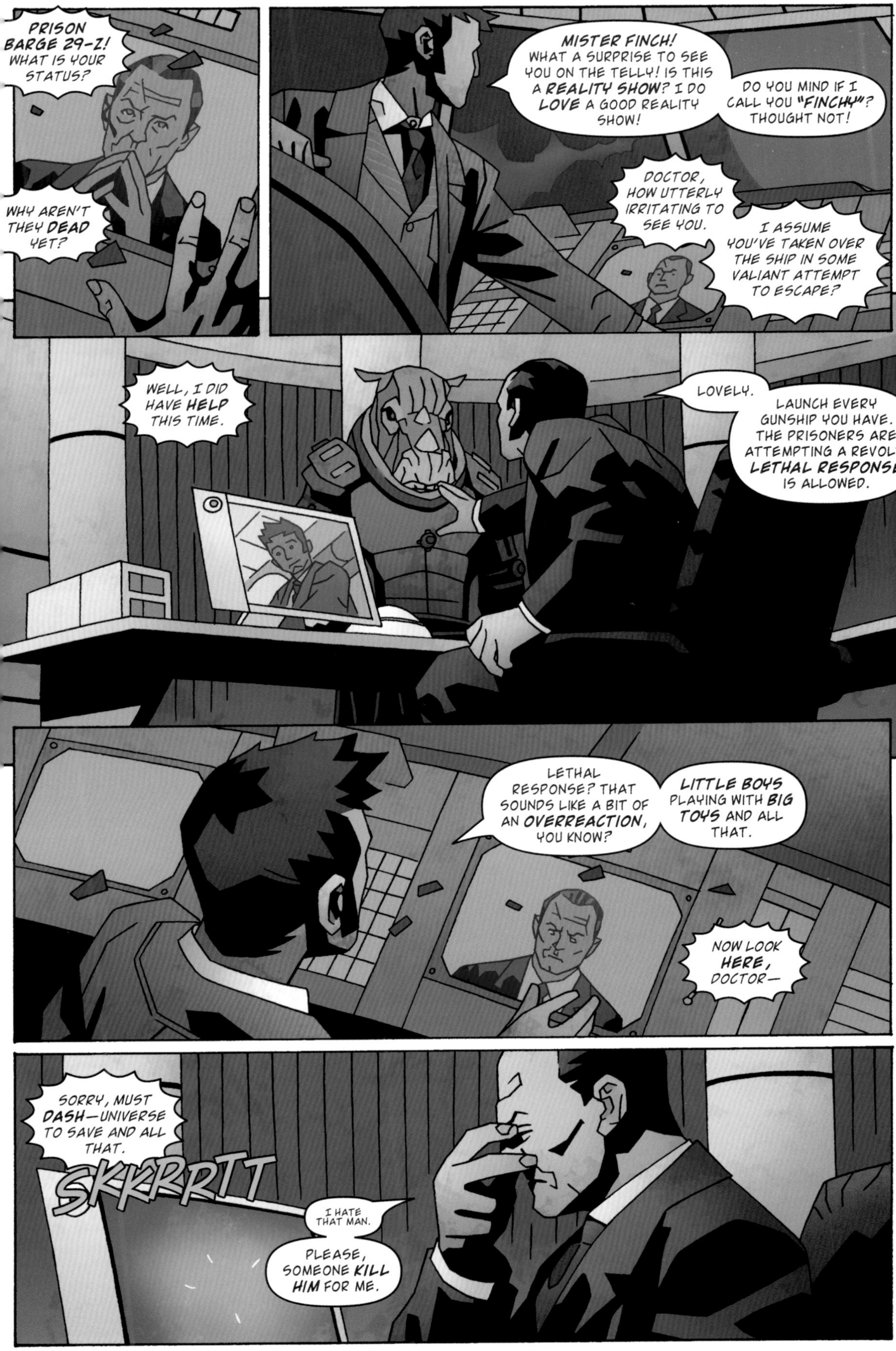
PRISON BARGE 29-Z! WHAT IS YOUR STATUS?
WHY AREN'T THEY DEAD YET?
MISTER FINCH! WHAT A SURPRISE TO SEE YOU ON THE TELLY! IS THIS A REALITY SHOW? I DO LOVE A GOOD REALITY SHOW!
DO YOU MIND IF I CALL YOU "FINCHY"? THOUGHT NOT!
DOCTOR, HOW UTTERLY IRRITATING TO SEE YOU.
I ASSUME YOU'VE TAKEN OVER THE SHIP IN SOME VALIANT ATTEMPT TO ESCAPE?
WELL, I DID HAVE HELP THIS TIME.
LOVELY.
LAUNCH EVERY GUNSHIP YOU HAVE. THE PRISONERS ARE ATTEMPTING A REVOLT. LETHAL RESPONSE IS ALLOWED.
LETHAL RESPONSE? THAT SOUNDS LIKE A BIT OF AN OVERREACTION, YOU KNOW?
LITTLE BOYS PLAYING WITH BIG TOYS AND ALL THAT.
NOW LOOK HERE, DOCTOR—
SORRY, MUST DASH—UNIVERSE TO SAVE AND ALL THAT.
SKKRRTT
I HATE THAT MAN.
PLEASE, SOMEONE KILL HIM FOR ME.

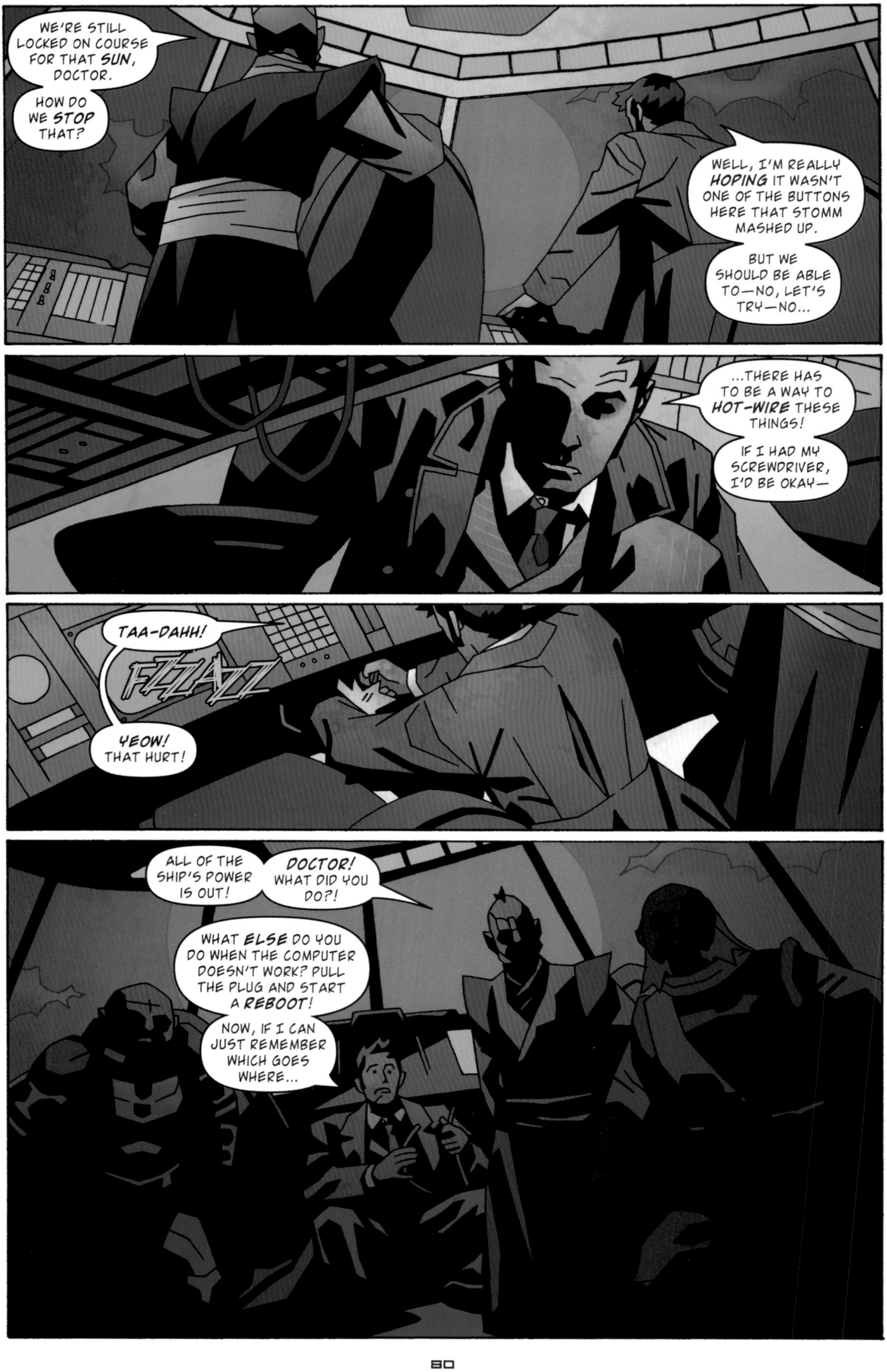
WE'RE STILL LOCKED ON COURSE FOR THAT SUN, DOCTOR.
HOW DO WE STOP THAT?
WELL, I'M REALLY HOPING IT WASN'T ONE OF THE BUTTONS HERE THAT STOMM MASHED UP.
BUT WE SHOULD BE ABLE TO—NO, LET'S TRY—NO...
...THERE HAS TO BE A WAY TO HOT-WIRE THESE THINGS!
IF I HAD MY SCREWDRIVER, I'D BE OKAY—
TAA-DAHH!
FZZAZZ
YEOW! THAT HURT!
ALL OF THE SHIP'S POWER IS OUT!
DOCTOR! WHAT DID YOU DO?!
WHAT ELSE DO YOU DO WHEN THE COMPUTER DOESN'T WORK? PULL THE PLUG AND START A REBOOT!
NOW, IF I CAN JUST REMEMBER WHICH GOES WHERE...

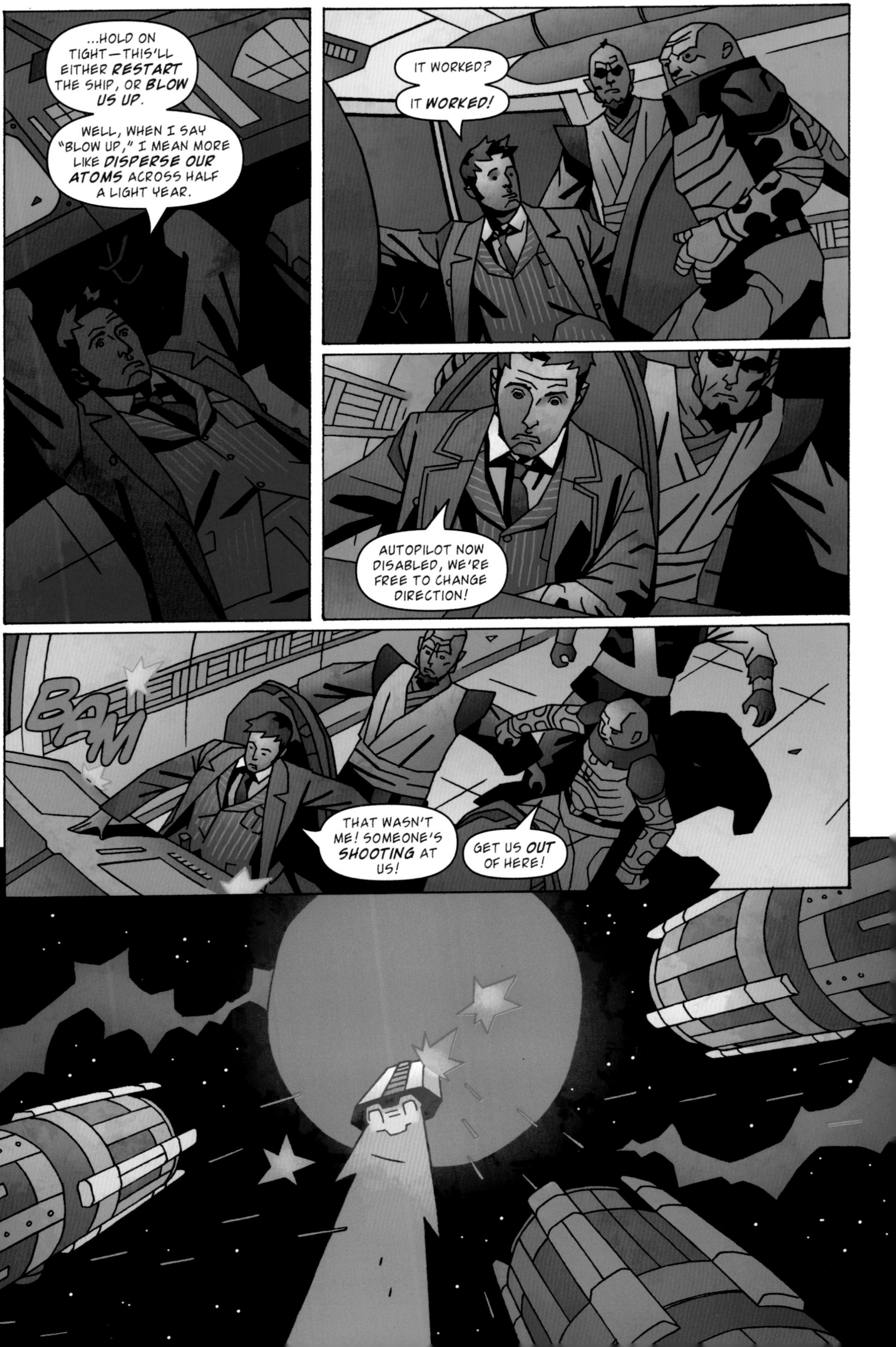
...HOLD ON TIGHT—THIS'LL EITHER RESTART THE SHIP, OR BLOW US UP.
WELL, WHEN I SAY "BLOW UP," I MEAN MORE LIKE DISPERSE OUR ATOMS ACROSS HALF A LIGHT YEAR.
IT WORKED?
IT WORKED!
AUTOPILOT NOW DISABLED, WE'RE FREE TO CHANGE DIRECTION!
BAM
THAT WASN'T ME! SOMEONE'S SHOOTING AT US!
GET US OUT OF HERE!

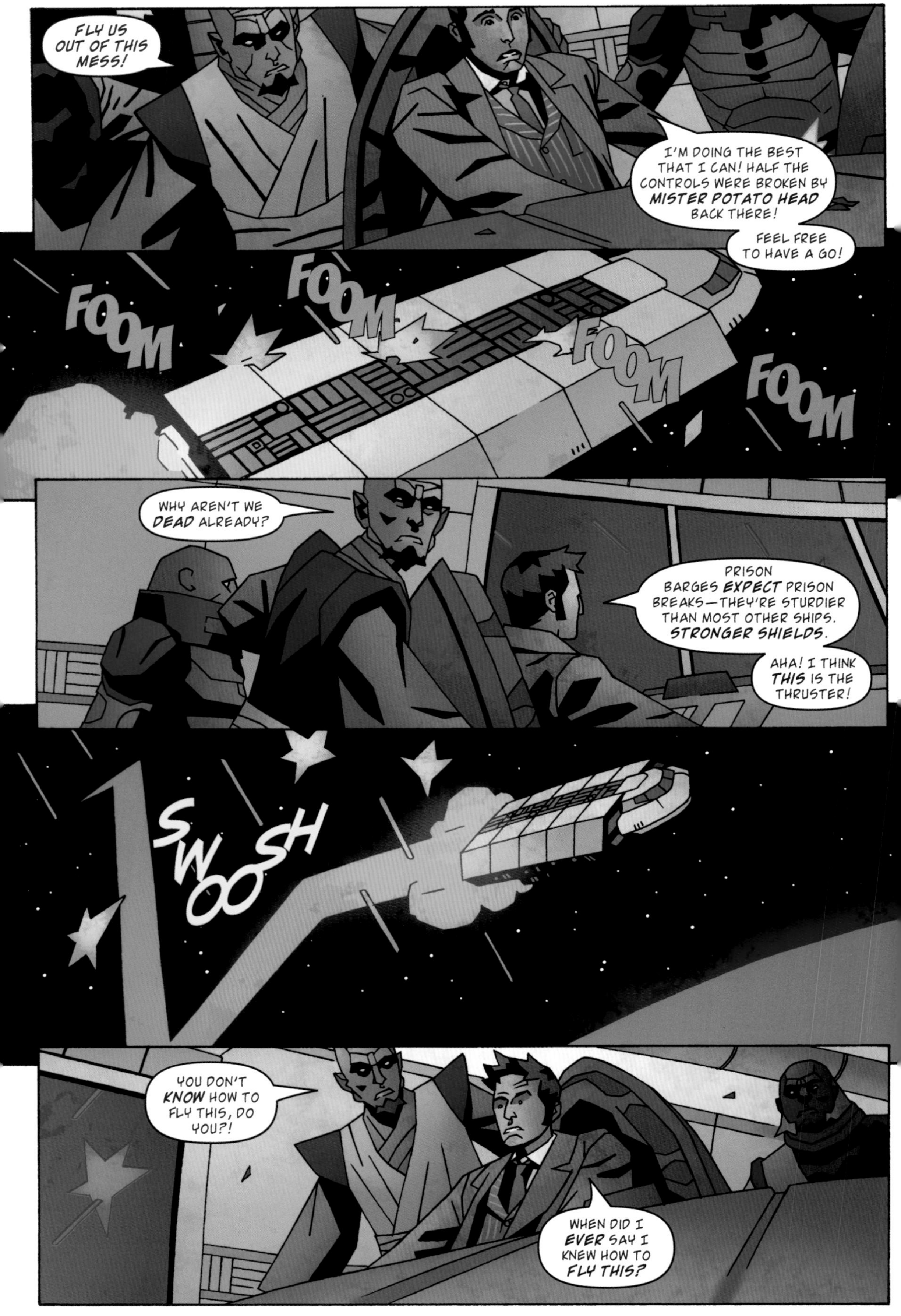
FLY US OUT OF THIS MESS!
I'M DOING THE BEST THAT I CAN! HALF THE CONTROLS WERE BROKEN BY MISTER POTATO HEAD BACK THERE!
FEEL FREE TO HAVE A GO!
FOOM
FOOM
FOOM
FOOM
WHY AREN'T WE DEAD ALREADY?
PRISON BARGES EXPECT PRISON BREAKS—THEY'RE STURDIER THAN MOST OTHER SHIPS. STRONGER SHIELDS.
AHA! I THINK THIS IS THE THRUSTER!
SWOOSH
YOU DON'T KNOW HOW TO FLY THIS, DO YOU?!
WHEN DID I EVER SAY I KNEW HOW TO FLY THIS?

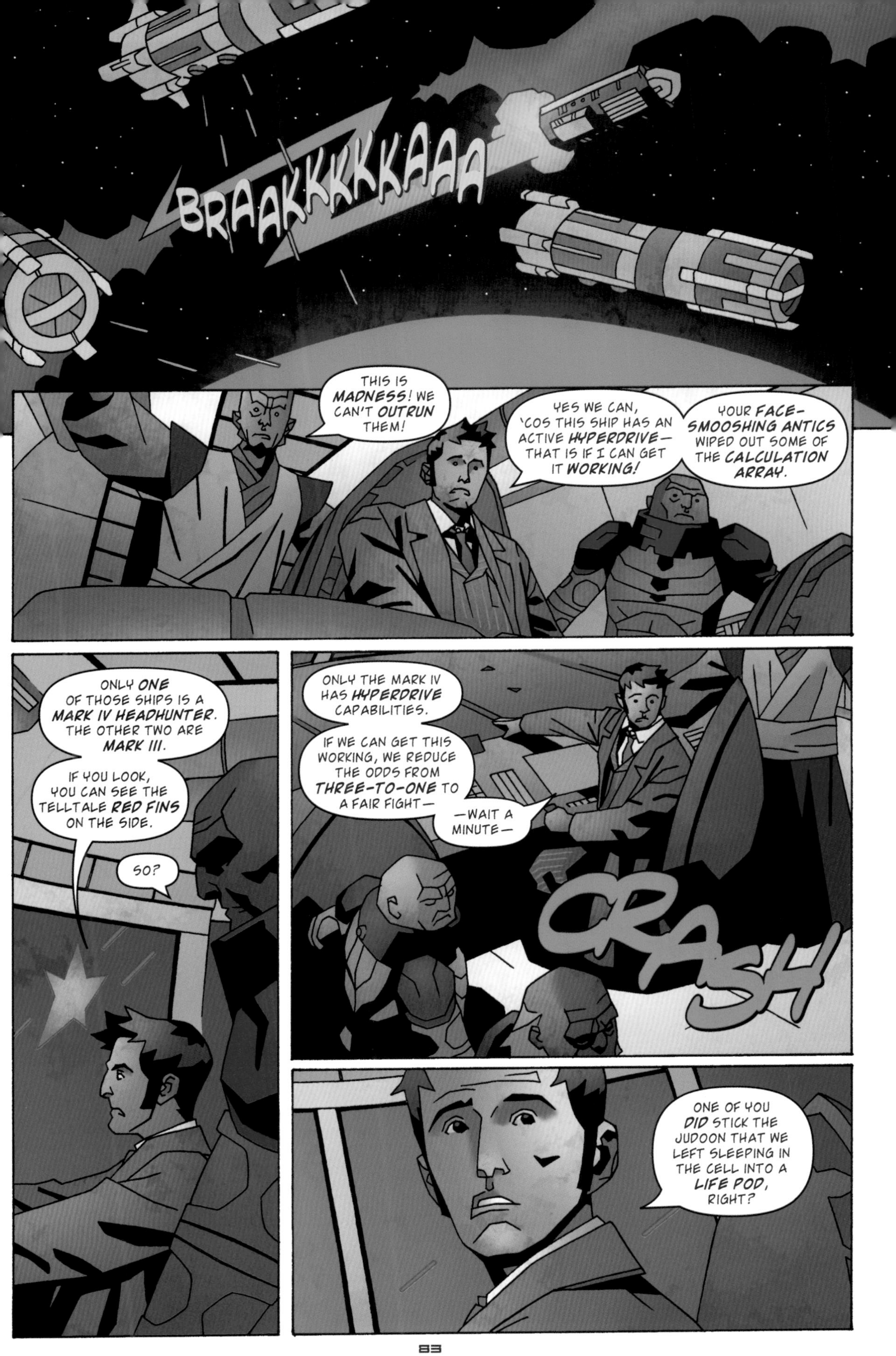
BRAAKKKKKAAA
THIS IS MADNESS! WE CAN'T OUTRUN THEM!
YES WE CAN, 'COS THIS SHIP HAS AN ACTIVE HYPERDRIVE— THAT IS IF I CAN GET IT WORKING!
YOUR FACE-SMOOSHING ANTICS WIPED OUT SOME OF THE CALCULATION ARRAY.
ONLY ONE OF THOSE SHIPS IS A MARK IV HEADHUNTER. THE OTHER TWO ARE MARK III.
IF YOU LOOK, YOU CAN SEE THE TELLTALE RED FINS ON THE SIDE.
SO?
ONLY THE MARK IV HAS HYPERDRIVE CAPABILITIES.
IF WE CAN GET THIS WORKING, WE REDUCE THE ODDS FROM THREE-TO-ONE TO A FAIR FIGHT—
—WAIT A MINUTE—
CRASH
ONE OF YOU DID STICK THE JUDOON THAT WE LEFT SLEEPING IN THE CELL INTO A LIFE POD, RIGHT?

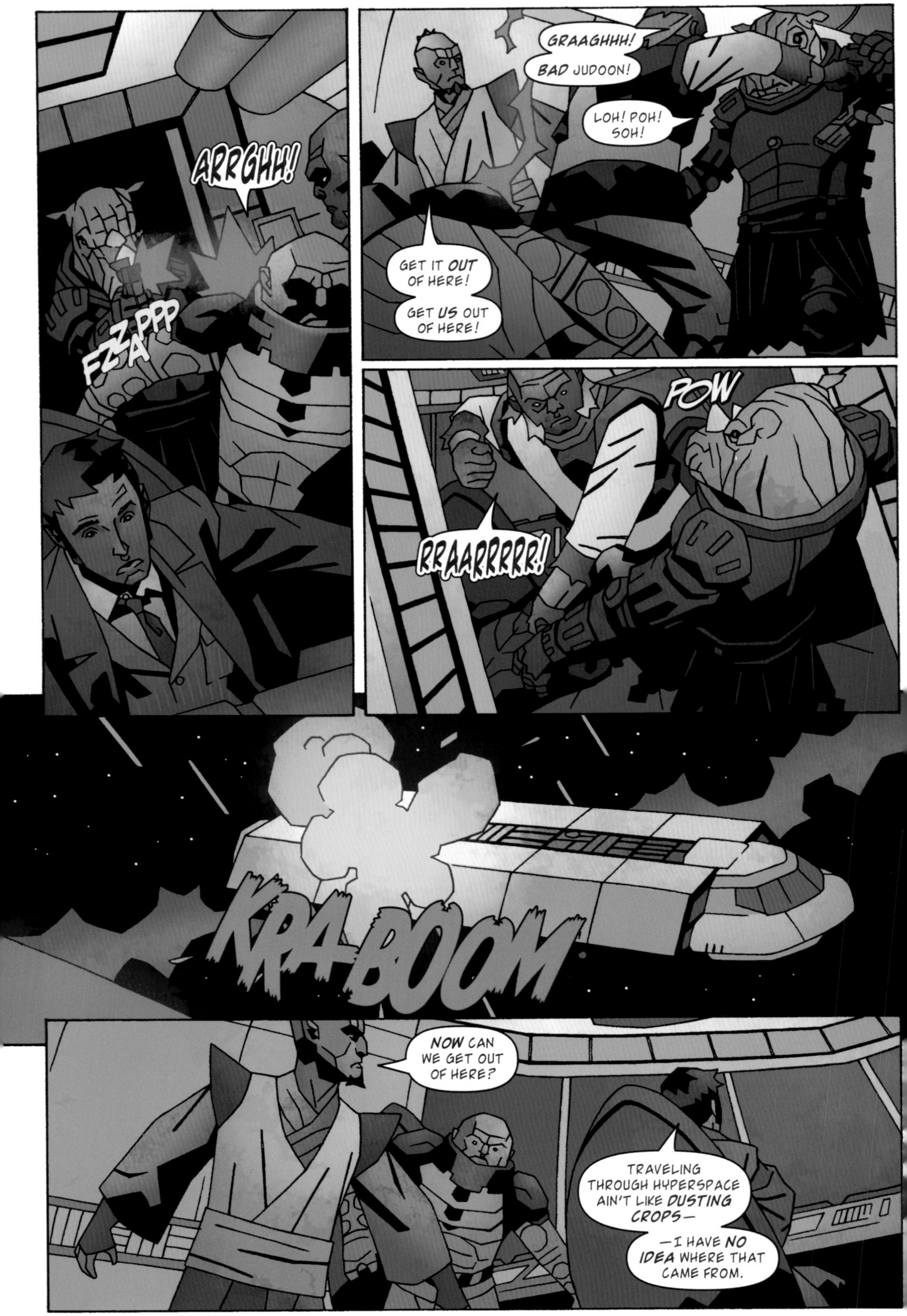
ARRGHH!
FZZAPPP
GRAAGHHH!
BAD JUDOON!
LOH! POH! SOH!
GET IT OUT OF HERE!
GET US OUT OF HERE!
POW
RRAARRRRR!
KRA BOOM
NOW CAN WE GET OUT OF HERE?
TRAVELING THROUGH HYPERSPACE AIN'T LIKE DUSTING CROPS—
—I HAVE NO IDEA WHERE THAT CAME FROM.

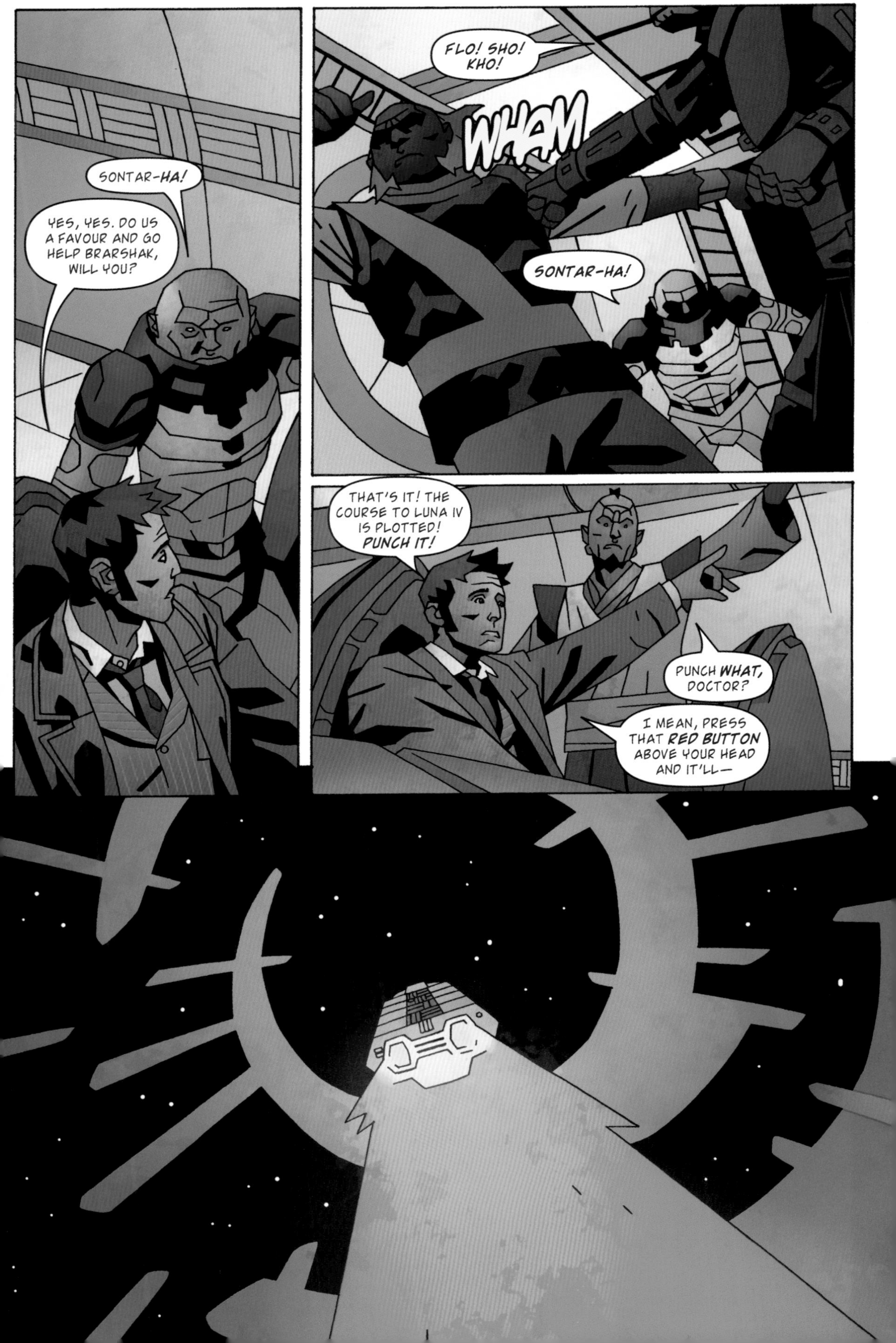
SONTAR-HA!
YES, YES. DO US A FAVOUR AND GO HELP BRARSHAK, WILL YOU?
FLO! SHO! KHO!
WHAM
SONTAR-HA!
THAT'S IT! THE COURSE TO LUNA IV IS PLOTTED! PUNCH IT!
PUNCH WHAT, DOCTOR?
I MEAN, PRESS THAT RED BUTTON ABOVE YOUR HEAD AND IT'LL—

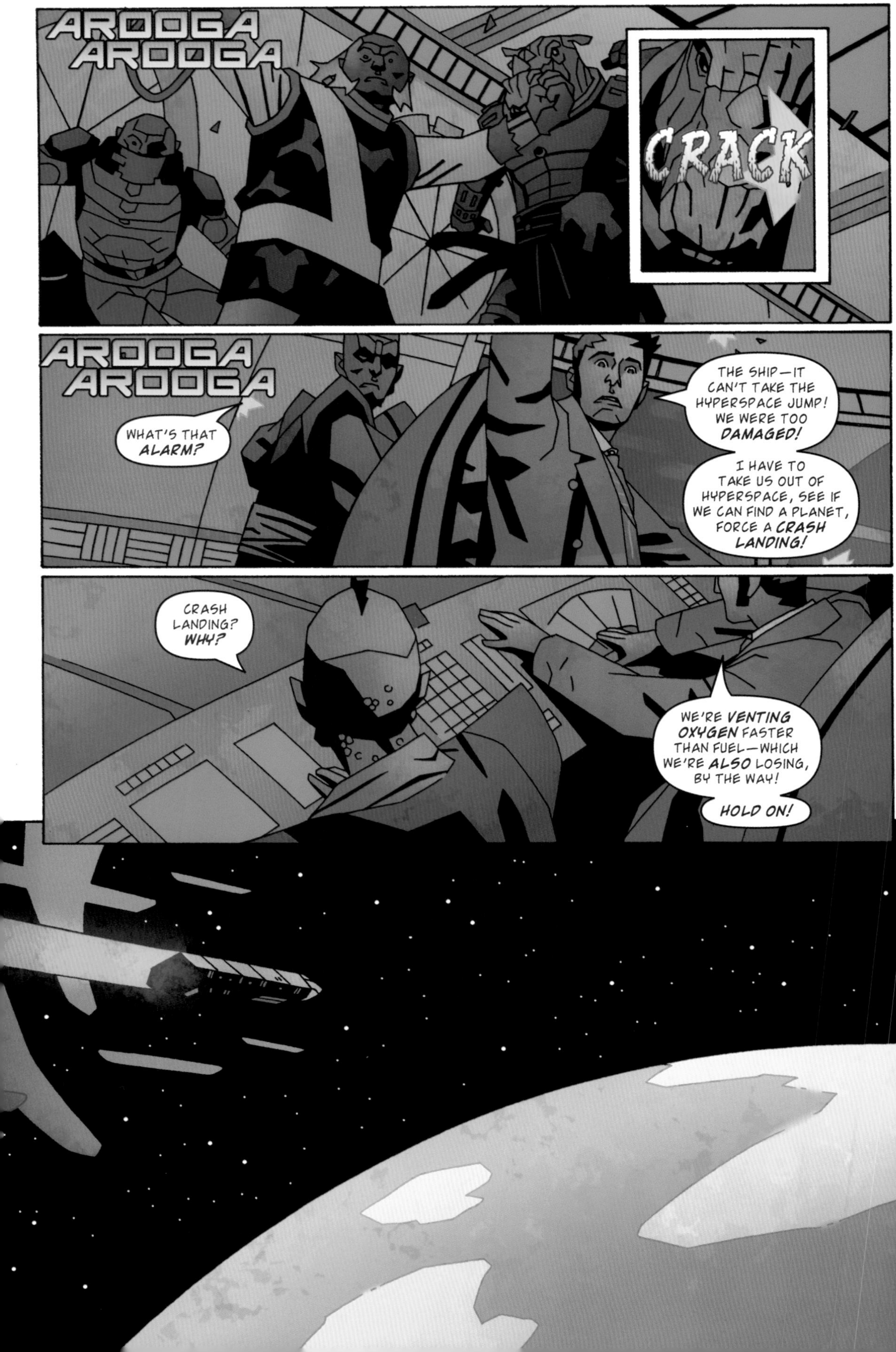
AROOGA AROOGA
CRACK
AROOGA AROOGA
WHAT'S THAT ALARM?
THE SHIP—IT CAN'T TAKE THE HYPERSPACE JUMP! WE WERE TOO DAMAGED!
I HAVE TO TAKE US OUT OF HYPERSPACE, SEE IF WE CAN FIND A PLANET, FORCE A CRASH LANDING!
CRASH LANDING? WHY?
WE'RE VENTING OXYGEN FASTER THAN FUEL—WHICH WE'RE ALSO LOSING, BY THE WAY!
HOLD ON!

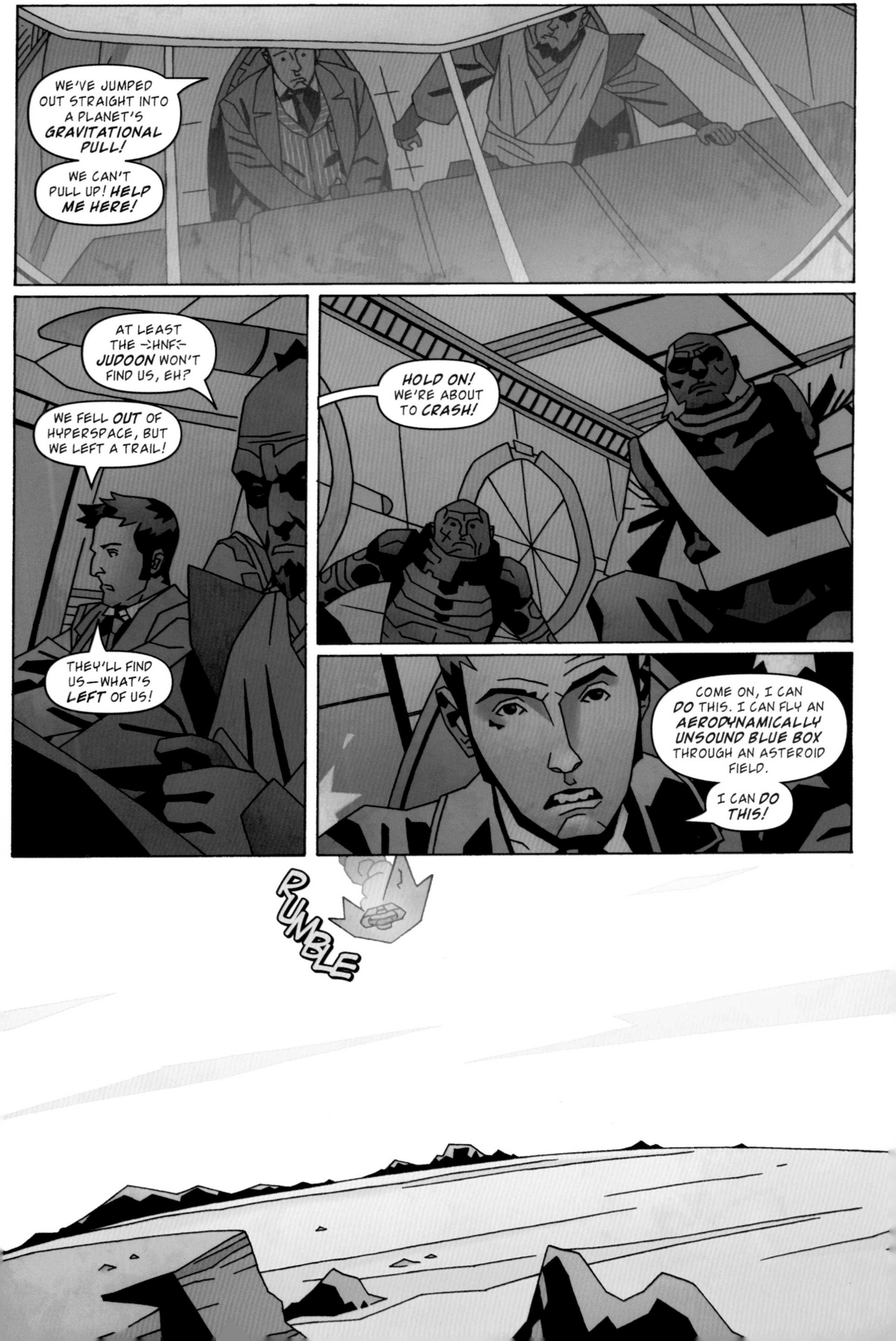
WE'VE JUMPED OUT STRAIGHT INTO A PLANET'S GRAVITATIONAL PULL!
WE CAN'T PULL UP! HELP ME HERE!
AT LEAST THE -HNF- JUDOON WON'T FIND US, EH?
WE FELL OUT OF HYPERSPACE, BUT WE LEFT A TRAIL!
THEY'LL FIND US—WHAT'S LEFT OF US!
HOLD ON! WE'RE ABOUT TO CRASH!
COME ON, I CAN DO THIS. I CAN FLY AN AERODYNAMICALLY UNSOUND BLUE BOX THROUGH AN ASTEROID FIELD.
I CAN DO THIS!
RUMBLE

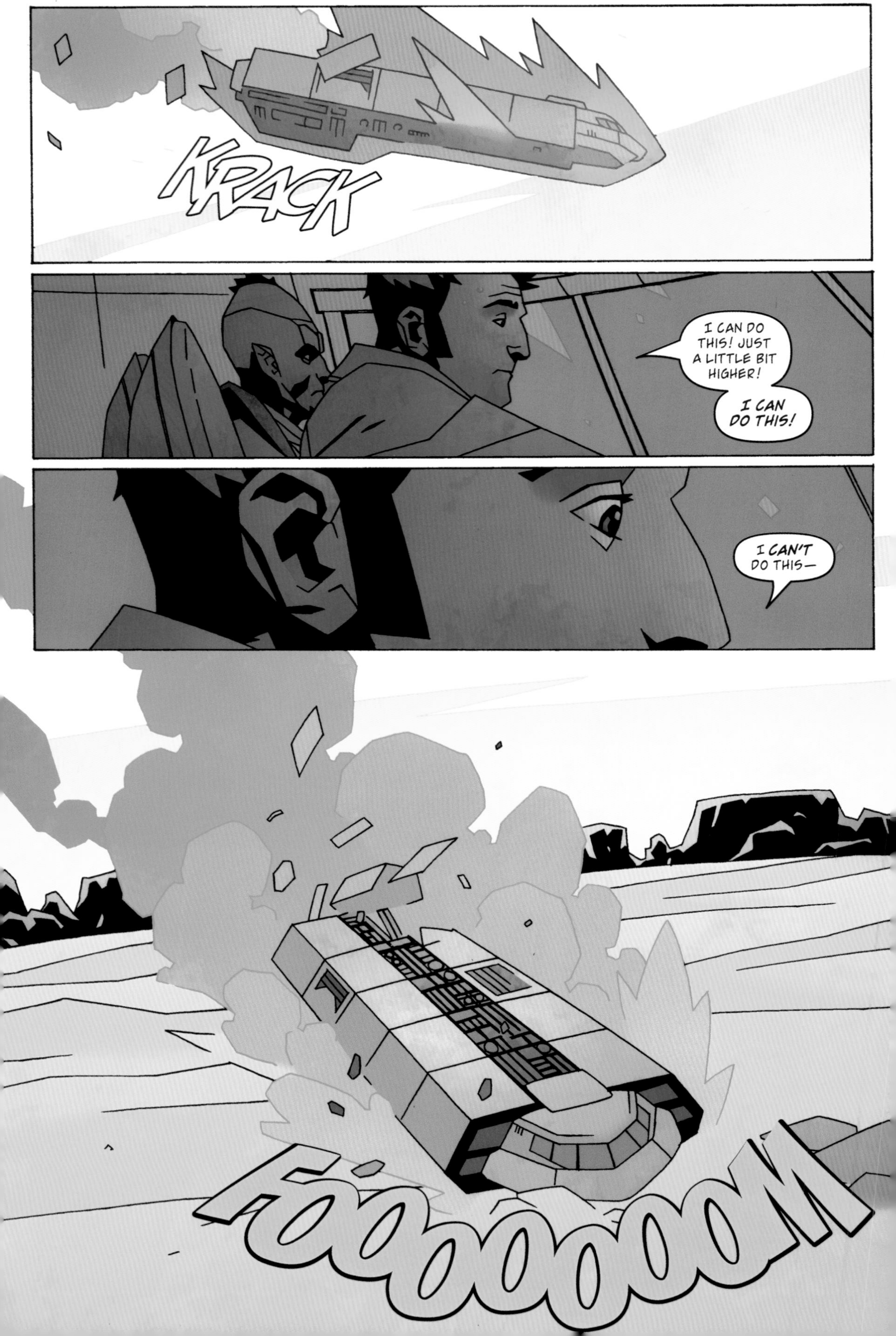
KRACK
I CAN DO THIS! JUST A LITTLE BIT HIGHER!
I CAN DO THIS!
I CAN'T DO THIS—
FOOOOOOOM

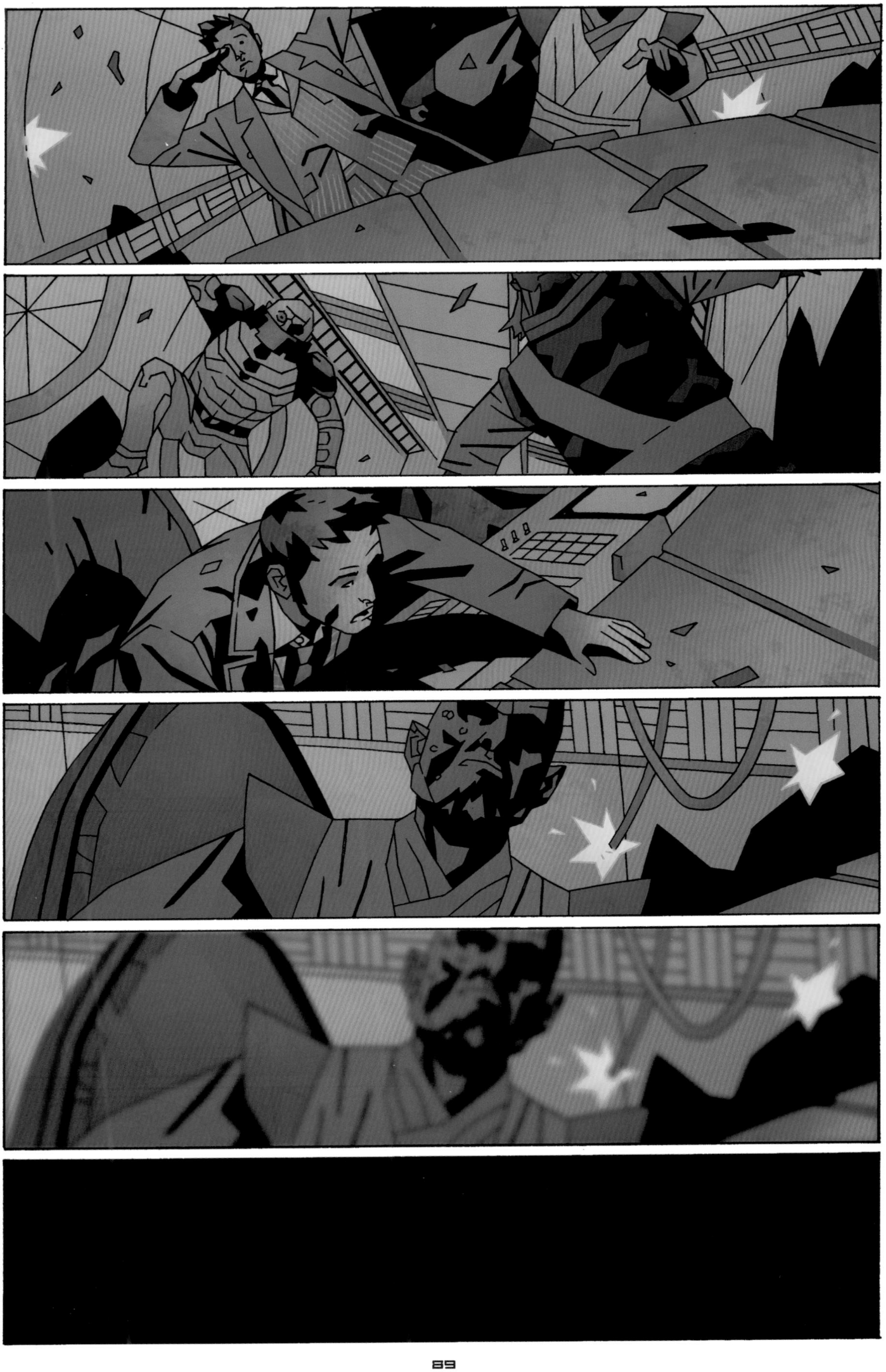

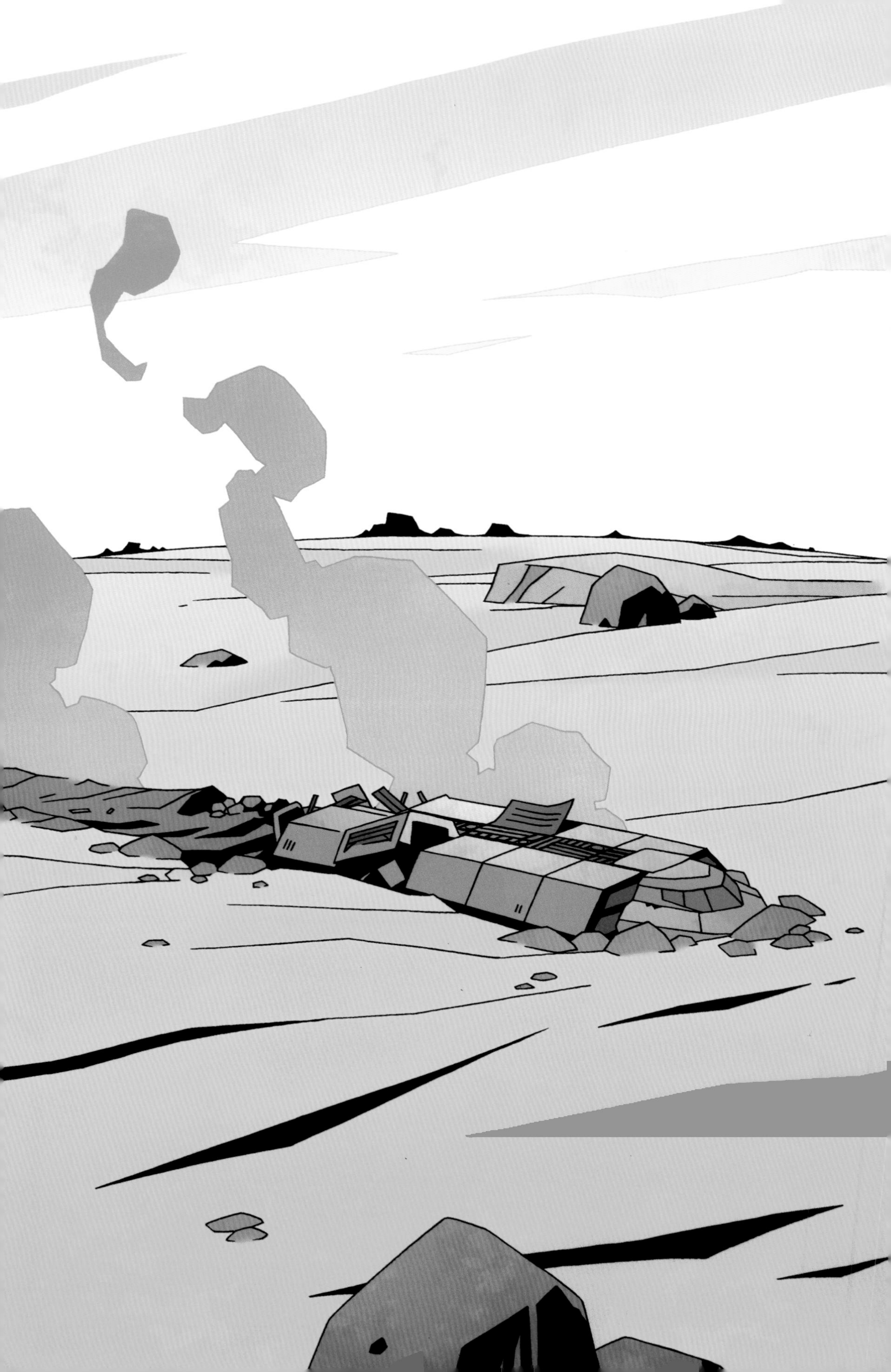

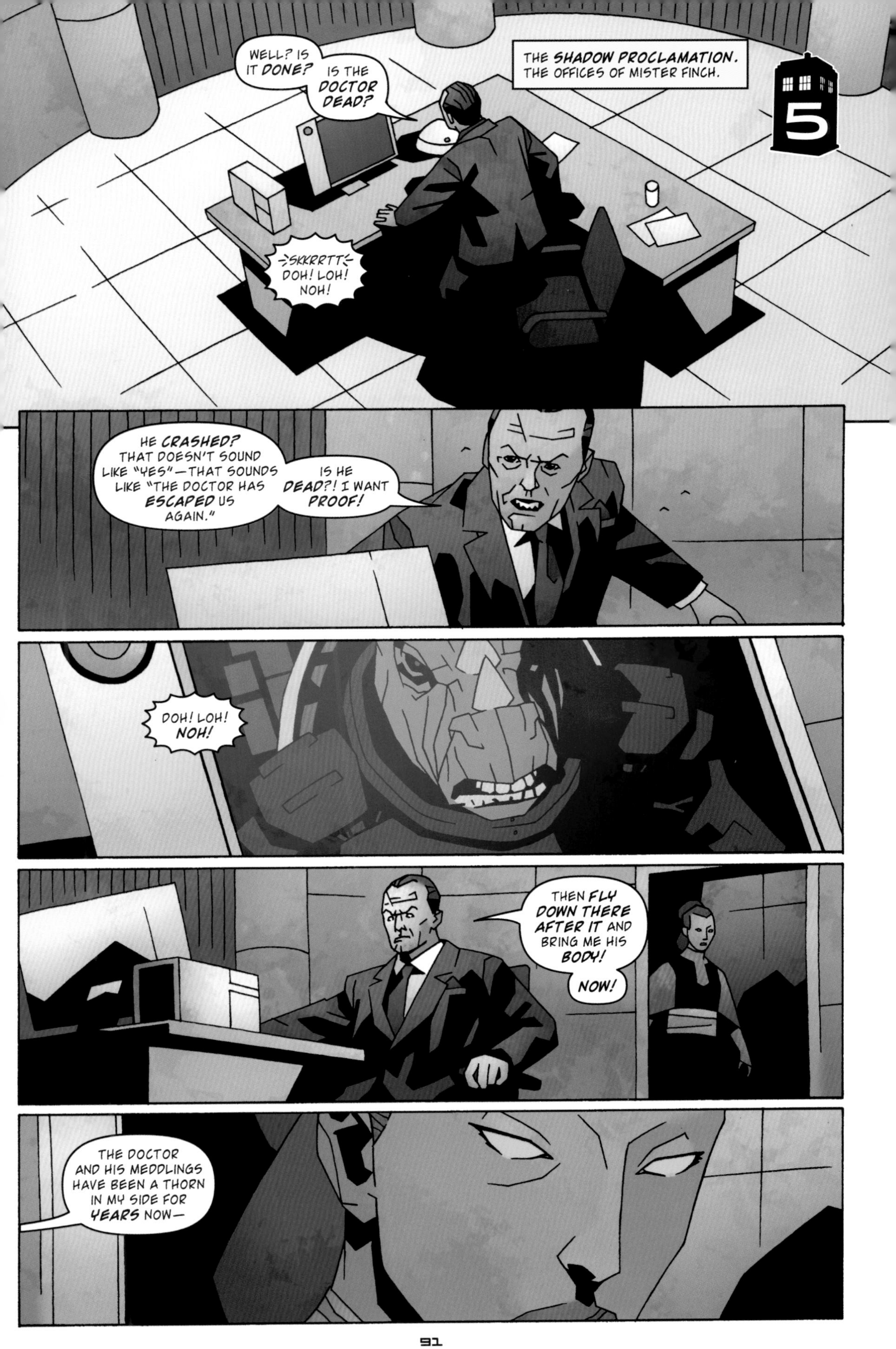

THE SHADOW PROCLAMATION. THE OFFICES OF MISTER FINCH.
5
WELL? IS IT DONE?
IS THE DOCTOR DEAD?
SKKRRTT DOH! LOH! NOH!
HE CRASHED? THAT DOESN'T SOUND LIKE "YES"—THAT SOUNDS LIKE "THE DOCTOR HAS ESCAPED US AGAIN."
IS HE DEAD?! I WANT PROOF!
DOH! LOH! NOH!
THEN FLY DOWN THERE AFTER IT AND BRING ME HIS BODY!
NOW!
THE DOCTOR AND HIS MEDDLINGS HAVE BEEN A THORN IN MY SIDE FOR YEARS NOW—

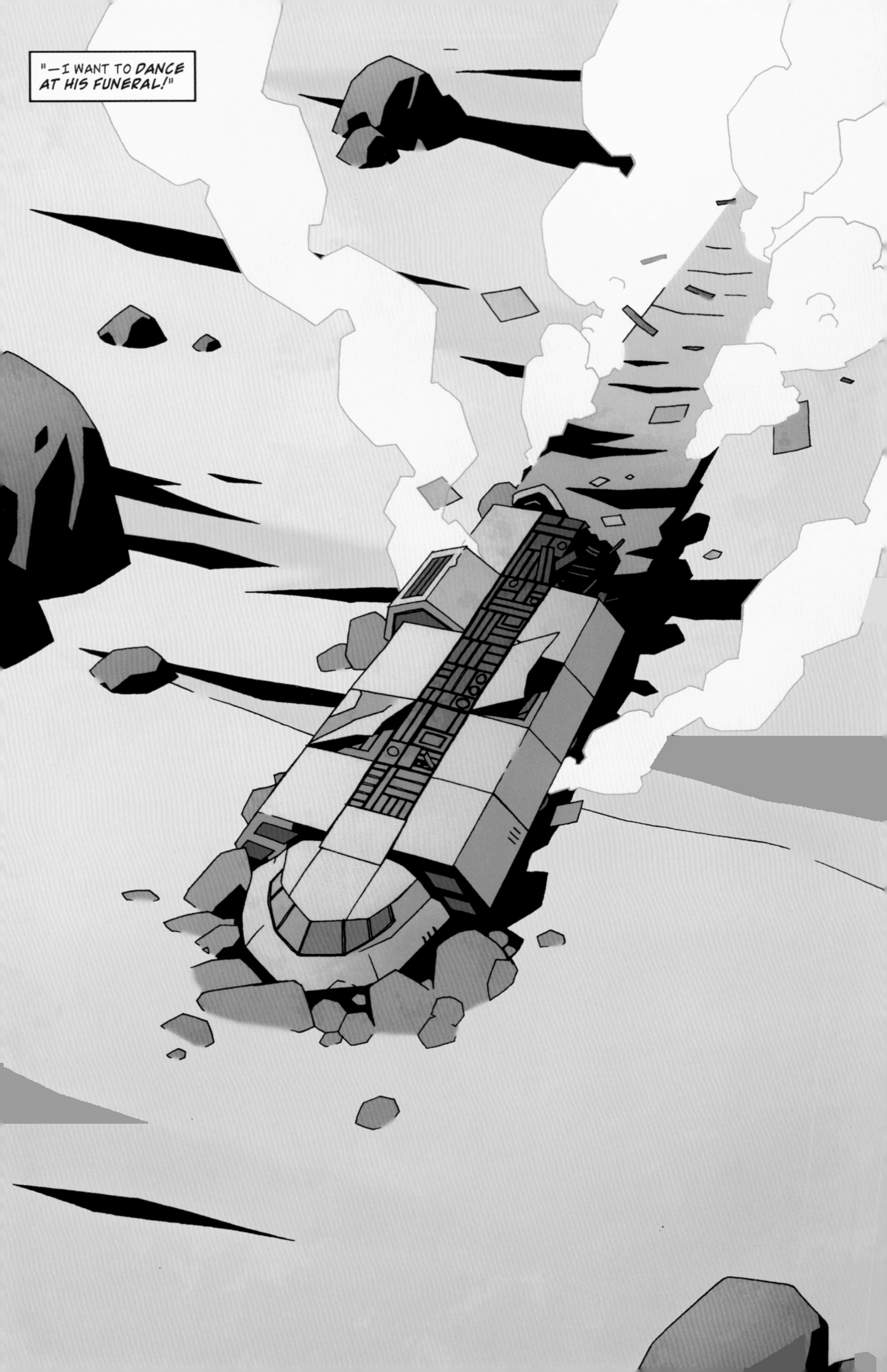
"—I WANT TO DANCE AT HIS FUNERAL!"

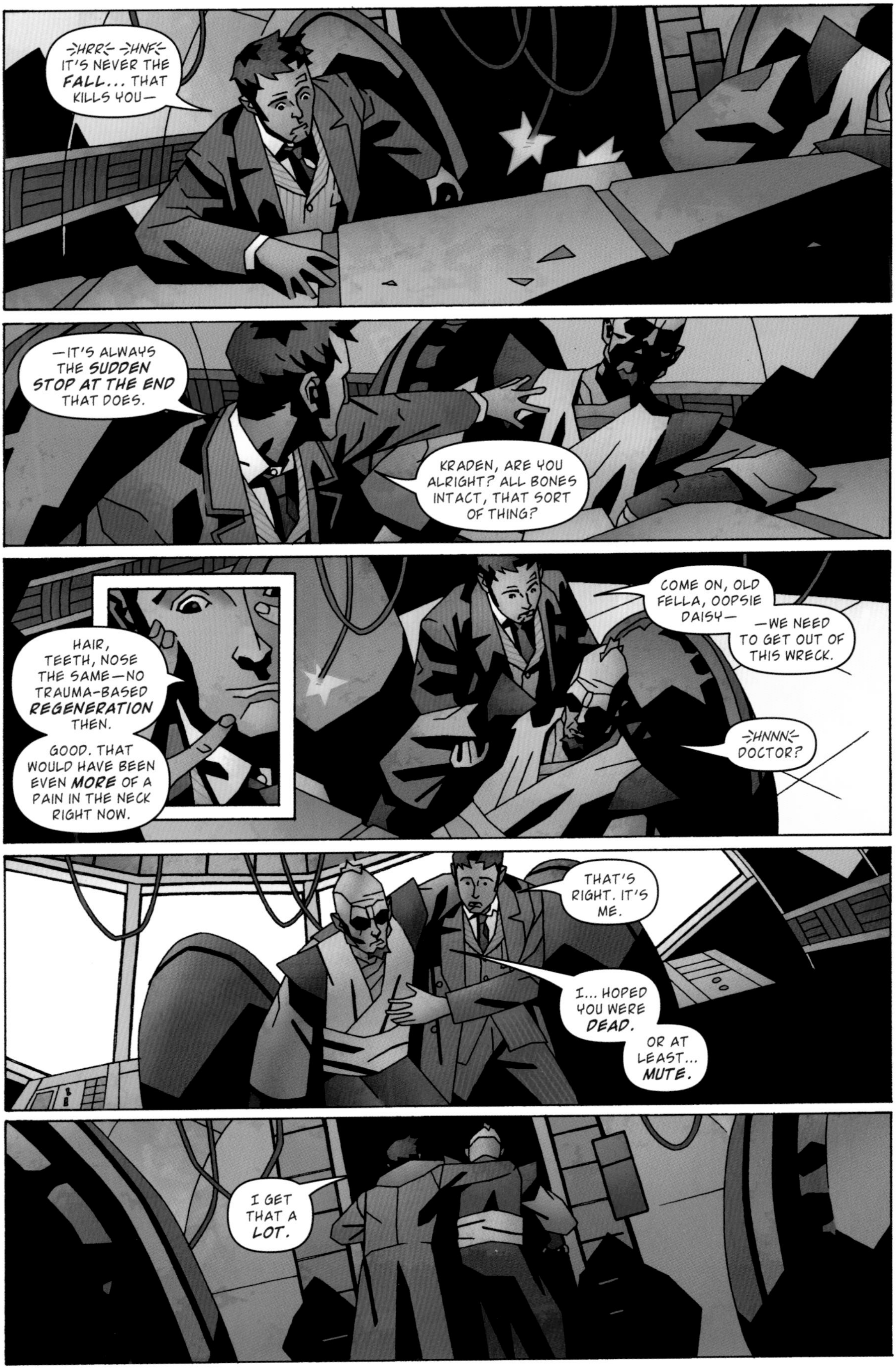

⇒HRR⇐ ⇒HNF⇐ IT'S NEVER THE FALL... THAT KILLS YOU—
—IT'S ALWAYS THE SUDDEN STOP AT THE END THAT DOES.
KRADEN, ARE YOU ALRIGHT? ALL BONES INTACT, THAT SORT OF THING?
HAIR, TEETH, NOSE THE SAME—NO TRAUMA-BASED REGENERATION THEN.
GOOD. THAT WOULD HAVE BEEN EVEN MORE OF A PAIN IN THE NECK RIGHT NOW.
COME ON, OLD FELLA, OOPSIE DAISY—
—WE NEED TO GET OUT OF THIS WRECK.
⇒HNNN⇐ DOCTOR?
THAT'S RIGHT. IT'S ME.
I... HOPED YOU WERE DEAD.
OR AT LEAST... MUTE.
I GET THAT A LOT.

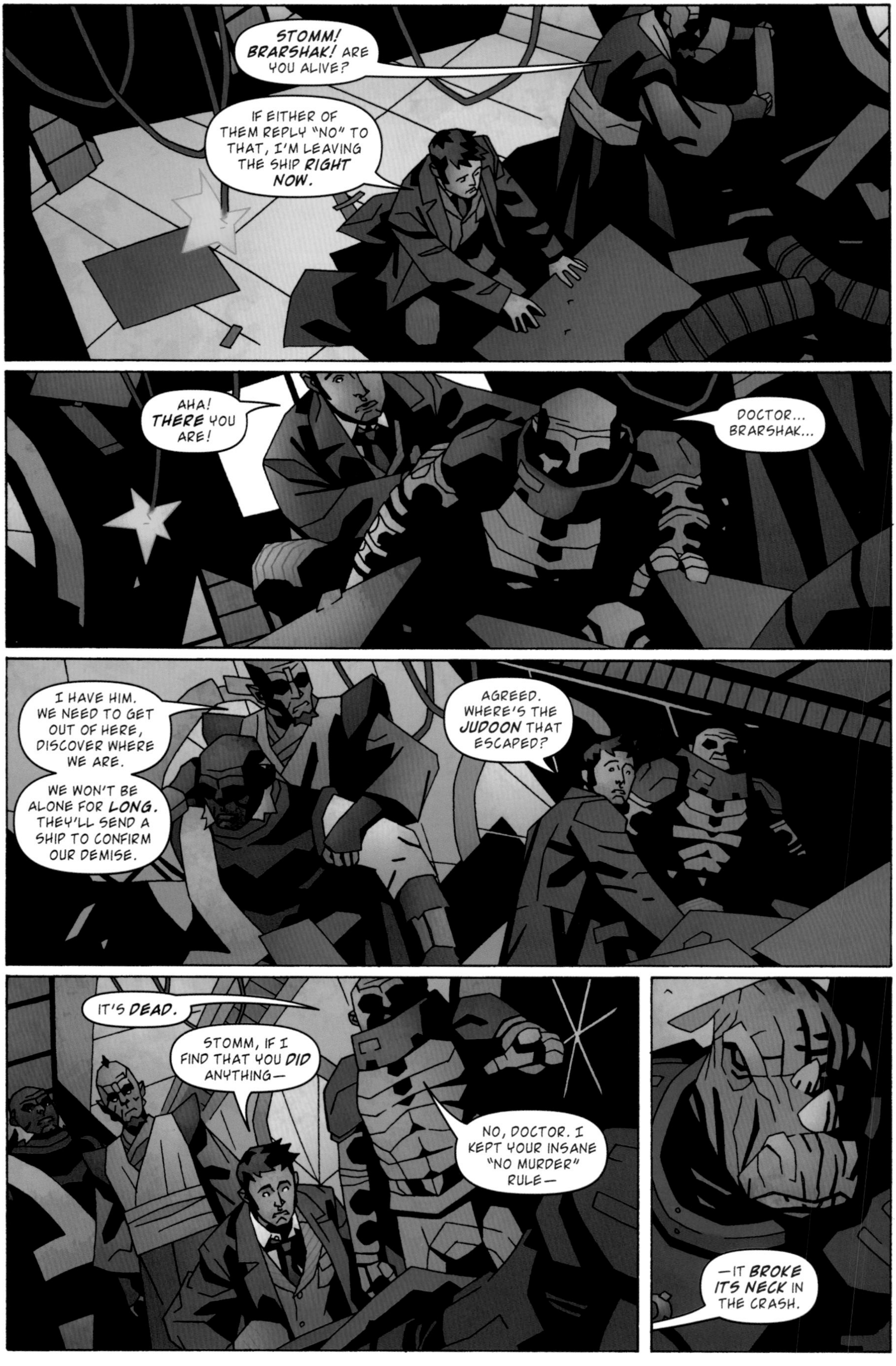
STOMM! BRARSHAK! ARE YOU ALIVE?
IF EITHER OF THEM REPLY "NO" TO THAT, I'M LEAVING THE SHIP RIGHT NOW.
AHA! THERE YOU ARE!
DOCTOR... BRARSHAK...
I HAVE HIM. WE NEED TO GET OUT OF HERE, DISCOVER WHERE WE ARE.
WE WON'T BE ALONE FOR LONG. THEY'LL SEND A SHIP TO CONFIRM OUR DEMISE.
AGREED. WHERE'S THE JUDOON THAT ESCAPED?
IT'S DEAD.
STOMM, IF I FIND THAT YOU DID ANYTHING—
NO, DOCTOR. I KEPT YOUR INSANE "NO MURDER" RULE—
—IT BROKE ITS NECK IN THE CRASH.

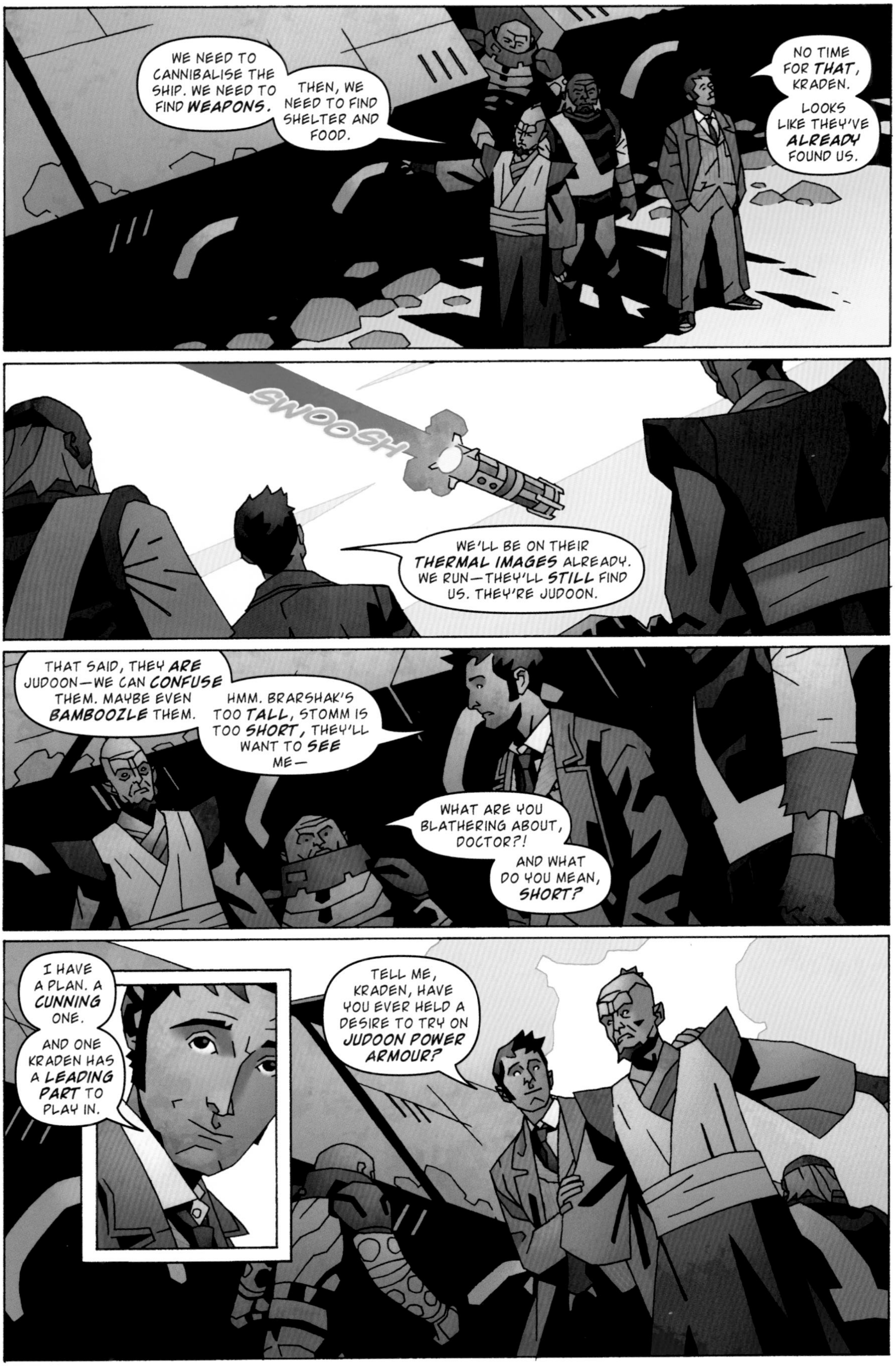
WE NEED TO CANNIBALISE THE SHIP. WE NEED TO FIND WEAPONS.
THEN, WE NEED TO FIND SHELTER AND FOOD.
NO TIME FOR THAT, KRADEN.
LOOKS LIKE THEY'VE ALREADY FOUND US.
SWOOSH
WE'LL BE ON THEIR THERMAL IMAGES ALREADY. WE RUN—THEY'LL STILL FIND US. THEY'RE JUDOON.
THAT SAID, THEY ARE JUDOON—WE CAN CONFUSE THEM. MAYBE EVEN BAMBOOZLE THEM.
HMM. BRARSHAK'S TOO TALL, STOMM IS TOO SHORT, THEY'LL WANT TO SEE ME—
WHAT ARE YOU BLATHERING ABOUT, DOCTOR?!
AND WHAT DO YOU MEAN, SHORT?
I HAVE A PLAN. A CUNNING ONE.
AND ONE KRADEN HAS A LEADING PART TO PLAY IN.
TELL ME, KRADEN, HAVE YOU EVER HELD A DESIRE TO TRY ON JUDOON POWER ARMOUR?

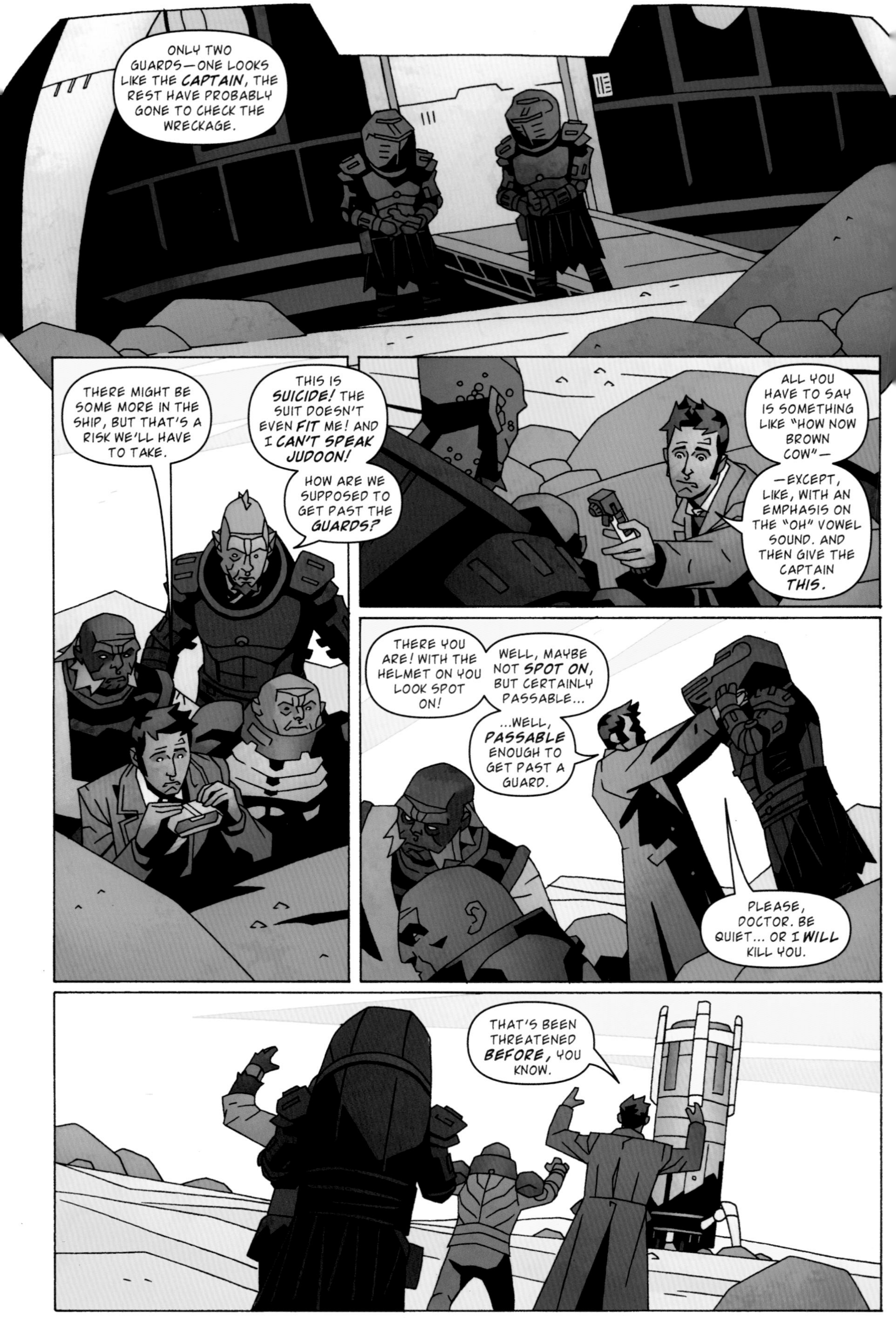
ONLY TWO GUARDS—ONE LOOKS LIKE THE CAPTAIN, THE REST HAVE PROBABLY GONE TO CHECK THE WRECKAGE.
THERE MIGHT BE SOME MORE IN THE SHIP, BUT THAT'S A RISK WE'LL HAVE TO TAKE.
THIS IS SUICIDE! THE SUIT DOESN'T EVEN FIT ME! AND I CAN'T SPEAK JUDOON!
HOW ARE WE SUPPOSED TO GET PAST THE GUARDS?
ALL YOU HAVE TO SAY IS SOMETHING LIKE "HOW NOW BROWN COW"—
—EXCEPT, LIKE, WITH AN EMPHASIS ON THE "OH" VOWEL SOUND. AND THEN GIVE THE CAPTAIN THIS.
THERE YOU ARE! WITH THE HELMET ON YOU LOOK SPOT ON!
WELL, MAYBE NOT SPOT ON, BUT CERTAINLY PASSABLE...
...WELL, PASSABLE ENOUGH TO GET PAST A GUARD.
PLEASE, DOCTOR. BE QUIET... OR I WILL KILL YOU.
THAT'S BEEN THREATENED BEFORE, YOU KNOW.

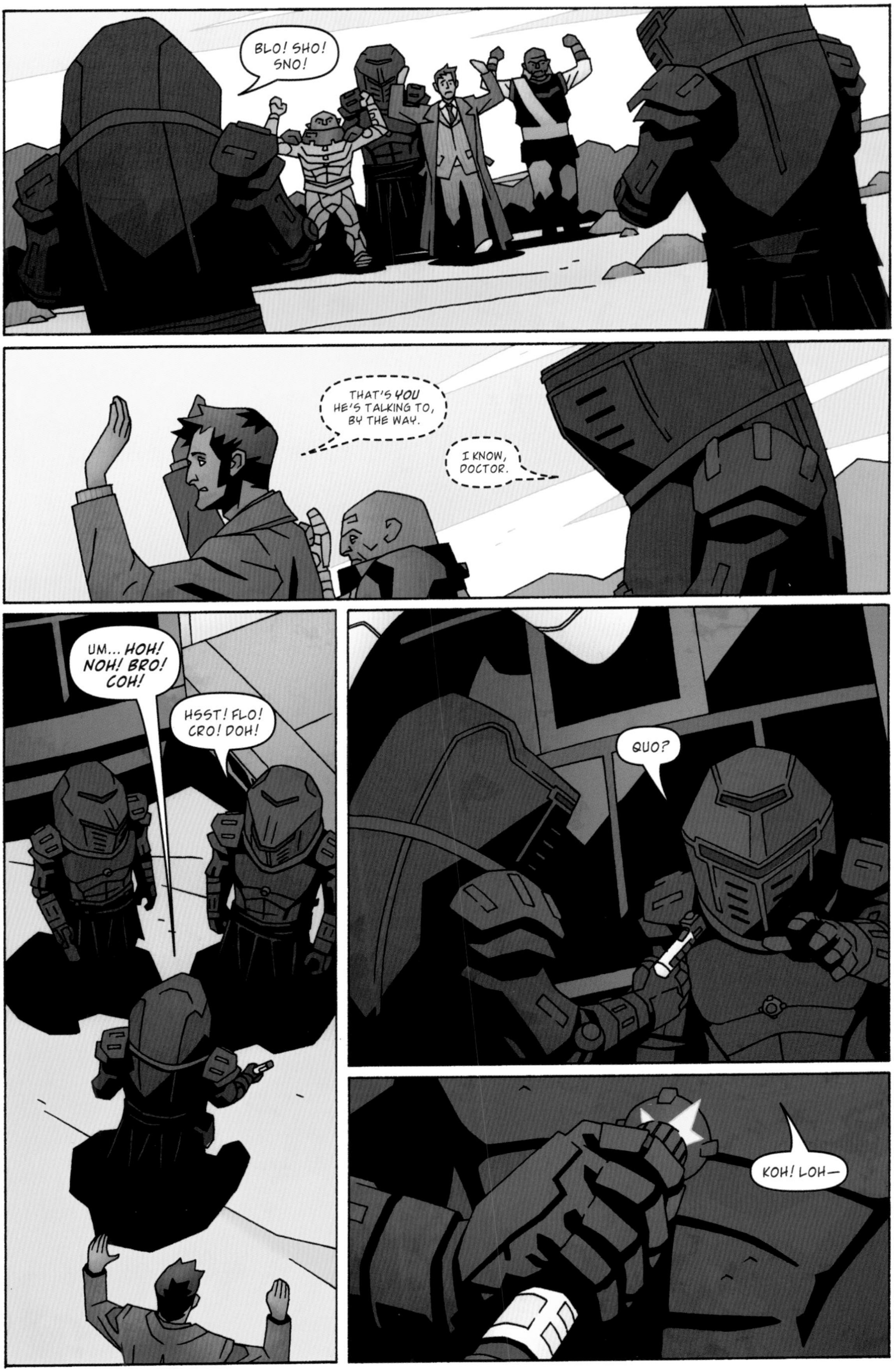
BLO! SHO! SNO!
THAT'S YOU HE'S TALKING TO, BY THE WAY.
I KNOW, DOCTOR.
UM... HOH! NOH! BRO! COH!
HSST! FLO! CRO! DOH!
QUO?
KOH! LOH—

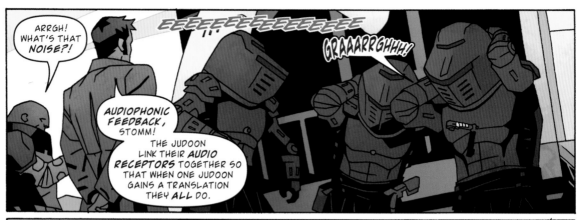

ARRGH! WHAT'S THAT NOISE?!

EEEEEEEEEEEEEEEE

GRAAAARRGHHH!

AUDIOPHONIC FEEDBACK, STOMM!

THE JUDOON LINK THEIR **AUDIO RECEPTORS** TOGETHER SO THAT WHEN ONE JUDOON GAINS A TRANSLATION THEY **ALL DO.**

INSTANTLY **DOWNLOADED** INTO THE CORTEX THROUGH THEIR SUITS.

KRADEN SAID SOMETHING LIKE "MANGO, BICYCLE, BOOKCASE" IN JUDOON. THE CAPTAIN HAD TO CHECK IF HIS **TRANSLATION CIRCUITS** WERE WORKING.

AND THE MOMENT HE INSERTED THE TRANSLATOR, I SENT THEM AN **AUDIAL VIRUS**—SOMETHING THAT, ONCE UPLOADED, WOULD STRIKE AT THEIR CORTEX, PARALYSING THEM.

BUT WHY DIDN'T **I** GET HIT BY IT?

DRACONIANS HAVE A HIGHER FREQUENCY TOLERANCE—

—AH. LOOK OUT!

FZAPP

FZAPP

SO WHY AREN'T **THEY** AFFECTED?

IT'S ONLY GOT A LIMITED RANGE. WE NEED TO—

DON'T WORRY, DOCTOR...

...LET **WARRIORS** DO THIS ONE.

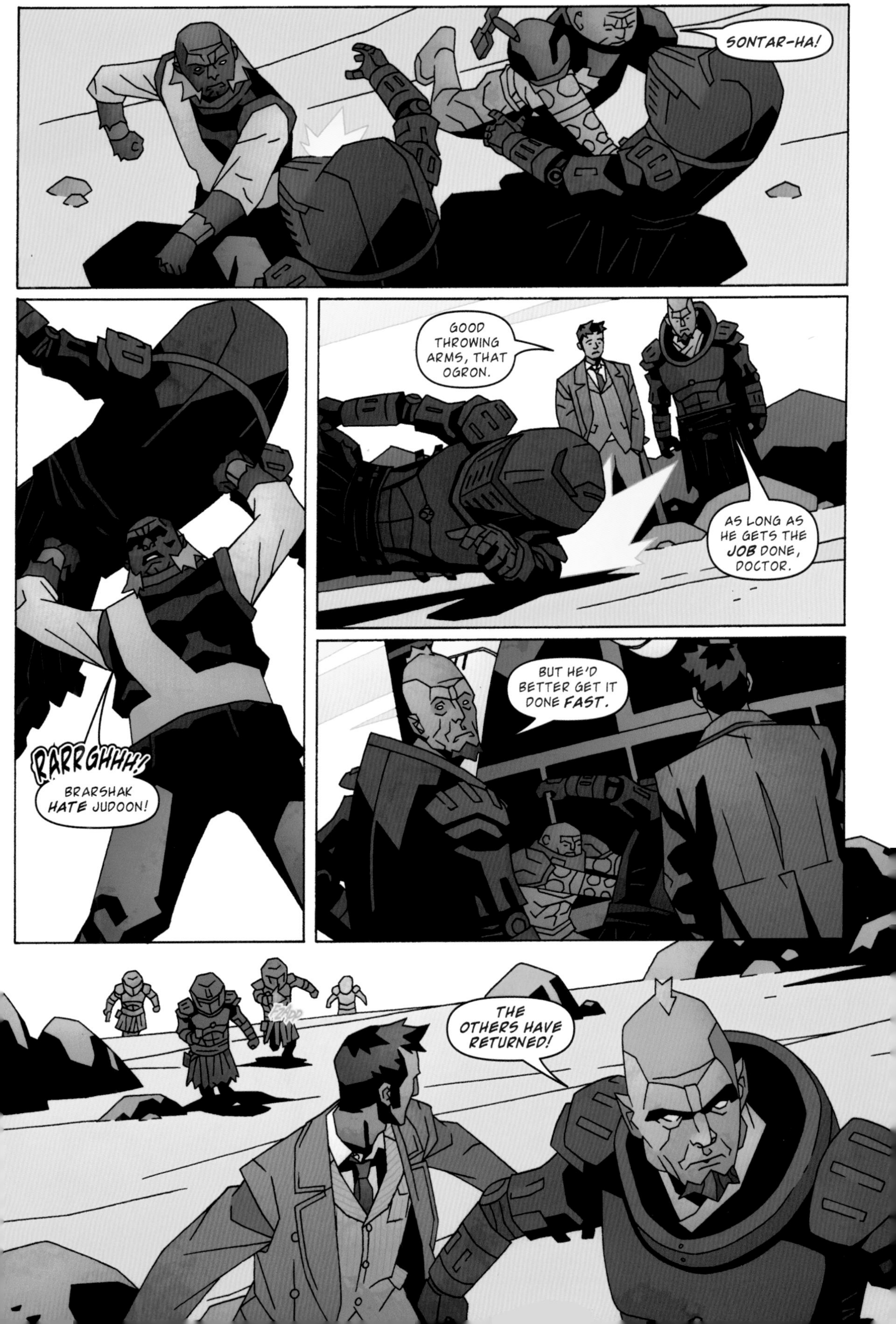
SONTAR-HA!
RARRGHHH!
BRARSHAK HATE JUDOON!
GOOD THROWING ARMS, THAT OGRON.
AS LONG AS HE GETS THE JOB DONE, DOCTOR.
BUT HE'D BETTER GET IT DONE FAST.
FZAPP
THE OTHERS HAVE RETURNED!

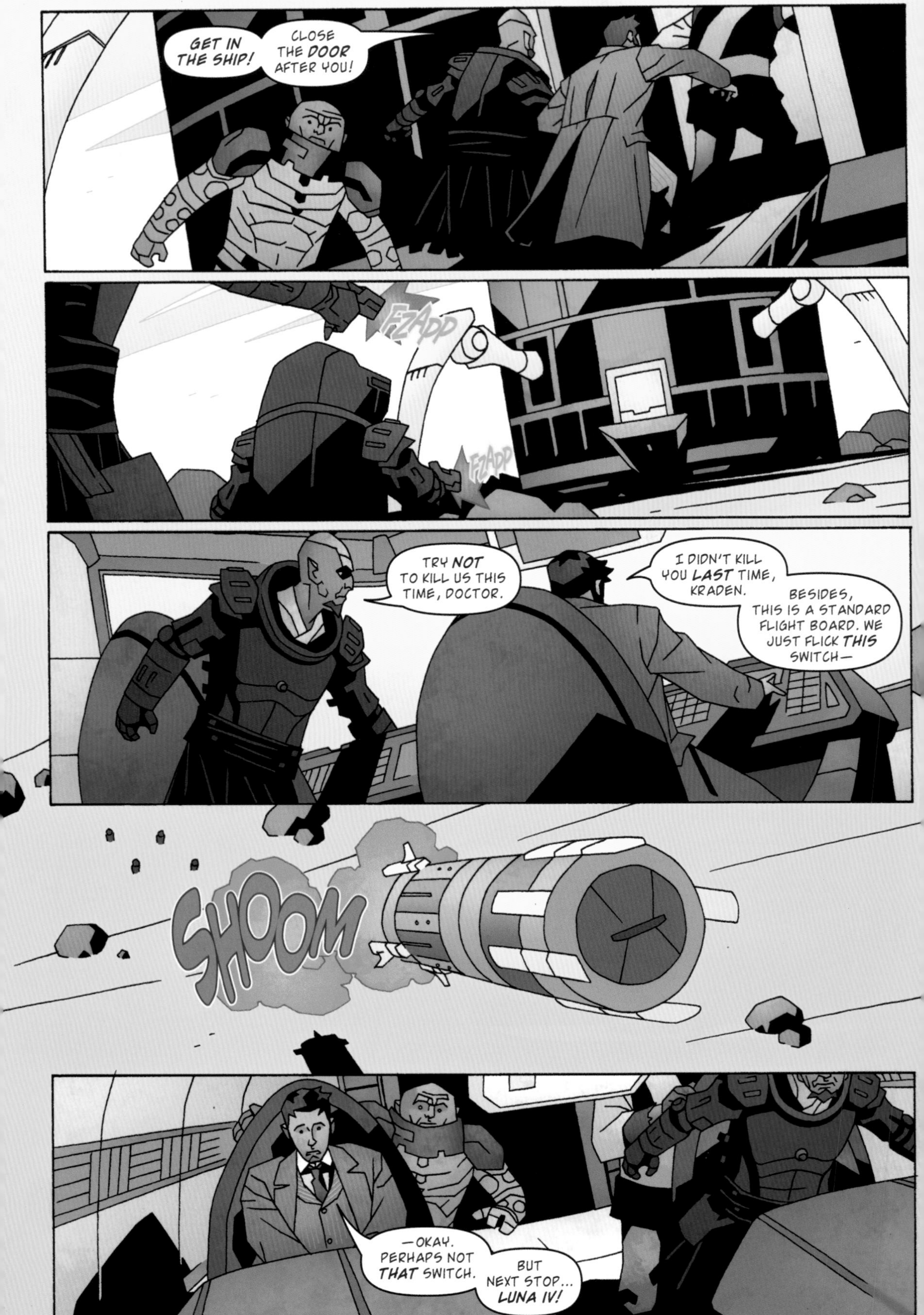
GET IN THE SHIP!
CLOSE THE DOOR AFTER YOU!
FZAPP
FZAPP
TRY NOT TO KILL US THIS TIME, DOCTOR.
I DIDN'T KILL YOU LAST TIME, KRADEN.
BESIDES, THIS IS A STANDARD FLIGHT BOARD. WE JUST FLICK THIS SWITCH—
SHOOM
—OKAY. PERHAPS NOT THAT SWITCH.
BUT NEXT STOP... LUNA IV!

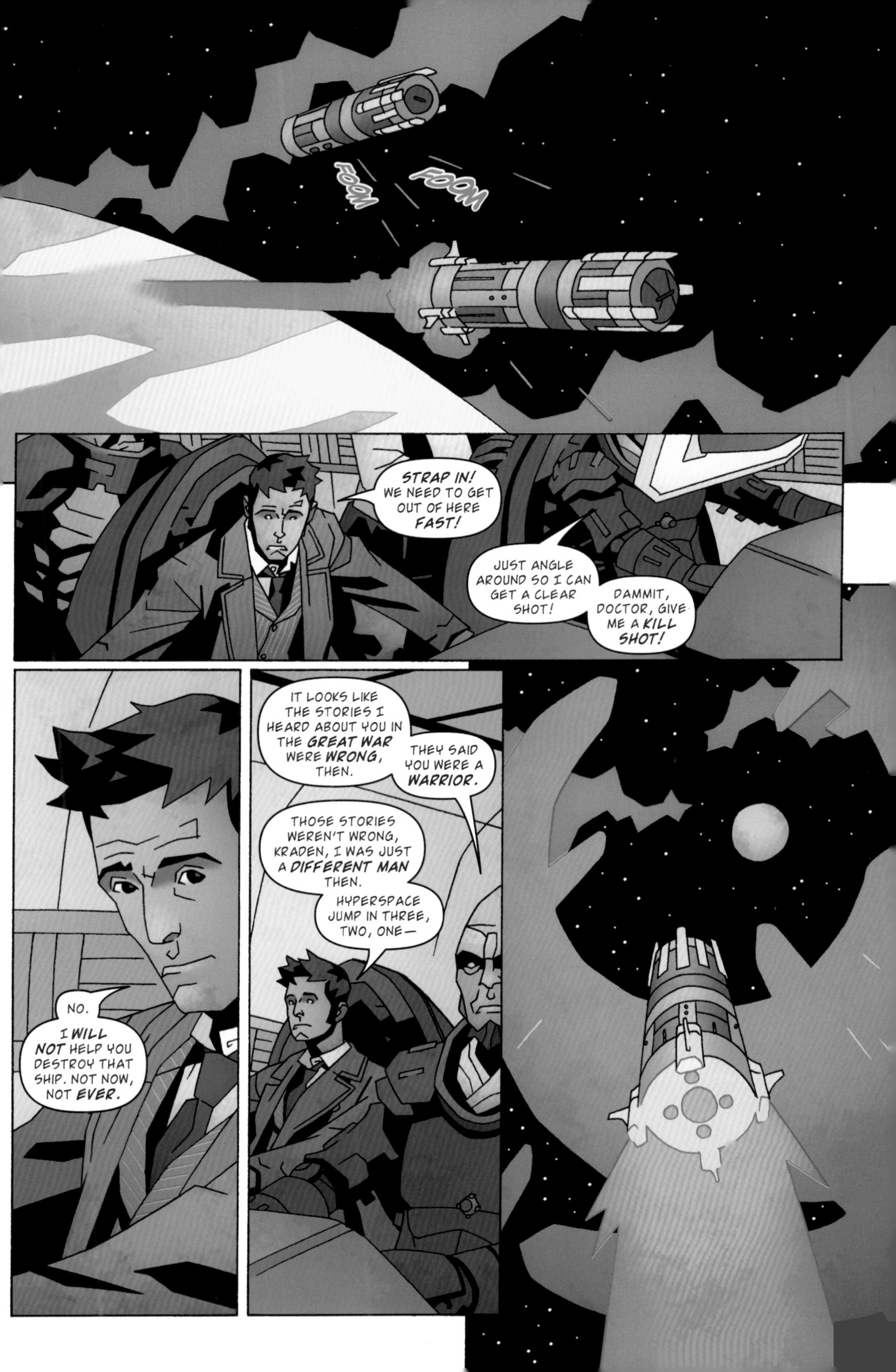
FOOM
FOOM
STRAP IN! WE NEED TO GET OUT OF HERE FAST!
JUST ANGLE AROUND SO I CAN GET A CLEAR SHOT!
DAMMIT, DOCTOR, GIVE ME A KILL SHOT!
NO.
I WILL NOT HELP YOU DESTROY THAT SHIP. NOT NOW, NOT EVER.
IT LOOKS LIKE THE STORIES I HEARD ABOUT YOU IN THE GREAT WAR WERE WRONG, THEN.
THEY SAID YOU WERE A WARRIOR.
THOSE STORIES WEREN'T WRONG, KRADEN, I WAS JUST A DIFFERENT MAN THEN.
HYPERSPACE JUMP IN THREE, TWO, ONE—

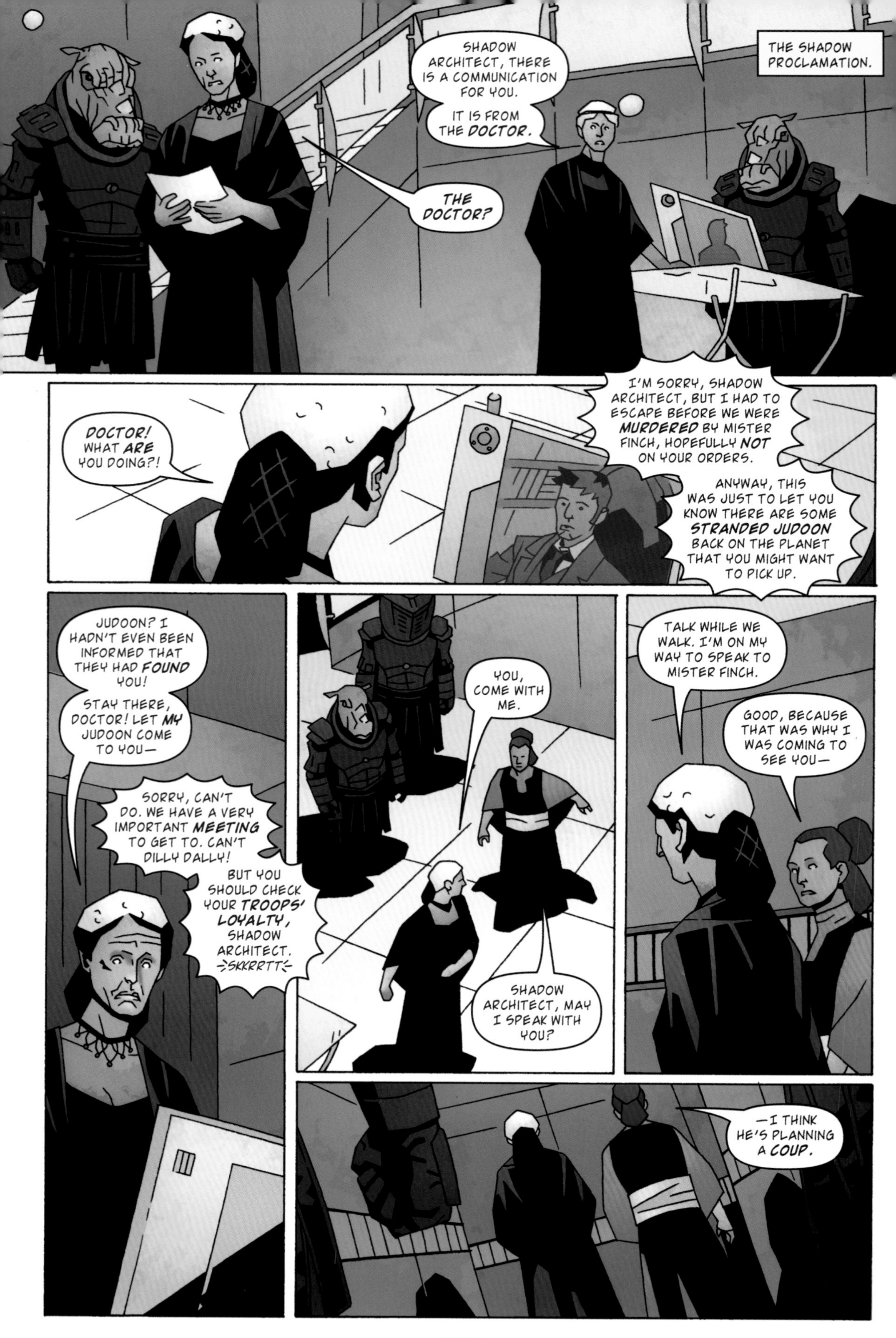

THE SHADOW PROCLAMATION.
SHADOW ARCHITECT, THERE IS A COMMUNICATION FOR YOU.
IT IS FROM THE DOCTOR.
THE DOCTOR?
DOCTOR! WHAT ARE YOU DOING?!
I'M SORRY, SHADOW ARCHITECT, BUT I HAD TO ESCAPE BEFORE WE WERE MURDERED BY MISTER FINCH, HOPEFULLY NOT ON YOUR ORDERS.
ANYWAY, THIS WAS JUST TO LET YOU KNOW THERE ARE SOME STRANDED JUDOON BACK ON THE PLANET THAT YOU MIGHT WANT TO PICK UP.
JUDOON? I HADN'T EVEN BEEN INFORMED THAT THEY HAD FOUND YOU!
STAY THERE, DOCTOR! LET MY JUDOON COME TO YOU—
SORRY, CAN'T DO. WE HAVE A VERY IMPORTANT MEETING TO GET TO. CAN'T DILLY DALLY!
BUT YOU SHOULD CHECK YOUR TROOPS' LOYALTY, SHADOW ARCHITECT.
SKKRRTT
YOU, COME WITH ME.
SHADOW ARCHITECT, MAY I SPEAK WITH YOU?
TALK WHILE WE WALK. I'M ON MY WAY TO SPEAK TO MISTER FINCH.
GOOD, BECAUSE THAT WAS WHY I WAS COMING TO SEE YOU—
—I THINK HE'S PLANNING A COUP.

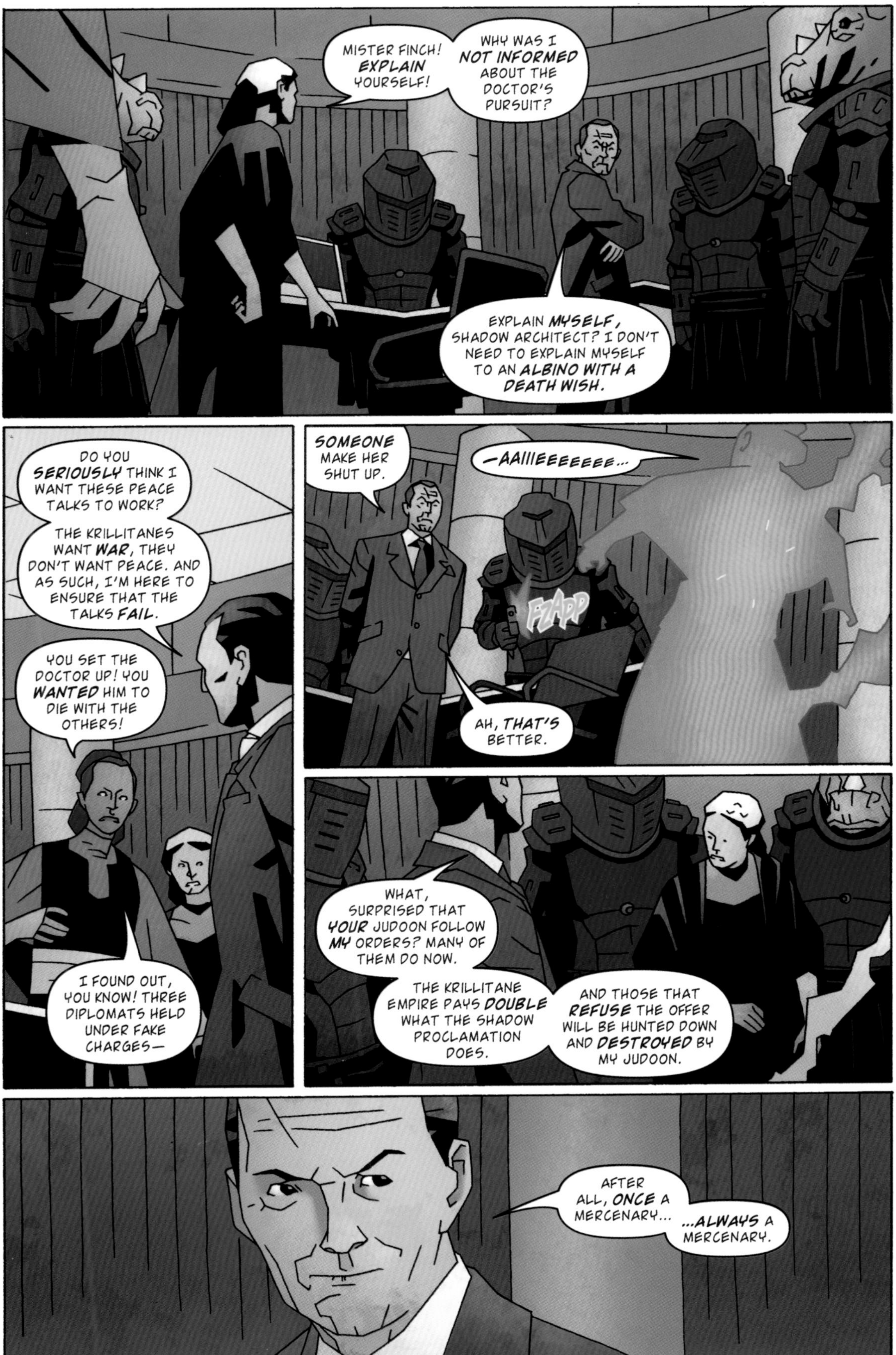

MISTER FINCH! EXPLAIN YOURSELF!
WHY WAS I NOT INFORMED ABOUT THE DOCTOR'S PURSUIT?
EXPLAIN MYSELF, SHADOW ARCHITECT? I DON'T NEED TO EXPLAIN MYSELF TO AN ALBINO WITH A DEATH WISH.
DO YOU SERIOUSLY THINK I WANT THESE PEACE TALKS TO WORK?
THE KRILLITANES WANT WAR, THEY DON'T WANT PEACE. AND AS SUCH, I'M HERE TO ENSURE THAT THE TALKS FAIL.
YOU SET THE DOCTOR UP! YOU WANTED HIM TO DIE WITH THE OTHERS!
I FOUND OUT, YOU KNOW! THREE DIPLOMATS HELD UNDER FAKE CHARGES—
SOMEONE MAKE HER SHUT UP.
—AAIIIEEEEEEE...
FZAPP
AH, THAT'S BETTER.
WHAT, SURPRISED THAT YOUR JUDOON FOLLOW MY ORDERS? MANY OF THEM DO NOW.
THE KRILLITANE EMPIRE PAYS DOUBLE WHAT THE SHADOW PROCLAMATION DOES.
AND THOSE THAT REFUSE THE OFFER WILL BE HUNTED DOWN AND DESTROYED BY MY JUDOON.
AFTER ALL, ONCE A MERCENARY...
...ALWAYS A MERCENARY.

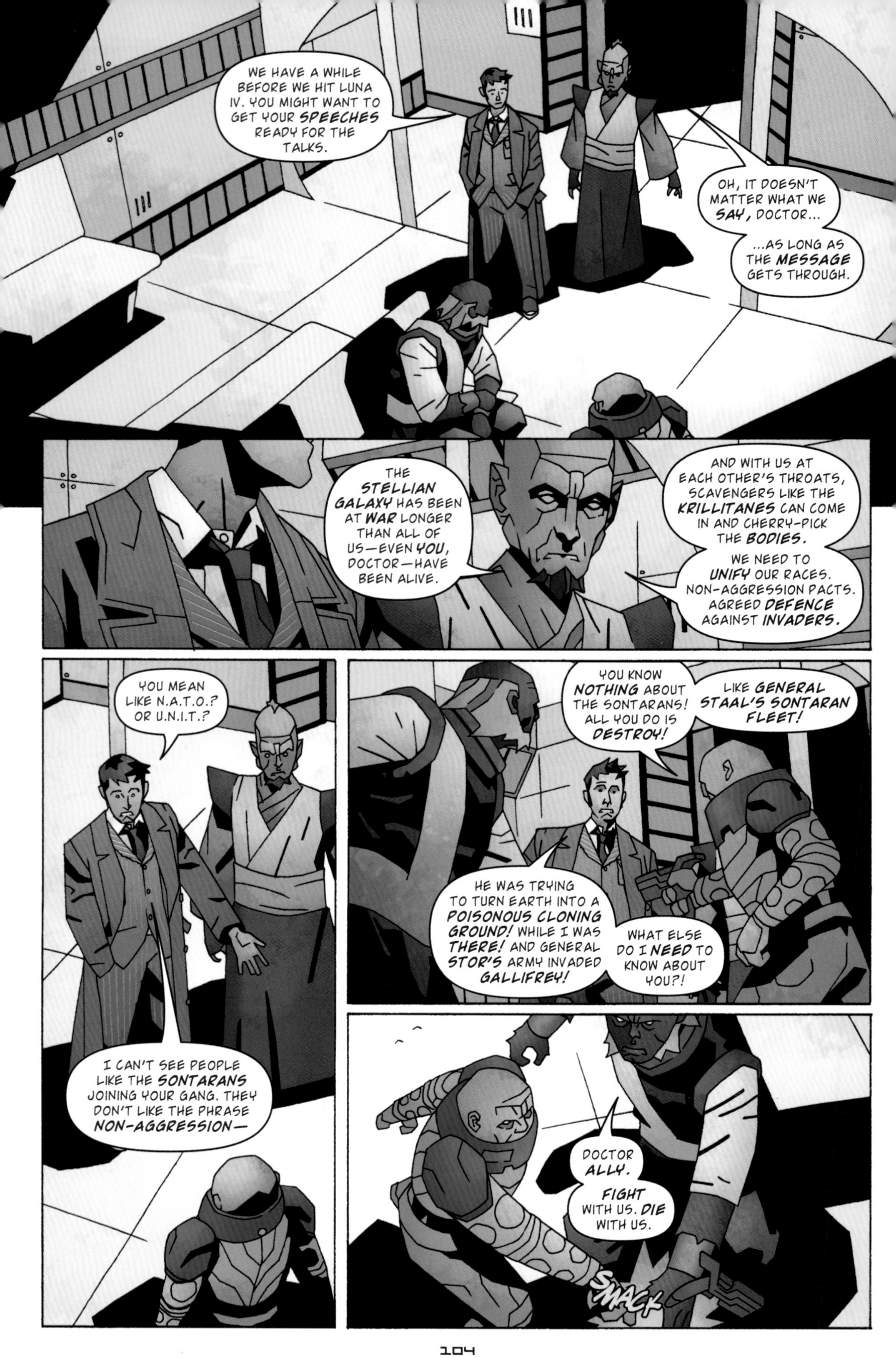
WE HAVE A WHILE BEFORE WE HIT LUNA IV. YOU MIGHT WANT TO GET YOUR SPEECHES READY FOR THE TALKS.
OH, IT DOESN'T MATTER WHAT WE SAY, DOCTOR...
...AS LONG AS THE MESSAGE GETS THROUGH.
THE STELLIAN GALAXY HAS BEEN AT WAR LONGER THAN ALL OF US—EVEN YOU, DOCTOR—HAVE BEEN ALIVE.
AND WITH US AT EACH OTHER'S THROATS, SCAVENGERS LIKE THE KRILLITANES CAN COME IN AND CHERRY-PICK THE BODIES.
WE NEED TO UNIFY OUR RACES. NON-AGGRESSION PACTS. AGREED DEFENCE AGAINST INVADERS.
YOU MEAN LIKE N.A.T.O.? OR U.N.I.T.?
I CAN'T SEE PEOPLE LIKE THE SONTARANS JOINING YOUR GANG. THEY DON'T LIKE THE PHRASE NON-AGGRESSION—
YOU KNOW NOTHING ABOUT THE SONTARANS! ALL YOU DO IS DESTROY!
LIKE GENERAL STAAL'S SONTARAN FLEET!
HE WAS TRYING TO TURN EARTH INTO A POISONOUS CLONING GROUND! WHILE I WAS THERE! AND GENERAL STOR'S ARMY INVADED GALLIFREY!
WHAT ELSE DO I NEED TO KNOW ABOUT YOU?!
DOCTOR ALLY.
FIGHT WITH US. DIE WITH US.
SMACK

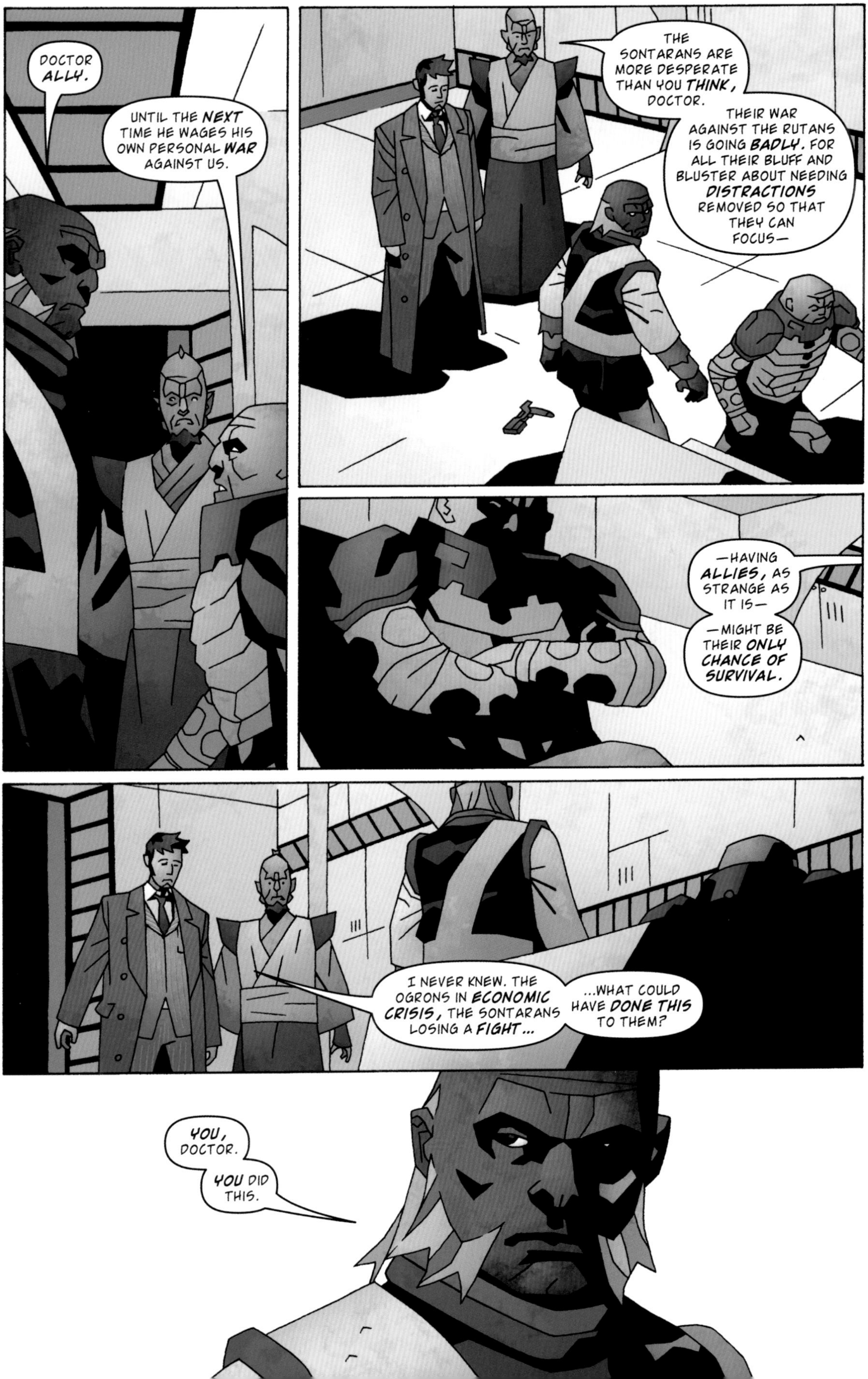
DOCTOR ALLY.
UNTIL THE NEXT TIME HE WAGES HIS OWN PERSONAL WAR AGAINST US.
THE SONTARANS ARE MORE DESPERATE THAN YOU THINK, DOCTOR.
THEIR WAR AGAINST THE RUTANS IS GOING BADLY. FOR ALL THEIR BLUFF AND BLUSTER ABOUT NEEDING DISTRACTIONS REMOVED SO THAT THEY CAN FOCUS—
—HAVING ALLIES, AS STRANGE AS IT IS—
—MIGHT BE THEIR ONLY CHANCE OF SURVIVAL.
I NEVER KNEW. THE OGRONS IN ECONOMIC CRISIS, THE SONTARANS LOSING A FIGHT...
...WHAT COULD HAVE DONE THIS TO THEM?
YOU, DOCTOR.
YOU DID THIS.

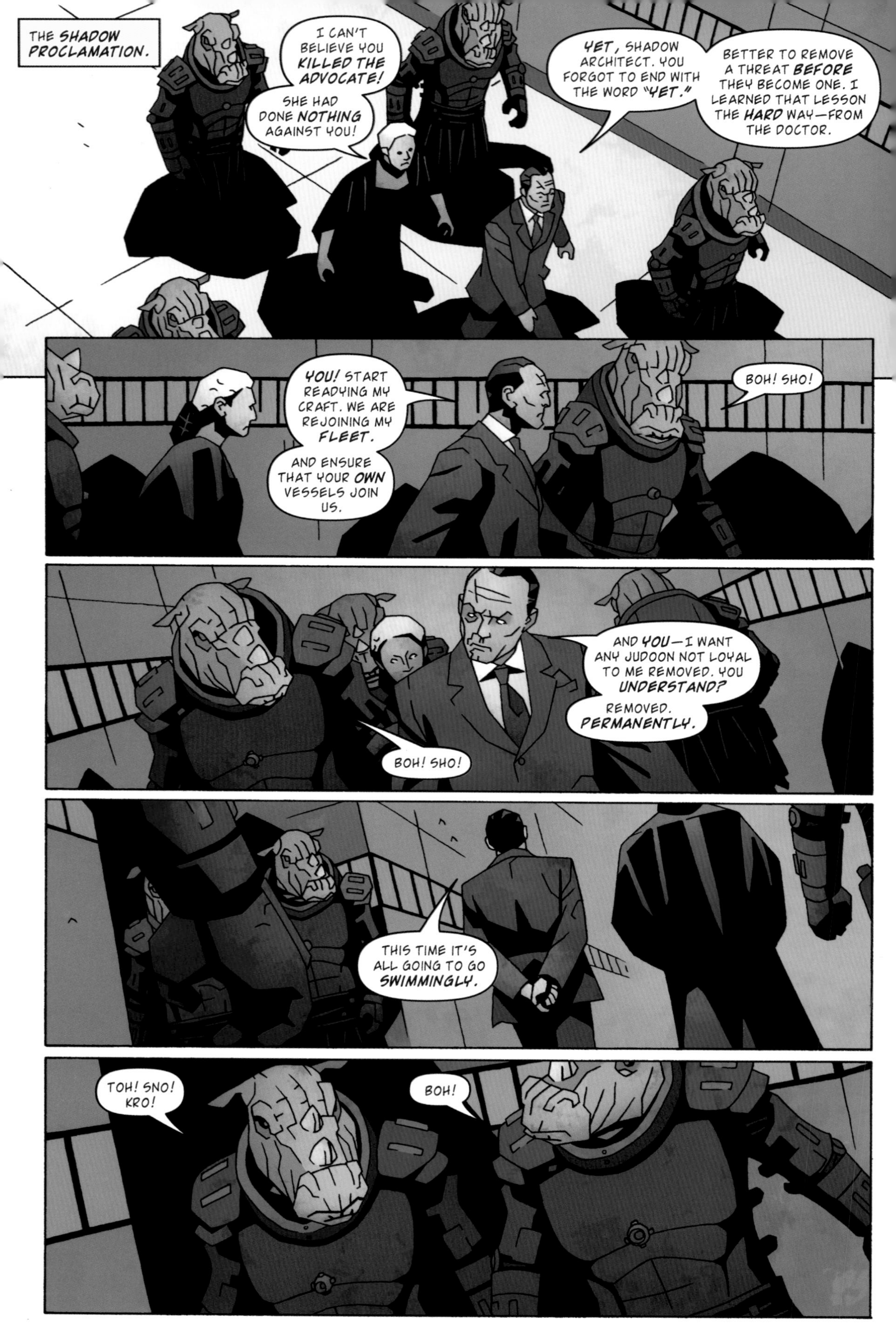
THE SHADOW PROCLAMATION.
I CAN'T BELIEVE YOU KILLED THE ADVOCATE!
SHE HAD DONE NOTHING AGAINST YOU!
YET, SHADOW ARCHITECT. YOU FORGOT TO END WITH THE WORD "YET."
BETTER TO REMOVE A THREAT BEFORE THEY BECOME ONE. I LEARNED THAT LESSON THE HARD WAY—FROM THE DOCTOR.
YOU! START READYING MY CRAFT. WE ARE REJOINING MY FLEET.
AND ENSURE THAT YOUR OWN VESSELS JOIN US.
BOH! SHO!
AND YOU—I WANT ANY JUDOON NOT LOYAL TO ME REMOVED. YOU UNDERSTAND?
REMOVED. PERMANENTLY.
BOH! SHO!
THIS TIME IT'S ALL GOING TO GO SWIMMINGLY.
TOH! SNO! KRO!
BOH!

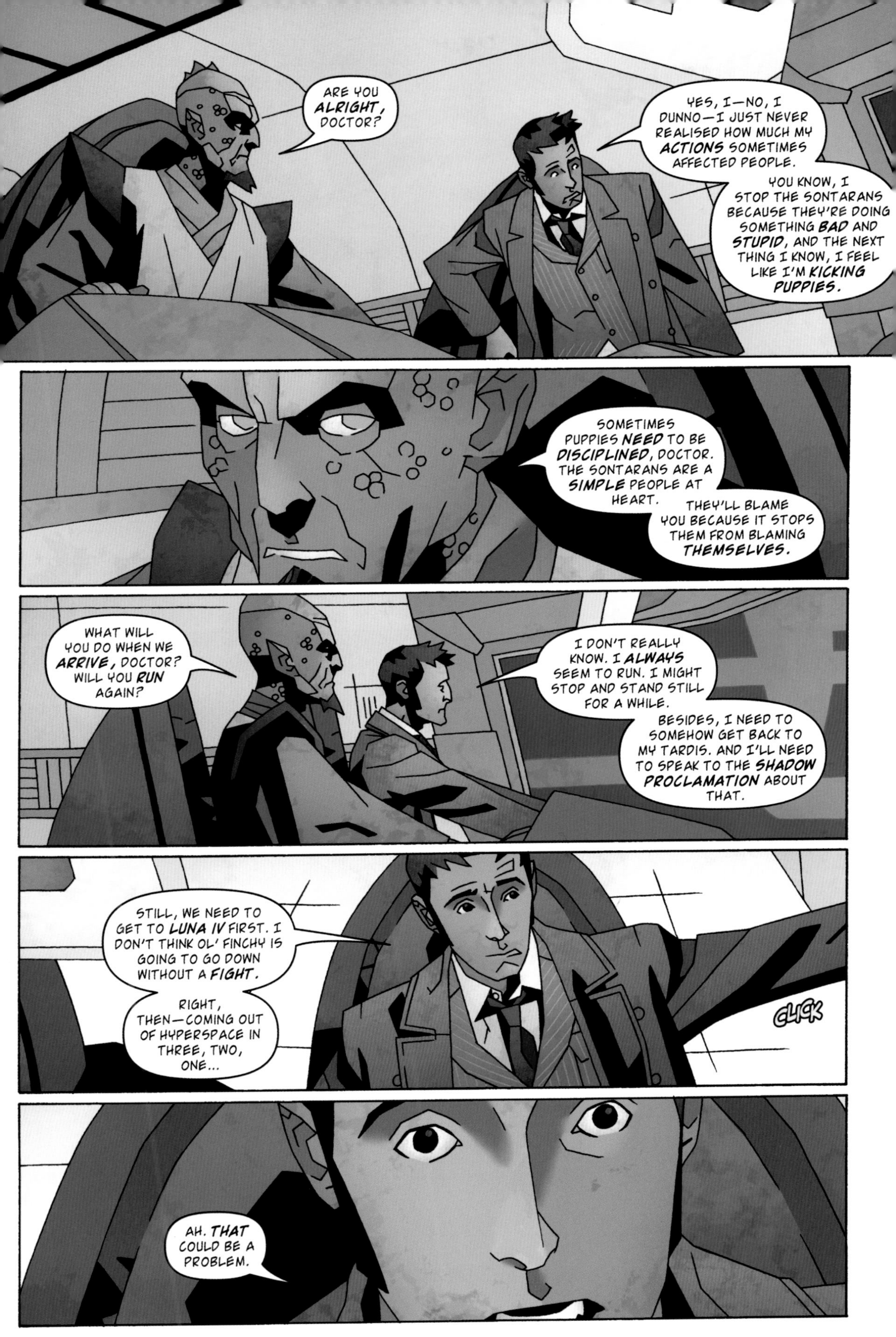
ARE YOU ALRIGHT, DOCTOR?
YES, I—NO, I DUNNO—I JUST NEVER REALISED HOW MUCH MY ACTIONS SOMETIMES AFFECTED PEOPLE.
YOU KNOW, I STOP THE SONTARANS BECAUSE THEY'RE DOING SOMETHING BAD AND STUPID, AND THE NEXT THING I KNOW, I FEEL LIKE I'M KICKING PUPPIES.
SOMETIMES PUPPIES NEED TO BE DISCIPLINED, DOCTOR. THE SONTARANS ARE A SIMPLE PEOPLE AT HEART.
THEY'LL BLAME YOU BECAUSE IT STOPS THEM FROM BLAMING THEMSELVES.
WHAT WILL YOU DO WHEN WE ARRIVE, DOCTOR? WILL YOU RUN AGAIN?
I DON'T REALLY KNOW. I ALWAYS SEEM TO RUN. I MIGHT STOP AND STAND STILL FOR A WHILE.
BESIDES, I NEED TO SOMEHOW GET BACK TO MY TARDIS. AND I'LL NEED TO SPEAK TO THE SHADOW PROCLAMATION ABOUT THAT.
STILL, WE NEED TO GET TO LUNA IV FIRST. I DON'T THINK OL' FINCHY IS GOING TO GO DOWN WITHOUT A FIGHT.
RIGHT, THEN—COMING OUT OF HYPERSPACE IN THREE, TWO, ONE...
CLICK
AH. THAT COULD BE A PROBLEM.

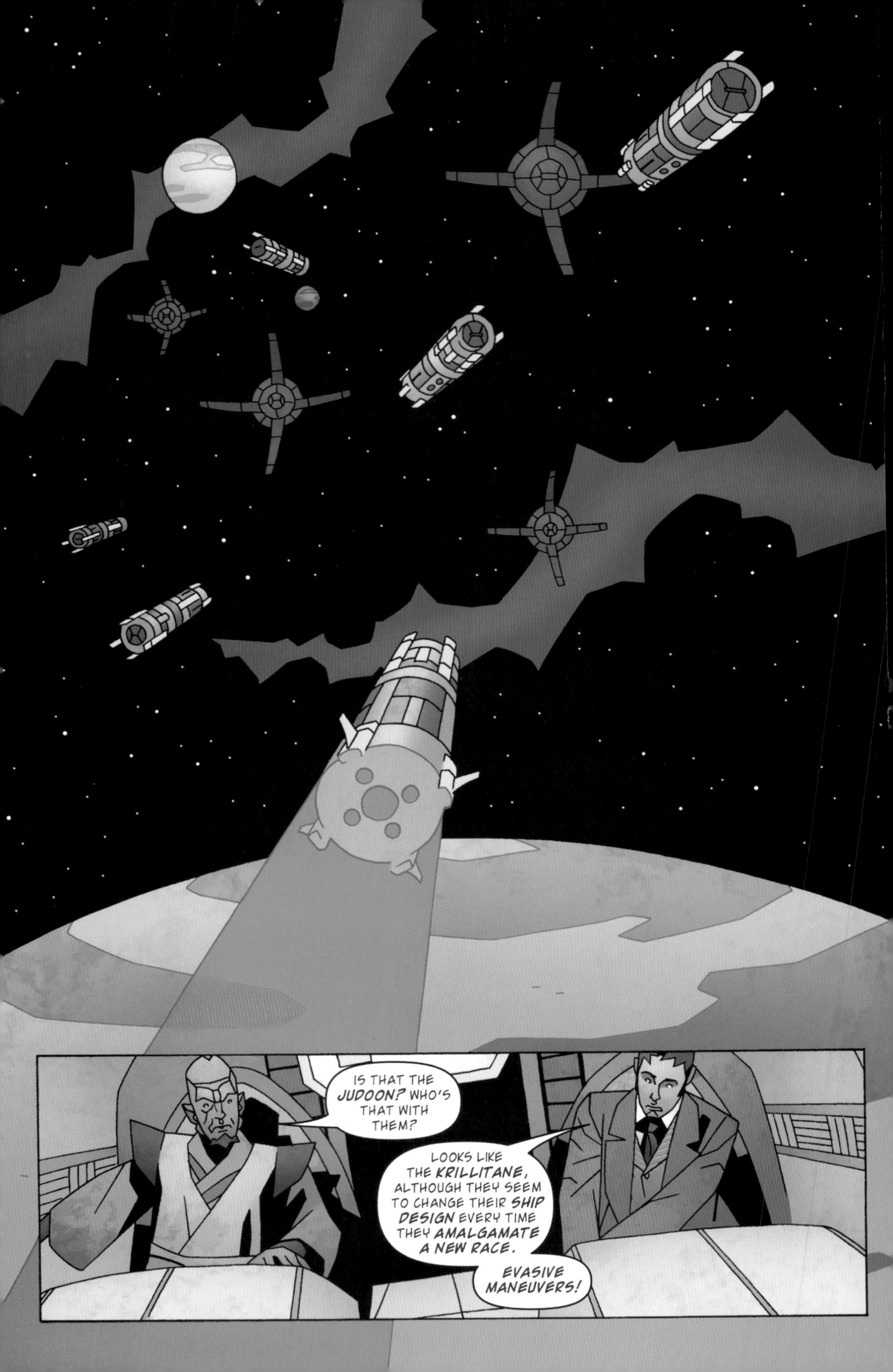
IS THAT THE JUDOON? WHO'S THAT WITH THEM?
LOOKS LIKE THE KRILLITANE, ALTHOUGH THEY SEEM TO CHANGE THEIR SHIP DESIGN EVERY TIME THEY AMALGAMATE A NEW RACE.
EVASIVE MANEUVERS!

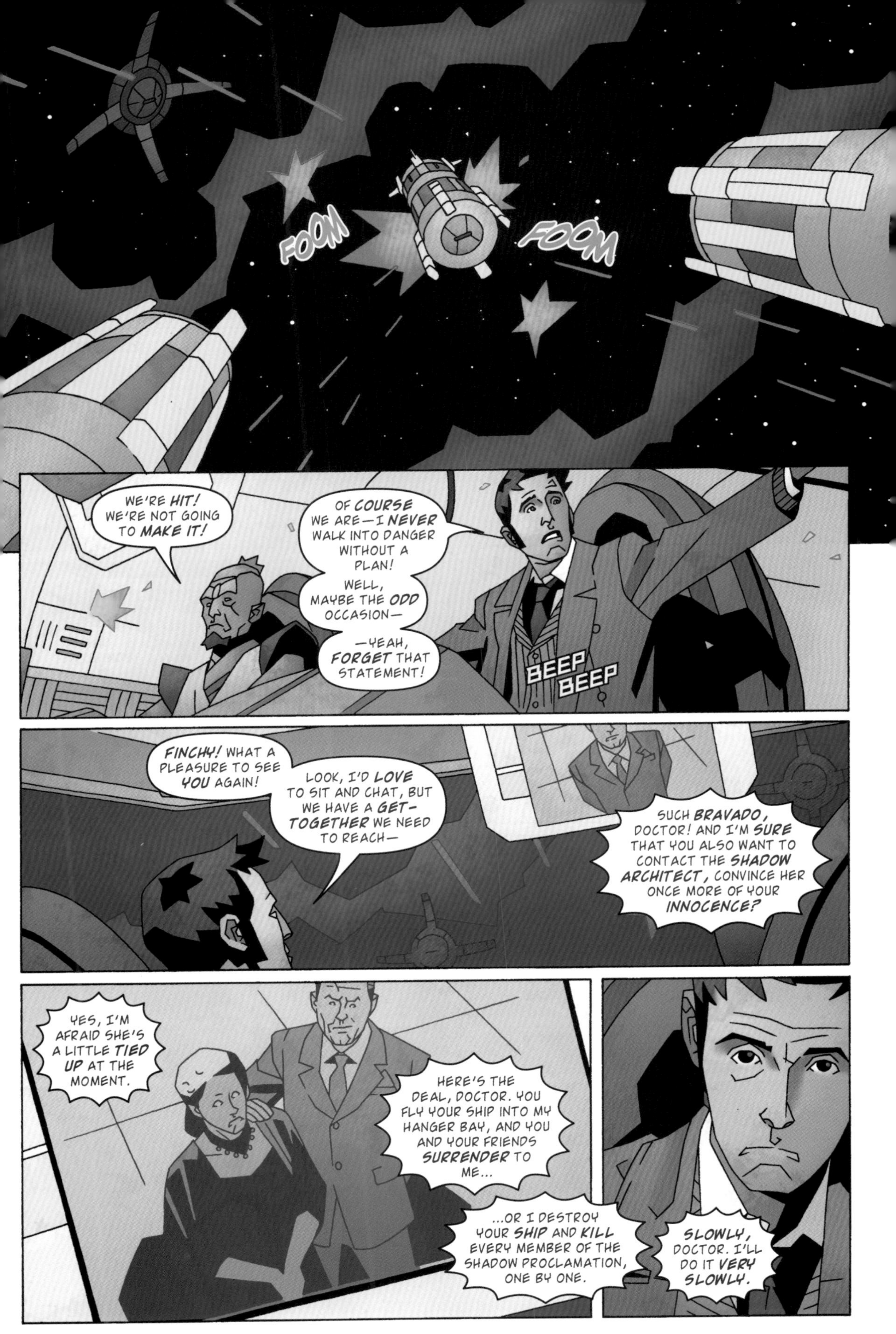
FOOM
FOOM
WE'RE HIT! WE'RE NOT GOING TO MAKE IT!
OF COURSE WE ARE—I NEVER WALK INTO DANGER WITHOUT A PLAN!
WELL, MAYBE THE ODD OCCASION—
—YEAH, FORGET THAT STATEMENT!
BEEP BEEP
FINCHY! WHAT A PLEASURE TO SEE YOU AGAIN!
LOOK, I'D LOVE TO SIT AND CHAT, BUT WE HAVE A GET-TOGETHER WE NEED TO REACH—
SUCH BRAVADO, DOCTOR! AND I'M SURE THAT YOU ALSO WANT TO CONTACT THE SHADOW ARCHITECT, CONVINCE HER ONCE MORE OF YOUR INNOCENCE?
YES, I'M AFRAID SHE'S A LITTLE TIED UP AT THE MOMENT.
HERE'S THE DEAL, DOCTOR. YOU FLY YOUR SHIP INTO MY HANGER BAY, AND YOU AND YOUR FRIENDS SURRENDER TO ME...
...OR I DESTROY YOUR SHIP AND KILL EVERY MEMBER OF THE SHADOW PROCLAMATION, ONE BY ONE.
SLOWLY, DOCTOR. I'LL DO IT VERY SLOWLY.

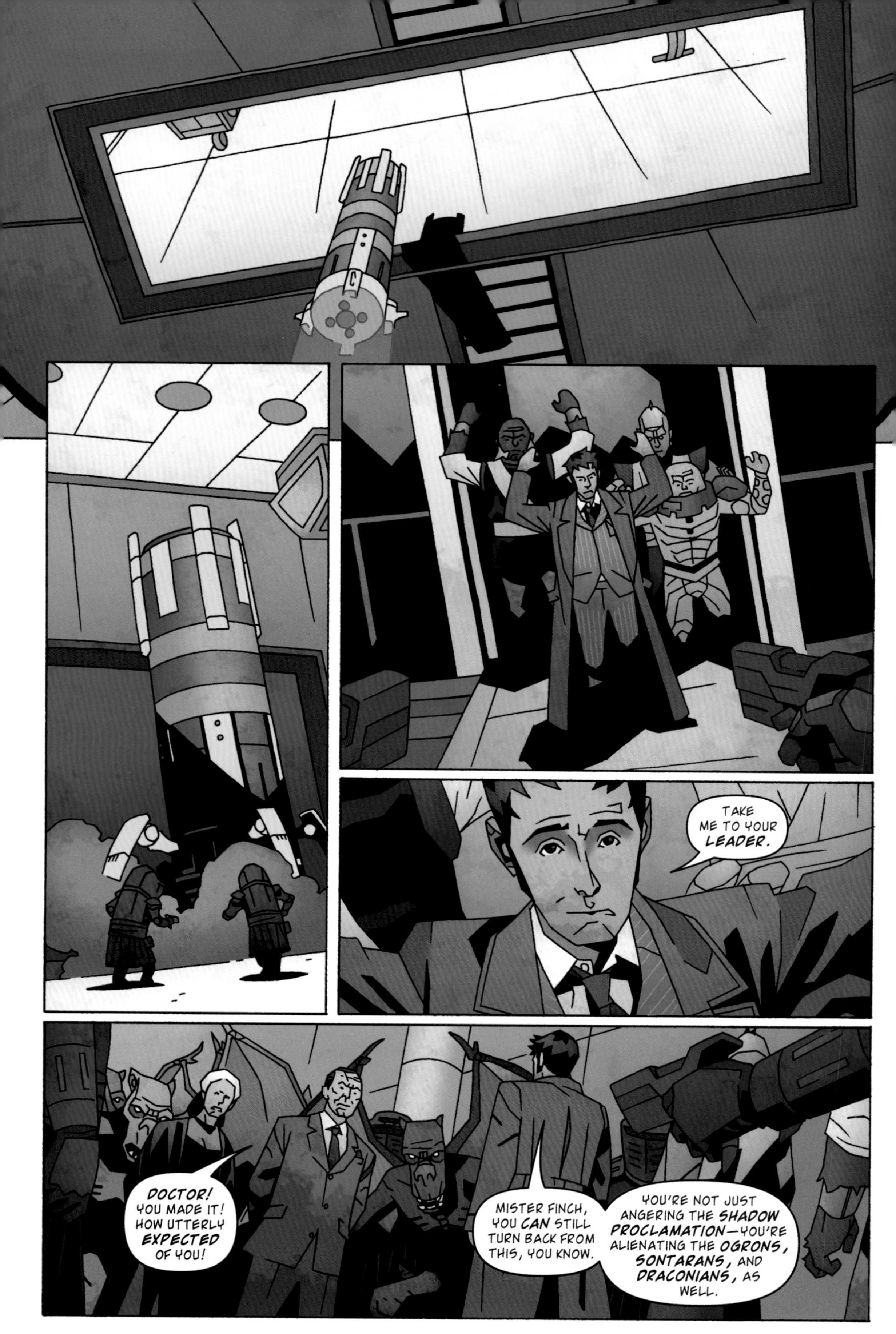
TAKE ME TO YOUR LEADER.
DOCTOR! YOU MADE IT! HOW UTTERLY EXPECTED OF YOU!
MISTER FINCH, YOU CAN STILL TURN BACK FROM THIS, YOU KNOW.
YOU'RE NOT JUST ANGERING THE SHADOW PROCLAMATION—YOU'RE ALIENATING THE OGRONS, SONTARANS, AND DRACONIANS, AS WELL.

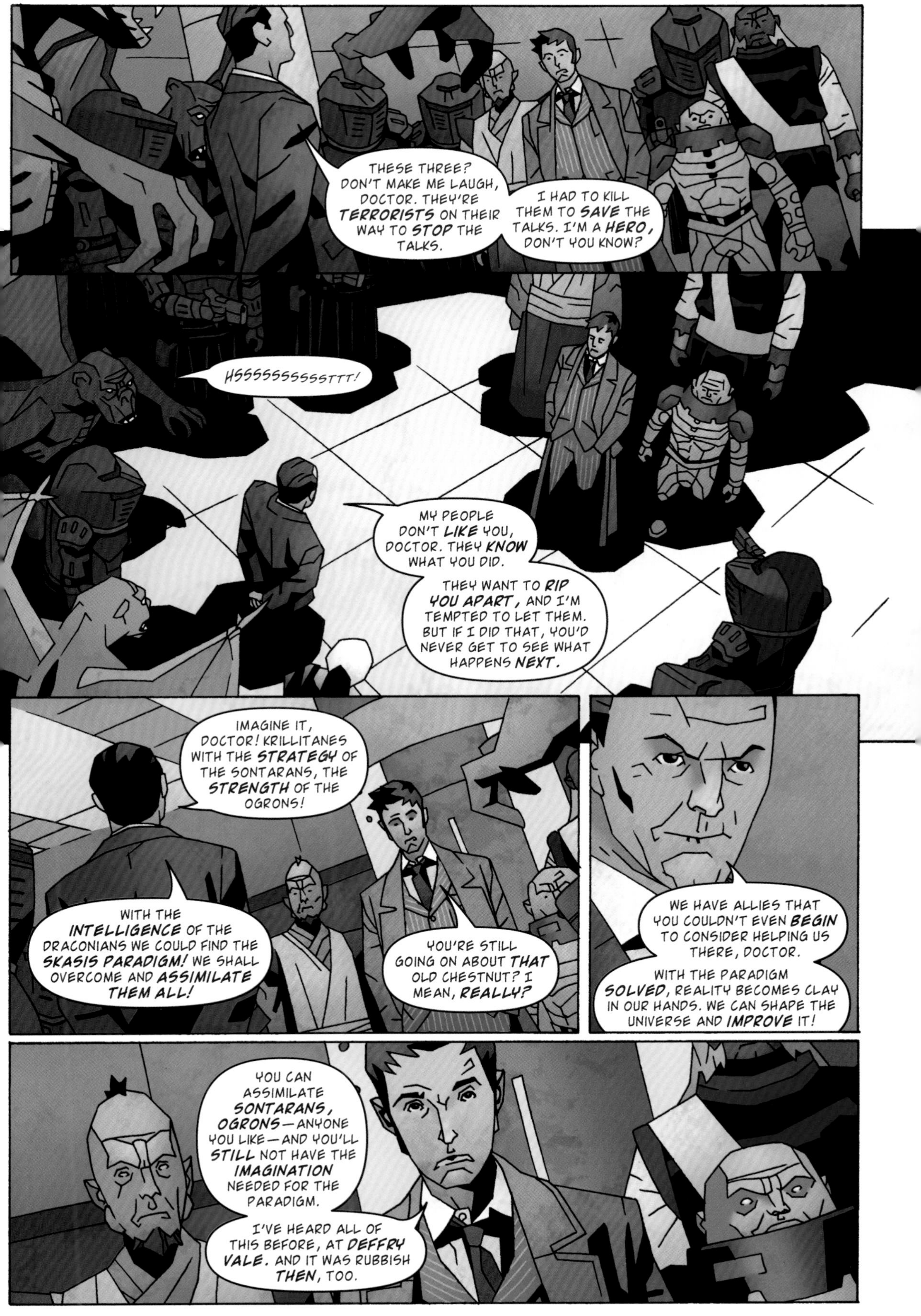
THESE THREE? DON'T MAKE ME LAUGH, DOCTOR. THEY'RE TERRORISTS ON THEIR WAY TO STOP THE TALKS.
I HAD TO KILL THEM TO SAVE THE TALKS. I'M A HERO, DON'T YOU KNOW?
HSSSSSSSSSSTTT!
MY PEOPLE DON'T LIKE YOU, DOCTOR. THEY KNOW WHAT YOU DID.
THEY WANT TO RIP YOU APART, AND I'M TEMPTED TO LET THEM. BUT IF I DID THAT, YOU'D NEVER GET TO SEE WHAT HAPPENS NEXT.
IMAGINE IT, DOCTOR! KRILLITANES WITH THE STRATEGY OF THE SONTARANS, THE STRENGTH OF THE OGRONS!
WITH THE INTELLIGENCE OF THE DRACONIANS WE COULD FIND THE SKASIS PARADIGM! WE SHALL OVERCOME AND ASSIMILATE THEM ALL!
YOU'RE STILL GOING ON ABOUT THAT OLD CHESTNUT? I MEAN, REALLY?
WE HAVE ALLIES THAT YOU COULDN'T EVEN BEGIN TO CONSIDER HELPING US THERE, DOCTOR.
WITH THE PARADIGM SOLVED, REALITY BECOMES CLAY IN OUR HANDS. WE CAN SHAPE THE UNIVERSE AND IMPROVE IT!
YOU CAN ASSIMILATE SONTARANS, OGRONS—ANYONE YOU LIKE—AND YOU'LL STILL NOT HAVE THE IMAGINATION NEEDED FOR THE PARADIGM.
I'VE HEARD ALL OF THIS BEFORE, AT DEFFRY VALE. AND IT WAS RUBBISH THEN, TOO.

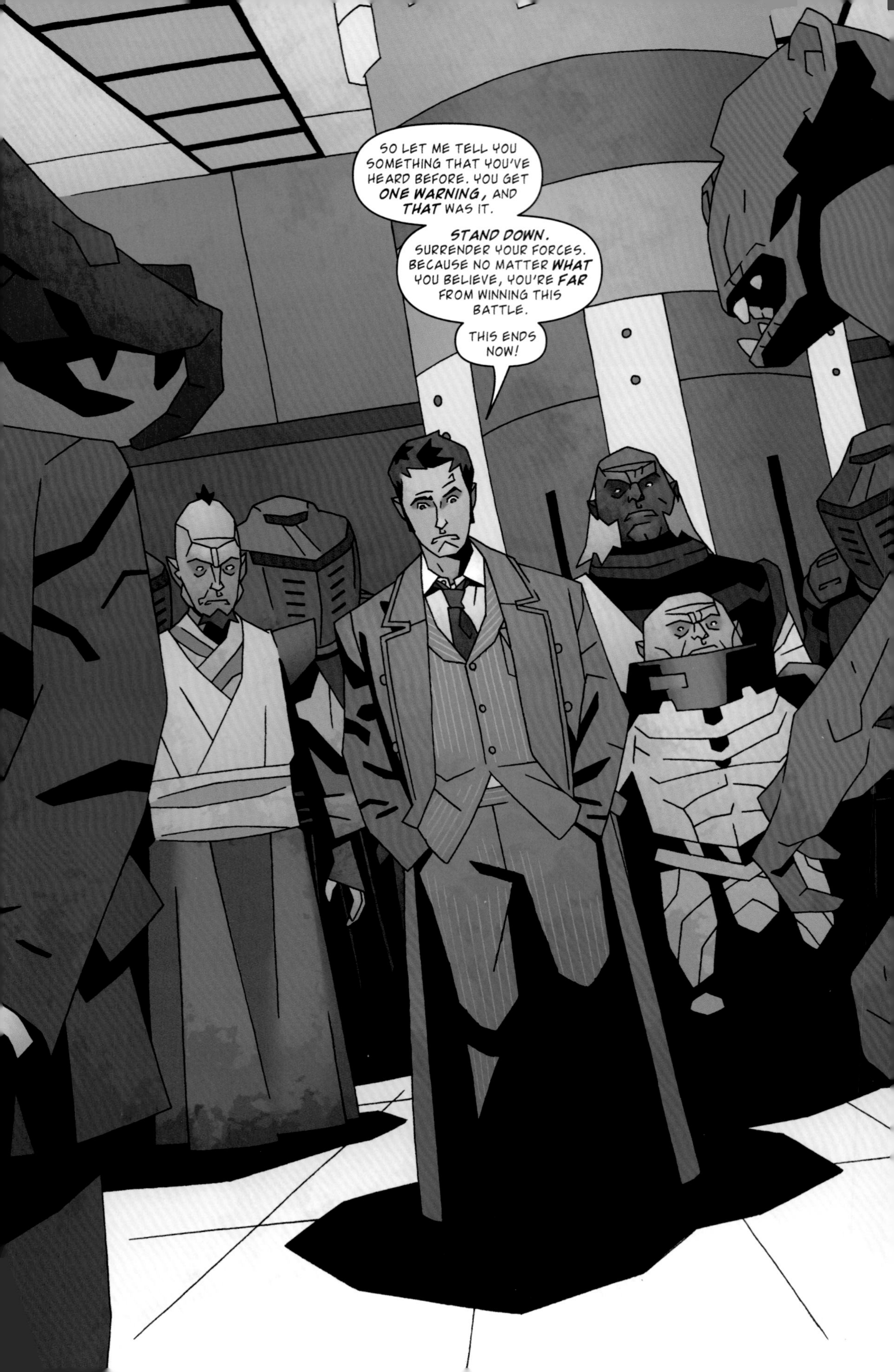
SO LET ME TELL YOU SOMETHING THAT YOU'VE HEARD BEFORE. YOU GET ONE WARNING, AND THAT WAS IT.
STAND DOWN. SURRENDER YOUR FORCES. BECAUSE NO MATTER WHAT YOU BELIEVE, YOU'RE FAR FROM WINNING THIS BATTLE.
THIS ENDS NOW!

MR. FINCH'S KRILLITANE
BATTLECRUISER.

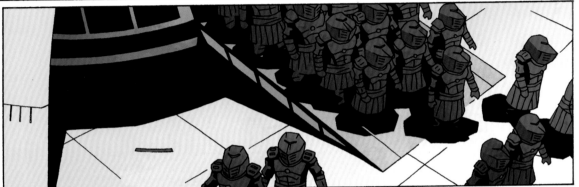

BOH! SHO!

**FOH! DOH!
NOH!**

KOH.

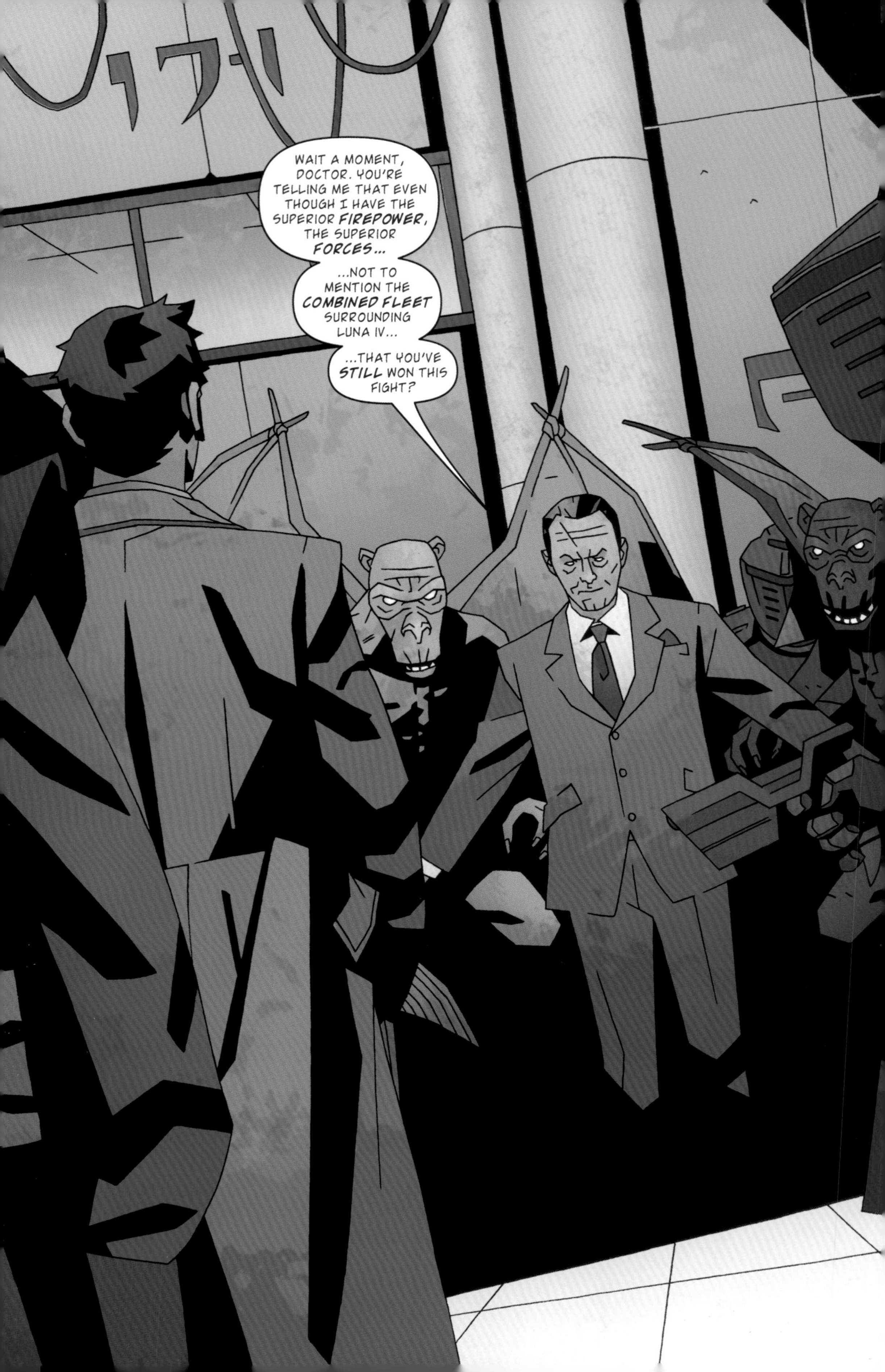
WAIT A MOMENT, DOCTOR. YOU'RE TELLING ME THAT EVEN THOUGH I HAVE THE SUPERIOR FIREPOWER, THE SUPERIOR FORCES...
...NOT TO MENTION THE COMBINED FLEET SURROUNDING LUNA IV...
...THAT YOU'VE STILL WON THIS FIGHT?

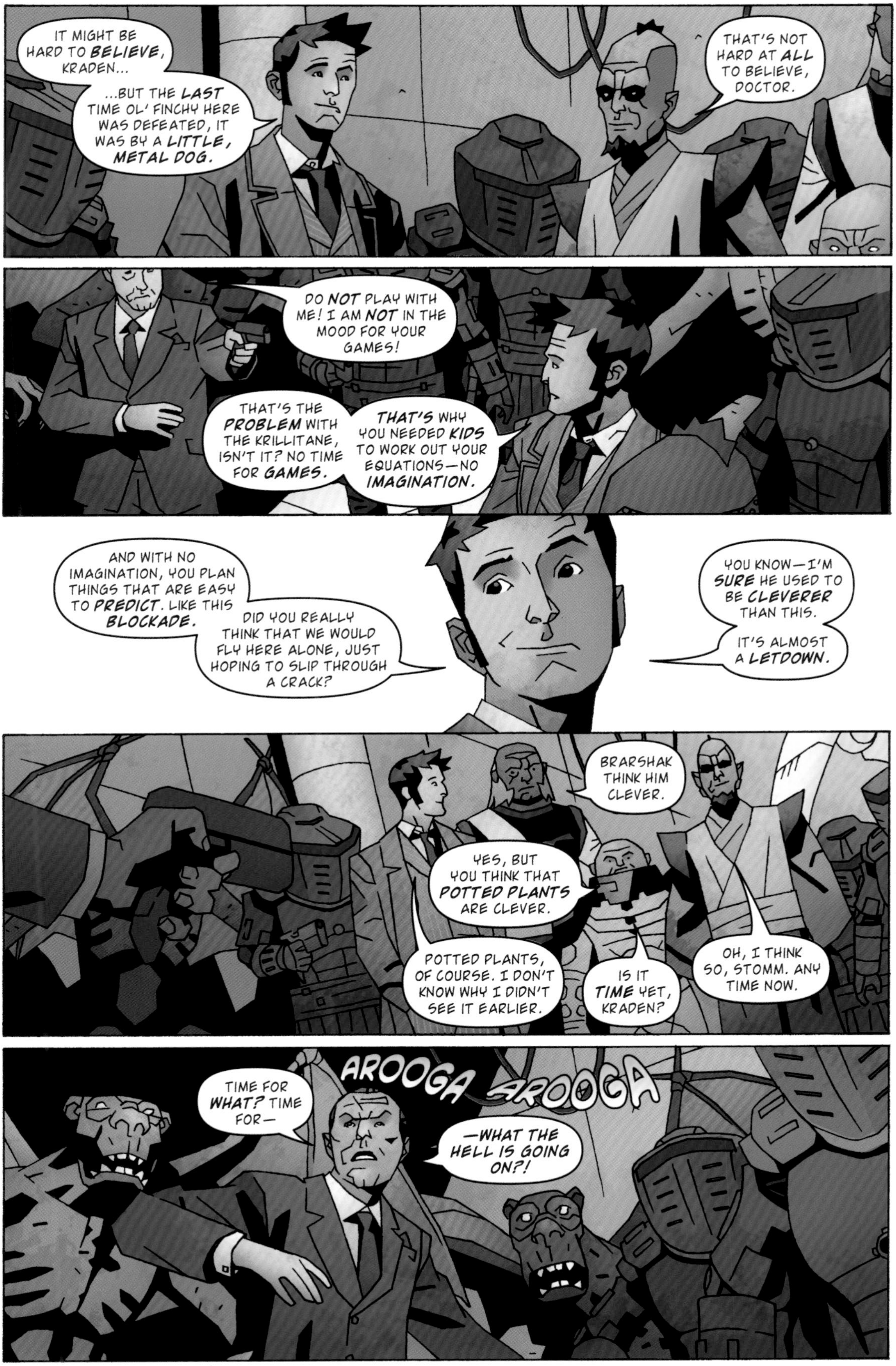

IT MIGHT BE HARD TO BELIEVE, KRADEN...
...BUT THE LAST TIME OL' FINCHY HERE WAS DEFEATED, IT WAS BY A LITTLE, METAL DOG.
THAT'S NOT HARD AT ALL TO BELIEVE, DOCTOR.
DO NOT PLAY WITH ME! I AM NOT IN THE MOOD FOR YOUR GAMES!
THAT'S THE PROBLEM WITH THE KRILLITANE, ISN'T IT? NO TIME FOR GAMES.
THAT'S WHY YOU NEEDED KIDS TO WORK OUT YOUR EQUATIONS—NO IMAGINATION.
AND WITH NO IMAGINATION, YOU PLAN THINGS THAT ARE EASY TO PREDICT. LIKE THIS BLOCKADE.
DID YOU REALLY THINK THAT WE WOULD FLY HERE ALONE, JUST HOPING TO SLIP THROUGH A CRACK?
YOU KNOW—I'M SURE HE USED TO BE CLEVERER THAN THIS.
IT'S ALMOST A LETDOWN.
BRARSHAK THINK HIM CLEVER.
YES, BUT YOU THINK THAT POTTED PLANTS ARE CLEVER.
POTTED PLANTS, OF COURSE. I DON'T KNOW WHY I DIDN'T SEE IT EARLIER.
IS IT TIME YET, KRADEN?
OH, I THINK SO, STOMM. ANY TIME NOW.
AROOGA AROOGA
TIME FOR WHAT? TIME FOR—
—WHAT THE HELL IS GOING ON?!

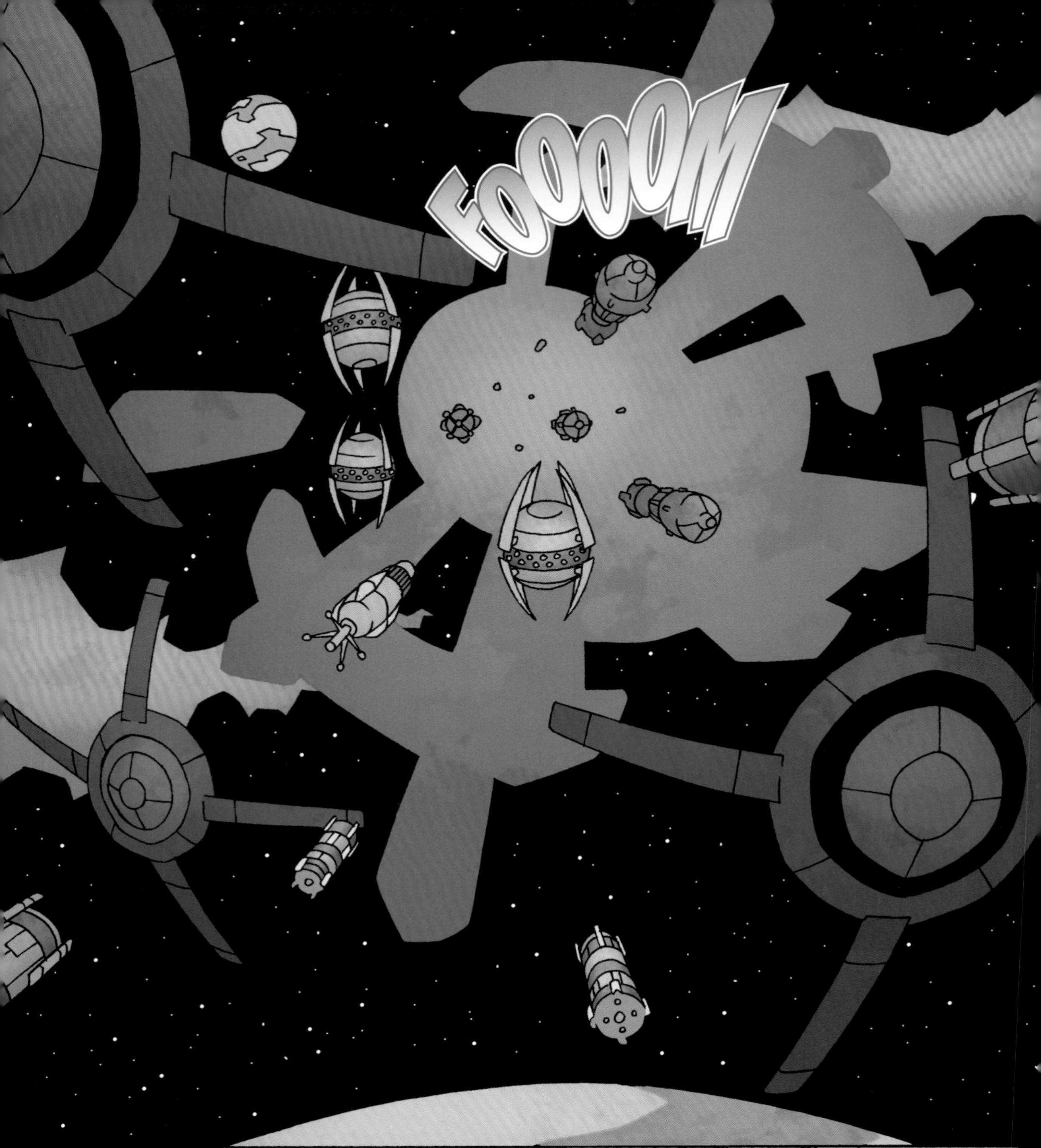
FOOOOM

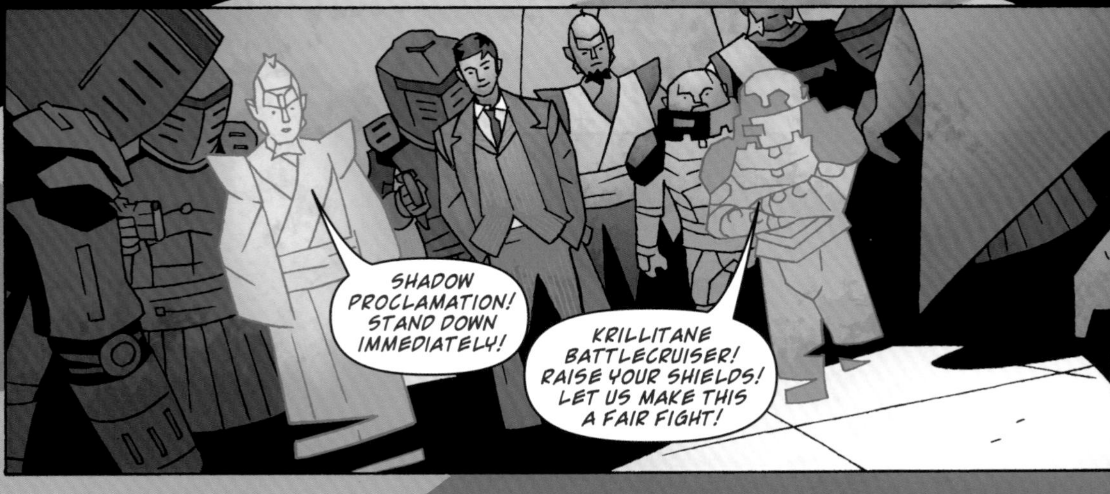
SHADOW PROCLAMATION! STAND DOWN IMMEDIATELY!
KRILLITANE BATTLECRUISER! RAISE YOUR SHIELDS! LET US MAKE THIS A FAIR FIGHT!

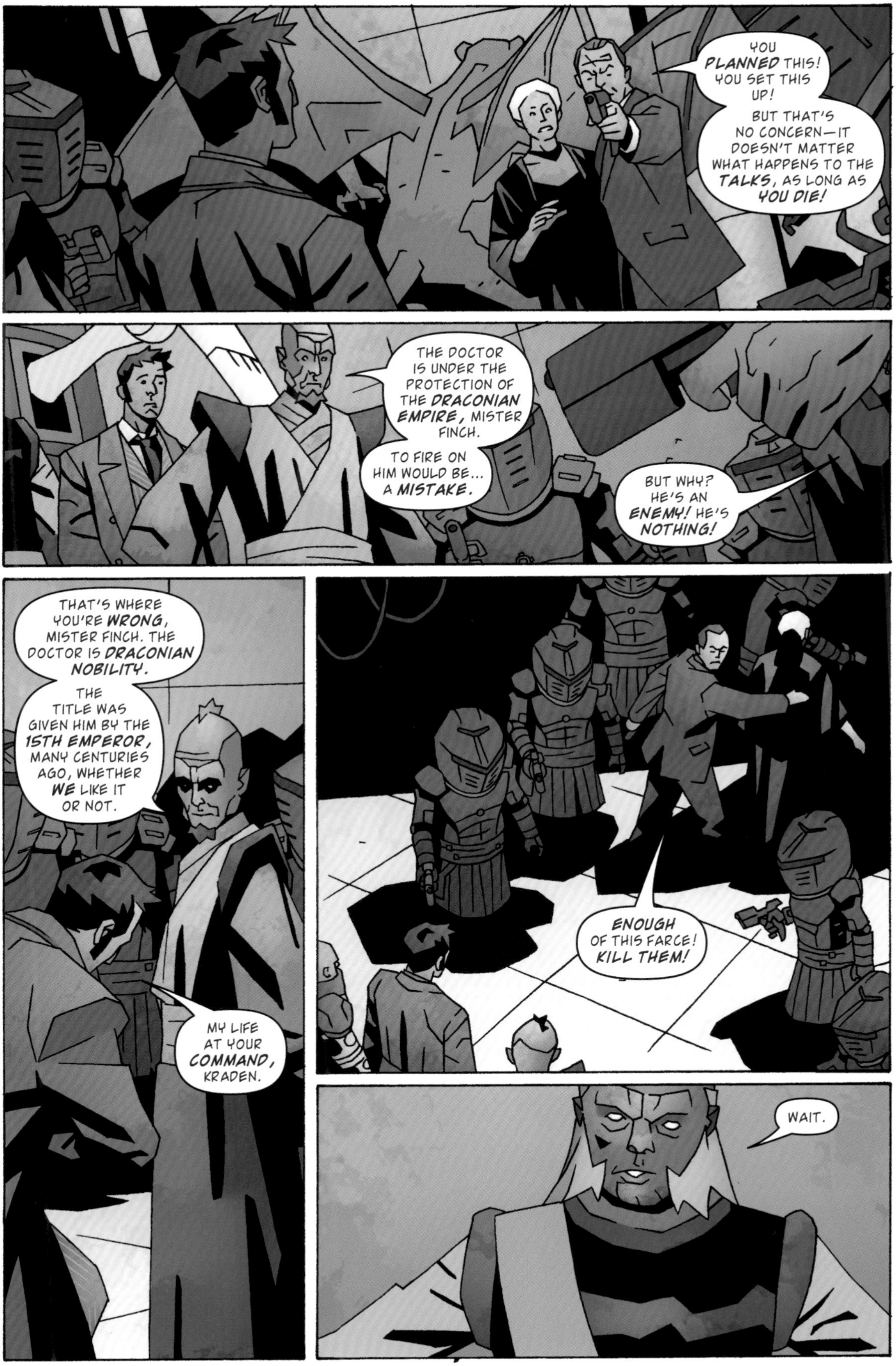
YOU PLANNED THIS! YOU SET THIS UP!
BUT THAT'S NO CONCERN—IT DOESN'T MATTER WHAT HAPPENS TO THE TALKS, AS LONG AS YOU DIE!
THE DOCTOR IS UNDER THE PROTECTION OF THE DRACONIAN EMPIRE, MISTER FINCH.
TO FIRE ON HIM WOULD BE... A MISTAKE.
BUT WHY? HE'S AN ENEMY! HE'S NOTHING!
THAT'S WHERE YOU'RE WRONG, MISTER FINCH. THE DOCTOR IS DRACONIAN NOBILITY.
THE TITLE WAS GIVEN HIM BY THE 15TH EMPEROR, MANY CENTURIES AGO, WHETHER WE LIKE IT OR NOT.
MY LIFE AT YOUR COMMAND, KRADEN.
ENOUGH OF THIS FARCE! KILL THEM!
WAIT.

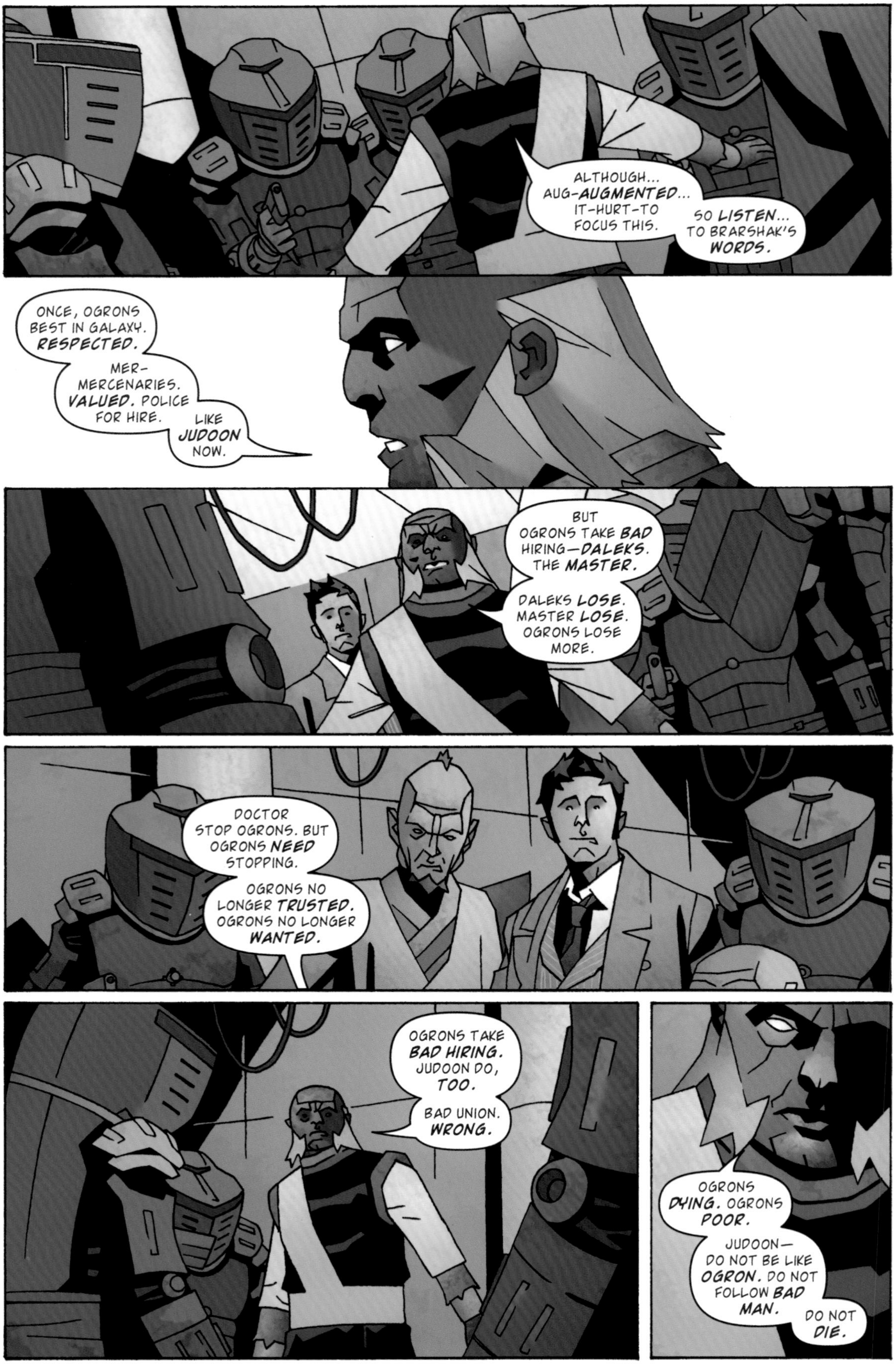
ALTHOUGH... AUG-AUGMENTED... IT-HURT-TO FOCUS THIS.
SO LISTEN... TO BRARSHAK'S WORDS.
ONCE, OGRONS BEST IN GALAXY. RESPECTED.
MER- MERCENARIES. VALUED. POLICE FOR HIRE.
LIKE JUDOON NOW.
BUT OGRONS TAKE BAD HIRING—DALEKS. THE MASTER.
DALEKS LOSE. MASTER LOSE. OGRONS LOSE MORE.
DOCTOR STOP OGRONS. BUT OGRONS NEED STOPPING.
OGRONS NO LONGER TRUSTED. OGRONS NO LONGER WANTED.
OGRONS TAKE BAD HIRING. JUDOON DO, TOO.
BAD UNION. WRONG.
OGRONS DYING. OGRONS POOR.
JUDOON— DO NOT BE LIKE OGRON. DO NOT FOLLOW BAD MAN.
DO NOT DIE.

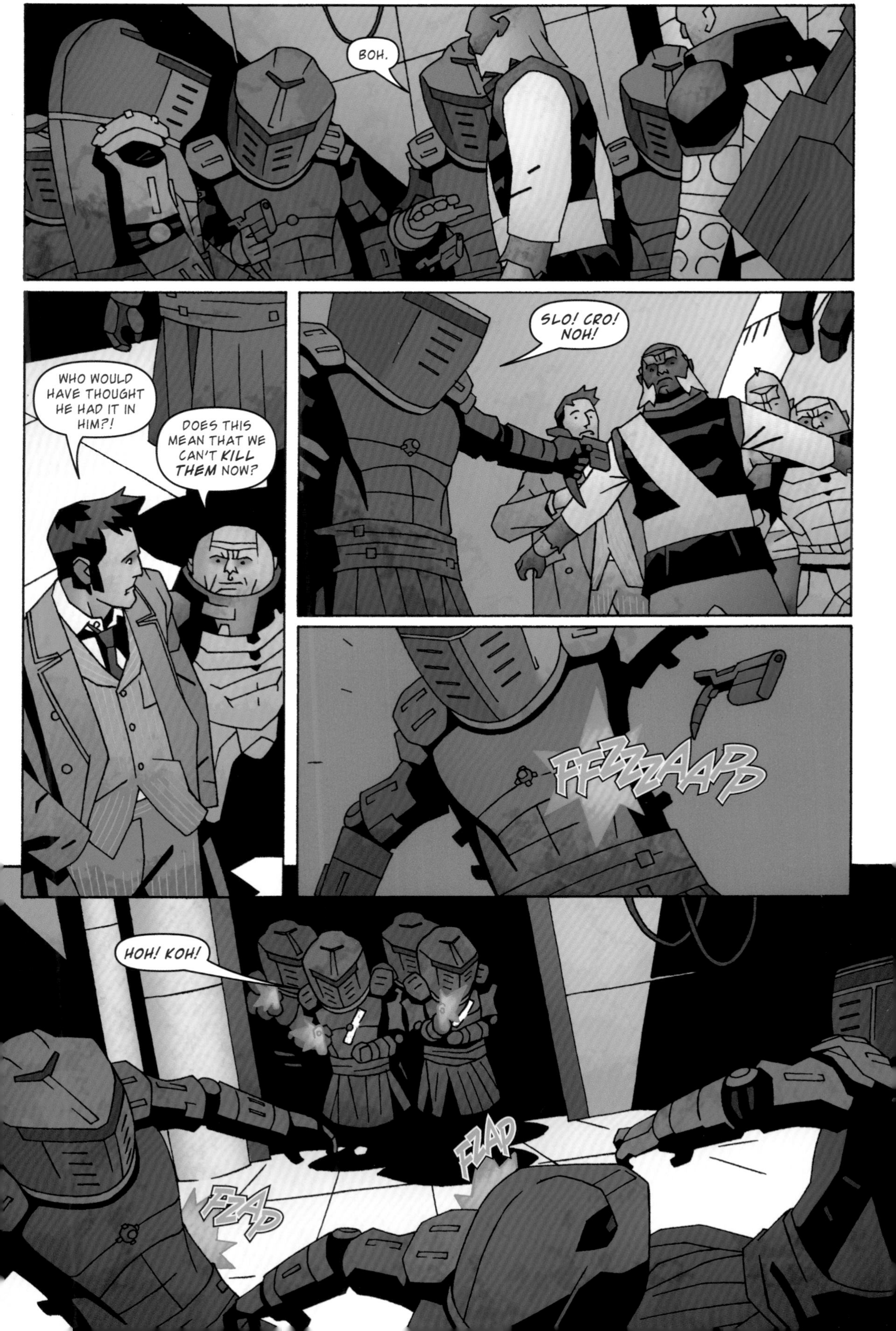
BOH.
WHO WOULD HAVE THOUGHT HE HAD IT IN HIM?!
DOES THIS MEAN THAT WE CAN'T **KILL THEM** NOW?
SLO! CRO! NOH!
FFZZZAAPP
HOH! KOH!
FZAP
FZAP

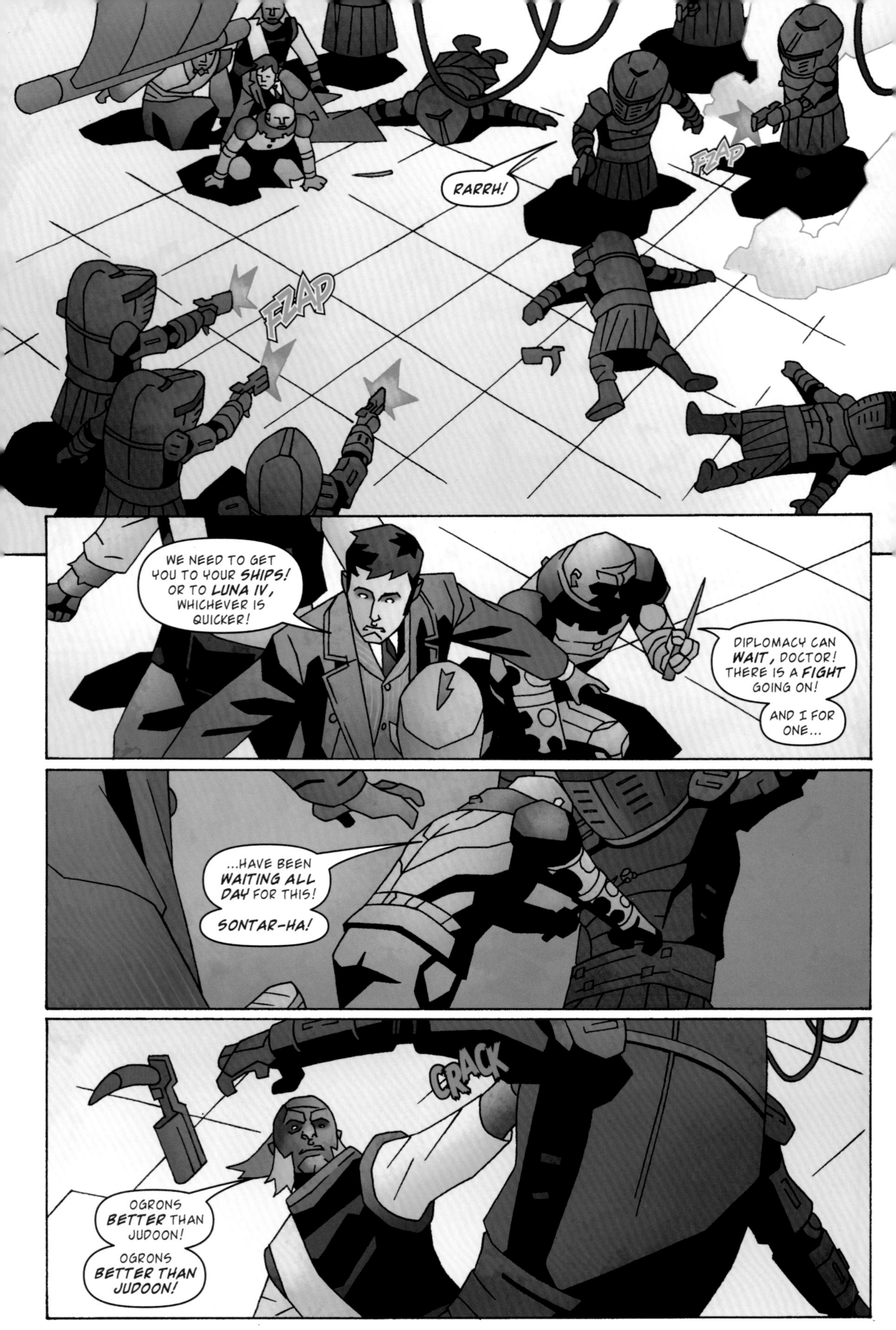
RARRH!
FZAP
FZAP
WE NEED TO GET YOU TO YOUR SHIPS! OR TO LUNA IV, WHICHEVER IS QUICKER!
DIPLOMACY CAN WAIT, DOCTOR! THERE IS A FIGHT GOING ON!
AND I FOR ONE...
...HAVE BEEN WAITING ALL DAY FOR THIS!
SONTAR-HA!
CRACK
OGRONS BETTER THAN JUDOON!
OGRONS BETTER THAN JUDOON!

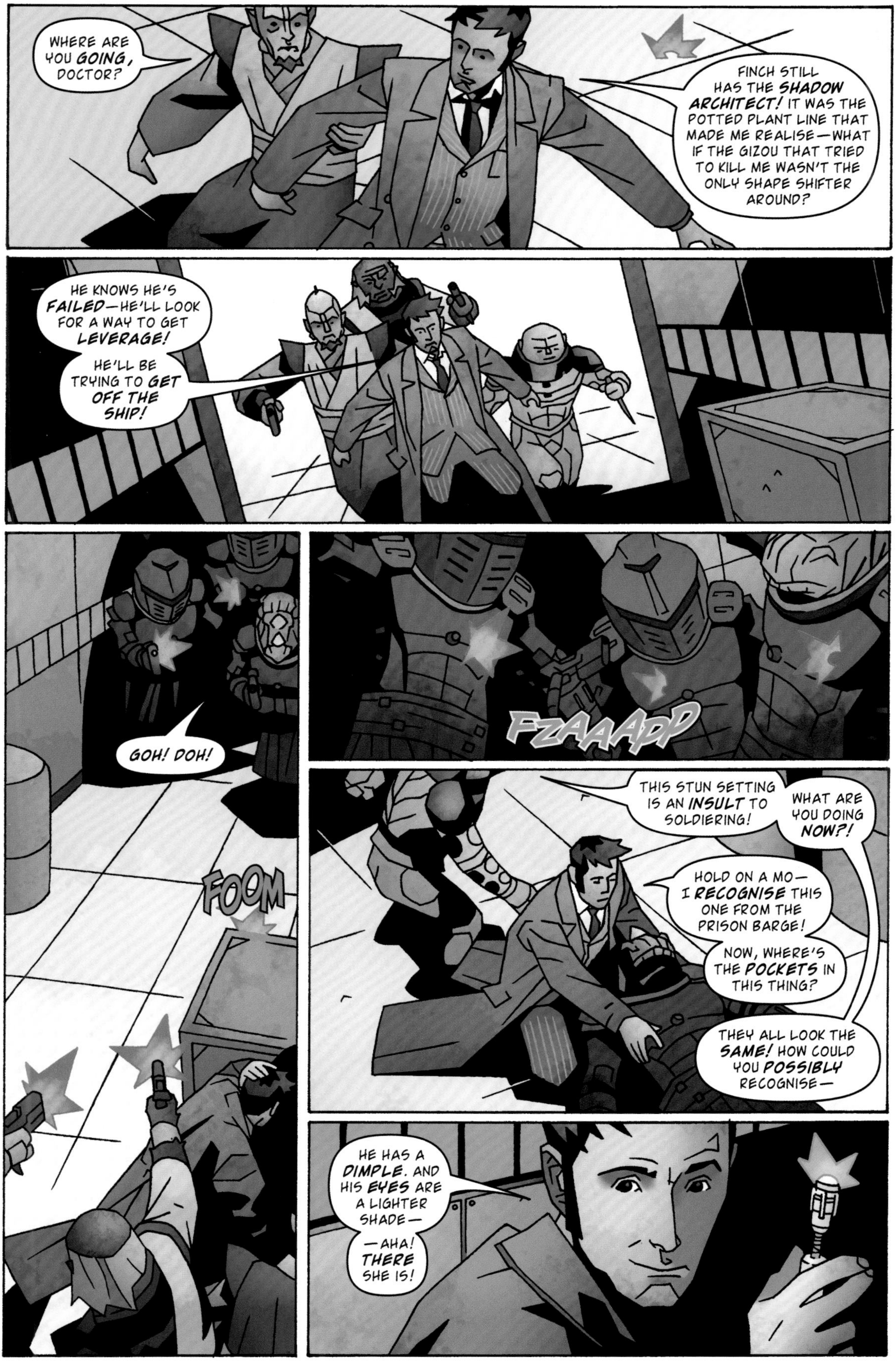
WHERE ARE YOU GOING, DOCTOR?
FINCH STILL HAS THE SHADOW ARCHITECT! IT WAS THE POTTED PLANT LINE THAT MADE ME REALISE—WHAT IF THE GIZOU THAT TRIED TO KILL ME WASN'T THE ONLY SHAPE SHIFTER AROUND?
HE KNOWS HE'S FAILED—HE'LL LOOK FOR A WAY TO GET LEVERAGE!
HE'LL BE TRYING TO GET OFF THE SHIP!
GOH! DOH!
FOOM
FZAAAADP
THIS STUN SETTING IS AN INSULT TO SOLDIERING!
WHAT ARE YOU DOING NOW?!
HOLD ON A MO—I RECOGNISE THIS ONE FROM THE PRISON BARGE!
NOW, WHERE'S THE POCKETS IN THIS THING?
THEY ALL LOOK THE SAME! HOW COULD YOU POSSIBLY RECOGNISE—
HE HAS A DIMPLE. AND HIS EYES ARE A LIGHTER SHADE—
—AHA! THERE SHE IS!

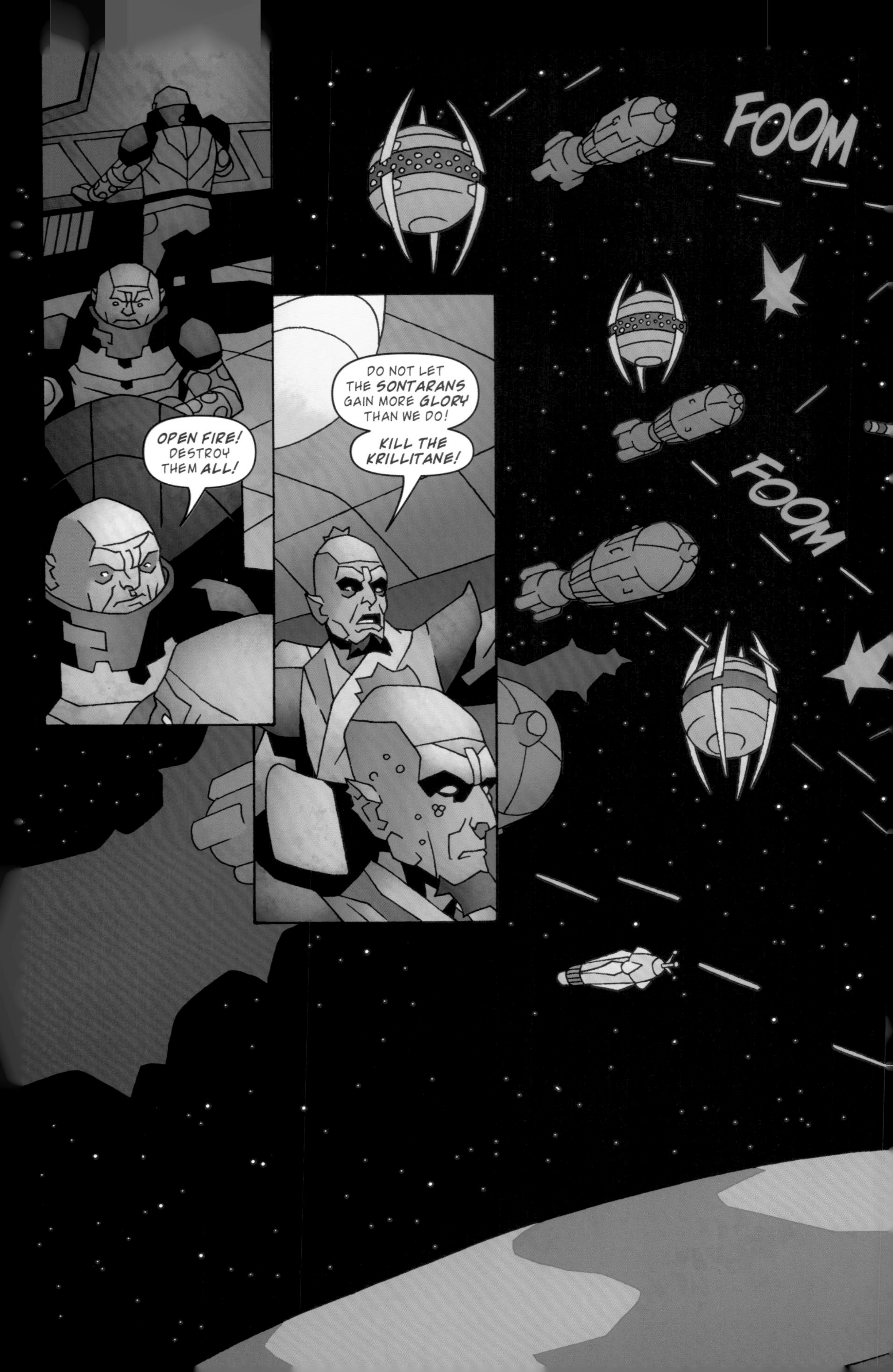

OPEN FIRE! DESTROY THEM ALL!
DO NOT LET THE SONTARANS GAIN MORE GLORY THAN WE DO!
KILL THE KRILLITANE!
FOOM
FOOM

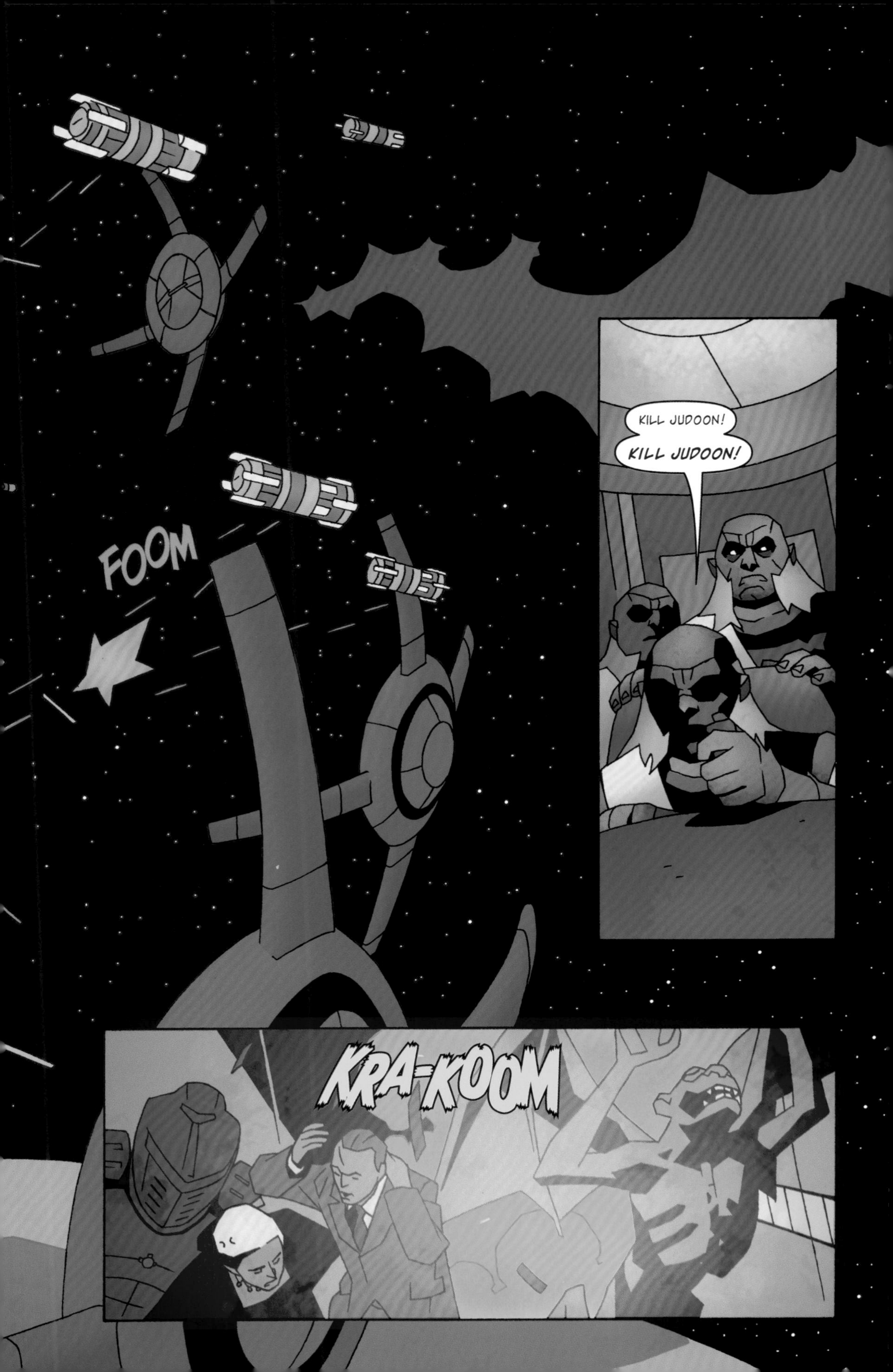
FOOM
KILL JUDOON!
KILL JUDOON!
KRA-KOOM

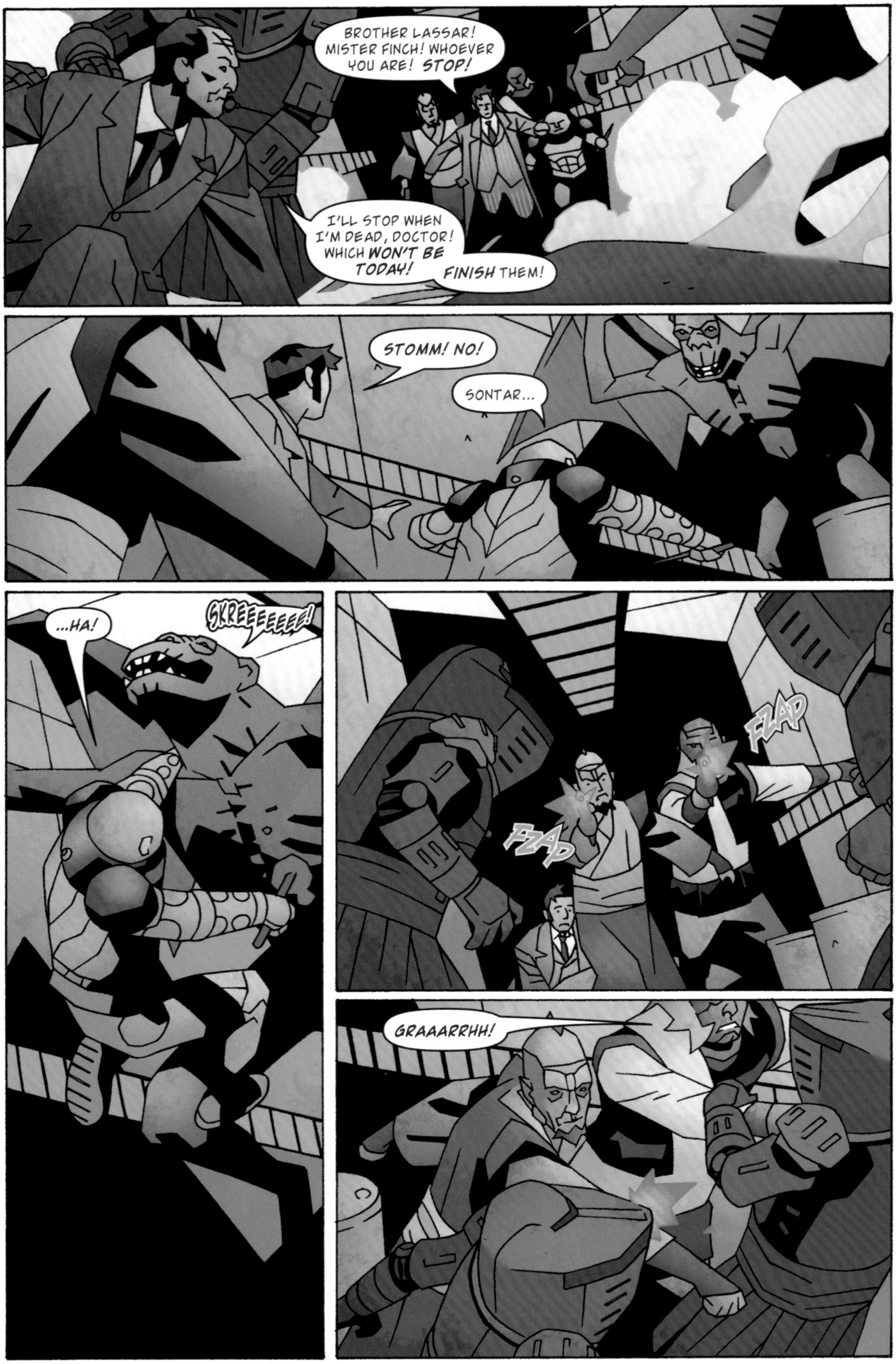
BROTHER LASSAR! MISTER FINCH! WHOEVER YOU ARE! STOP!
I'LL STOP WHEN I'M DEAD, DOCTOR! WHICH WON'T BE TODAY!
FINISH THEM!
STOMM! NO!
SONTAR...
...HA!
SKREEEEEEEE!
FZAP
FZAP
GRAAARRHH!

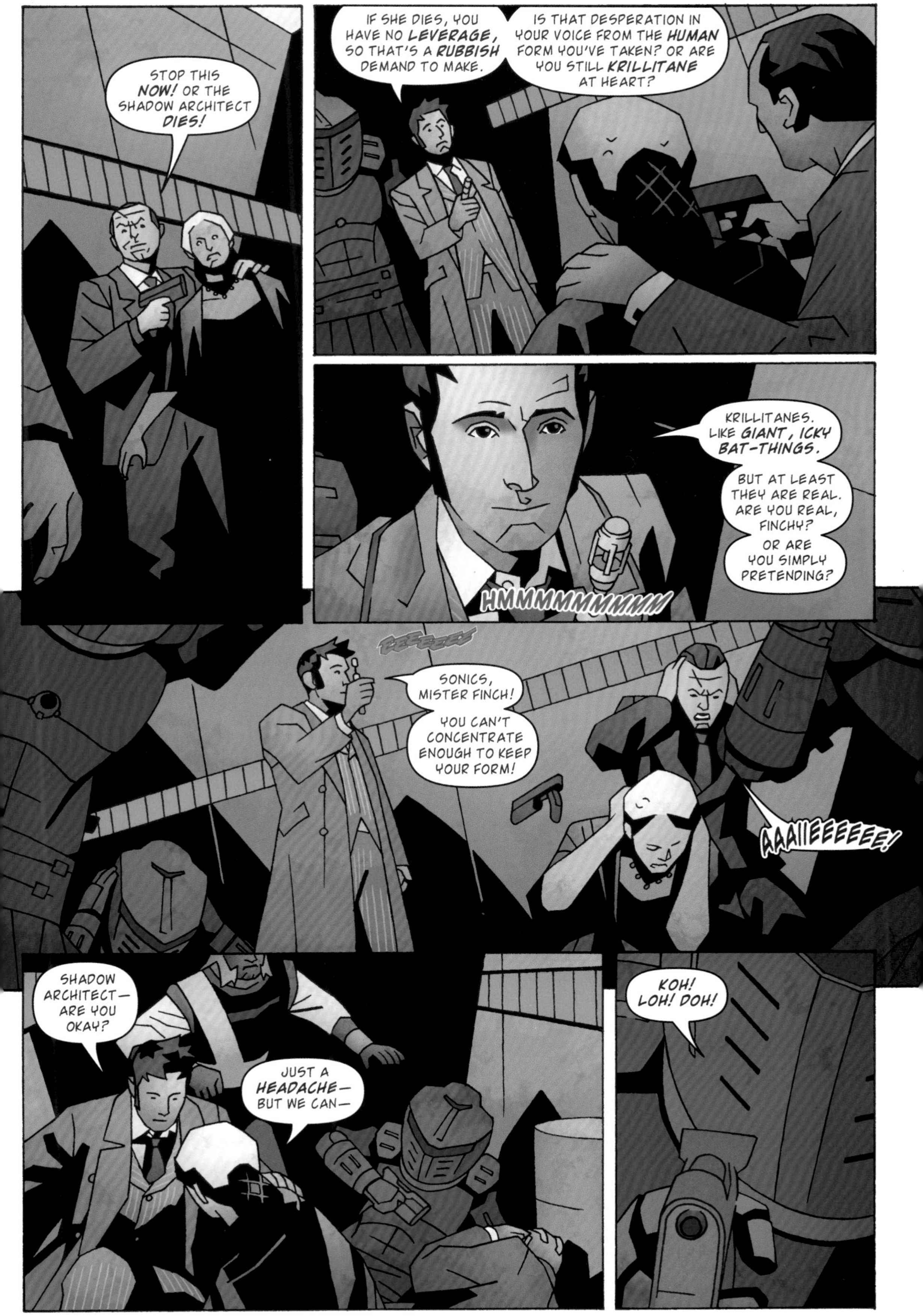
STOP THIS NOW! OR THE SHADOW ARCHITECT DIES!
IF SHE DIES, YOU HAVE NO LEVERAGE, SO THAT'S A RUBBISH DEMAND TO MAKE.
IS THAT DESPERATION IN YOUR VOICE FROM THE HUMAN FORM YOU'VE TAKEN? OR ARE YOU STILL KRILLITANE AT HEART?
KRILLITANES. LIKE GIANT, ICKY BAT-THINGS.
BUT AT LEAST THEY ARE REAL. ARE YOU REAL, FINCHY?
OR ARE YOU SIMPLY PRETENDING?
HMMMMMMMMMM
SONICS, MISTER FINCH!
YOU CAN'T CONCENTRATE ENOUGH TO KEEP YOUR FORM!
AAAIIEEEEEE!
SHADOW ARCHITECT— ARE YOU OKAY?
JUST A HEADACHE— BUT WE CAN—
KOH! LOH! DOH!

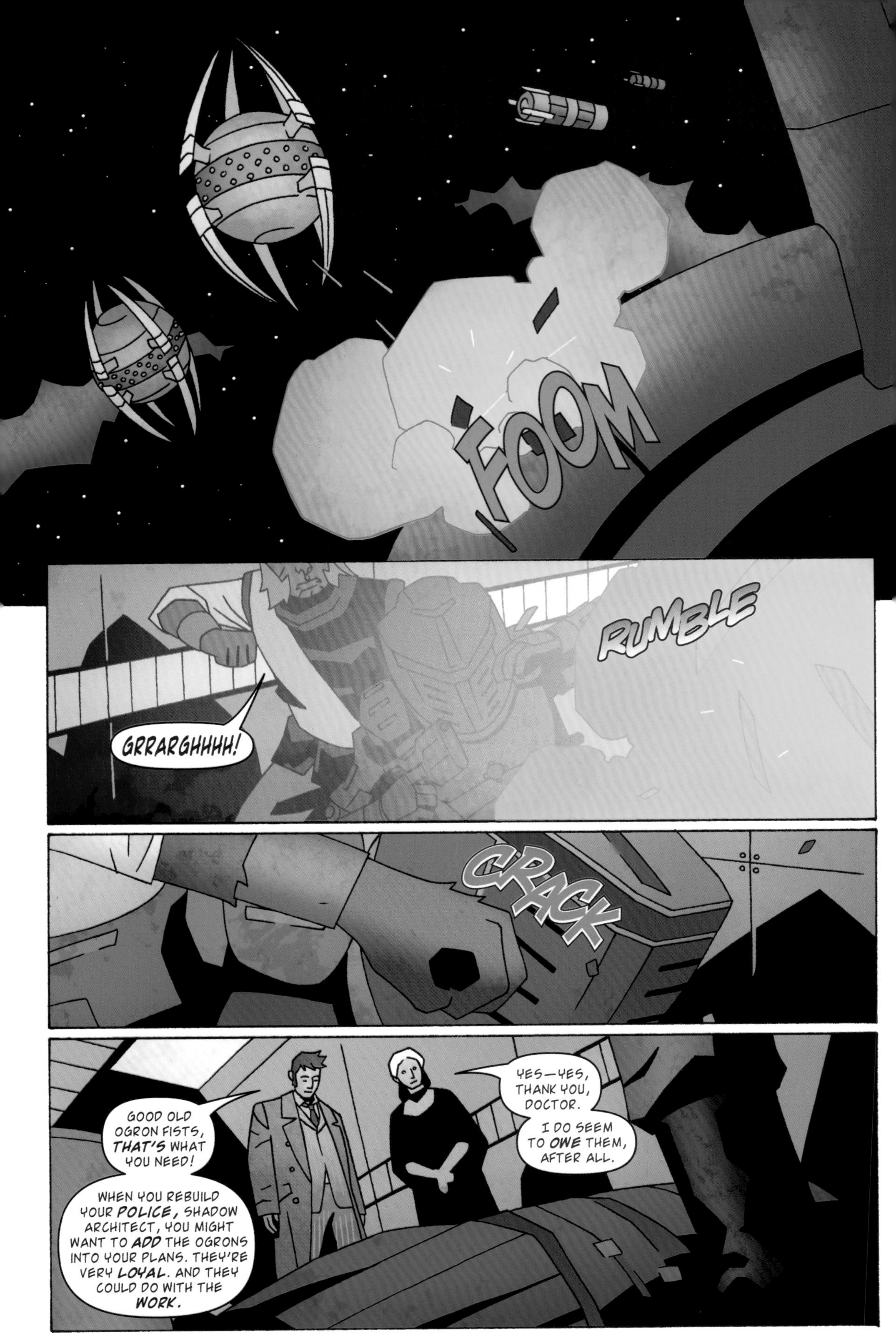
FOOM
RUMBLE
GRRARGHHHH!
CRACK
GOOD OLD OGRON FISTS, THAT'S WHAT YOU NEED!
WHEN YOU REBUILD YOUR POLICE, SHADOW ARCHITECT, YOU MIGHT WANT TO ADD THE OGRONS INTO YOUR PLANS. THEY'RE VERY LOYAL. AND THEY COULD DO WITH THE WORK.
YES—YES, THANK YOU, DOCTOR.
I DO SEEM TO OWE THEM, AFTER ALL.

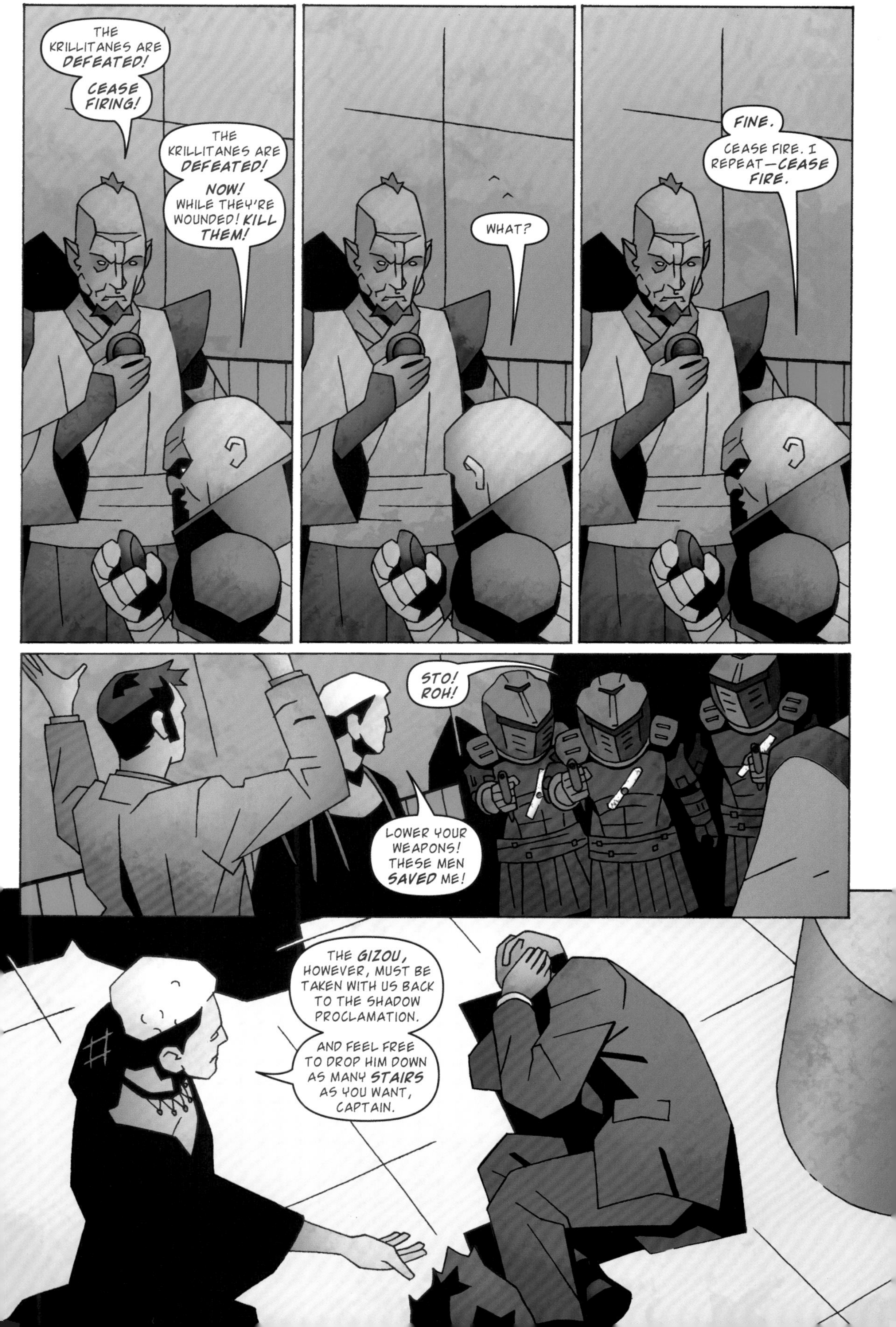
THE KRILLITANES ARE DEFEATED!
CEASE FIRING!
THE KRILLITANES ARE DEFEATED!
NOW! WHILE THEY'RE WOUNDED! KILL THEM!
WHAT?
FINE.
CEASE FIRE. I REPEAT—CEASE FIRE.
STO! ROH!
LOWER YOUR WEAPONS! THESE MEN SAVED ME!
THE GIZOU, HOWEVER, MUST BE TAKEN WITH US BACK TO THE SHADOW PROCLAMATION.
AND FEEL FREE TO DROP HIM DOWN AS MANY STAIRS AS YOU WANT, CAPTAIN.

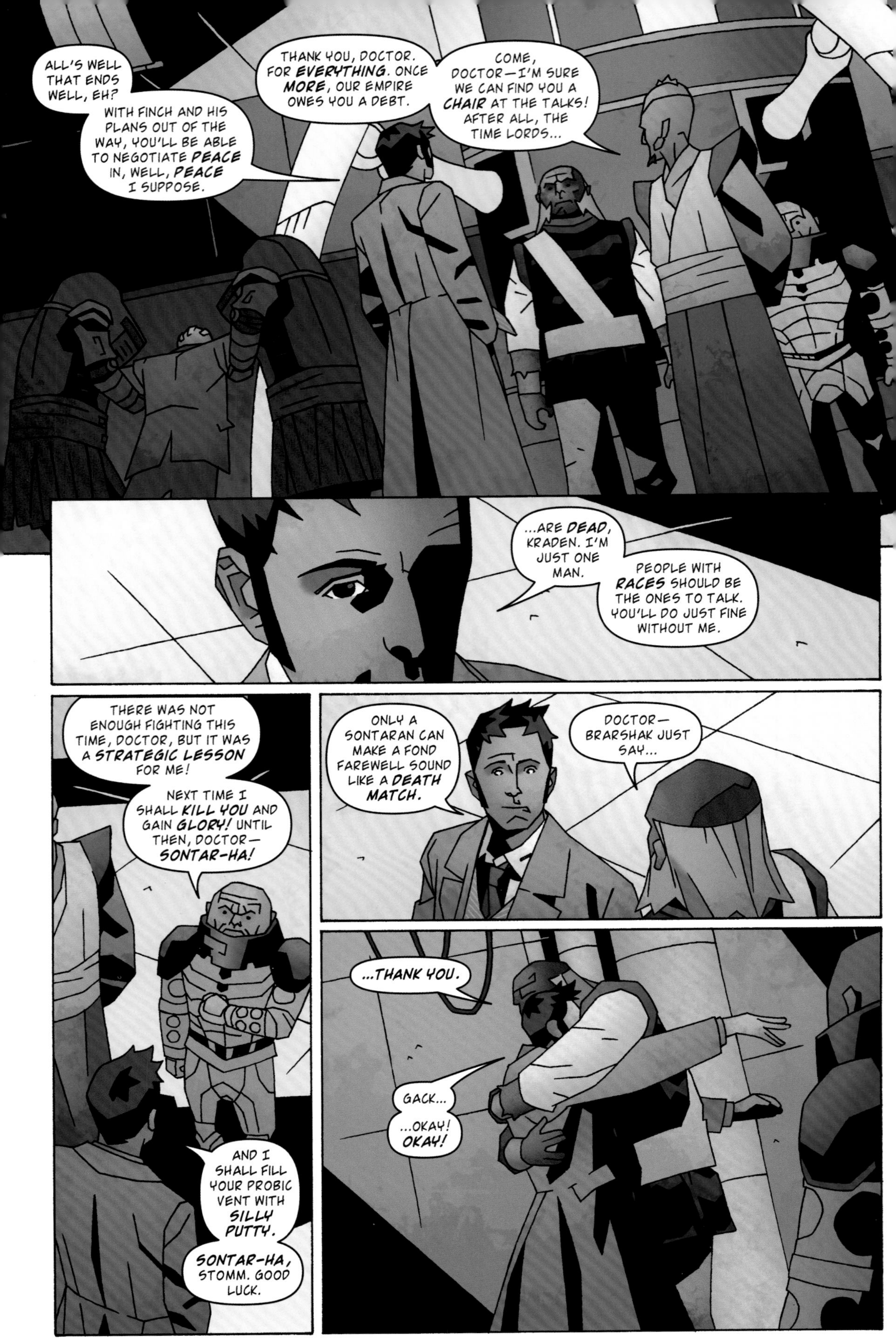
ALL'S WELL THAT ENDS WELL, EH?
WITH FINCH AND HIS PLANS OUT OF THE WAY, YOU'LL BE ABLE TO NEGOTIATE PEACE IN, WELL, PEACE I SUPPOSE.
THANK YOU, DOCTOR. FOR EVERYTHING. ONCE MORE, OUR EMPIRE OWES YOU A DEBT.
COME, DOCTOR—I'M SURE WE CAN FIND YOU A CHAIR AT THE TALKS! AFTER ALL, THE TIME LORDS...
...ARE DEAD, KRADEN. I'M JUST ONE MAN.
PEOPLE WITH RACES SHOULD BE THE ONES TO TALK. YOU'LL DO JUST FINE WITHOUT ME.
THERE WAS NOT ENOUGH FIGHTING THIS TIME, DOCTOR, BUT IT WAS A STRATEGIC LESSON FOR ME!
NEXT TIME I SHALL KILL YOU AND GAIN GLORY! UNTIL THEN, DOCTOR— SONTAR-HA!
AND I SHALL FILL YOUR PROBIC VENT WITH SILLY PUTTY.
SONTAR-HA, STOMM. GOOD LUCK.
ONLY A SONTARAN CAN MAKE A FOND FAREWELL SOUND LIKE A DEATH MATCH.
DOCTOR— BRARSHAK JUST SAY...
...THANK YOU.
GACK...
...OKAY! OKAY!

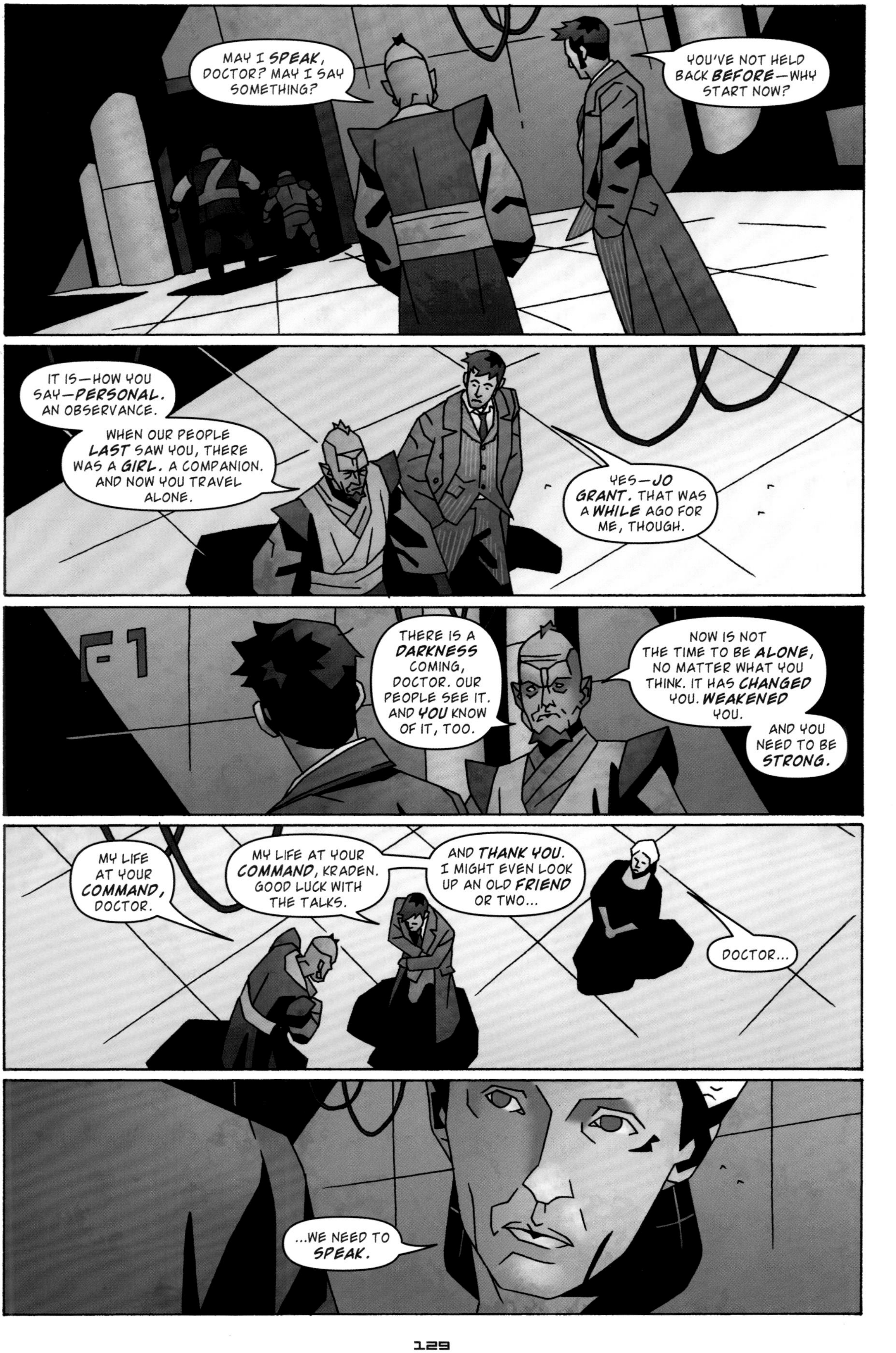
MAY I SPEAK, DOCTOR? MAY I SAY SOMETHING?
YOU'VE NOT HELD BACK BEFORE—WHY START NOW?
IT IS—HOW YOU SAY—PERSONAL. AN OBSERVANCE.
WHEN OUR PEOPLE LAST SAW YOU, THERE WAS A GIRL. A COMPANION. AND NOW YOU TRAVEL ALONE.
YES—JO GRANT. THAT WAS A WHILE AGO FOR ME, THOUGH.
F-1
THERE IS A DARKNESS COMING, DOCTOR. OUR PEOPLE SEE IT. AND YOU KNOW OF IT, TOO.
NOW IS NOT THE TIME TO BE ALONE, NO MATTER WHAT YOU THINK. IT HAS CHANGED YOU. WEAKENED YOU.
AND YOU NEED TO BE STRONG.
MY LIFE AT YOUR COMMAND, DOCTOR.
MY LIFE AT YOUR COMMAND, KRADEN. GOOD LUCK WITH THE TALKS.
AND THANK YOU. I MIGHT EVEN LOOK UP AN OLD FRIEND OR TWO...
DOCTOR...
...WE NEED TO SPEAK.

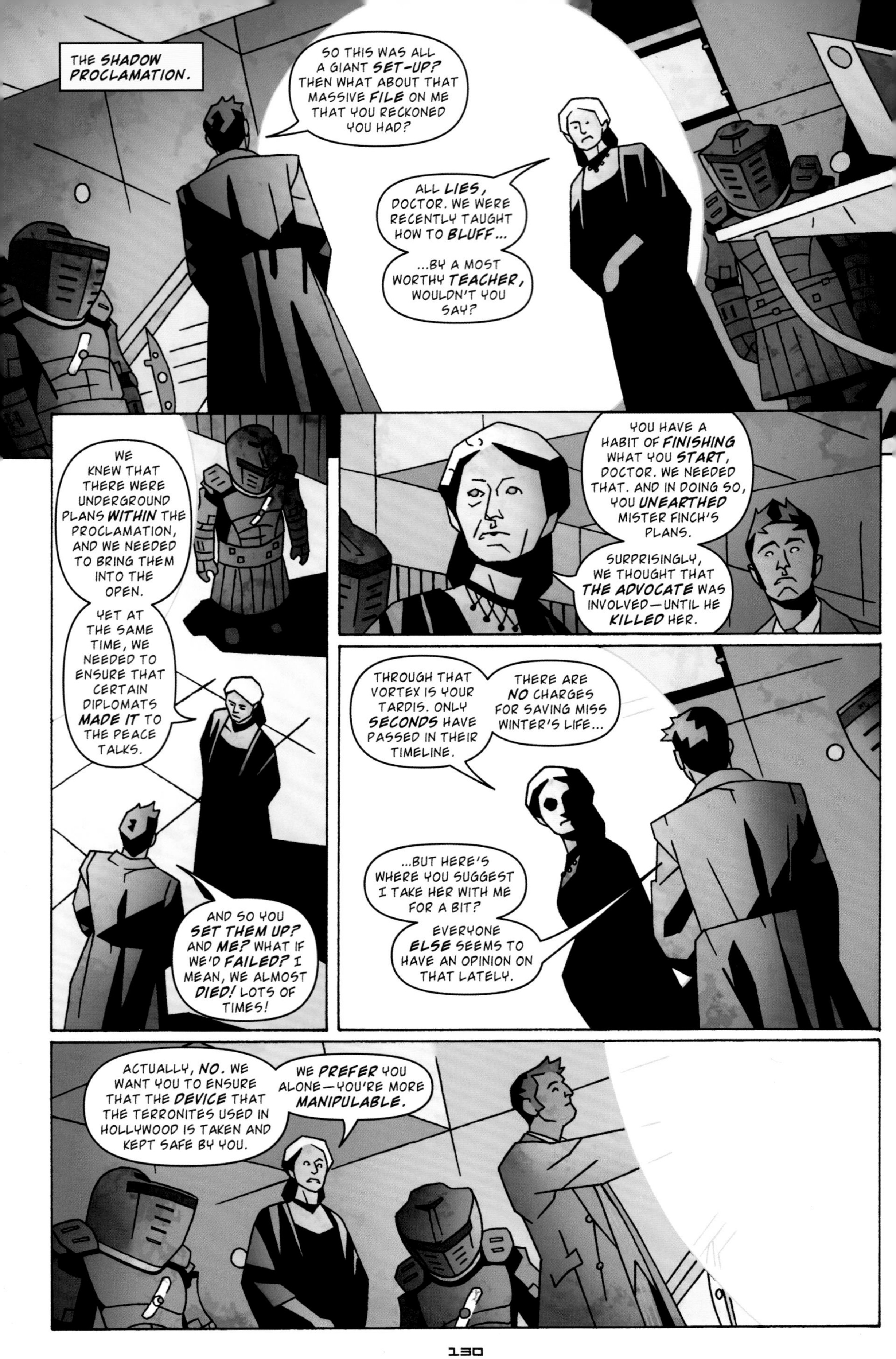
THE SHADOW PROCLAMATION.
SO THIS WAS ALL A GIANT SET-UP? THEN WHAT ABOUT THAT MASSIVE FILE ON ME THAT YOU RECKONED YOU HAD?
ALL LIES, DOCTOR. WE WERE RECENTLY TAUGHT HOW TO BLUFF...
...BY A MOST WORTHY TEACHER, WOULDN'T YOU SAY?
WE KNEW THAT THERE WERE UNDERGROUND PLANS WITHIN THE PROCLAMATION, AND WE NEEDED TO BRING THEM INTO THE OPEN.
YET AT THE SAME TIME, WE NEEDED TO ENSURE THAT CERTAIN DIPLOMATS MADE IT TO THE PEACE TALKS.
AND SO YOU SET THEM UP? AND ME? WHAT IF WE'D FAILED? I MEAN, WE ALMOST DIED! LOTS OF TIMES!
YOU HAVE A HABIT OF FINISHING WHAT YOU START, DOCTOR. WE NEEDED THAT. AND IN DOING SO, YOU UNEARTHED MISTER FINCH'S PLANS.
SURPRISINGLY, WE THOUGHT THAT THE ADVOCATE WAS INVOLVED—UNTIL HE KILLED HER.
THROUGH THAT VORTEX IS YOUR TARDIS. ONLY SECONDS HAVE PASSED IN THEIR TIMELINE.
THERE ARE NO CHARGES FOR SAVING MISS WINTER'S LIFE...
...BUT HERE'S WHERE YOU SUGGEST I TAKE HER WITH ME FOR A BIT?
EVERYONE ELSE SEEMS TO HAVE AN OPINION ON THAT LATELY.
ACTUALLY, NO. WE WANT YOU TO ENSURE THAT THE DEVICE THAT THE TERRONITES USED IN HOLLYWOOD IS TAKEN AND KEPT SAFE BY YOU.
WE PREFER YOU ALONE—YOU'RE MORE MANIPULABLE.

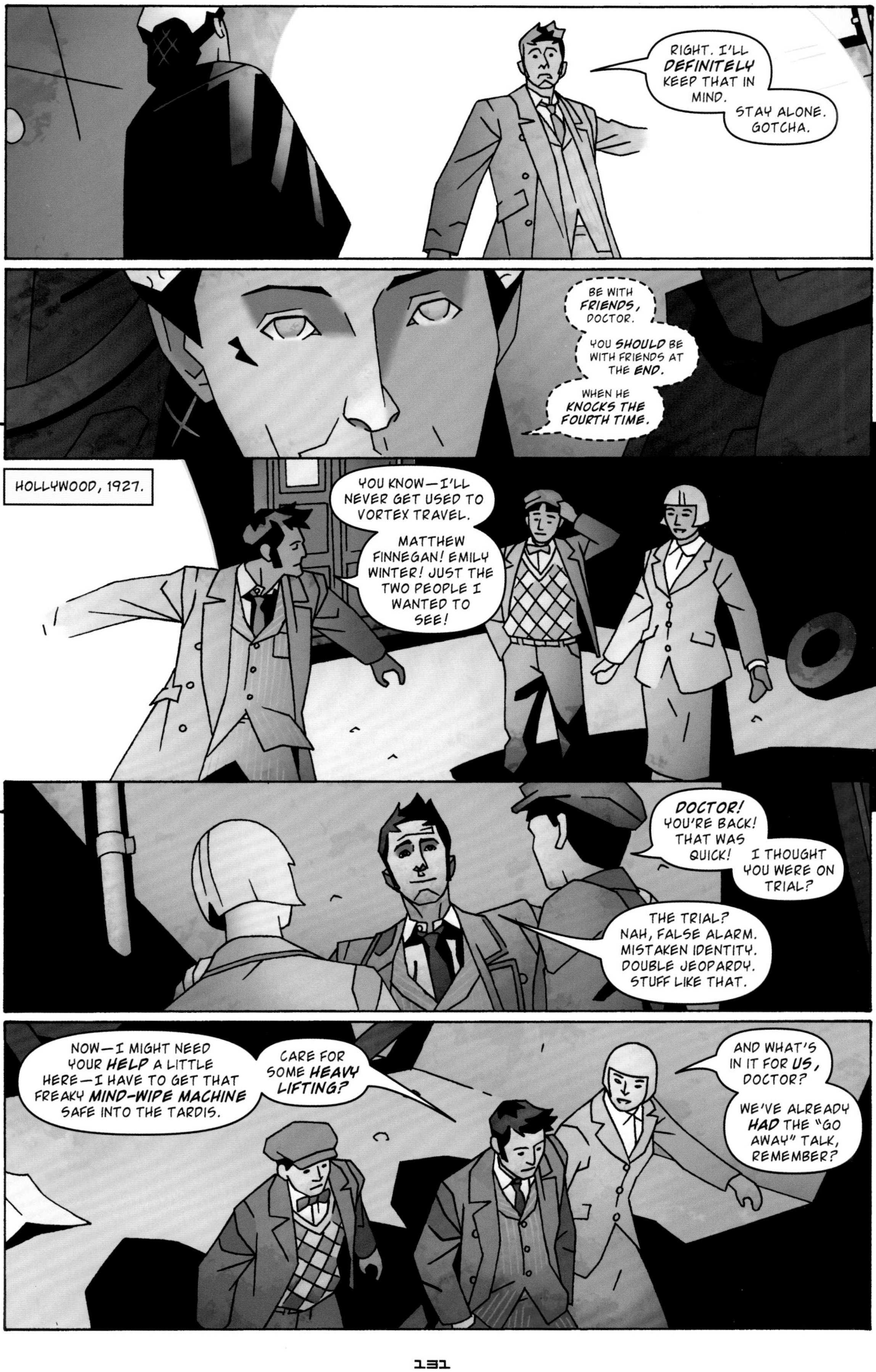
RIGHT. I'LL DEFINITELY KEEP THAT IN MIND.
STAY ALONE. GOTCHA.
BE WITH FRIENDS, DOCTOR.
YOU SHOULD BE WITH FRIENDS AT THE END.
WHEN HE KNOCKS THE FOURTH TIME.
HOLLYWOOD, 1927.
YOU KNOW—I'LL NEVER GET USED TO VORTEX TRAVEL.
MATTHEW FINNEGAN! EMILY WINTER! JUST THE TWO PEOPLE I WANTED TO SEE!
DOCTOR! YOU'RE BACK! THAT WAS QUICK!
I THOUGHT YOU WERE ON TRIAL?
THE TRIAL? NAH, FALSE ALARM. MISTAKEN IDENTITY. DOUBLE JEOPARDY. STUFF LIKE THAT.
NOW—I MIGHT NEED YOUR HELP A LITTLE HERE—I HAVE TO GET THAT FREAKY MIND-WIPE MACHINE SAFE INTO THE TARDIS.
CARE FOR SOME HEAVY LIFTING?
AND WHAT'S IN IT FOR US, DOCTOR?
WE'VE ALREADY HAD THE "GO AWAY" TALK, REMEMBER?

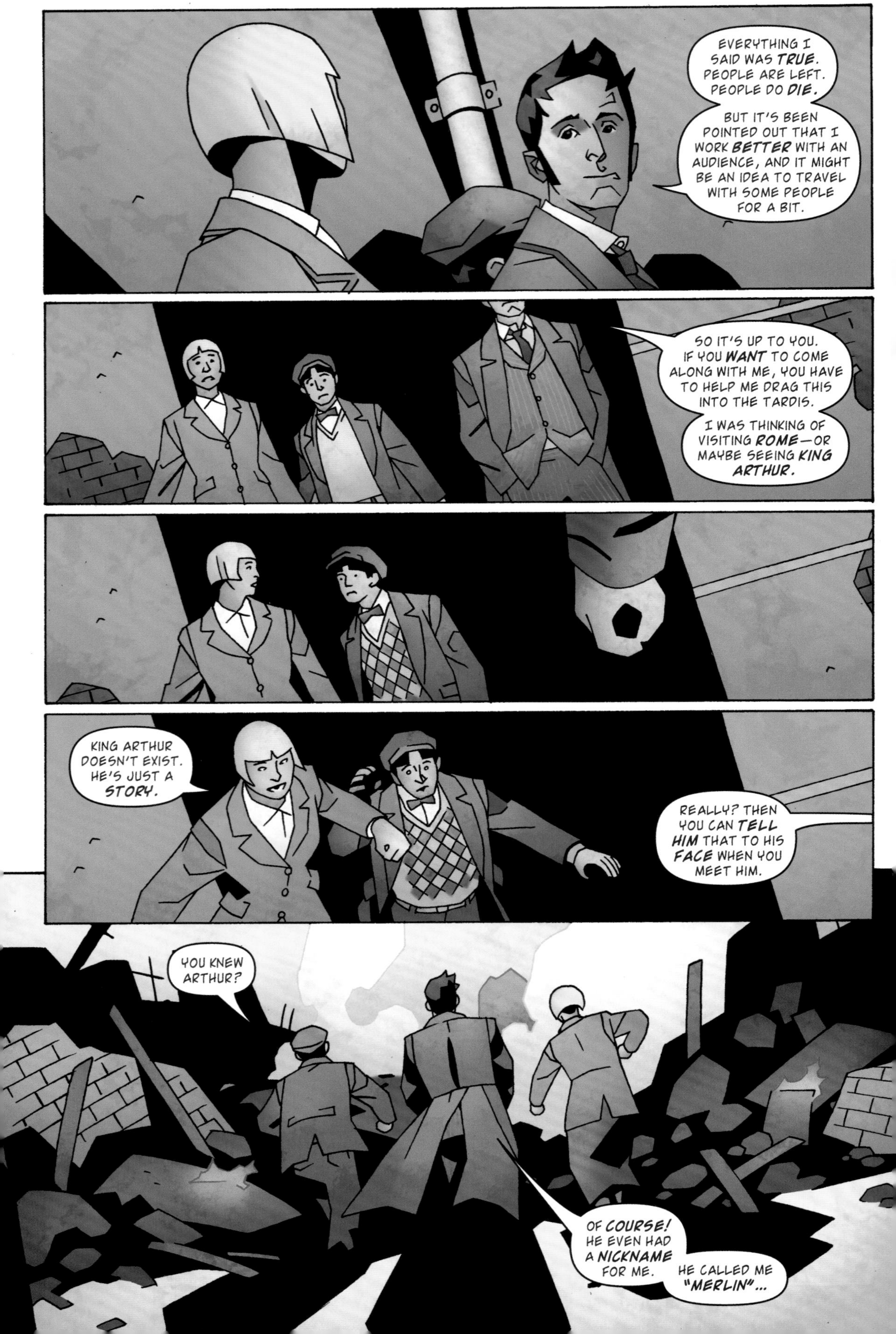
EVERYTHING I SAID WAS TRUE. PEOPLE ARE LEFT. PEOPLE DO DIE.
BUT IT'S BEEN POINTED OUT THAT I WORK BETTER WITH AN AUDIENCE, AND IT MIGHT BE AN IDEA TO TRAVEL WITH SOME PEOPLE FOR A BIT.
SO IT'S UP TO YOU. IF YOU WANT TO COME ALONG WITH ME, YOU HAVE TO HELP ME DRAG THIS INTO THE TARDIS.
I WAS THINKING OF VISITING ROME—OR MAYBE SEEING KING ARTHUR.
KING ARTHUR DOESN'T EXIST. HE'S JUST A STORY.
REALLY? THEN YOU CAN TELL HIM THAT TO HIS FACE WHEN YOU MEET HIM.
YOU KNEW ARTHUR?
OF COURSE! HE EVEN HAD A NICKNAME FOR ME.
HE CALLED ME "MERLIN"...

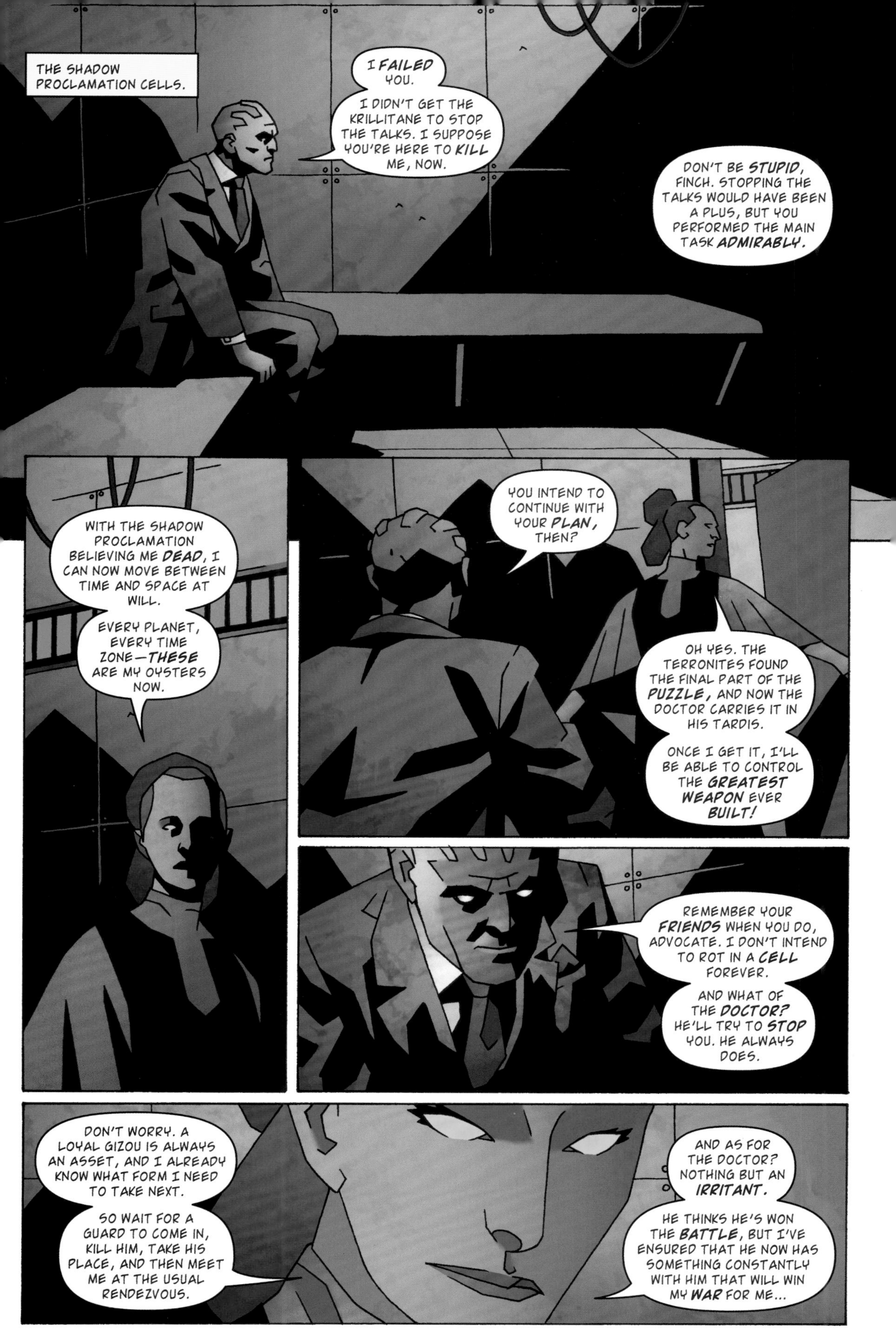

THE SHADOW PROCLAMATION CELLS.
I FAILED YOU.
I DIDN'T GET THE KRILLITANE TO STOP THE TALKS. I SUPPOSE YOU'RE HERE TO KILL ME, NOW.
DON'T BE STUPID, FINCH. STOPPING THE TALKS WOULD HAVE BEEN A PLUS, BUT YOU PERFORMED THE MAIN TASK ADMIRABLY.
WITH THE SHADOW PROCLAMATION BELIEVING ME DEAD, I CAN NOW MOVE BETWEEN TIME AND SPACE AT WILL.
EVERY PLANET, EVERY TIME ZONE—THESE ARE MY OYSTERS NOW.
YOU INTEND TO CONTINUE WITH YOUR PLAN, THEN?
OH YES. THE TERRONITES FOUND THE FINAL PART OF THE PUZZLE, AND NOW THE DOCTOR CARRIES IT IN HIS TARDIS.
ONCE I GET IT, I'LL BE ABLE TO CONTROL THE GREATEST WEAPON EVER BUILT!
REMEMBER YOUR FRIENDS WHEN YOU DO, ADVOCATE. I DON'T INTEND TO ROT IN A CELL FOREVER.
AND WHAT OF THE DOCTOR? HE'LL TRY TO STOP YOU. HE ALWAYS DOES.
DON'T WORRY. A LOYAL GIZOU IS ALWAYS AN ASSET, AND I ALREADY KNOW WHAT FORM I NEED TO TAKE NEXT.
SO WAIT FOR A GUARD TO COME IN, KILL HIM, TAKE HIS PLACE, AND THEN MEET ME AT THE USUAL RENDEZVOUS.
AND AS FOR THE DOCTOR? NOTHING BUT AN IRRITANT.
HE THINKS HE'S WON THE BATTLE, BUT I'VE ENSURED THAT HE NOW HAS SOMETHING CONSTANTLY WITH HIM THAT WILL WIN MY WAR FOR ME...

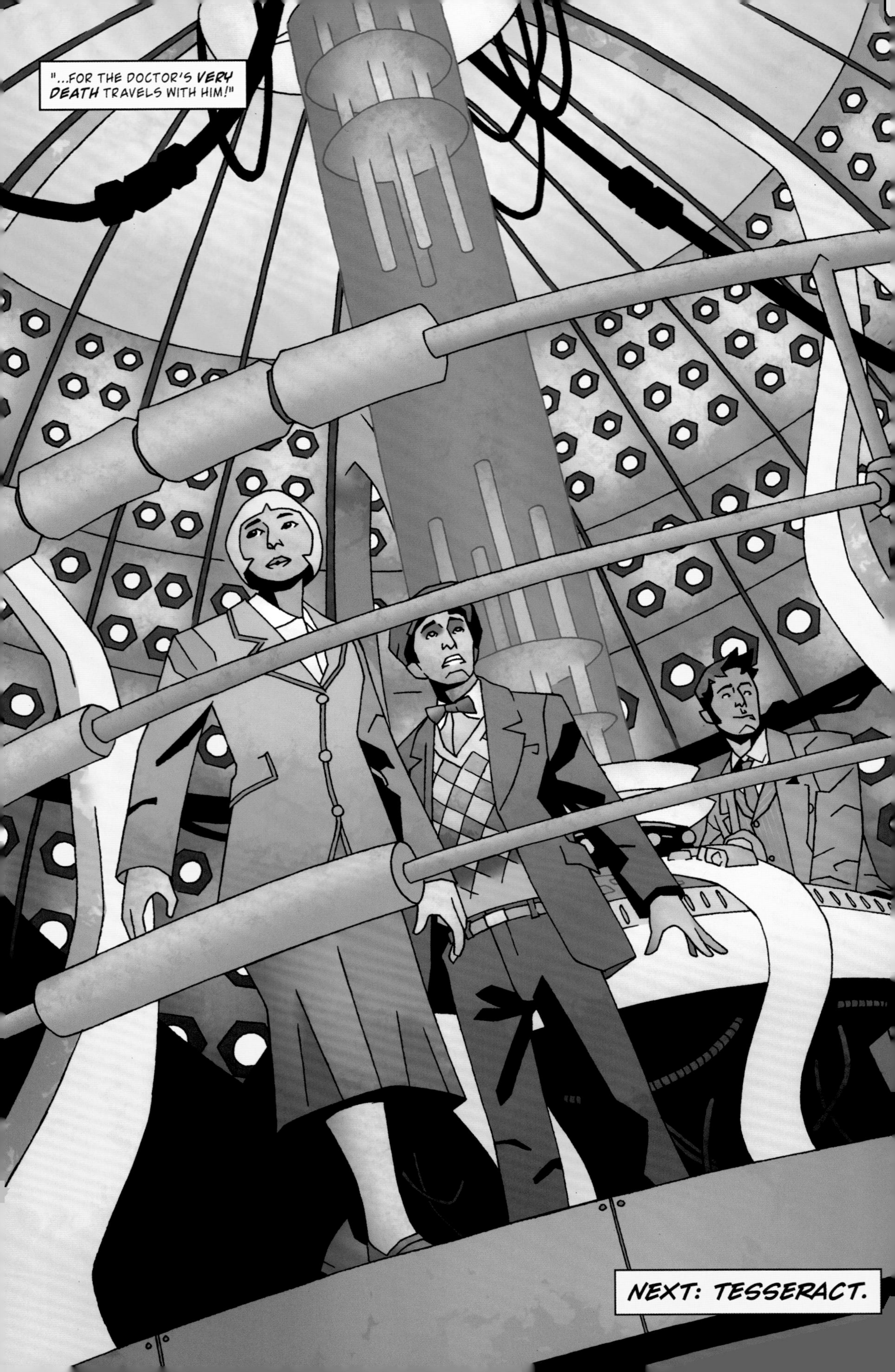
"...FOR THE DOCTOR'S VERY DEATH TRAVELS WITH HIM!"
NEXT: TESSERACT.

ART GALLERY

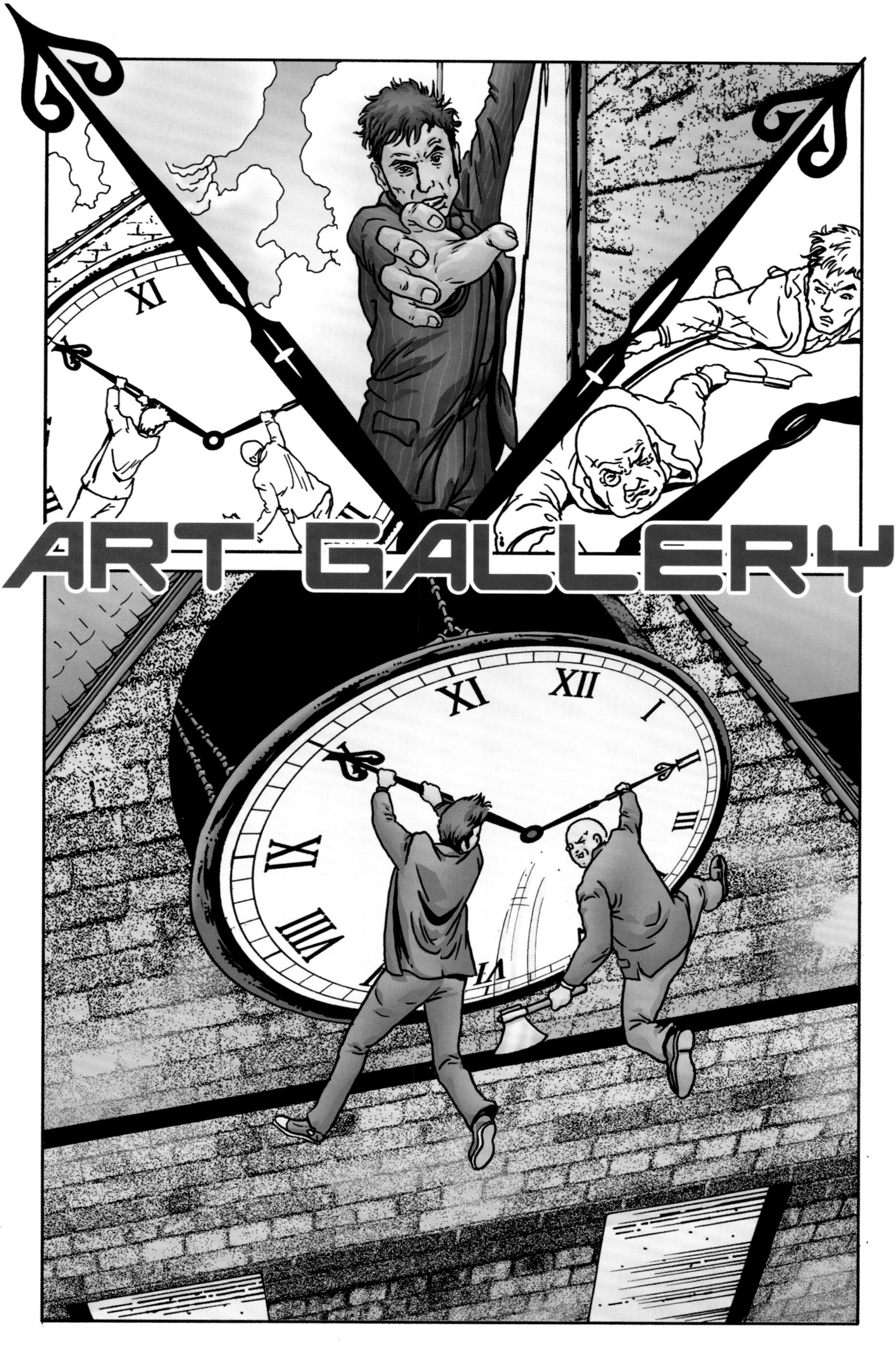

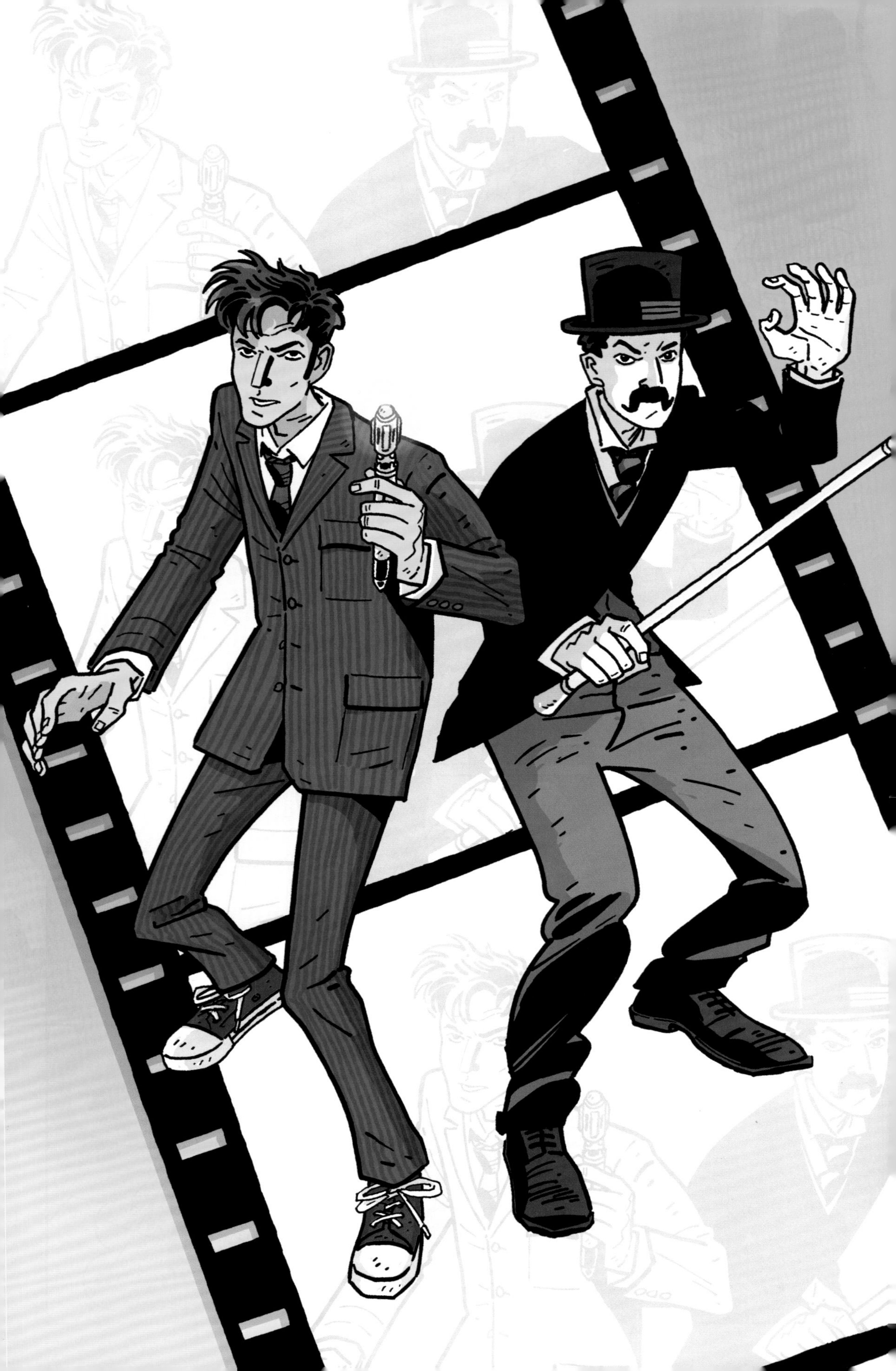

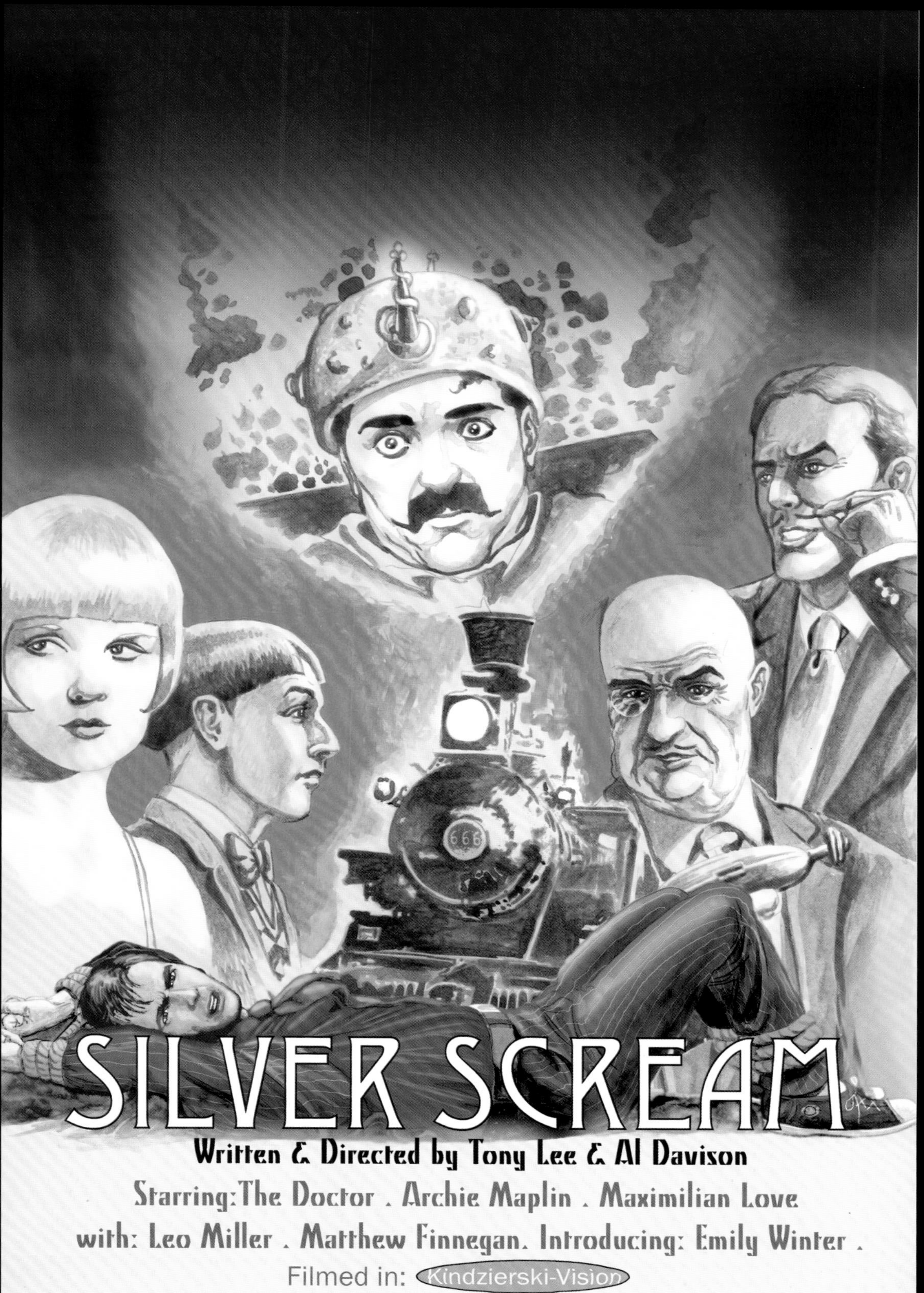

SILVER SCREAM
Written & Directed by Tony Lee & Al Davison
Starring: The Doctor . Archie Maplin . Maximilian Love
with: Leo Miller . Matthew Finnegan. Introducing: Emily Winter .
Filmed in: Kindzierski-Vision

previous page
art by Paul Grist : colors by Phil Elliott

this page
art by Al Davison

next page
art by Tommy Lee Edwards

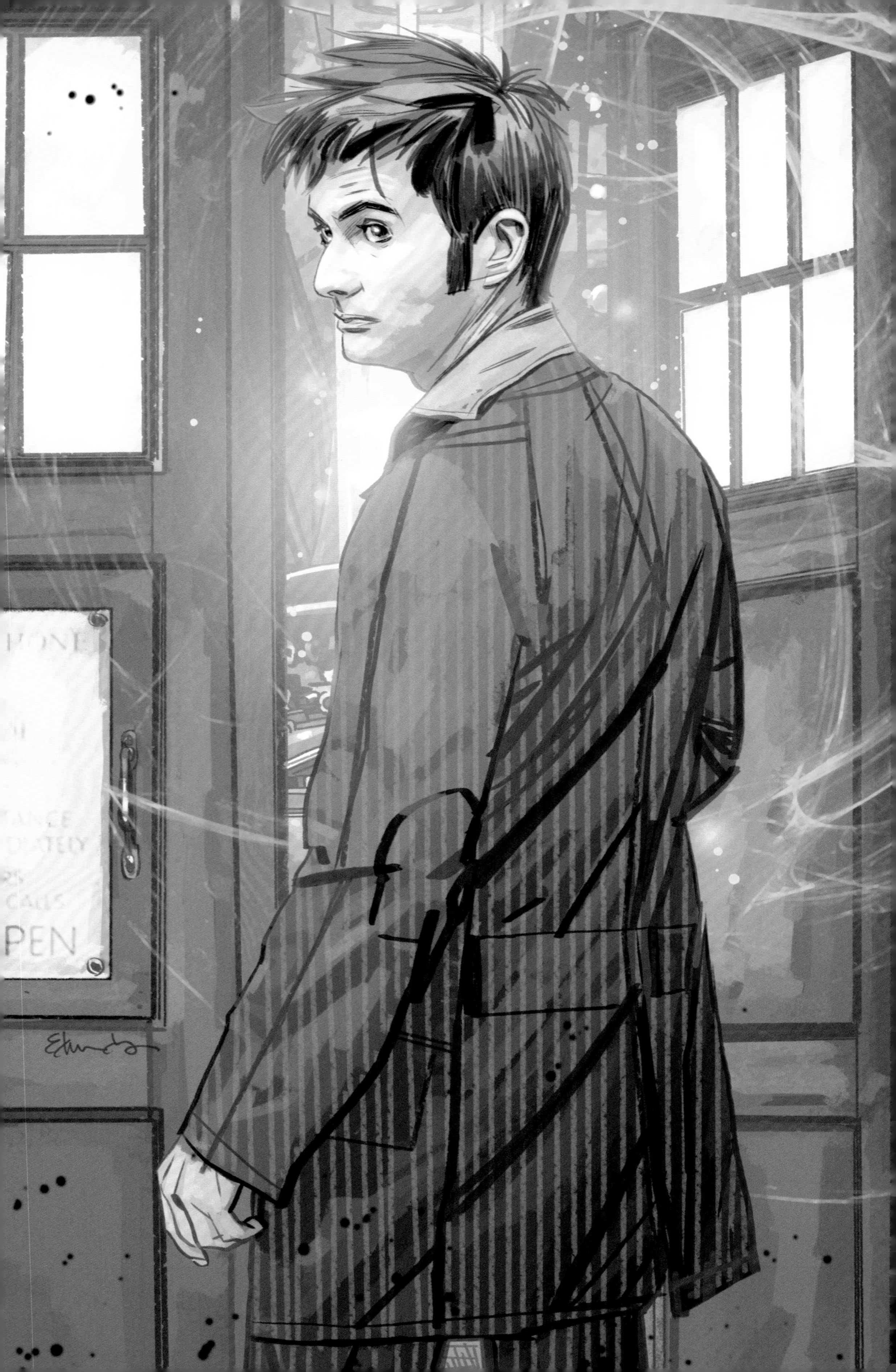

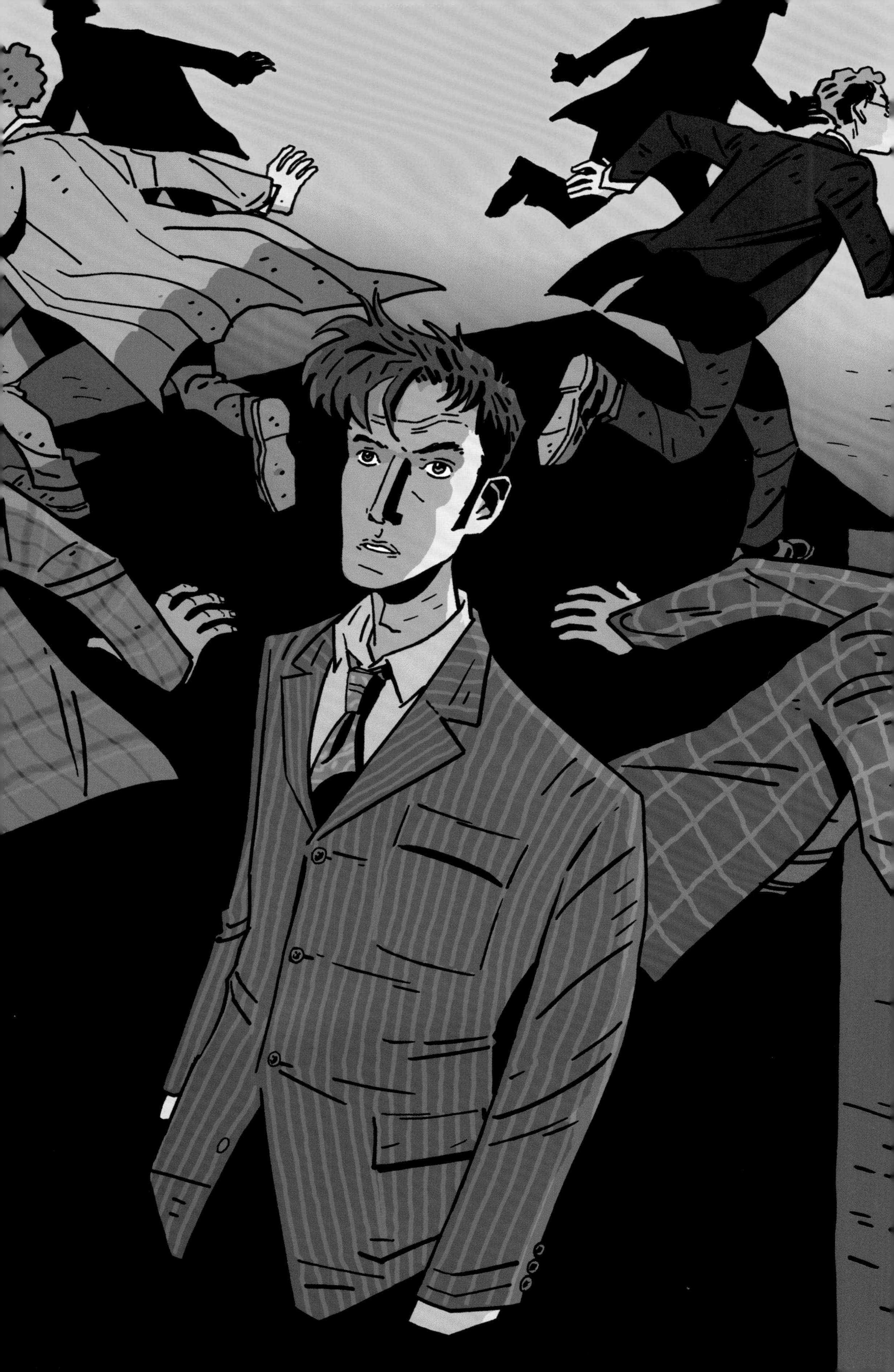

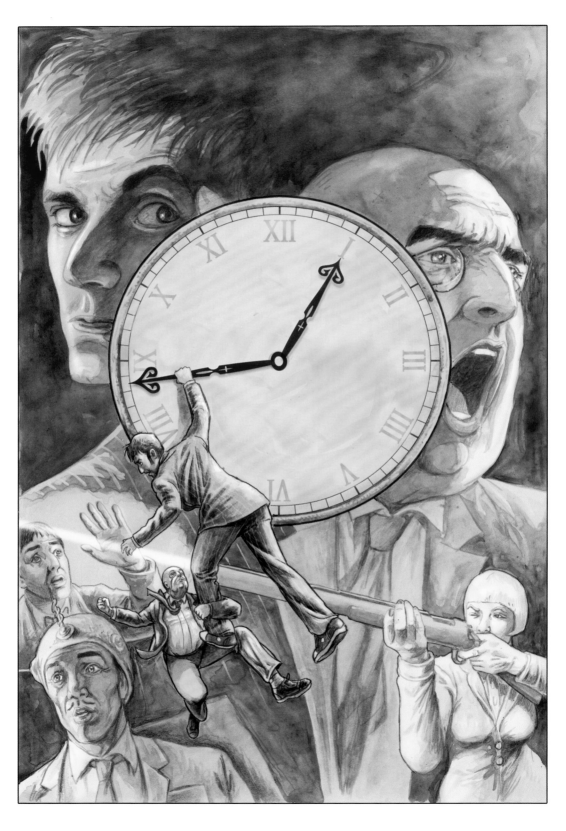

previous page
art by Paul Grist : colors by Phil Elliott

this page
art by Al Davison

next page
art by Paul Grist : colors by Phil Elliott

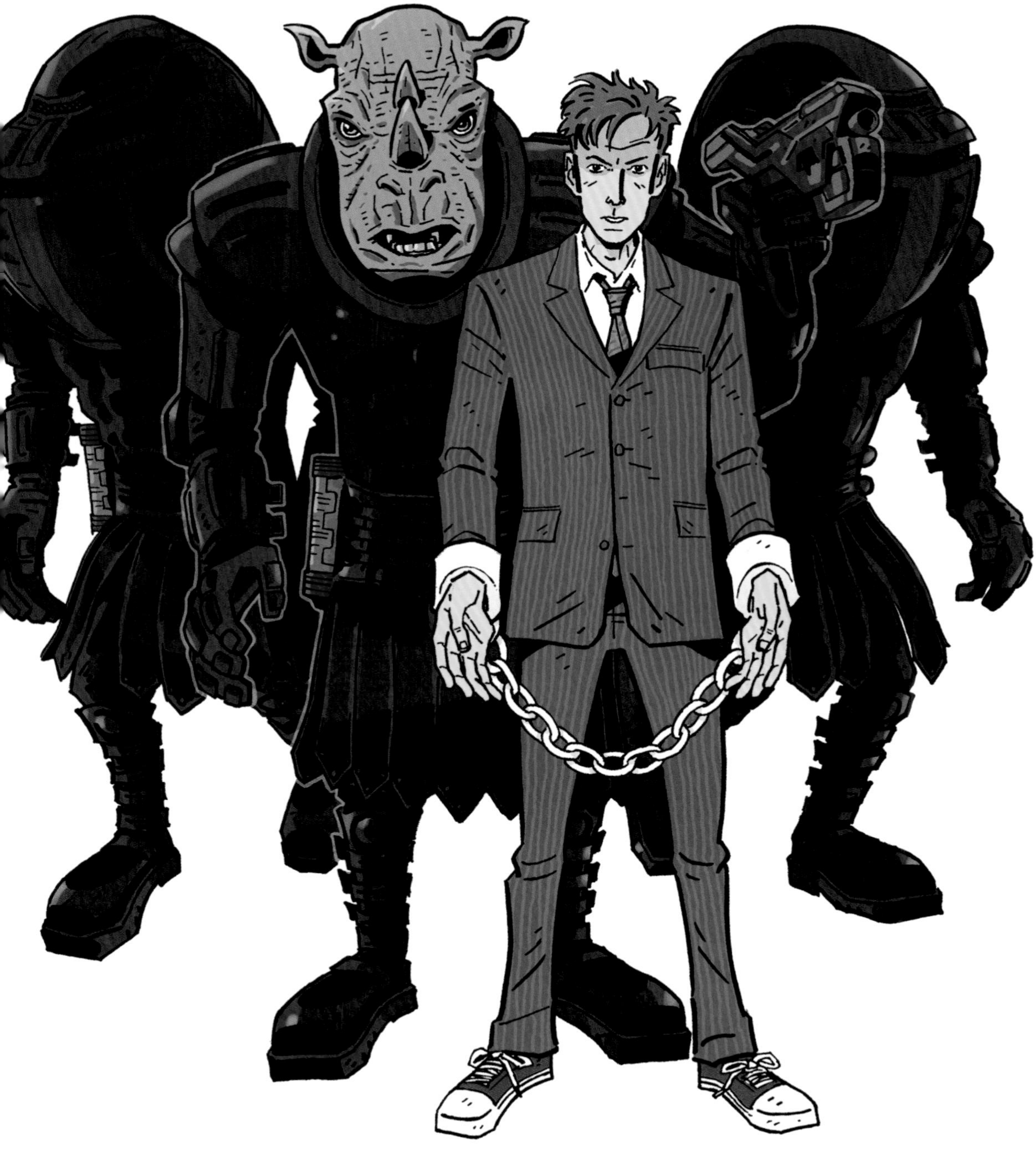

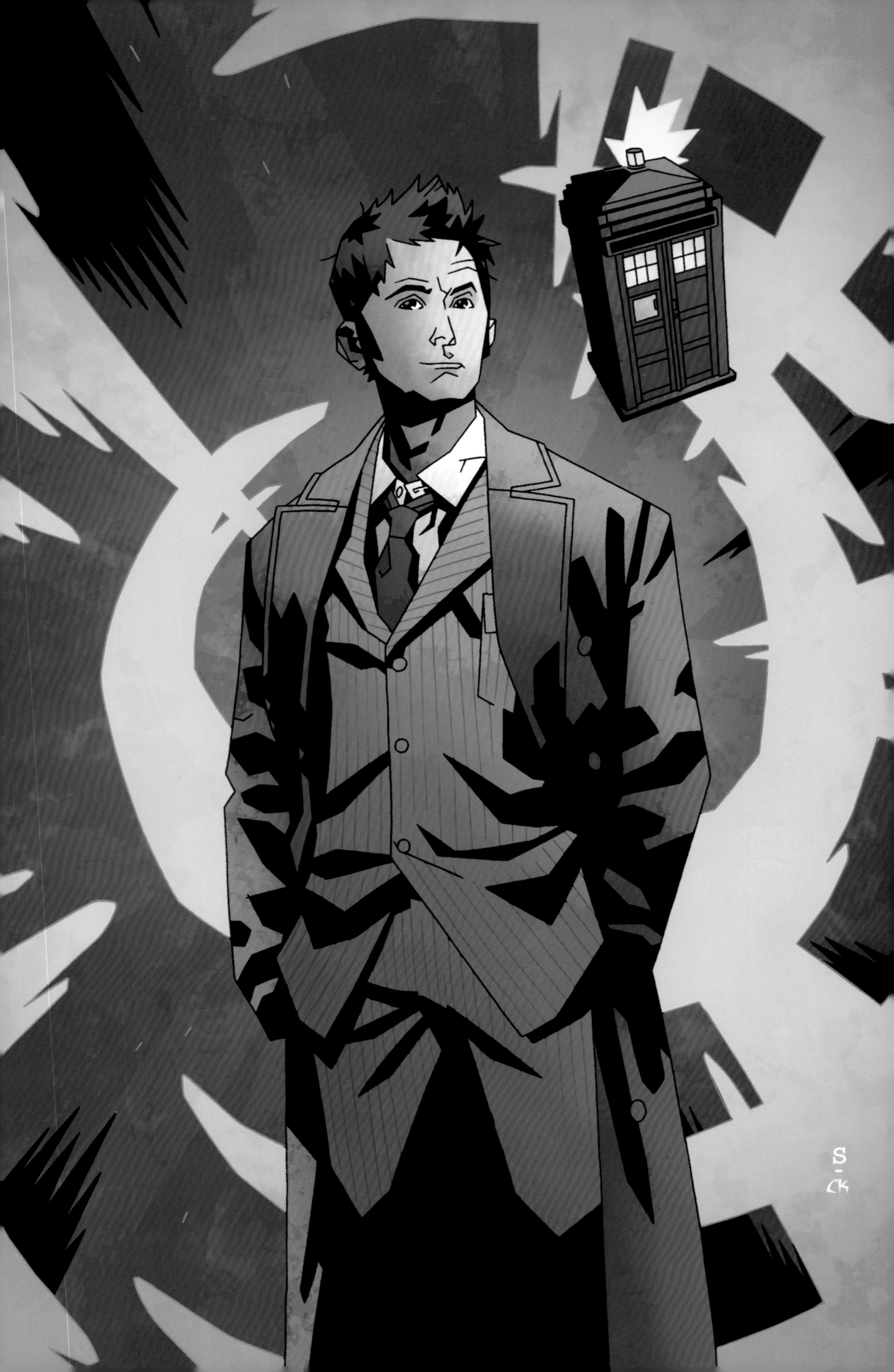

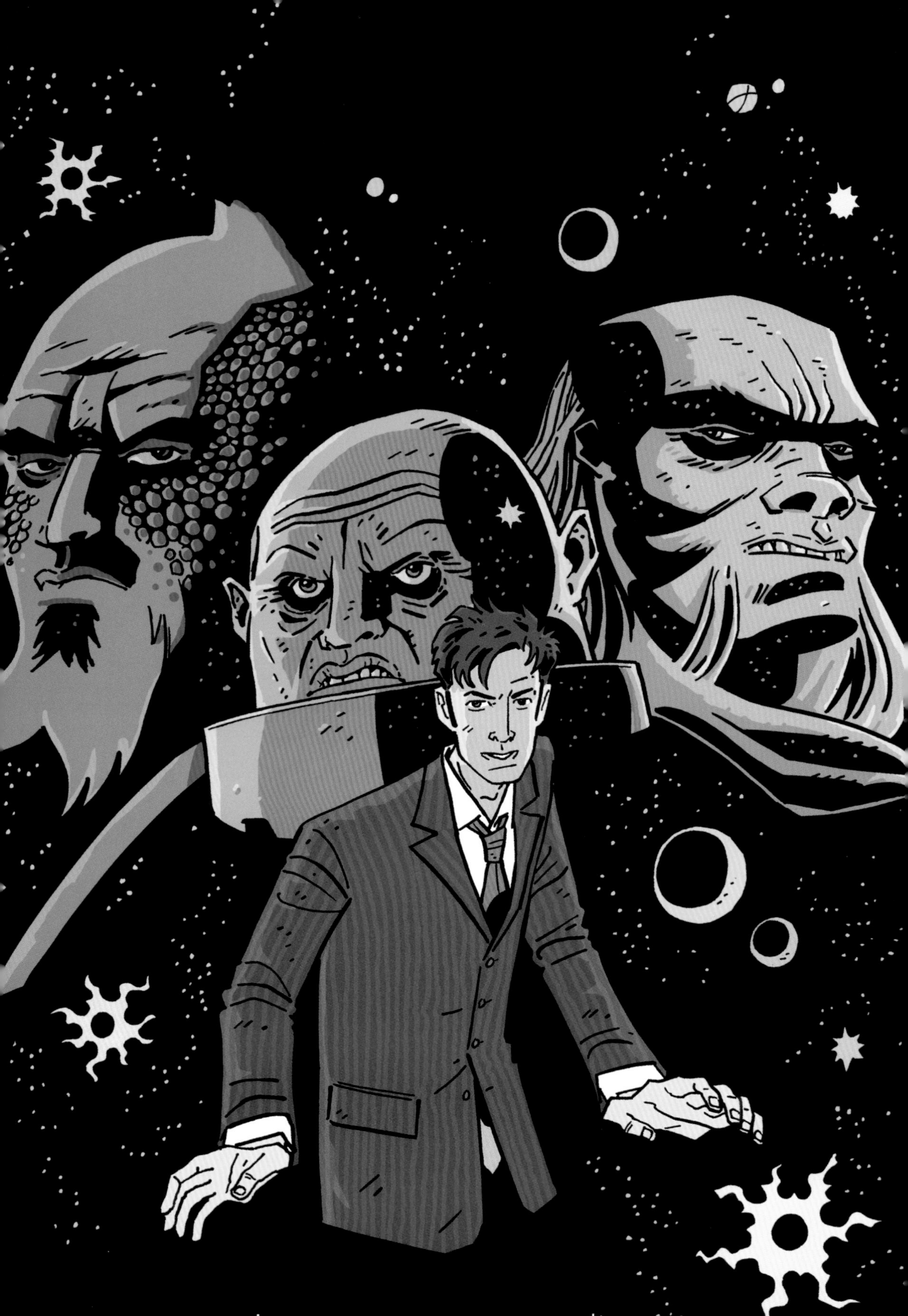

previous page
art by Matthew Dow Smith : colors by Charlie Kirchoff

this page
art by Paul Grist : colors by Phil Elliott

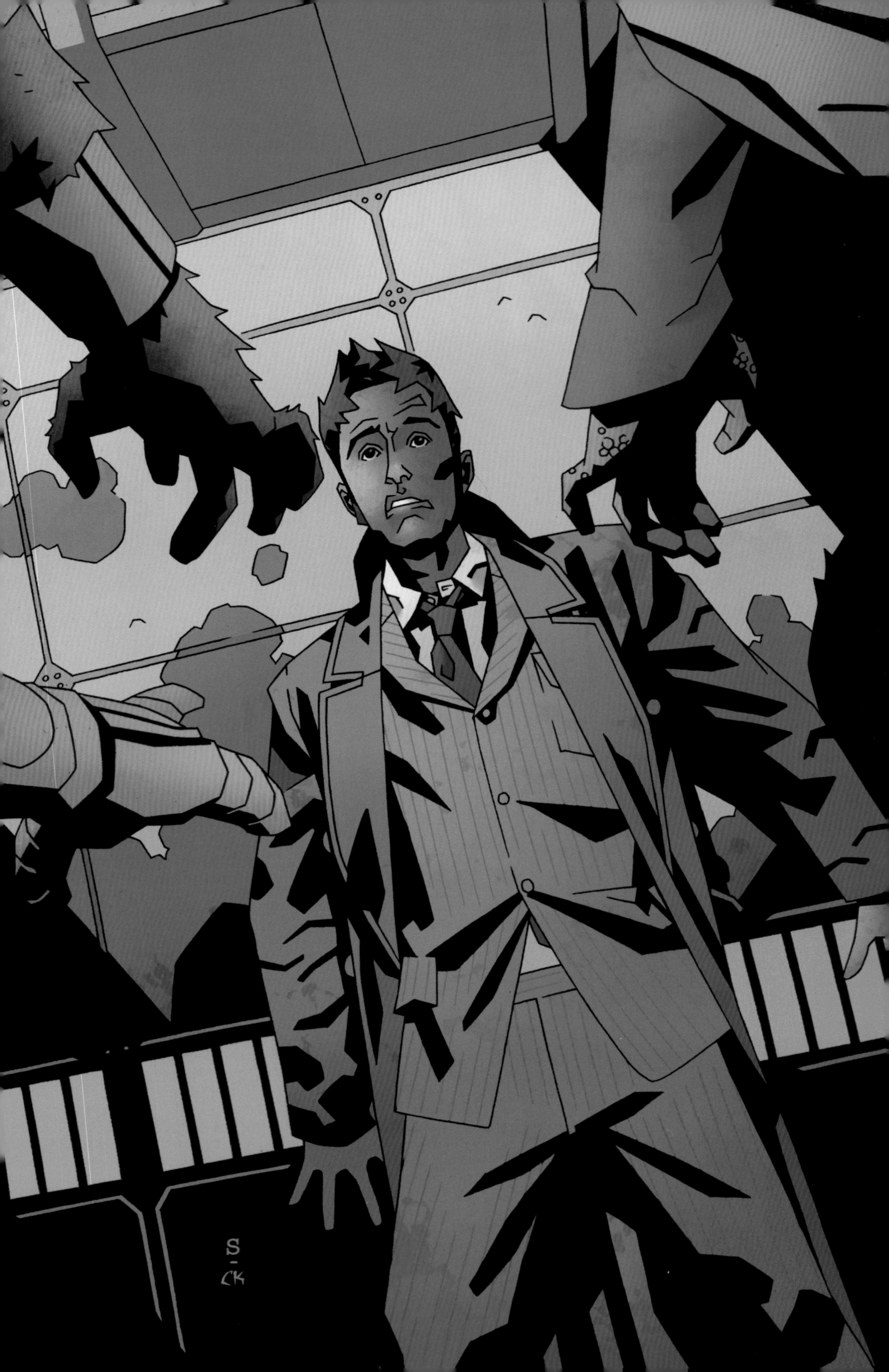

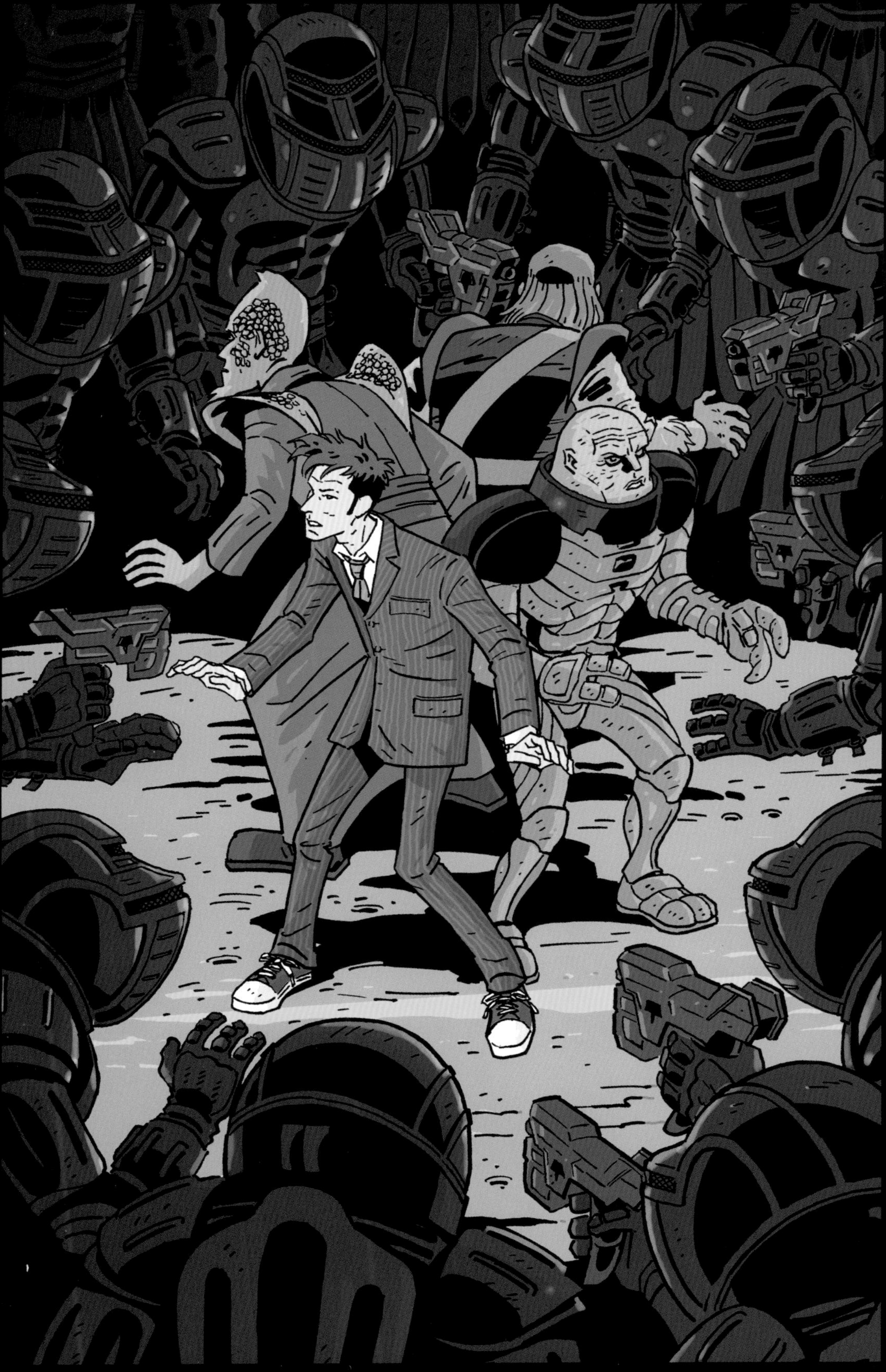

previous page
art by Matthew Dow Smith : colors by Charlie Kirchoff

this page
art by Paul Grist : colors by Phil Elliott

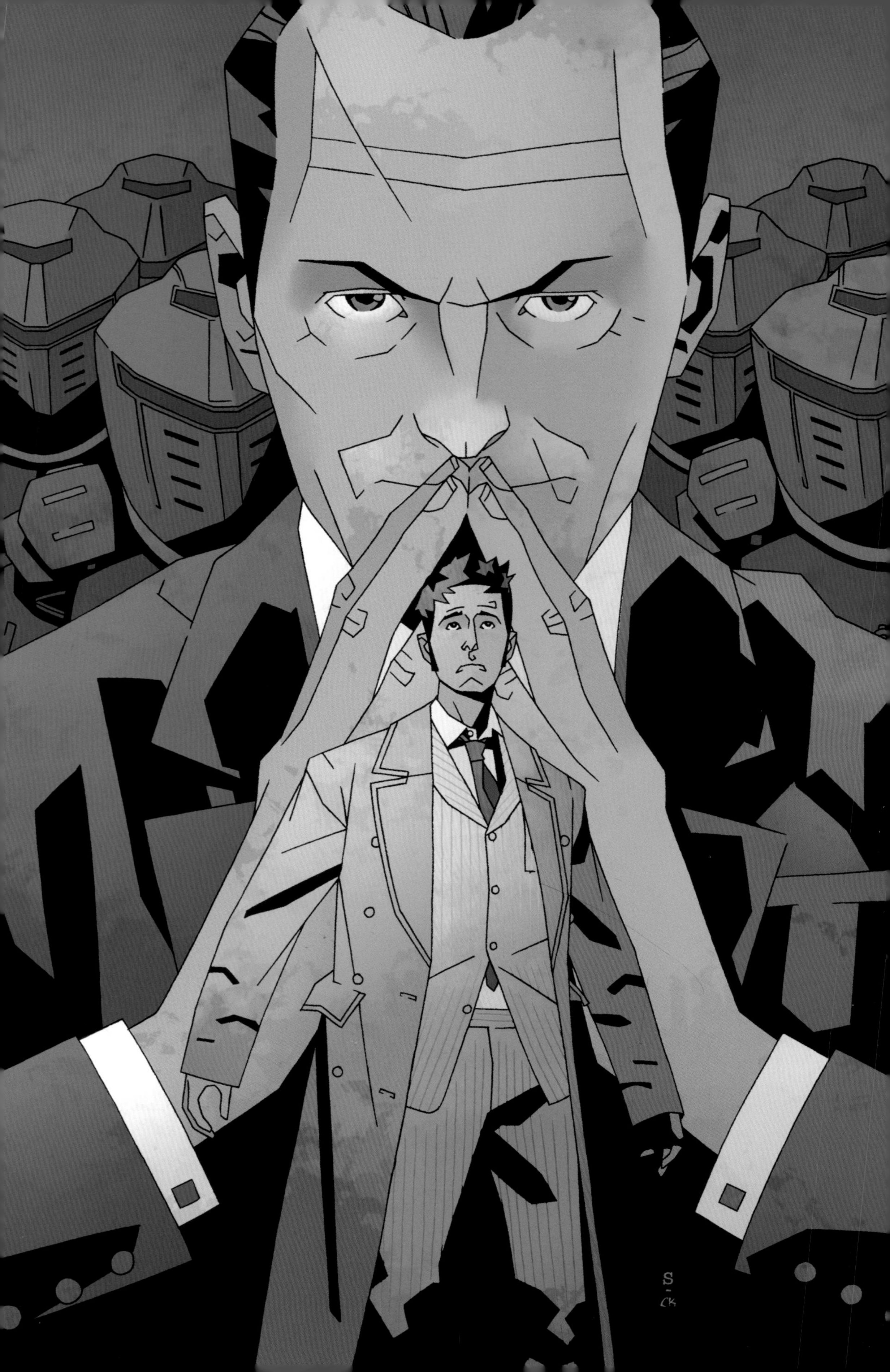

previous page
art by Matthew Dow Smith : colors by Charlie Kirchoff

this page
art by Paul Grist : colors by Phil Elliott

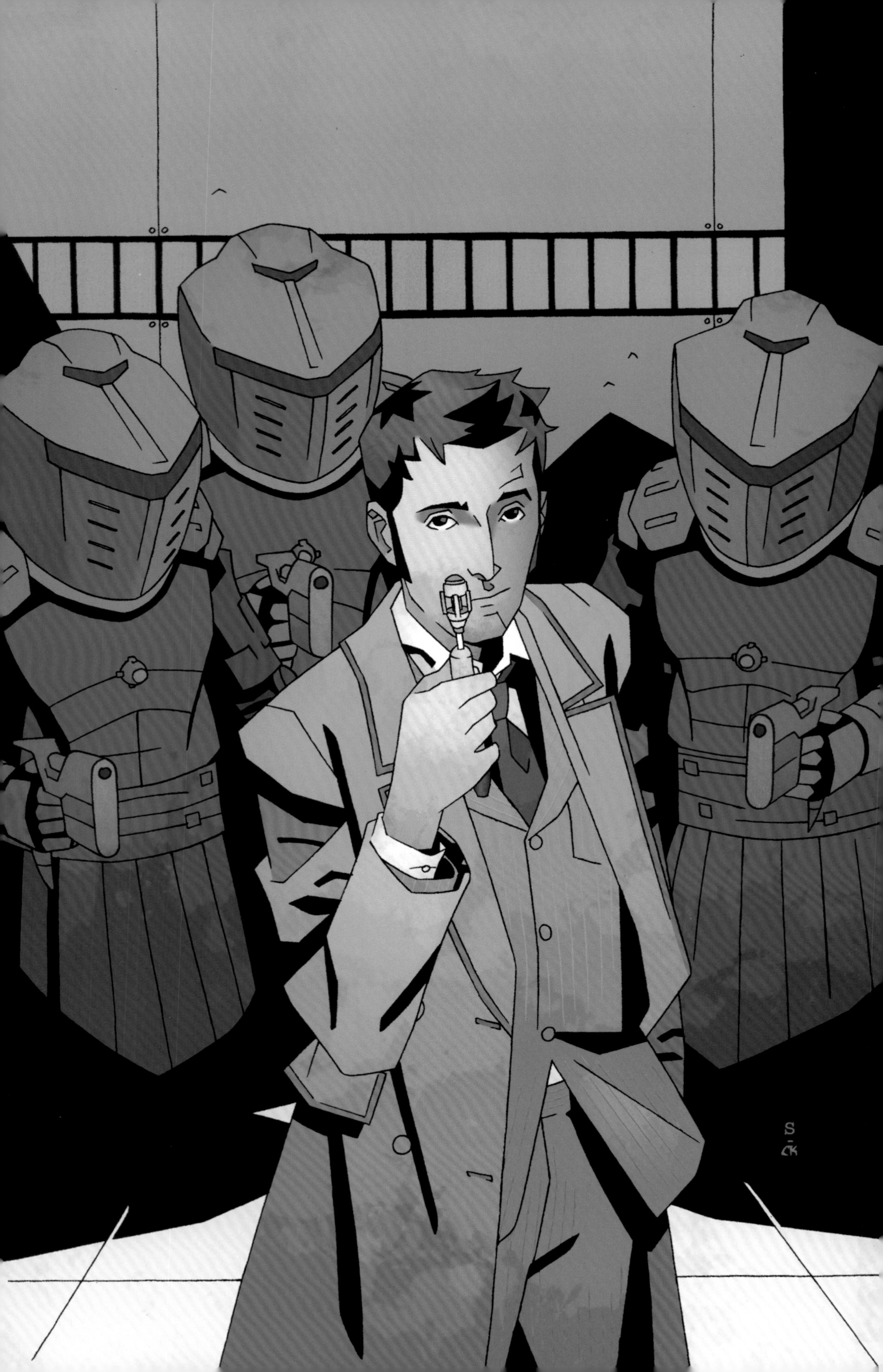

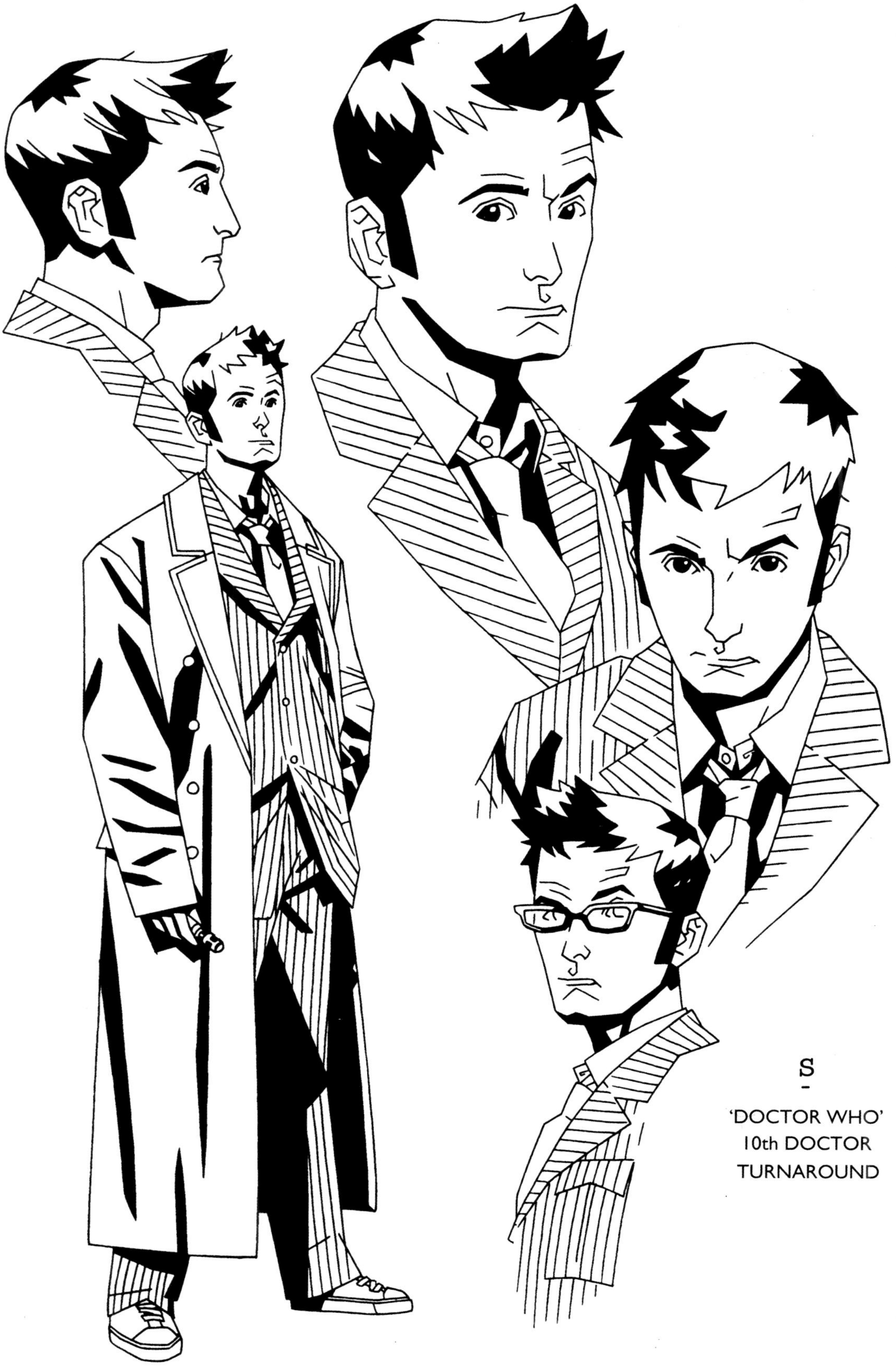
S
'DOCTOR WHO'
10th DOCTOR
TURNAROUND

previous page
art by Matthew Dow Smith : colors by Charlie Kirchoff

this page
sketch by Matthew Dow Smith

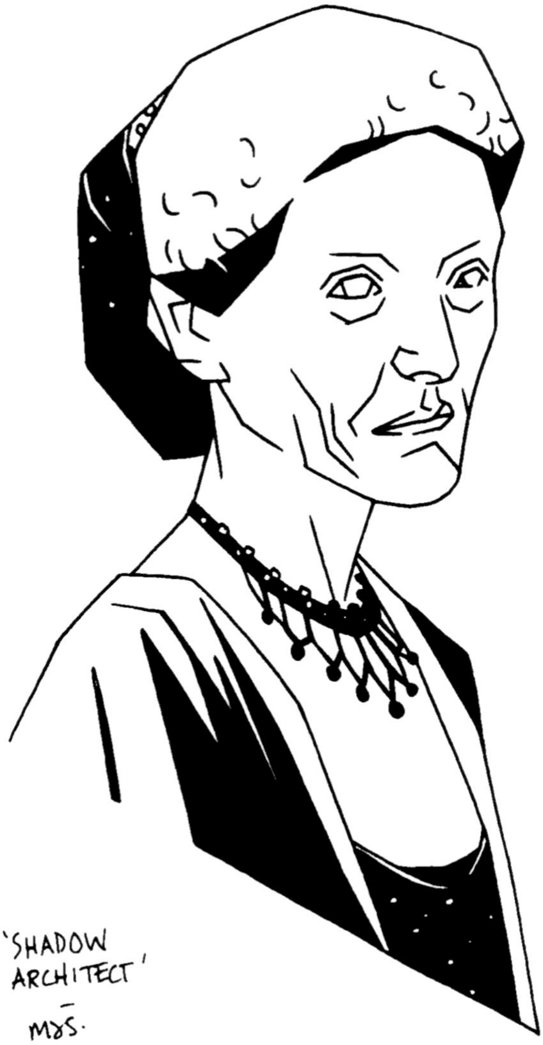

'SHADOW ARCHITECT'
-
MJS.

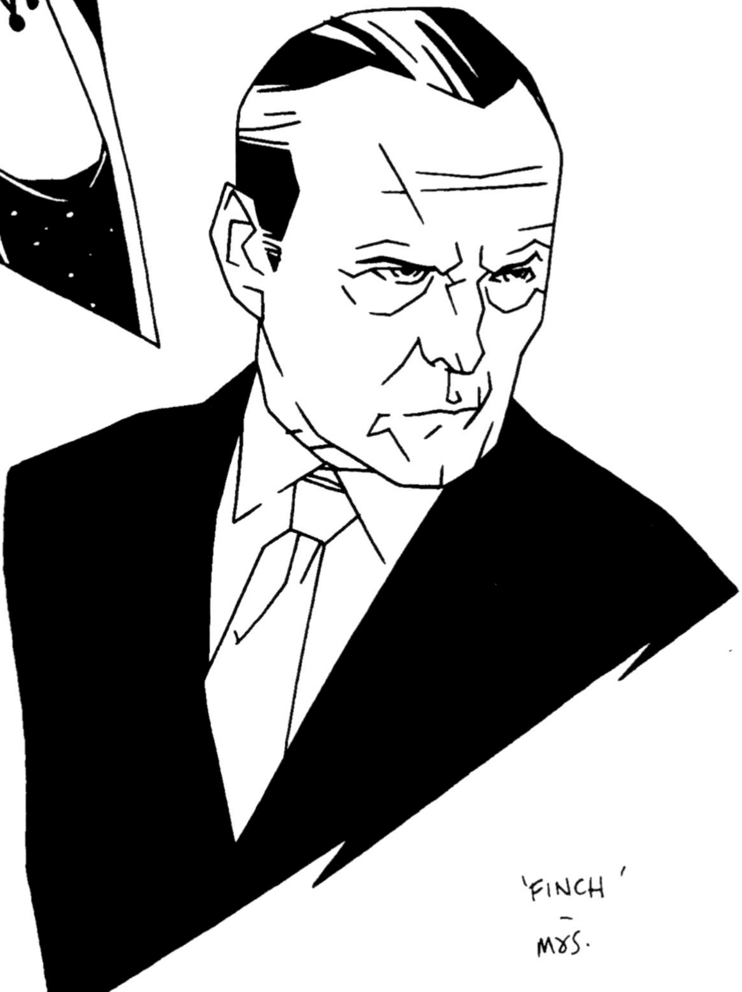

'FINCH'
-
MJS.

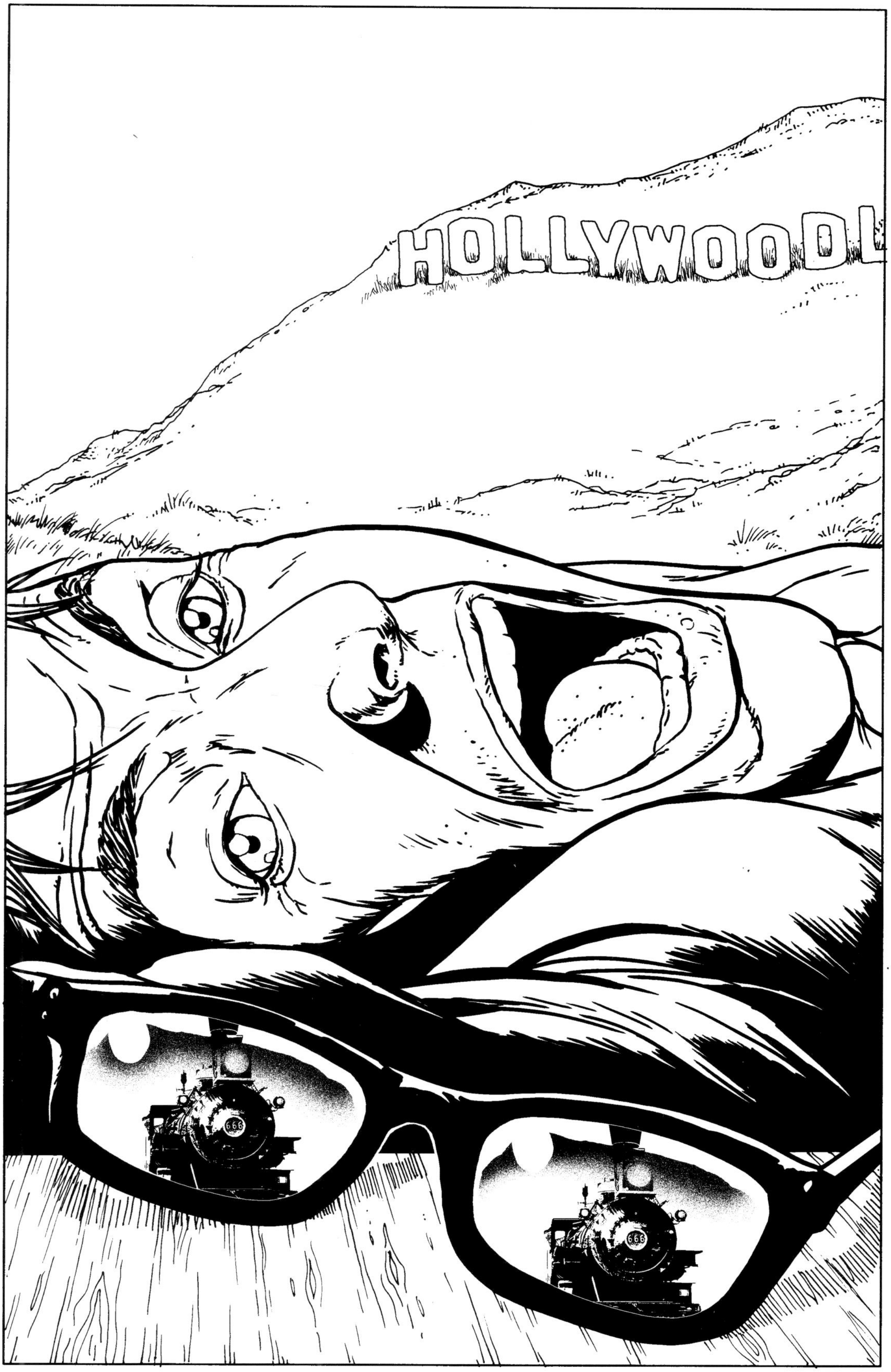
HOLLYWOOD
666
666

previous page
sketch by Matthew Dow Smith

this page
sketch by Al Davison

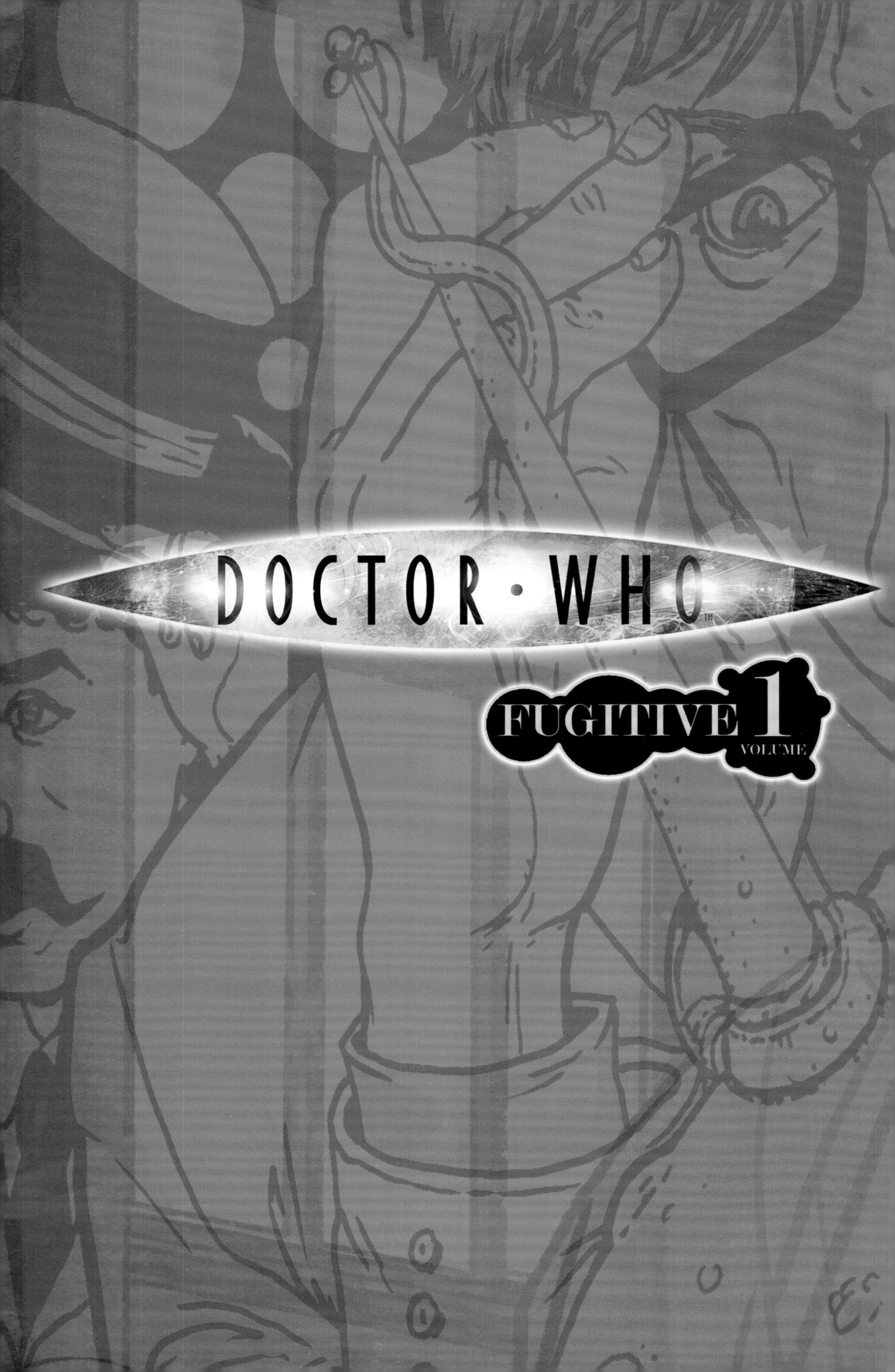
DOCTOR · WHO™
FUGITIVE 1
VOLUME

DOCTOR WHO

The Doctor

He's a Time Lord from the planet Gallifrey. He's more than 900 years old. If there's danger, he's the man who's going to save your life—and everyone on your planet. Got a problem with that?

POLICE PUBLIC CALL BOX

The TARDIS

The Doctor's dimensionally transcendental time/space machine, cunningly disguised as a police public call box. The trip of a lifetime is guaranteed with every journey!

Written by >> Tony Lee

Art by >> Al Davison and Matthew Dow Smith

Colors by >> Lovern Kindzierski and Charlie Kirchoff

Letters by >> Chris Mowry, Robbie Robbins, and Neil Uyetake

Original Series Edits by >> Denton J. Tipton

Collection Edits by >> Justin Eisinger

Collection Design by >> Neil Uyetake

ISBN: 978-1-60010-607-1 16 15 14 13 4 5 6 7

Special thanks to Gary Russell and David Turbitt for their invaluable assistance.
IDW founded by Ted Adams, Alex Garner, Kris Oprisko, and Robbie Robbins

IDW®

Ted Adams, CEO & Publisher
Greg Goldstein, President & COO
Robbie Robbins, EVP/Sr. Graphic Artist
Chris Ryall, Chief Creative Officer/Editor-in-Chief
Matthew Ruzicka, CPA, Chief Financial Officer
Alan Payne, VP of Sales
Dirk Wood, VP of Marketing
Lorelei Bunjes, VP of Digital Services

Become our fan on Facebook **facebook.com/idwpublishing**
Follow us on Twitter **@idwpublishing**
Check us out on YouTube **youtube.com/idwpublishing**
www.IDWPUBLISHING.com

Originally published as DOCTOR WHO Issues #1–6.

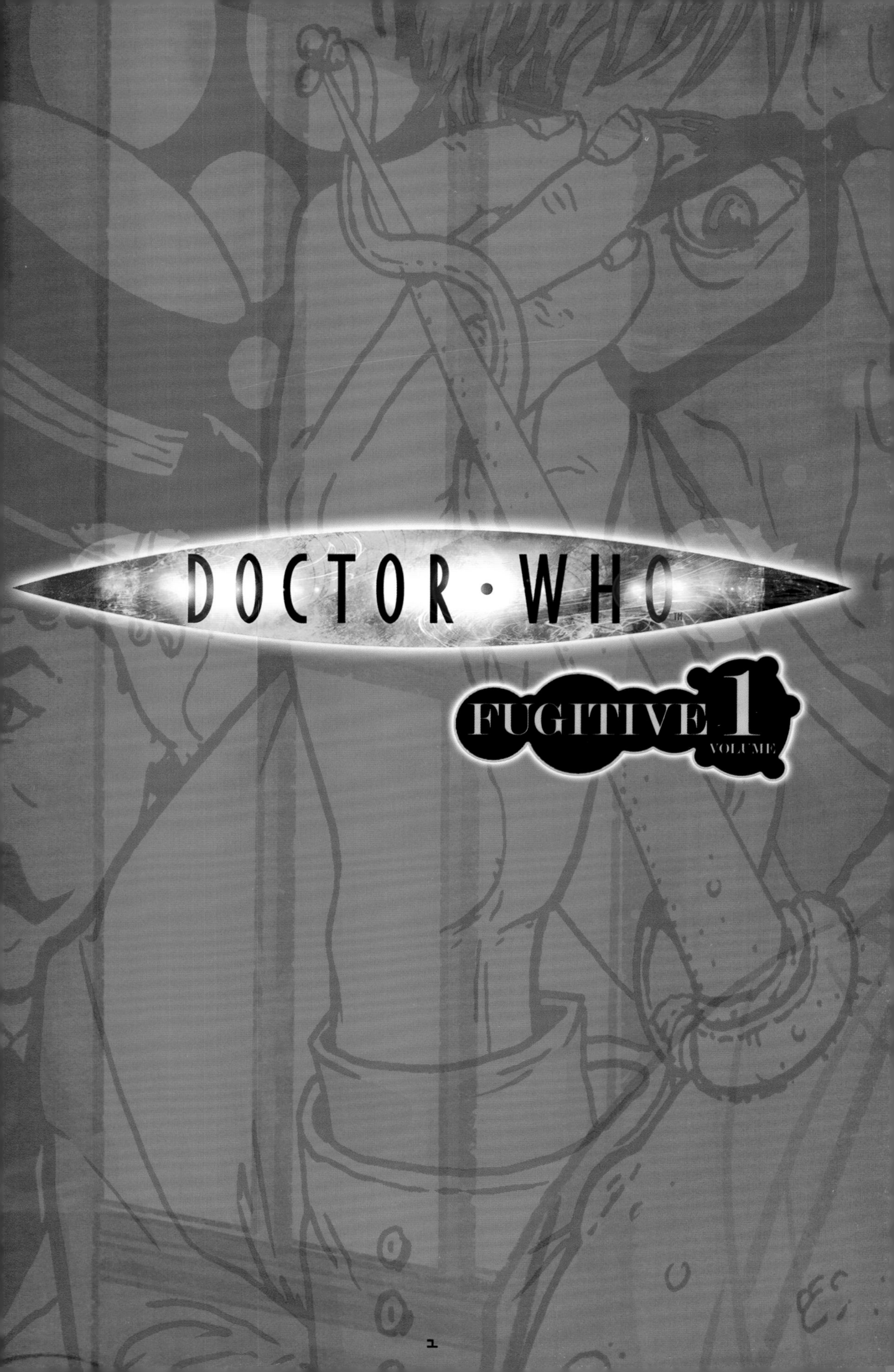

DOCTOR WHO™

FUGITIVE VOLUME 1